6th Workshop on South and Southeast Asian Natural Language Processing (WSSANLP 2016)

Osaka, Japan
11 – 16 December 2016

ISBN: 978-1-5108-3317-3

WSSANLP 2016

6th Workshop on South and Southeast Asian Natural Language Processing

Proceedings of the Conference

December 11-16, 2016
Osaka, Japan

Preface

Welcome to the 6th Workshop on South and Southeast Asian Natural Language Processing (WSSANLP - 2016), a collocated event at the 26th International Conference on Computational Linguistics (COLING 2016) , December 11 - 16, 2016 at Osaka International Convention Center, Osaka, Japan.

South and Southeast Asia comprise of the countries, Afghanistan, Bangladesh, Bhutan, India, Maldives, Nepal, Pakistan and Sri Lanka. Southeast Asia, on the other hand, consists of Brunei, Burma, Cambodia, East Timor, Indonesia, Laos, Malaysia, Philippines, Singapore, Thailand and Vietnam. This area is the home to thousands of languages that belong to different language families like Indo-Aryan, Indo-Iranian, Dravidian, Sino-Tibetan, Austro-Asiatic, Kradai, Hmong-Mien, etc. In terms of population, South Asian and Southeast Asia represent 35 percent of the total population of the world which means as much as 2.5 billion speakers. Some of the languages of these regions have a large number of native speakers: Hindi (5th largest according to number of its native speakers), Bengali (6th), Punjabi (12th), Tamil(18th), and Urdu (20th).

As internet and electronic devices including PCs and hand held devices including mobile phones have spread far and wide in the region, it has become imperative to develop language technology for these languages. It is important for economic development as well as for social and individual progress.

A characteristic of these languages is that they are under-resourced. The words of these languages show rich variations in morphology. Moreover they are often heavily agglutinated and synthetic, making segmentation an important issue. The intellectual motivation for this workshop comes from the need to explore ways of harnessing the morphology of these languages for higher level processing. The task of morphology, however, in South and Southeast Asian Languages is intimately linked with segmentation for these languages.

The goal of WSSANLP is:

• Providing a platform to linguistic and NLP communities for sharing and discussing ideas and work on South and Southeast Asian languages and combining efforts.

• Development of useful and high quality computational resources for under resourced South and Southeast Asian languages.

We are delighted to present to you this volume of proceedings of the 6th Workshop on South and Southeast Asian Natural Language Processing. We have received total 37 submissions in the categories of long paper and short paper. On the basis of our review process, we have competitively selected 19 full papers and 3 short papers.

We look forward to an invigorating workshop.

Dekai Wu (Chair WSSANLP-2016),
Hong Kong University of Science and Technology, Hong Kong

Pushpak Bhattacharyya (Co-Chair WSSANLP-2016),
Indian Institute of Technology Patna, India

Workshop Chair

Dekai Wu, Hong Kong University of Science and Technology, Hong Kong

Workshop Co-Chair

Pushpak Bhattacharyya, Indian Institute of Technology Patna, India

Key Note Speaker

Alain Désoulières, INALCO - CERLOM, France

Organisers

M. G. Abbas Malik, Auckland University of Technology, Auckland, New Zealand (chair)

Sadaf Abdul Rauf, Fatima Jinnah Women University, Islamabad, Pakistan

Mahsa Mohaghegh, Unitec Institute of Technology, Auckland, New Zealand

Programme Committee

Sadaf Abdul Rauf, Fatima Jinnah Women University, Pakistan

Naveed Afzal, Cardiovascular Biomarkers Laboratory, Mayo Clinic, USA

Tafseer Ahmed, DHA Suffa University, Pakistan

Aasim Ali, University of the Punjab, Pakistan

Jalal S. Alowibdi, University of Jeddah, Saudi Arabia

Saleh Alshomrani, University of Jeddah, Saudi Arabia

Amer Alzaidi, University of Jeddah, Saudi Arabia

M. Waqas Anwar, COMSATS Institute of Technology Abbottabad, Pakistan

Bal Krishna Bal, Kathmandu University, Nepal

Sivaji Bandyopadhyay, Jadavpur University, India

Vincent Berment, GETALP-LIG and INALCO, France

Laurent Besacier, University of Grenoble, France

Pushpak Bhattacharyya, Indian Institute of Technology Patna, India

Hervé Blanchon, University of Grenoble, France

Christian Boitet, University of Grenoble, France

Miriam Butt, University of Konstanz, Germany

Eric Castelli, International Research Center MICA, Vietnam

Amitava Das, Indian Institute of Information Technology, Sri City, India

Alain Desoulieres, INALCO - CERLOM, France

Alexander Gelbukh, Center for Computing Research, CIC, Mexico

Choochart Haruechaiyasak, National Electronics and Computer Technology Center (NECTEC), Thailand

Sarmad Hussain, University of Engineering and Technology Lahore, Pakistan

Aravind K. Joshi, University of Pennsylvania, USA

Amba Kulkarni, University of Hyderabad, India

Gurpreet Singh Lehal, Punjabi University, Patiala, India

Haizhou Li, Institute for Infocomm Research, Singapore

M. G. Abbas Malik, Auckland University of Technology, New Zealand

Mahsa Mohaghegh, Unitec Institute of Technology, New Zealand

Ajit Narayanan, Auckland University of Technology, New Zealand

K. V. S. Prasad, Chalmers University of Technology, Sweden

Bali Ranaivo-Malançon, University of Malaysia Sarawak, Malaysia

Paolo Rosso, Universitat Politècnica de València, Spain

Huda Sarfraz, Beacon house National University, Pakistan

Hossein Sarrafzadeh, High Technology Transdisciplinary Research Network, Unitec Auckland, New Zealand

L. Sobha, AU-KBC Research Centre, India

Virach Sornlertlamvanich, TCL, National Institute of Information and Communication Technology, Thailand

Ruvan Weerasinghe, University of Colombo School of Computing, Sri Lanka

Table of Contents

Full Papers

Compound Type Identification in Sanskrit: What Roles do the Corpus and Grammar Play?
Amrith Krishna, Pavankumar Satuluri, Shubham Sharma, Apurv Kumar and Pawan Goyal 1

Comparison of Grapheme-to-Phoneme Conversion Methods on a Myanmar Pronunciation Dictionary
Ye Kyaw Thu, Win Pa Pa, Yoshinori Sagisaka and Naoto Iwahashi 11

Character-Aware Neural Networks for Arabic Named Entity Recognition for Social Media
Mourad Gridach 23

Development of a Bengali parser by cross-lingual transfer from Hindi
Ayan Das, Agnivo Saha and Sudeshna Sarkar 33

Sinhala Short Sentence Similarity Calculation using Corpus-Based and Knowledge-Based Similarity Measures
Jcs Kadupitiya, Surangika Ranathunga and Gihan Dias 44

Enriching Source for English-to-Urdu Machine Translation
Bushra Jawaid, Amir Kamran and Ondřej Bojar 54

The IMAGACT4ALL Ontology of Animated Images: Implications for Theoretical and Machine Translation of Action Verbs from English-Indian Languages
Pitambar Behera, Sharmin Muzaffar, Atul kr. Ojha and Girish Jha 64

Crowdsourcing-based Annotation of Emotions in Filipino and English Tweets
Fermin Roberto Lapitan, Riza Theresa Batista-Navarro and Eliezer Albacea 74

Temporal Information Extraction in Clinical Domain (TIECA)
Shujeevan Kanapathipillai, Viraj Welgama and Ruwan Weerasinghe 83

Sentiment Analysis of Tweets in Three Indian Languages
Shanta Phani, Shibamouli Lahiri and Arindam Biswas 93

Dealing with Linguistic Divergences in English-Bhojpuri Machine Translation
Pitambar Behera, Neha Mourya and Vandana Pandey 103

The development of a web corpus of Hindi language and corpus-based comparative studies to Japanese
Miki Nishioka and Shiro Akasegawa 114

Automatic Creation of a Sentence Aligned Sinhala-Tamil Parallel Corpus
Riyafa Abdul Hameed, Nadeeshani Pathirennehelage, Anusha Ihalapathirana, Maryam Ziyad Mohamed, Surangika Ranathunga, Sanath Jayasena, Gihan Dias and Sandareka Fernando 124

Clustering-based Phonetic Projection in Mismatched Crowdsourcing Channels for Low-resourced ASR
Wenda Chen, Mark Hasegawa-Johnson, Nancy Chen, Preethi Jyothi and Lav Varshney 133

Improving the Morphological Analysis of Classical Sanskrit
Oliver Hellwig 142

Query Translation for Cross-Language Information Retrieval using Multilingual Word Clusters
Paheli Bhattacharya, Pawan Goyal and Sudeshna Sarkar 152

A study of attention-based neural machine translation model on Indian languages
Ayan Das, Pranay Yerra, Ken Kumar and Sudeshna Sarkar 163

Comprehensive Part-Of-Speech Tag Set and SVM based POS Tagger for Sinhala
Sandareka Fernando, Surangika Ranathunga, Sanath Jayasena and Gihan Dias 173

Short Papers

Align Me: A framework to generate Parallel Corpus Using OCRs and Bilingual Dictionaries
Priyam Bakliwal, Devadath V V and C V Jawahar 183

Learning Indonesian-Chinese Lexicon with Bilingual Word Embedding Models and Monolingual Signals
Xinying Qiu and Gangqin Zhu 188

Creating rich online dictionaries for the Lao–French language pair, reusable for Machine Translation
Vincent Berment 194

Conference Program

Sunday, December 11, 2016

WSSANLP 2016 Openning

9:00–9:10   *Openning Remarks*

9:10–10:00   *Key Note by Alain Désoulières, INALCO, CERLOM, France*

10:00–10:20   **Coffee and Tea Break**

10:20–12:00   **WSSANLP Session 1: Oral Presentations**

Session Chair: Dekai Wu

10:20–10:40   *Compound Type Identification in Sanskrit: What Roles do the Corpus and Grammar Play?*
Amrith Krishna, Pavankumar Satuluri, Shubham Sharma, Apurv Kumar and Pawan Goyal

10:40–11:00   *Comparison of Grapheme-to-Phoneme Conversion Methods on a Myanmar Pronunciation Dictionary*
Ye Kyaw Thu, Win Pa Pa, Yoshinori Sagisaka and Naoto Iwahashi

11:00–11:20   *Character-Aware Neural Networks for Arabic Named Entity Recognition for Social Media*
Mourad Gridach

11:20–11:40   *Development of a Bengali parser by cross-lingual transfer from Hindi*
Ayan Das, Agnivo Saha and Sudeshna Sarkar

11:40–12:00   *Sinhala Short Sentence Similarity Calculation using Corpus-Based and Knowledge-Based Similarity Measures*
Jcs Kadupitiya, Surangika Ranathunga and Gihan Dias

12:00–13:30   **Lunch Break**

13:30–14:55   WSSANLP Session 2: Poster Presentations

Session Chair: M G Abbas Malik

Full Papers

Enriching Source for English-to-Urdu Machine Translation
Bushra Jawaid, Amir Kamran and Ondřej Bojar

The IMAGACT4ALL Ontology of Animated Images: Implications for Theoretical and Machine Translation of Action Verbs from English-Indian Languages
Pitambar Behera, Sharmin Muzaffar, Atul kr. Ojha and Girish Jha

Crowdsourcing-based Annotation of Emotions in Filipino and English Tweets
Fermin Roberto Lapitan, Riza Theresa Batista-Navarro and Eliezer Albacea

Temporal Information Extraction in Clinical Domain (TIECA)
Shujeevan Kanapathipillai, Viraj Welgama and Ruwan Weerasinghe

Sentiment Analysis of Tweets in Three Indian Languages
Shanta Phani, Shibamouli Lahiri and Arindam Biswas

Dealing with Linguistic Divergences in English-Bhojpuri Machine Translation
Pitambar Behera, Neha Mourya and Vandana Pandey

The development of a web corpus of Hindi language and corpus-based comparative studies to Japanese
Miki Nishioka and Shiro Akasegawa

Automatic Creation of a Sentence Aligned Sinhala-Tamil Parallel Corpus
Riyafa Abdul Hameed, Nadeeshani Pathirennehelage, Anusha Ihalapathirana, Maryam Ziyad Mohamed, Surangika Ranathunga, Sanath Jayasena, Gihan Dias and Sandareka Fernando

Short Papers

Align Me: A framework to generate Parallel Corpus Using OCRs and Bilingual Dictionaries
Priyam Bakliwal, Devadath V V and C V Jawahar

Learning Indonesian-Chinese Lexicon with Bilingual Word Embedding Models and Monolingual Signals
Xinying Qiu and Gangqin Zhu

Creating rich online dictionaries for the Lao–French language pair, reusable for Machine Translation
Vincent Berment

15:00–16:50 WSSANLP Session 3: Oral Presentations

Session Chair: Christian Boitet

15:00–15:10 *Introduction of Language Resources and Evaluation (LRE) Map by Laurent Besacier, member European Language Resources Association (ELRA)*

15:10–15:30 *Clustering-based Phonetic Projection in Mismatched Crowdsourcing Channels for Low-resourced ASR*
Wenda Chen, Mark Hasegawa-Johnson, Nancy Chen, Preethi Jyothi and Lav Varshney

15:30–15:50 *Improving the Morphological Analysis of Classical Sanskrit*
Oliver Hellwig

15:50–16:10 *Query Translation for Cross-Language Information Retrieval using Multilingual Word Clusters*
Paheli Bhattacharya, Pawan Goyal and Sudeshna Sarkar

16:10–16:30 *A study of attention-based neural machine translation model on Indian languages*
Ayan Das, Pranay Yerra, Ken Kumar and Sudeshna Sarkar

16:30–16:50 *Comprehensive Part-Of-Speech Tag Set and SVM based POS Tagger for Sinhala*
Sandareka Fernando, Surangika Ranathunga, Sanath Jayasena and Gihan Dias

WSSANLP 2016 Closing

16:50–17:00 *Closing Remarks*

Compound Type Identification in Sanskrit : What Roles do the Corpus and Grammar Play?

Amrith Krishna, Pavankumar Satuluri, Shubham Sharma,
Apurv Kumar and Pawan Goyal
Department of Computer Science & Engineering
Indian Institute of Technology, Kharagpur, WB, India
amrith@iitkgp.ac.in

Abstract

We propose a classification framework for semantic type identification of compounds in Sanskrit. We broadly classify the compounds into four different classes namely, *Avyayībhāva*, *Tatpuruṣa*, *Bahuvrīhi* and *Dvandva*. Our classification is based on the traditional classification system as mentioned in the ancient grammar treatise *Aṣṭādhyāyī* by Pāṇini, written 25 centuries back. We construct an elaborate feature space for our system by combining conditional rules from the grammar *Aṣṭādhyāyī*, semantic relations between the compound components from a lexical database *Amarakoṣa* and linguistic structures from the data using Adaptor Grammars. Our in-depth analysis of the feature space highlights the inadequacy of *Aṣṭādhyāyī*, a generative grammar, in classifying the data samples. Our experimental results validate the effectiveness of using lexical databases as suggested by Kulkarni and Kumar (2013) and put forward a new research direction by introducing linguistic patterns obtained from Adaptor grammars for effective identification of compound type. We utilise an ensemble based approach, specifically designed for handling skewed datasets and we achieve an overall accuracy of 0.77 using random forest classifiers.

1 Introduction

Compounding is a productive process of vocabulary expansion in languages where two or more nouns are used together to generate a new lexeme. Compound analysis is computationally challenging primarily due to three factors: i). compounds are highly productive in nature, ii). the relation between the components is implicit and iii). the correct interpretation of a compound is often dependent on contextual or pragmatic features (Kim and Baldwin, 2005). For example, 'houseboat' and 'boathouse'[1] are compounds formed from the same pair of nouns, 'house' and 'boat', but do not mean the same. Similarly, the relation between 'olive' and 'oil' in 'olive oil' does not hold between 'baby' and 'oil' in 'baby oil'.

Identifying the head of a compound can lead to significant improvements in semantic analysis tasks like Machine Translation, Question Answering etc. (Weller et al., 2014; Tiedemann, 2005). The head of a compound, in general is indicative of the referent(s) of the compound, in addition to determining the syntactic properties of the compound. For example, in 'paleface' paraphrased as 'a person who has a pale face', the head of the compound is an external entity. Here a word to word translation of the components would yield undesirable results. In 'bittersweet', both the stems 'bitter' and 'sweet' are the heads of the compound. In both 'houseboat' and 'boathouse', the final component forms the head.

On our empirical investigation of the Digital Corpus of Sanskrit (DCS)[2], we find a rich use of compounds with a presence of about 198,000 unique compound words occurring 373,000 times in a corpus of 2.5 million tokens (after stop-word removal). This is almost double in comparison to languages like German, which report 5.5-7% of corpus presence of the compounds (Schiller, 2005; Baroni et al., 2002). In DCS, 75% of the vocabulary consists of compounds, as against 47% vocabulary share

[1] http://wikidiff.com/houseboat/boathouse
[2] http://kjc-sv013.kjc.uni-heidelberg.de/dcs/

1

Proceedings of the 6th Workshop on South and Southeast Asian Natural Language Processing,
pages 1–10, Osaka, Japan, December 11-17 2016.

(Baroni et al., 2002) of compounds in German. We also find that 43% of the 66,000 lemmas in the corpus vocabulary were part of the compound formation as compared to 3-4% in English (Séaghdha and Copestake, 2013). In Sanskrit literature, especially in poetry, use of long compounds with multiple components is common. In DCS, more than 41 % of compounds have 3 or more components. For example, "*pravaramukuṭamaṇimarīcimañjarīcayacarcitacaraṇayugalaḥ*" is an exocentric compound used from the text "*Pañcatantram (kathāmukham)*" which translates to "The pair of whose feet was covered with a stream of rays originating from the gems in wreaths of eminent noble kings". This compound is composed of 9 components (Krishna et al., 2016).

Aṣṭādhyāyī, an ancient grammar treatise on Sanskrit, discusses the generation of four broad classes of compounds, namely, *Avyayībhāva, Tatpuruṣa, Bahuvrīhi* and *Dvandva*. We propose a classifier model to identify the semantic type of Sanskrit compounds i.e. one of the four classes. We find that the aforementioned notion of 'head' in compounds is discriminative as per this categorization. For our classification task, we successfully combine features extracted from rules in *Aṣṭādhyāyī*, taxonomy information and semantic relations inferred from *Amarakośa* ontology (Nair and Kulkarni, 2010), and linguistic structural information from the data using Adaptor grammar (Johnson et al., 2006). We perform an in-depth analysis of the performance of the system and highlight where the existing rules of *Aṣṭādhyāyī*, a generative grammar, are inadequate in classifying the data samples and show how additional features help us improve the performance of the classifier, by using our results obtained on a held-out dataset.

2 Compounds in Sanskrit

The compounds in Sanskrit exhibit numerous regularities that characterise them (Gillon, 1991). Compounds in Sanskrit are concatenative in nature, with a strict preference for the ordering of the components. A generated compound is treated as a fully qualified word (pada), such that the compound is subject to all the inflectional and derivational modifications applicable to nouns. Affixation occurs at the end of the compound similar to languages like that of Greek and not within the components (Ziering and van der Plas, 2016; Gillon, 1991). Any compound can be analysed by decomposing it into two immediate component nouns.

Linguists in Sanskrit have deeply discussed exceptions for the aforementioned regularities leading to different categorisations and further sub-categorisations of the compound types (Kulkarni and Kumar, 2013; Gillon, 2009). We only consider the four broad categorisations of the compounds. We now explain four classes of compounds and discuss various discriminative aspects about the broad level classes that we can abstract out from the generated forms and use in our system. In Sanskrit Grammar, compounds are classified into four general categories, namely, *Avyayībhāva, Tatpuruṣa, Bahuvrīhi* and *Dvandva*.

1. *Avyayībhāva* Compounds - In *Avyayībhāva* compound, the first component is an indeclinable or *avyaya*, which generally forms the head of the compound. The compound so generated will also become an indeclinable. For instance, in '*upakṛṣṇam*' (near to *Kṛṣṇa*), the word '*upa*' (near) is an indeclinable and the second component '*kṛṣṇa*' bears an inflectional affix, but the compound becomes an indeclinable.

2. *Tatpuruṣa* Compounds or Determinative compounds - They are endocentric compounds in which the second component is generally the head of the entire compound. For example, the phrase '*rājñaḥ puruṣaḥ*' (King's man) yields *rājapuruṣaḥ*. The second component, '*puruṣaḥ*' forms the head in the canonical paraphrase and hence the head of the compound (Gillon, 1991). The relation between the components is marked by the genitive case inflection of the first component *rājñaḥ*. *Tatpuruṣa* compounds constitute a distinctive sub-categorization, namely, Descriptive compounds or *Karmadhāraya*. In *karmadhāraya* compounds, one of the components needs to be an adjective and it is observed that generally the adjective comes as the first component. For example, in '*nīlameghaḥ*' (blue cloud) the first component, '*nīla*' (blue), is qualifying the head word, '*megha*' (cloud).

3. *Bahuvrīhi* Compounds or Exocentric Compounds - When the components in the compound refer to some external entity, say a person or an object, we call it a *Bahuvrīhi* compound. Here, the referent of the compound becomes the head of the compound. For example, '*pītāmbaraḥ*' is paraphrased as '*pītam ambaram yasya saḥ*'. Here the words *pītam* (yellow) and *ambaram* (cloth) together form the

compound referring to the Lord Vishnu. In absence of the paraphrase, the referent or headword often needs to be inferred from the context in which the compound is used. However, the gender differences between the final component and that of the compound is a convenient heuristic that can be used to identify the compound type in some of the cases (Goyal and Huet, 2013).

4. Dvandva or Copulative compounds - They are conjunctive compounds where the components are compounded to show the collectiveness of the individuals. The components involved may be nouns or adjectives. Since the components share a conjunctive relation, often multiple components are compounded together in a single process. In *Dvandva* compounds, the compound generally assumes the gender of the final component. But deciding the final component can be tricky especially in a free word order language like Sanskrit. For example, a *Dvandva* compound formed from the paraphrases '*pitā ca mātā ca*' and '*mātā ca pitā ca*' (mother and father) will always be of the form '*mātāpitarau*', which is in masculine due to the masculine noun *pitā* (father), but will never be '*pitāmātarau*', which should be in feminine gender. The formation of the latter is prohibited in the grammar, thereby eliminating the possibility of a conflict.

It is often observed that the same pair of components can generate compounds belonging to different semantic types. For example, *pītāmbarah* (Lord Vishnu) and *pītāmbaram* (yellow cloth) are *Bahuvrīhi* and *Tatpuruṣa* compounds respectively, formed from the same components, *pīta* and *ambaram*. Here the gender of the compounds becomes a discriminative feature. In general, the stem '*ambara*' is in neuter and hence in *Tatpuruṣa* compounds, the compound also maintains the neuter gender. But, for *Bahuvrīhi* compounds, the gender is based on the referent, which in this case is masculine.

Now, if we consider a compound like *nīlotpalam*, which contains two components *nīla* and *utpala*, the compound maintains the same final form in the case of both *Tatpuruṣa* and *Bahuvrīhi*, leading to ambiguity in semantic type identification. To resolve this conflict, either the canonical paraphrase or the context of usage is necessary. The potential conflict in disambiguation is often expressed between the compounds of *Bahuvrīhi* and specifically *karmadhāraya* compounds. Similarly, for compounds where the first component denotes a negation marker, there can be conflicts between *Tatpuruṣa* and *Bahuvrīhi* classes. The specific sub-categories are called as *Nañ-Tatpuruṣa* and *Nañ-Bahuvrīhi* compounds respectively. For instance, the compound '*aputrah*' is paraphrased as '*na putrah*'(not a son) in the case of *Tatpuruṣa* and '*avidyamānah putrah yasya sah*'(having no son) in the case pf *Bahuvrīhi*. *Tatpuruṣa* compounds can conflict with *Avyayībhāva* compounds as well. For example in '*ativanam*', the compound consists of two components viz '*ati*' and '*vanam*'. Here the first component '*ati*' is an indeclinable, a strong characteristic of *Avyayībhāva* compounds. But, there exists a sub-categorisation of *Tatpuruṣa*, where the first component is an indeclinable. The paraphrase of '*ativanam*' in the case of *Avyayībhāva* is '*vanasya atyayah*' (past the forest) and '*vanam atikrāntah*' (having passed the forest) in the case of *Tatpuruṣa*.

The aforementioned instances show the challenges involved in identifying the semantic type of a compound. Sometimes, the task is non-trivial even for humans and human cognition often relies on the context in which the compound is used or on the world knowledge about the entities involved .

3   Method

In our current work, we treat the problem as follows. When given a compound word decomposed into two immediate components of the compound, we identify the semantic type of the given compound and classify it into one of the four classes as discussed in Section 2. We build a feature-rich multi-class classifier and analyse the effectiveness of the features for the classification task. In *Aṣṭādhyāyī*, the generation of a compound is assumed to start with the canonical paraphrase of the compound. The noun declensions, modifiers and relation words in the paraphrase are then elided to form the compound. In our current settings, we only consider the compound and its individual split components. In this section, we describe the various features used for this classification task.

3.1   Rules from *Aṣṭādhyāyī*

Kulkarni and Kumar (2013) provides a categorisation of the rules in *Aṣṭādhyāyī* which are useful for compound analysis. Table 1 provides a summary of the type of rules that we employ in our system. The

Rule Type	Rule	Example
Type 1: Lexical lists	*Aṣṭādhyāyī* Rules like A.2.1.40 enlist specific lists of stems to be used as a component in compound formation	**akṣaśauṇḍaḥ** - *śauṇḍa* is listed in the rule A.2.1.40
Type 2: Morphological Properties	Rules like A.2.1.25 use inflectional suffix, derivational suffix etc. of the components in paraphrase as conditions for compounding	*kṛta* in the compound **svayaṃkṛta** bears a derivational suffix *ta*.
Type 3: Semantic property of the component	Rules like A.2.1.45 state specific properties of objects as conditions for compounding, e.g., part of day.	Stem *pūrvāhṇa* (forenoon) in **pūrvāhṇakṛta** denotes a part of day.
Type 4: Semantic relations between the components	Rules like A.2.1.57 check for specific relations between the components, e.g., Modifier - Modified relation	**nīlotpalam** - *nīla* (blue) describes the second component utpalam (lotus).

Table 1: Various rule types in *Aṣṭādhyāyī* for compound analysis (Kulkarni and Kumar, 2013). A.2.1.40 etc. indicate the rule numbers in the book.

type 1 rules are lexical lists which contain lists of nouns and indeclinable that appear as a component in the compound. Type 2 considers the morphological properties of the components. Inflectional affixes are indicators of the case of the noun, gender and plurality. In our work, we utilise string patterns at the end of the components to infer inflectional and derivational affixes used. Obtaining the exact noun declensions from the final forms is not always deterministic as the same affix might be used for representing multiple noun declensions for a given word. Additionally, the current parsers in Sanskrit do not include analysers for derivational affixes. On an empirical analysis over a dataset of 8000 labelled compounds, we find that a little above 4000 of 10000 unique compound components are recognised by the Sanskrit Heritage Reader unambiguously (Goyal and Huet, 2016). This is primarily due to the fact that the parsers are lexicon driven, and also due to the absence of derivational suffix analysers. The last two rule types are semantic in nature. Rule type 3, i.e., rules that check for semantic property of the component, is captured using manually curated lists of lexicons such as list of rivers, parts of day and night, etc. It essentially contain word lists stated outside of *Aṣṭādhyāyī*. The last type of rule looks into the possible relations between the components. where we utilise the lexical database *Amarakoṣa*.

3.2 Relations from Lexicons

Lexical databases with annotated semantic networks are beneficial in identifying the semantic compatibility between individual nouns and hence can be used in compound analysis (Kim and Baldwin, 2005; Séaghdha and Copestake, 2013). We utilise '*Amarakoṣa*', an ancient dictionary which covers about 11580 words (9031 unique lemmas) in altogether 4035 *synsets*. With efforts from Nair and Kulkarni (2010), *Amarakoṣa* is digitised, forming a semantic network explicitly labelled with semantic relations between the words. The lexicon primarily consists of six relations, of which three of the relations, namely, 'part-whole','is a kind of' and 'master-possession', are useful in identifying *Tatpuruṣa* compounds. Two of the three remaining relations, namely, 'child-parent' and 'husband-wife', are helpful in identifying *Dvandva* compounds. An additional advantage with *Amarakoṣa* is that we get gender information about the individual nouns from the e-lexicon, which is a discriminative factor in identifying *Bahuvrīhi* compounds as mentioned in Section 2. For each component, the gender, head word and the corresponding word with which the component bears the relation, are used as features. We consider all the six relations in *Amarakoṣa* between the compound components.

3.3 Variable Length Character n-grams

We capture semantic class specific linguistic regularities present in our dataset using variable length character n-grams and character n-gram collocations shared between compounds. In order to learn the character n-grams, we use Adaptor grammars (Johnson et al., 2006), a non-parametric Bayesian approach towards learning productions for a probabilistic context free grammar (PCFG).

The grammar obtained from the Adaptor Grammar (AG) is a probabilistic context free grammar, where the productions form a set of fixed non-terminals and the probabilities for the productions to be invoked are learnt from the data. In Adaptor Grammar, a skeletal context free grammar is defined as shown in Listing 1a, where the set of non-terminals to be adapted is fixed a priori and will be a subset of the entire set of non-terminals in the skeletal grammar. For each of the adapted non-terminal, marked with a '@', the grammar learns a distribution over trees rooted at each of the adapted non-terminal (Zhai et al., 2014). We learn grammars G1, G2 and G3 with the same skeletal structure in Listing 1a, but with different data samples belonging to *Tatpuruṣa*, *Bahuvrīhi* and *Dvandva* respectively. We did not learn a grammar for *Avyayībhāva*, due to insufficient data samples for learning the patterns. We use a '$' marker to indicate the word boundary between the components and a '#' symbol to mark the beginning and ending of the first and the final components respectively. We also learn a grammar G4, where the entire dataset is taken together along with additional 4000 random pair of words from the DCS corpus, where none of the words appeared as a compound component in the corpus.

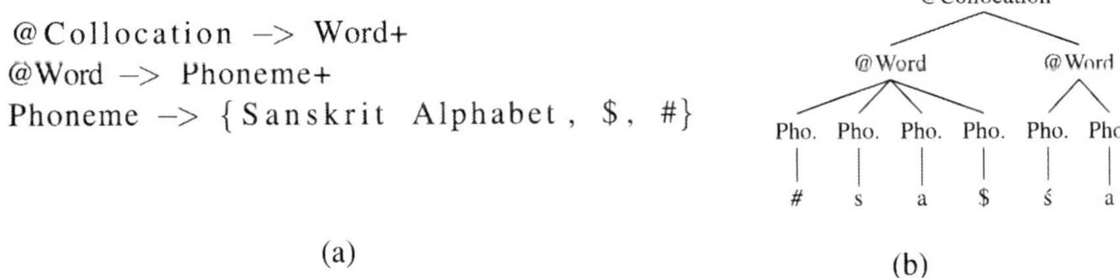

```
@Collocation  ->  Word+
@Word  ->  Phoneme+
Phoneme  ->  {Sanskrit  Alphabet ,  $,  #}
```

(a)

(b)

Listing 1: a) Skeletal grammar for the adaptor grammar (Johnson et al., 2006). b) Derivation tree for an instance of a production '#sa$ śa' for the non-terminal @collocation

Every production in the learned grammars has a probability to be invoked, where likelihood of all the productions of a non-terminal sums to one. To obtain discriminative productions from G1, G2 and G3, we find conditional entropy of the production with that of G4 and filter only those productions above a threshold. We also consider all the unique productions in each of the Grammars in G1 to G3. We further restrict the productions based on the frequency of the production in the data and the length of the sub-string produced by the production, both of them were kept at the value of three.

We show an instance of one such production for a variable length character n-gram collocation. Here, for the adapted non-terminal @Collocation, we find that one of the production finally derives '#sa$ śa', which actually is derived as two @Word derivations as shown in the Listing 1b. We use this as a regular expression, which captures some properties that need to satisfied by the concatenated components. The particular production mandates that the first component must be exactly *sa*, as it is sandwiched between the symbols # and $. Now, since *śa* occurs after the previous substring which contains $ the boundary for both the components, *śa* should belong to the second component. Now, since as per the grammar both the substrings are independent @word productions, we relax the constraint that both the susbtrings should occur immediately one after the other. We treat the same as a regular expression, such that *śa* should occur after *sa*, and any number of characters can come in between both the substrings. For the particular susbtring, we had 22 compounds, all of them belonging to *Bahuvrīhi*, which satisfied the criteria. Now, compounds where first component is 'sa' are mostly *Bahuvrīhi* compounds, and this is obvious to Sanskrit linguists. But here, the system was not provided with any such prior information or possible patterns. The system learnt the pattern from the data. Incidentally, our dataset consisted of a few compound samples belonging to different classes where the first component was '*sa*'.

3.4   Other Features

We look for specific patterns that check for the lexical similarity between components. For example, consider the compound *bhāvābhāvau* where the final component *a-bhāva* is the negation for the first component *bhāva*. The prepositions '*a*' and '*an*' represent negation of entities. We identify those compounds, where the first and second components differ only by *a* or *an*. This heuristic has its own limitations, as not all negations are marked by the markers. We also use Jaro-Winkler distance, an edit distance variant, between both the components as an additional feature to capture the lexical similarity between the

5

Word	Component Position	Compound Class
iti	First	*Bahuvrīhi*
sva	First	*Tatpuruṣa*
manāḥ	Final	*Bahuvrīhi*
mātā	First	*Dvandva*
dharmā	Final	*Bahuvrīhi*

Table 2: Sample of filtered words and their position in the compound.

Classifiers	P	R	F	A
Random Forests	0.76	0.75	0.74	0.74
Extreme Random Forests (ERF)	0.76	0.75	0.74	0.75
Gradient Boosting Methods (GBM)	0.62	0.54	0.53	0.54
Adaboost Classifier	0.71	0.69	0.69	0.69

Table 3: Precision (P), Recall (R), F-Score (F) & Accuracy (A) for the competing systems on held-out dataset.

components. We find that the mean Jaro-Winkler distance between components of *Dvandva* compounds (0.48) is higher than that of other compounds (0.31 - 0.38). We also consider the last three characters of the second component, where the second component bears the nominal inflections of the compound word. We also used a handful of specific suffix patterns based on the entropy score of the patterns in discriminating the classes. The patterns are indicative of the affix information. We finally filtered 34 words and patterns by manual inspection, that had lower entropy score as well as there is a linguistic motivation for their inclusion. Table 2 shows a sample of such filtered words; we skip the linguistic motivation behind the filtering of each lemma due to space constraints.

4 Experiments

4.1 Dataset

We obtained a labelled dataset of compounds and the decomposed pairs of components from the Sanskrit studies department, UoHyd[3]. The dataset contains more than 32000 unique compounds. The compounds were obtained from ancient digitised texts including *Śrīmad Bhagavat Gīta, Caraka saṃhitā* among others. The dataset contains the *sandhi* split components along with the compounds. With more than 75 % of the dataset containing *Tatpuruṣa* compounds, we down-sample the *Tatpuruṣa* compounds to a count of 4000, to match with the second highest class, *Bahuvrīhi*. We find that the *Avyayībhāva* compounds are severely under-represented in the data-set, with about 5 % of the *Bahuvrīhi* class. From the dataset, we filtered 9952 different data-points split into 7957 data points for training and the remaining as held-out dataset. For all the features mentioned in Section 3, we have considered data points which are in the training set and we have not considered data from the held-out in calculating any of the features, including Adaptor grammar.

4.2 Results

Probably due to a large feature space of 2737 features we employ, and an imbalanced dataset, the performance of the classifier models like SVM and decision tree were near to chance with SVM making no predictions to the *Avyayībhāva* class. We use ensemble based approaches for our system and the results are presented in Table 3. The results presented in the table are predictions over held-out data, where the classifier was trained with the entire training data. We find that the Extreme Random Forests (ERF) (Geurts et al., 2006; Pedregosa et al., 2011) gives the best performance amongst all the compared systems in Table 3. The performance of the Random Forests and the ERF were almost similar with reported performance measures varying only from the third decimal point. Table 4b shows the result for the ERF classifier over training data when trained with 10 fold cross validation. The class-wise precision and recall for the model over held out dataset is presented in Table 4a. We find that the classifier fares poorly for *Avyayībhāva* and *Dvandva*, primarily due to sparsity in the data as they both amount to about 5% and 33% of the other two classes respectively.

To measure the impact of different types of features we have incorporated, we train the classifier incrementally with different feature types as reported in Section 3. We report the results over the held-out

---

[3]http://sanskrit.uohyd.ac.in/scl/

Class	P	R	F
A	0.92	0.43	0.58
B	0.85	0.74	0.79
D	0.69	0.39	0.49
T	0.68	0.88	0.77

(a)

Class	P	R	F
A	0.85	0.48	0.61
B	0.84	0.76	0.80
D	0.94	0.25	0.39
T	0.75	0.85	0.80

(b)

Class	P	R	F
A	0.84	0.67	0.74
B	0.88	0.73	0.79
D	0.69	0.61	0.65
T	0.72	0.87	0.79

(c)

Table 4: Classwise Precision (P), Recall (R) and F-Score (F) results for three different setups. a) on held-out data (Accuracy - 0.75). b) with 10-fold cross validation over training data (Accuracy - 0.79). c) Easy ensemble on held-out data (Accuracy - 0.77). A, B, D and T represent the classes *Avyayībhāva*, *Bahuvrīhi*, *Dvandva* and *Tatpuruṣa* respectively.

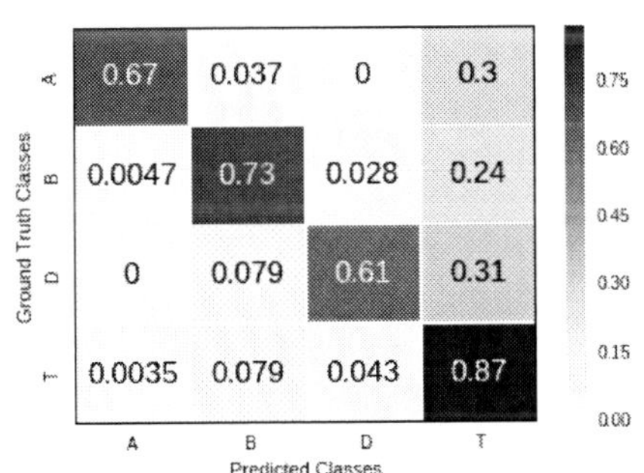

Figure 1: Confusion Matrix heat map for the easy ensemble classifier

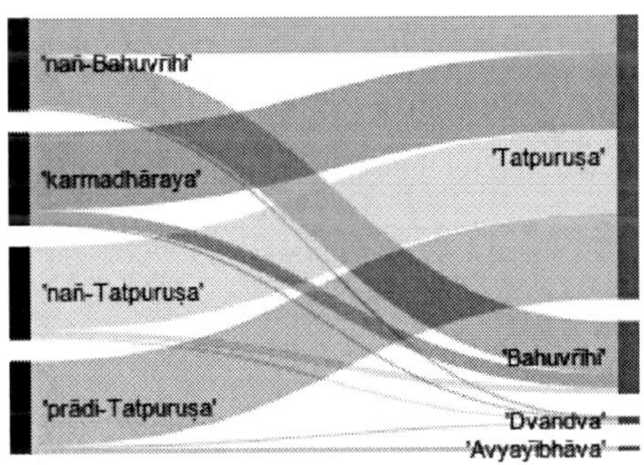

Figure 2: Alluvial graph showing the classification outcome for specific sub-classes

data. At first we train the system with only *Aṣṭādhyāyī* rules and features discussed in Section 3.4. We find that the overall accuracy of the system is about 59.34%. We do not report the accuracy of the system when we use *Aṣṭādhyāyī* rules alone as it was not sufficient to cover all the samples. Then we augmented the classifier by adding features from *Amarakoṣa* as described in Section 3.2. We find that the overall accuracy of the system has increased to 63.81%. Notably, the precision for *Dvandva* and *Bahuvrīhi* increased by absolute values 0.15 and 0.06 respectively. We then add the Adaptor grammar features to the feature set and Table 4a presents the result of the system with the entire feature set. We perform feature ranking based on entropy measure. We try to iteratively drop the least ranked features in steps of 50, till 1700 of 2737 features are dropped. We find that the accuracy does not change much, but mostly drops from the reported accuracy of 0.75 by a maximum of 0.38% (0.747).

To handle the imbalanced data set, we employed easy ensemble (Liu et al., 2009) approach. In easy ensemble approach, we form multiple training sets, where each of the set is a subset of the original training set such that the data samples in the minority classes remain intact whereas the majority classes are under-sampled to a defined proportion. In effect, we have multiple training sets where the data samples in the majority class are distributed across the subsets. Now with each of the subset, we run ERF classifier and average out the results. As can be seen from Table 4c, this approach gives consistent results across the four classes, with significant improvements in F-Score for *Dvandva* and *Avyayībhāva* classes. We further look into specific cases of compound classes which get misclassified. Figure 1 shows the confusion matrix heat-map for our best performing system, the easy ensemble classifier. From the heat-map we can observe that most of the mis-classifications go to *Tatpuruṣa*, resulting in a lower precision of 0.72 for *Tatpuruṣa*. It can also be noted that there are no *Dvandva* and *Avyayībhāva* mis-classifications. Figure 2 represents classification of the specific cases of sub-types as discussed in Section 2. *Avyayībhāva* and *Tatpuruṣa* can potentially be conflicting as there exists specific types of *Tatpuruṣa* where the first component can be an *avyaya*. We find that 6 data samples of *Tatpuruṣa* have been misclassified into *Avyayībhāva* and all the 6 data points have their first component as an *avyaya*. From Figure 1, it is already clear that majority of mis-classifications in *Avyayībhāva* go to *Tatpuruṣa*. Out of 70 mis-classifications of

Tatpuruṣa to *Bahuvrīhi*, 38 belong to *karmadhāraya* class. Also only 2 of the *karmadhāraya* compounds got mis-classified to a different class other than *Bahuvrīhi*. 83.81 % of the *karmadhāraya* compounds got correctly classified into *Tatpuruṣa*. *Nañ-Bahuvrīhi* and *Nañ-Tatpuruṣa* are also potentially conflicting cases, and we find that in *Nañ-Tatpuruṣa*, 8 of 11 mis-classifications happen to *Bahuvrīhi* class and in *Nañ-Bahuvrīhi* 13 of 14 mis-classifications happen to *Tatpuruṣa* class. But in all the aforementioned cases, the majority of the data samples got correctly classified.

5 Related Work

Semantic analysis of compounds has attracted much traction from the computational linguistics community, especially on languages like English, German, Italian, Afrikaans and Dutch (Verhoeven et al., 2014). Lexical databases like Wordnet (Kim and Baldwin, 2005) and Wikipedia (Strube and Ponzetto, 2006) were extensively used to infer semantic relations between the components in a compound. Effectiveness of verb-semantics and word sense disambiguation of the components involved were also studied (Kim and Baldwin, 2006; Kim and Baldwin, 2013). Séaghdha (2009) defines wordnet kernel functions for identifying the relational similarity between the components. Works like Séaghdha and Copestake (2013) use corpus-based approaches where co-occurrence measures between the components are utilised. Nastase et al. (2006) combine both the corpus-based approaches and lexical database based approaches for semantic analysis of compounds. Ziering and van der Plas (2016) presents a corpus-based approach for splitting of German compounds The authors augment the model by incorporating distributional information in Ziering et al. (2016). Botha et al. (2012) builds a language model by using a hierarchical Bayesian model where the models for head word and the other component are conditioned differently. The *samarthāhnika* (Joshi, 1968) gives a detailed account of the discussion involved in the Indian tradition on the semantic compatibility of constituents and the compositionality of the meaning of a compound. Pataskar (1996) has discussed the use of the *Dvandva* compounds in relation to their case endings and how *Pāṇini* dealt with the *sūtras* in *Aṣṭādhyāyī*. Bhandare (1995) has discussed the structural and semantic aspects of *Dvandva* compounds. Mahavir (1986) has discussed various transformations that take place on the canonical paraphrase of a compound (*vigrahavākya*) to generate the final form. Gillon (2009) proposes an extended phrase structure syntax to represent the underlying constituent structure of the compounds. Kumar (2012) has described the computational analysis of Sanskrit compounds in his doctoral dissertation. Goyal and Huet (2013) describes various morphological phenomena involved in the generation and analysis of *Avyayībhāva* compounds. Pavankumar (2015) built a Sanskrit compound generator, adhering to the tradition followed in *Aṣṭādhyāyī*, as a part of his doctoral dissertation.

6 Conclusion

In this work, we built an automated classifier for identifying the semantic type of a compound in Sanskrit. With an ensemble based classifier approach, we tackle the challenge of an imbalanced dataset and our system effectively classifies data into appropriate semantic classes. We successfully incorporate rules from the ancient grammar treatise *Aṣṭādhyāyī*, lexical relations from *Amarakoṣa* and we also learn linguistic structures from the data using adaptor grammars. In our work, we show the improvement in performance after incorporating each of the aforementioned feature types. We also discuss the specific cases of conflicts between the semantic types.

Our primary motivation for this work was to understand the computational challenges involved in automated means of classifying compounds in Sanskrit. Our work can be seen as an extension in the line of works suggested in Kulkarni and Kumar (2013), and ours is the first such system for Sanskrit to incorporate semantic relations in taxonomy as well as class specific linguistic structures for the task. Results from our system demonstrate the effectiveness of a lexical database for the task and that it is a promising direction to be explored. We can extend the current system by incorporating other lexicons such as Indo-wordnet (Sinha et al., 2006) along with *amarakoṣa*. The improvement gained by using adaptor grammar productions look promising, as the grammar was not exposed to the data from the held-out dataset and yet was able to classify the data samples into appropriate classes. We will be further investigating the utility of Adaptor grammar in defining skeletal grammars as per the rules mentioned in Gillon (2009) and some of the conditional rules in *Aṣṭādhyāyī* itself. From multiple instances discussed in Section 2, the role of context in determining compound type is evident. But such systems should be designed only after giving enough thought on solving the obvious resource constraints that the language currently faces.

Acknowledgements

The authors would like to thank Mr. Nishant Nikhil and Ms. Survi Makharia, IIT Kharagpur, for their contributions towards the implementation of the framework.

References

Marco Baroni, Johannes Matiasek, and Harald Trost. 2002. Wordform-and class-based prediction of the components of german nominal compounds in an aac system. In *Proceedings of the 19th international conference on Computational linguistics-Volume 1*, pages 1–7. Association for Computational Linguistics.

V. V. Bhandare. 1995. Structural and Semantic Aspects of the Dvandva Compound. *Annals of the Bhandarkar Oriental Research Institute*, 76(1-4):89–96.

Jan Botha, Chris Dyer, and Phil Blunsom. 2012. Bayesian language modelling of german compounds. In *Proceedings of COLING 2012*.

Pierre Geurts, Damien Ernst, and Louis Wehenkel. 2006. Extremely randomized trees. *Machine learning*, 63(1):3–42.

Brendan Gillon. 1991. Sanskrit word formation and context free rules. *Toronto Working Papers in Linguistics*, 11.

Brendan S. Gillon. 2009. Tagging Classical Sanskrit Compounds. In Amba Kulkarni and Gérard Huet, editors, *Sanskrit Computational Linguistics 3*, pages 98–105. Springer-Verlag LNAI 5406.

Pawan Goyal and Gérard Huet. 2013. Completeness analysis of a sanskrit reader. In *Proceedings, 5th International Symposium on Sanskrit Computational Linguistics. DK Printworld (P) Ltd*, pages 130–171.

Pawan Goyal and Gérard Huet. 2016. Design and analysis of a lean interface for sanskrit corpus annotation. *Journal of Language Modelling*, 4(2):145–182.

Mark Johnson, Thomas L Griffiths, and Sharon Goldwater. 2006. Adaptor grammars: A framework for specifying compositional nonparametric bayesian models. In *Advances in neural information processing systems*, pages 641–648.

S. D. Joshi. 1968. *Patañjali's Vyākaraṇa - Mahābhāṣya Samarthāhnika (P. 2.1.1)*. Centre of Advanced Study in Sanskrit, University of Poona, Poona.

Su Nam Kim and Timothy Baldwin. 2005. Automatic interpretation of noun compounds using wordnet similarity. In *International Conference on Natural Language Processing*, pages 945–956. Springer.

Su Nam Kim and Timothy Baldwin. 2006. Interpreting semantic relations in noun compounds via verb semantics. In *Proceedings of the COLING/ACL on Main conference poster sessions*, pages 491–498. Association for Computational Linguistics.

Su Nam Kim and Timothy Baldwin. 2013. Word sense and semantic relations in noun compounds. *ACM Transactions on Speech and Language Processing (TSLP)*, 10(3):9.

Amrith Krishna, Bishal Santra, Pavan Kumar Satuluri, Sasi Prasanth Bandaru, Bhumi Faldu, Yajuvendra Singh, and Pawan Goyal. 2016. Word segmentation in sanskrit using path constrained random walks. In *Proceedings of COLING 2016*.

Amba Kulkarni and Anil Kumar. 2013. Clues from aṣṭādhyāyī for compound type identification. In *5th International Sanskrit Computational Linguistics Symposium (SCLS)*.

Anil Kumar. 2012. An Automatic Sanskrit Compound Processor. In *Proceedings of the International Sanskrit Computational Linguistics Symposium*. Springer-Verlag LNAI 5406.

Xu-Ying Liu, Jianxin Wu, and Zhi-Hua Zhou. 2009. Exploratory undersampling for class-imbalance learning. *IEEE Transactions on Systems, Man, and Cybernetics, Part B (Cybernetics)*, 39(2):539–550.

Mahavir. 1986. Treatment of Samāsa in Pāṇini. *Annals of the Bhandarkar Oriental Research Institute*, 67(1-4):147–158.

Sivaja S Nair and Amba Kulkarni. 2010. The knowledge structure in amarakośa. In *Sanskrit Computational Linguistics*, pages 173–189. Springer.

Vivi Nastase, Jelber Sayyad-Shirabad, Marina Sokolova, and Stan Szpakowicz. 2006. Learning noun-modifier semantic relations with corpus-based and wordnet-based features. In *Proceedings of the National Conference on Artificial Intelligence*, volume 21, page 781. Menlo Park, CA; Cambridge, MA; London; AAAI Press; MIT Press; 1999.

Bhagyalata Pataskar. 1996. Some Observations about the Compound Structure of Aṣṭādhyāyī. *Annals of the Bhandarkar Oriental Research Institute*, 77(1-4):121–131.

Pavankumar. 2015. *Sanskrit Compound Generation: With a Focus on the Order of the Operations (Doctoral Dissertation)*. University of Hyderabad.

F. Pedregosa, G. Varoquaux, A. Gramfort, V. Michel, B. Thirion, O. Grisel, M. Blondel, P. Prettenhofer, R. Weiss, V. Dubourg, J. Vanderplas, A. Passos, D. Cournapeau, M. Brucher, M. Perrot, and E. Duchesnay. 2011. Scikit-learn: Machine learning in Python. *Journal of Machine Learning Research*, 12:2825–2830.

Anne Schiller. 2005. German compound analysis with wfsc. In *International Workshop on Finite-State Methods and Natural Language Processing*, pages 239–246. Springer.

Diarmuid O Séaghdha and Ann Copestake. 2013. Interpreting compound nouns with kernel methods. *Natural Language Engineering*, 19(03):331–356.

Diarmuid Séaghdha. 2009. Semantic classification with wordnet kernels. In *Proceedings of Human Language Technologies: The 2009 Annual Conference of the North American Chapter of the Association for Computational Linguistics, Companion Volume: Short Papers*, pages 237–240. Association for Computational Linguistics.

Manish Sinha, Mahesh Reddy, and Pushpak Bhattacharyya. 2006. An approach towards construction and application of multilingual indo-wordnet. In *3rd Global Wordnet Conference (GWC 06), Jeju Island, Korea*.

Michael Strube and Simone Paolo Ponzetto. 2006. Wikirelate! computing semantic relatedness using wikipedia. In *AAAI*, volume 6, pages 1419–1424.

Jörg Tiedemann. 2005. Improving passage retrieval in question answering using nlp. In *Portuguese Conference on Artificial Intelligence*, pages 634–646. Springer.

Ben Verhoeven, Walter Daelemans, Menno Van Zaanen, and Gerhard Van Huyssteen. 2014. Automatic compound processing: Compound splitting and semantic analysis for afrikaans and dutch. *ComAComA 2014*, page 20.

Marion Weller, Fabienne Cap, Stefan Müller, Sabine Schulte im Walde, and Alexander Fraser. 2014. Distinguishing degrees of compositionality in compound splitting for statistical machine translation. In *Proceedings of the First Workshop on Computational Approaches to Compound Analysis (ComAComA 2014)*, pages 81–90.

Ke Zhai, Jordan Boyd-Graber, and Shay B Cohen. 2014. Online adaptor grammars with hybrid inference. *Transactions of the Association for Computational Linguistics*, 2:465–476.

Patrick Ziering and Lonneke van der Plas. 2016. Towards unsupervised and language-independent compound splitting using inflectional morphological transformations. In *Proceedings of the NAACL 2016*.

Patrick Ziering, Stefan Müller, and Lonneke van der Plas. 2016. Top a splitter: Using distributional semantics for improving compound splitting. *The 12th Workshop on Multiword Expressions, ACL 2016*, page 50.

Comparison of Grapheme–to–Phoneme Conversion Methods on a Myanmar Pronunciation Dictionary

Ye Kyaw Thu[λ,†], Win Pa Pa[‡], Yoshinori Sagisaka[†] and Naoto Iwahashi[λ]

[λ]Artificial Intelligence Lab., Okayama Prefectural University, Japan
[‡]Natural Language Processing Lab., University of Computer Studies Yangon, Myanmar
[†]Language and Speech Science Research Lab., Waseda University, Japan
{ye, iwahashi}@c.oka-pu.ac.jp, winpapa@ucsy.edu.mm, ysagisaka@gmail.com

Abstract

Grapheme-to-Phoneme (G2P) conversion is the task of predicting the pronunciation of a word given its graphemic or written form. It is a highly important part of both automatic speech recognition (ASR) and text-to-speech (TTS) systems. In this paper, we evaluate seven G2P conversion approaches: Adaptive Regularization of Weight Vectors (AROW) based structured learning (S-AROW), Conditional Random Field (CRF), Joint-sequence models (JSM), phrase-based statistical machine translation (PBSMT), Recurrent Neural Network (RNN), Support Vector Machine (SVM) based point-wise classification, Weighted Finite-state Transducers (WFST) on a manually tagged Myanmar phoneme dictionary. The G2P bootstrapping experimental results were measured with both automatic phoneme error rate (PER) calculation and also manual checking in terms of voiced/unvoiced, tones, consonant and vowel errors. The result shows that CRF, PBSMT and WFST approaches are the best performing methods for G2P conversion on Myanmar language.

1 Introduction

Grapheme-to-Phoneme (G2P) conversion models are important for natural language processing (NLP), automatic speech recognition (ASR) and text-to-speech (TTS) developments. Although many machine learning approaches are applicable for G2P conversion, most of them are supervised learning approaches and as a prerequisite we have to prepare clean annotated training data and this is costly. As a consequence, G2P models are rarely available for under-resourced languages such as South and Southeast Asian languages. In practice, we need to perform bootstrapping or active learning with a small manually annotated G2P dictionary for efficient development of G2P converters. In this paper, we examine seven G2P conversion methodologies for incremental training with a small Myanmar language G2P lexicon. We used automatic evaluation in the form of phoneme error rate (PER) and also manually evaluated Myanmar language specific errors such as inappropriate voiced to unvoiced conversion and tones, on syllable units.

2 G2P Conversion for Myanmar Language

Myanmar language (Burmese) is one of the under-resourced Southeast Asian languages for NLP. It has SOV (Subject–Object–Verb) typology and syntactically is quite similar to Japanese and Korean in that functional morphemes succeed content morphemes, and verb phrases succeed noun phrases. In Myanmar text, words composed of single or multiple syllables are usually not separated by white space. Although spaces are used for separating phrases for easier reading, it is not strictly necessary, and these spaces are rarely used in short sentences. In this paper, we only consider phonetic conversion of syllables within words for G2P bootstrapping with a dictionary. Myanmar syllables are generally composed of sequences of consonants and (zero or more) vowel combinations starting with a consonant. Here, vowel combinations can be single vowels, sequences of vowels and sequences of vowels starting with a consonant that modifies the pronunciation of the first vowel. Some examples of Myanmar vowel combinations are အင်း(in:), အိန်း(ein:), အိုင်း(ain:), အန်း(an:) and အောင်း(aun:). The relationship between words and the pronunciation of Myanmar language is not completely consistent, ambiguous, and context dependent, depending on adjacent syllables. Moreover, there are many exceptional cases and rules that present difficulties for G2P conversion (Ye Kyaw Thu et al., 2015a).

Proceedings of the 6th Workshop on South and Southeast Asian Natural Language Processing,
pages 11–22, Osaka, Japan, December 11-17 2016.

Some Myanmar syllables can be pronounced in more than 4 ways depending on the context and Part-of-Speech (POS) of the syllable. As an example, consider the pronunciation of the two-syllable word ရောင်းဝယ် (meaning trade) with corresponding standard pronunciation of its syllables "ရောင်း" (pronunciation: `jaun:`) and "ဝယ်" (pronunciation: `we`). This is a simple pronunciation pattern of a Myanmar word and it has no pronunciation change (i.e. `jaun: + we => jaun:`). However, many pronunciations of syllables are changed depending on their combination such as in the Myanmar word မေတ္တာ (မေတ် syllable + တာ syllable), love in English; the pronunciation changes from "`mi' + ta`" to "`mji' + ta`", နား:ရွက် (နား: syllable + ရွက် syllable) , ear in English; the pronunciation changes from "`na: + jwe'`" to "`na- + jwe'`" .

POS is also a factor for pronunciation. The Myanmar word ထမင်းချက် can be pronounced in two ways; "`hta- min: che'`" when used as a **verb** "cook rice" and "`hta- min: gye'`" when used as a **noun** "a cook". In another example, the three syllable Myanmar word စာရင်းစစ် can be pronounced "`sa jin: si'`" when used to mean **verb** "audit" or "`sa- jin: zi'`" when used to mean a **noun** "auditor"; the single-syllable Myanmar word ချိုင့် can be pronounced "`chein`". for usage as an adjective "dented" or can be pronounced "`gyein.`". when used as a noun meaning "food carrier"; one syllable Myanmar word ချေ can be pronounced "`gyi`" when used as a noun meaning "barking deer" or can be pronounced "`chei`" when used as a verb.

The most common pronunciation change of Myanmar syllables is unvoiced to voiced and it is contextually dependent, for example the change from: "`pi. tau'`" to "`ba- dau'`" for the word ပိတောက် (Pterocarpus macrocarpus flower) , "`pja. tin: pau'`" to "`ba- din: bau'`" for ပြတင်းပေါက် (window) word. Some same syllables within a word can be pronounced differently, for example, the Myanmar consonant က pronounced "`ka.`" and "`ga-`" for three syllables Myanmar word ကကတစ် "`ka. ga- di'`" (giant sea perch in English). In some Myanmar words, the pronunciation of a syllable is totally different from its grapheme or spelling such as one old Myanmar name လူလင်ကျော် "`lu. lin kyo`" pronounced as "`na- lin gyo`".

3   Related Work

(Davel and Martirosian, 2009) designed a process for the development of pronunciation dictionaries in resource-scarce environments, and applied it to the development of pronunciation dictionaries for ten of the official languages of South Africa. The authors mentioned that it is a means of developing practically usable pronunciation dictionaries with minimal resources. (Schlippe, 2014) proposed efficient methods which contribute to rapid and economic semi-automatic pronunciation dictionary development and evaluated them on English, German, Spanish, Vietnamese, Swahili, and Haitian Creole. A novel modified Expectation-Maximization (EM)-driven G2P sequence alignment algorithm that supports joint-sequence language models, and several decoding solutions using weighted finite-state transducers (WFSTs) was presented in (Novak et al., 2012). G2P conversion using statistical machine translation (SMT) was proposed in (Laurent et al., 2009), (Karanasou and Lamel, 2011). In (Laurent et al., 2009), it is shown that applying SMT gives better results than a joint sequence model-based G2P converter for French. The automatic generation of a pronunciation dictionary is proposed in (Karanasou and Lamel, 2011), and their technique used Moses phrase-based SMT toolkit (Koehn et al., 2007) G2P conversion. (Damper et al., 1999) compared different G2P methods and found that data-driven methods outperform rule-based methods.

As far as the authors are aware, there have been only three published methodologies for Myanmar language G2P conversion. (Ei Phyu Phyu Soe, 2013) proposed a dictionary based approach and analyzed it only on pure Myanmar syllables without considering subscript consonants or Pali words. It is a simple approach with a dictionary that is not able to handle out-of-vocabulary (OOV) words. (Ye Kyaw Thu et al., 2015a) proposed four simple Myanmar syllable pronunciation patterns as features that can be used to augment the models in a CRF approach to G2P conversion. The results show that the new features can substantially improve the accuracy of G2P conversion especially on conversion of syllables specifically targeted by the new feature sets. (Ye Kyaw Thu et al., 2015b) applied a phrase-based SMT (PBSMT) approach to Myanmar

G2P conversion and found that G2P conversion using SMT outperformed a CRF approach, with a considerably faster training time. Their comparison between the CRF and PBSMT models shows that the PBSMT approach can handle pronunciation prediction on new compound words (a common form of OOV) well, and can also handle the influence of neighbouring words on the pronunciation of a word.

4 G2P Conversion Methodologies

In this section, we describe the G2P conversion methodologies used in the experiments in this paper.

4.1 Structured Adaptive Regularization of Weight Vectors (S-AROW)

(Kubo et al., 2014) proposed Structured AROW extending AROW (Crammer et al., 2013) to structured learning for G2P conversion. AROW is an online learning algorithm for binary classification that that has several useful properties: large margin training, confidence weighting, and the capacity to handle non-separable data. To overcome the overfitting problems encountered by competitive methods such as Margin Infused Relaxed Algorithm (MIRA) (Crammer and Singer, 2003) and the Confidence Weighted Algorithm (CW) (Dredze et al., 2008) AROW recasts the terms for the constraint of CW as regularizers. S-AROW is applicable for G2P conversion tasks and has a shorter learning time than MIRA. It also has been shown to have a lower phoneme and word error rate compared to MIRA (Kubo et al., 2014).

4.2 Conditional Random Fields

Linear-chain conditional random Fields (CRFs) (Lafferty et al., 2001) are models that consider dependencies among the predicted segmentation labels that are inherent in the state transitions of finite state sequence models and can incorporate domain knowledge effectively into segmentation. Unlike heuristic methods, they are principled probabilistic finite state models on which exact inference over sequences can be efficiently performed. The model computes the following probability of a label sequence $\mathbf{Y} = \{y_1, ..., y_T\}$ of a particular character string $\mathbf{W} = \{w_1, ..., w_T\}$.

$$P_\lambda(\mathbf{Y}|\mathbf{W}) = \frac{1}{Z(\mathbf{W})} exp(\sum_{t=1}^{T} \sum_{k=1}^{|\lambda|} \lambda_k f_k(y_{t-1}, \mathbf{W}, t)) \tag{1}$$

where $Z(\mathbf{W})$ is a normalization term, f_k is a feature function, and λ is a feature weight vector.

4.3 Joint-sequence models (JSM)

The joint-sequence models (JSM) approach for G2P was proposed by (Bisani and Ney, 2008) and it is also one of the most popular approaches for G2P conversion. The fundamental idea of JSM is that both the grapheme and phoneme sequences can be generated jointly by means of a sequence of joint units (graphones) which carry both grapheme and phoneme symbols. The goal of the JSM is to find a sequence of Y phonemes, $Q = Q_1^Y = \{q_1, q_2, ..., q_Y\}$, that given by a sequence of X graphemes defined by $G = G_1^X = \{g_1, g_2, ..., g_X\}$. This problem can be describe as the determination of the optimal sequence of phonemes, $\acute{Q}$, that maximizes their conditional probability, Q, given a sequence of graphemes, G:

$$\acute{Q} = \arg \max_Q P(Q|G). \tag{2}$$

The calculation for all possible sequences of Q directly from $P(Q|G)$ is difficult and we can express it using Bayes' Rule as follows:

$$\acute{Q} = \arg \max_Q P(Q|G) = \arg \max_Q \left\{ P(G|Q) \cdot P(Q)/P(G) \right\} \tag{3}$$

Here, $P(G)$ is common to all sequences Q. The above equation can be simplified as follows:

$$\acute{Q} = \arg \max_Q P(G|Q) \cdot P(Q) \tag{4}$$

4.4 Phrase-based Statistical Machine Translation (PBSMT)

A PBSMT translation model is based on joint phrasal units analogous to graphones (Koehn et al., 2003b), (Och and Marcu, 2003). A phrase-based translation system also includes length models, a language model on the target side, and a re-ordering model (which is typically not used for monotonic transduction such as G2P conversion. The models are integrated within a log-linear framework.

4.5 Recurrent Neural Network (RNN) Encoder-Decoder

The RNN Encoder-Decoder technique for machine translation (Cho et al., 2014), (Bahdanau et al., 2014) is a neural network model that links blocks of Long Short-Term Memory (LSTM) (Hochreiter and Schmidhuber, 1997) in an RNN that encodes the source language and decoder units that generate the target language. The basic architecture of the Encoder-Decoder model includes two networks: one encodes the source sentence into a real-valued vector, and the other decodes the vector into a target sentence. In the case of G2P, input is a sequence of graphemes of a Myanmar word, and the output is a phoneme sequence. For example, G2P conversion for Myanmar word ရှက်ပုန်:သီး (hidden talent in English), the model takes the graphemes of the source word as input: ရှက်, ပုန်:, သီး and outputs the target phoneme sequence jwe', poun: and dhi:, which is terminated by an end-of-sequence token (see Figure 1).

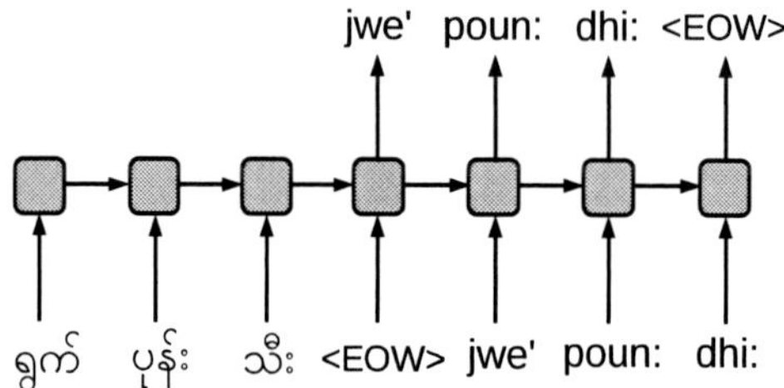

Figure 1: An Architecture of Encoder-Decoder Machine Translation for G2P conversion of Myanmar word ရှက်ပုန်:သီး (hidden talent in English)

4.6 Support Vector Machine (SVM) based Point-wise classification

Generally, sequence-based pronunciation prediction methods such as (Nagano et al., 2005) require a fully annotated training corpus. To reduce the cost of preparing a fully annotated corpus and also considering possible future work on domain adaptation from the general to the target domain, techniques involving only partial annotation have been developed (Ringger et al., 2007), (Tsuboi et al., 2008). (Neubig and Mori, 2010) proposed the combination of two separate techniques to achieve more efficient corpus annotation: point-wise estimation and word-based annotation. Point-wise estimation assumes that every decision about a segmentation point or word pronunciation is independent from the other decisions (Neubig and Mori, 2010). From this concept, a single annotation model can be trained on single annotated words, even if the surrounding words are not annotated such as ငါ/{ } ကျေး:ဇူ:/{kyei: zu:} တင်ပါတယ်/{tin ba de} (Thank you in English). In this paper, we applied this approach for phonemes of syllables within a word and thus the previous example will change to ငါ/{ } ကျေး:/{kyei:} ဇူ:/{zu:} တင်/{tin} ပါ/{ba} တယ်/{de}.

4.7 Weighted Finite-state Transducers (WFST)

(Novak et al.,) introduced a modified WFST-based many-to-many Expectation Maximization (EM) driven alignment algorithm for G2P conversion, and presented preliminary experimental results applying a RNN language model (RNNLM) as an N-best rescoring mechanism for G2P conversion. Their many-to-many approach contained three main modifications to G2P alignment, (1) only many-to-one and one-to-many arcs are trained, (2) a joint WFSA alignment lattice is built from each sequence pair using a log semiring (3) all remaining arcs (including deletion and substitution) are initialized to and constrained to maintain a non-zero weight. This approach provides EM training to produce better estimation for all possible transitions. The authors applied an RNNLM-based N-best rescoring method to G2P conversion.

5 Experimental Setup

5.1 Data Preparation

In the experiments, we used 25,300 words of Myanmar Language Commission (MLC) Dictionary data (Lwin, 1993). We randomized the original MLC dictionary and prepared 25,000 words for training, 300 words for three open test sets (100 words for each test set) for evaluation. In order to study how the seven G2P approaches behave with varying amounts of training data, we ran a sequence of experiments that trained G2P models from 2,500 words to 25,000 (2393 unique graphemes, 1864 unique pronunciations and 113 unique phonemes) words in increments of 2,500 words. 100 words from the training data also used for closed testing. The G2P mapping is used same mapping proposed by (Ye Kyaw Thu et al., 2015b) and some examples are given in Table 1.

Consonant	Vowel	Independent Vowel	Foreign Pronunciation
က => k	◌ွား => wa:	ဥ => au.	(က်) => K
ခ => kh	◌ွာ့ => wa.	ဦ => u	(ခ်) => KH
ဂ => g	ေ◌ွး => wei:	ဦး => u:	(လ်) => L
ဃ => gh	ေ◌ွ့ => wei.	ဣ => i.	(စ်) => S
င => ng	◌ွန် => un	ဤ => i	(ထ်) => HT

Table 1: An example of grapheme to phoneme mapping for Myanmar language

5.2 Software

We used following open source G2P converters, software frameworks and systems for our G2P experiments:

- Chainer: A framework for neural network development that provides an easy and straightforward way to implement complex deep learning architectures. (Tokui et al., 2015). A deep learning framework developed by Preferred Infrastructure, Inc. (PFI) (`https://preferred.jp/en/`) and Preferred Networks, Inc. (PFN) (`https://www.preferred-networks.jp/en/`). It was released as open source software in June, 2015 (`https://github.com/pfnet/chainer`). Some key features of Chainer are that it is supported as a Python library (PyPI: Chainer) and is able to run on both CUDA with multi-GPU computers. We used the Chainer Python module (version 1.15.0.1) for the G2P conversion experiments based on RNN and RNNA approaches. For both the RNN and the RNNA models, we trained for 100 epochs.

- CRFSuite: We used the CRFsuite tool (version 0.12) (Okazaki, 2007), (`https://github.com/chokkan/crfsuite`) for training and testing CRF models. The main reason was its speed relative to other CRF toolkits.

- KyTea: is a general toolkit (version 0.47) (Neubig and Mori, 2010), (`https://github.com/neubig/kytea`) and it is able to handle word segmentation and tagging. It uses a point-wise classifier-based (SVM or logistic regression) approach and the classifiers are trained with LIBLINEAR (`http://www.csie.ntu.edu.tw/~cjlin/liblinear/`). We used the KyTea toolkit for studying G2P bootstrapping with SVM based point-wise classification for Myanmar language.

- Moses: We used the PBSMT system provided by the Moses toolkit (`http://www.statmt.org/moses/`) for training the PBSMT model for G2P conversion. The word segmented source language was aligned with the word segmented target language using GIZA++ (Och

and Ney, 2000). The alignment was symmetrized by grow-diag-final-and heuristic (Koehn
et al., 2003a). The lexicalized reordering model was trained with the msd-bidirectional-fe
option (Tillmann, 2004). We used SRILM for training the 5-gram language model with
interpolated modified Kneser-Ney discounting (Stolcke, 2002), (Chen and Goodman, 1996).
Minimum error rate training (MERT) (Och, 2003) was used to tune the decoder parameters
and the decoding was done using the Moses decoder (version 2.1.1). We used default settings
of Moses for all experiments.

- Phonetisaurus: A WFST-driven G2P converter (Novak et al., 2012), (`https://github.com/AdolfVonKleist/Phonetisaurus`). Version 0.8a was used. An EM-based many-to-many aligner was applied to grapheme and phoneme sequences (training data) prior to building a G2P model. In the updated version of Phonetisaurus, dictionary alignment is performed with OpenFst (`http://www.openfst.org/twiki/bin/view/FST/WebHome`). In order to estimate an n-gram language model, any language model toolkit such as MITLM (`https://github.com/mitlm/mitlm`)or SRILM (`http://www.speech.sri.com/projects/srilm/`) can be used. We used MITLM toolkit and conversion from ARPA format to a binary FST representation was done with OpenFST.

- Sequitur: A data-driven G2P converter developed at RWTH Aachen University - Department of Computer Science by Maximilian Bisani (Bisani and Ney, 2008). The 2016-04-25 release version (`https://www-i6.informatik.rwth-aachen.de/web/Software/g2p.html`) was used for the JSM G2P conversion experiment.

- Slearp: Structured LEarning And Prediction (Kubo et al., 2014). We used Slearp (version 0.96) (`https://osdn.jp/projects/slearp/`) for S-AROW G2P model building.

We ran all above software with default parameters for building the G2P models. Although
feature engineering is usually an important component of machine-learning approaches, the G2P
models were built with features from only the grapheme and phoneme parallel data, to allow
for a fair comparison between the seven approaches.

5.3 Evaluation

To evaluate the quality of the G2P approaches, we used two evaluation criteria. One
is automatic evaluation of phoneme error rate (PER) with SCLITE (score speech recognition system output) program from the NIST scoring toolkit SCTK version 2.4.10
(`http://www1.icsi.berkeley.edu/Speech/docs/sctk-1.2/sclite.htm`). The other evaluation was done manually by counting voiced/unvoiced, tones, consonant and vowel errors on
G2P outputs.

The SCLITE scoring method for calculating the erroneous words in Word Error Rate (WER),
is as follows: first make an alignment of the G2P hypothesis (the output from the trained model)
and the reference (human transcribed) word strings and then perform a global minimization of
the Levenshtein distance function which weights the cost of correct words, insertions (I), deletions
(D) and substitutions (S). The formula for WER is as follows:

$$WER = (I + D + S) * 100/N \qquad (5)$$

In our case, we trained G2P models with syllable segmented words and thus alignment was
done on syllable units and the PER was derived from the Levenshtein distance at the phoneme
level rather than the word level. For example, phoneme level of syllable alignment, counting I, D
and S for Myanmar word "ချွင်းချက်" (exception in English), left column and "စိတ်ပျက်လက်ပျက်"
(disappointed in English), right column is as follows:

<table>
<tr><td>

```
Scores: (#C #S #D #I) 0 2 0 1
REF: *** CHWIN: GYE'
HYP: CHI NWIN: CHE'
Eval:   I    S    S
```

</td><td>

```
Scores: (#C #S #D #I) 2 1 1 0
REF: sei' PJEI le' PJAU'
HYP: sei' PJAUN: le' *****
Eval:       S         D
```

</td></tr>
</table>

6   Results

6.1   Automatic Evaluation with Phoneme Error Rate (PER)

We used PER to evaluate the performance of G2P conversion. We computed the PER scores using `sclite` (http://www1.icsi.berkeley.edu/Speech/docs/sctk-1.2/sclite.htm) on the hypotheses of G2P models and references. The results are presented in Figure 2 and lower PER is better in performance as we mentioned in Section 5.3. The experimental results also show the learning curve variations of seven G2P conversion approaches on the training data. We can clearly see that there is no significant learning improvement for the SVM based point-wise classification from the evaluation results on both the closed and the three open test sets (see Figure 2, (g)). Also, the PER results of S-AROW, JSM, PBSMT and RNNA on the closed test data are unstable. Each of the graphs show the performance of G2P conversion and the best PER scores (i.e. 0) was achieved on the closed test data by the RNN, S-AROW and WFST. The best PER scores of the CRF and PBSMT on closed test data were 6.4 and 7.5 respectively. On the other hand, the final models of the CRF and WFST achieved the lowest PER scores for all three open test data sets (open1, open2 and open3). A PER score 14.7 for open1 was achieved by WFST, 11.4 for open2, and 15.7 for open3 by both CRF and WFST. An interesting point is that the PBSMT approach achieved close to the lowest PERs for the three open test sets (16.1 for open1, 13.1 for open2 and 22.0 for open3). Figure 2, (e) shows the RNN approach is able to learn to reach zero PER score on the closed test data from epoch two (i.e. with 5,000 words). The PER of RNN is lower than RNNA approach for both the closed and the open test data (see Figure 2, (e) and (f)).

6.2   Manual Evaluation

Manual evaluation was mainly done on the results from the models trained with 25,000 words in terms of errors on voiced/unvoiced pronunciation change, vowel, consonant and tone. The results show that voiced/unvoiced error is the highest among them. (Ye Kyaw Thu et al., 2015a) discussed the importance of the pronunciation change patterns, and our experimental results also show how these patterns affect the G2P performance. Pronunciation error rates for PBSMT and WFST are comparable and the PBSMT approach gives the best performance overall. The SVM based point-wise classification approach produced the highest phoneme errors on unknown words (i.e. UNK tagging for OOV case by KyTea) among the seven G2P approaches. Generally, all methods can handle tone well and we assume that almost all the tonal information of Myanmar graphemes is covered in the training dictionary. The lowest error rate on tone was achieved by PBSMT. From the overall manual evaluation results from train1 (training number 1: trained with 2,500 words) to train10 (training number 2: trained with 25,000 words), we can see clearly that RNN, PBSMT and WFST approaches gradually improve with increasing training data set size. Some difficult pronunciation changes at the consonant level (such as pronunciation prediction from ljin to jin for the Myanmar word "kau'jin", "ကောက် လျှင်") can be predicted correctly by the PBSMT approach and the RNN but not by the other approaches. Although the training accuracy of RNN is higher than the other techniques, in the automatic evaluation, some OOV predictions are the worst (refer Table 2).

6.3   Discussion

As we presented in the previous section, some evaluation results of the G2P conversion approaches on closed test data are inconsistent especially for S-AROW and JSM (refer Figure 3, (a) and (c)). However all models are generally improve on the three open test evaluation sets. Here we investigate the OOV rates over test data. Figure 3 shows the OOV rate for graphemes of the three open test data sets over the incremental training process from train1 to train10. As expected, the OOV rate gradually decreases as the the training data size increases.

We performed a detailed analysis of each error type by manual evaluation, and the results are shown in Figure 4. From the results, we can clearly see that SVM based point-wise classification produced highest number of voiced/unvoiced errors, and we have already discussed UNK tags or KyTea pronunciation estimation errors in Section 6.2. We now turn to RNN specific errors. RNNs are capable sequence models with high potential for building G2P conversion models and thus we present a detailed error analysis. The RNN produced some reordering errors and the automatic evaluation counts one reordering error as one deletion and one insertion. For example,

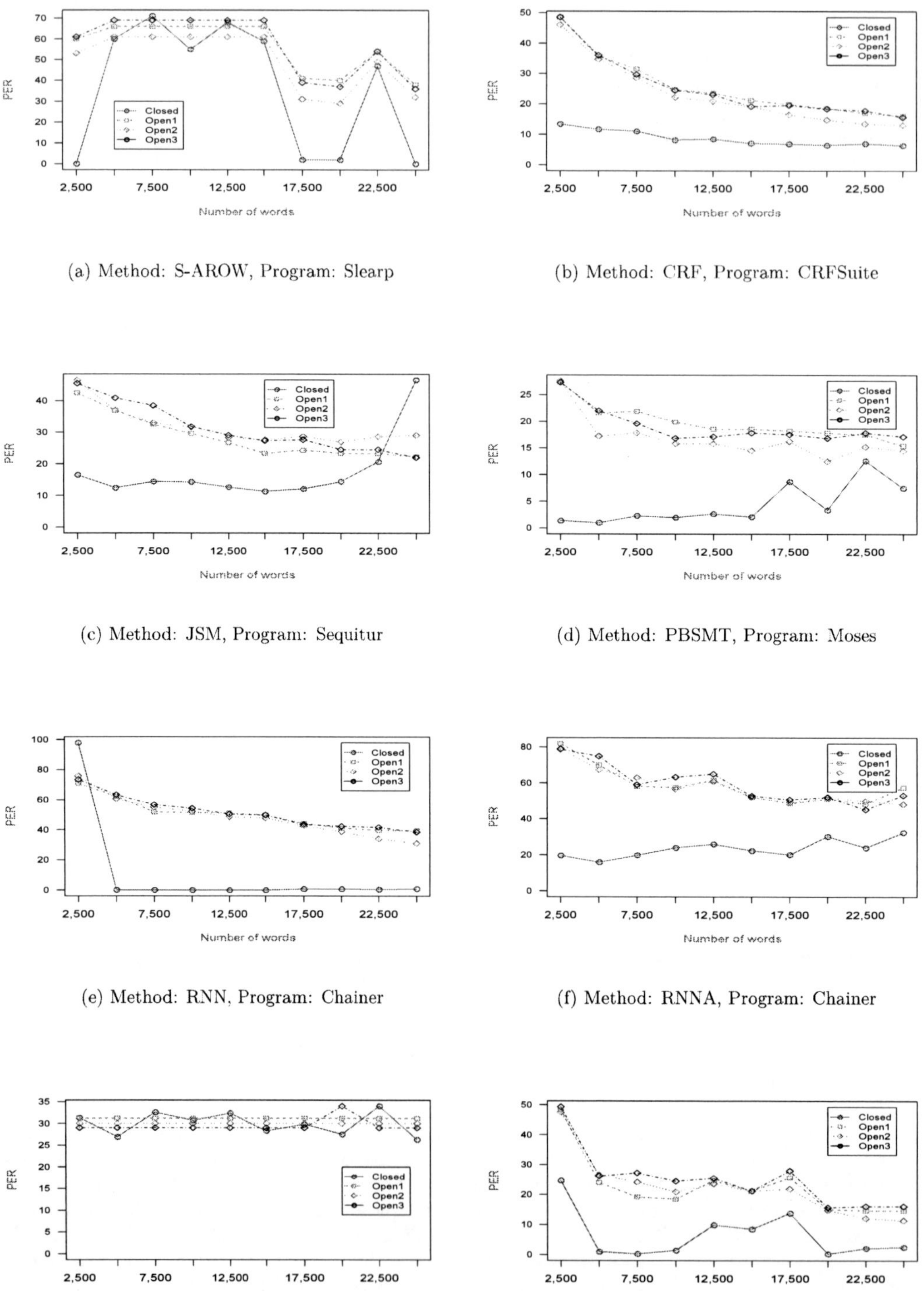

(a) Method: S-AROW, Program: Slearp

(b) Method: CRF, Program: CRFSuite

(c) Method: JSM, Program: Sequitur

(d) Method: PBSMT, Program: Moses

(e) Method: RNN, Program: Chainer

(f) Method: RNNA, Program: Chainer

(g) Method: SVM based point-wise classification, Program: KyTea

(h) Method: WFST, Program: Phonetisaurus

Figure 2: Phoneme Error Rate (PER) of G2P conversion methodologies

Method	Hypothesis	Note on Error
S-AROW	tha' ba. ja. nan baun:	tone error in "ba." and consonant error in "ja."
CRF	tha' ba- ja. nan baun:	consonant error in ja.
JSM	tha' ba. ra- baun:	tone error in "ba." and "ra-" one phoneme deletion
PBSMT	tha' ba. ja- nan baun:	tone error in "ba."
RNN	tha' ba- WA. SA MI:	3 syllables "WA. SA MI:" are predicted and they are far from the correct pronunciation
SVM based point-wise	UNK ba- ja- nan baun:	OOV error
WFST	tha' ba- ra. nan baun:	0 Error

Table 2: An example of phoneme prediction errors of G2P conversion methods.

the RNN model output for the Myanmar word "ထုံ့ပေပေ", htoun pei BEI (recalcitrantly in English). Its SCLITE alignment and scoring is shown in the left column below:

```
Scores: (#C #S #D #I) 2 0 1 1        Scores: (#C #S #D #I) 3 1 0 0
REF: *** htoun pei BEI               REF: mwei: tha- MI. gin
HYP: PEI htoun pei ***               HYP: mwei: tha- HPA. gin
Eval:    I            D              Eval:           S
```

Some RNN pronunciation prediction errors were semantic in nature, and we were surprised to discover them. For example, the RNN model output for the Myanmar word "မွေးသမိခင်", mwei: tha- MI. gin (mother in English) is similar word "မွေးသဖခင်", mwei: tha- HPA. gin (father in English). Similar semantic errors were also produced by the PBSMT approach. Another interesting point is that the RNN and WFST approaches can predict correctly for some rare patterns (i.e. where all syllable pronunciations of a word are changed) even when all other models made errors. For example, the errors for the Myanmar word "စားပွဲခင်:", za- bwe: gin: (tablecloth in English) made by the other approaches were: S-AROW: za- bwe: khin:, JSM: za- bwe: khin:, RNN: za- bwe: gin:, WFST: za- bwe: gin: and SVM based point-wise classification: za- bwe: khin:.

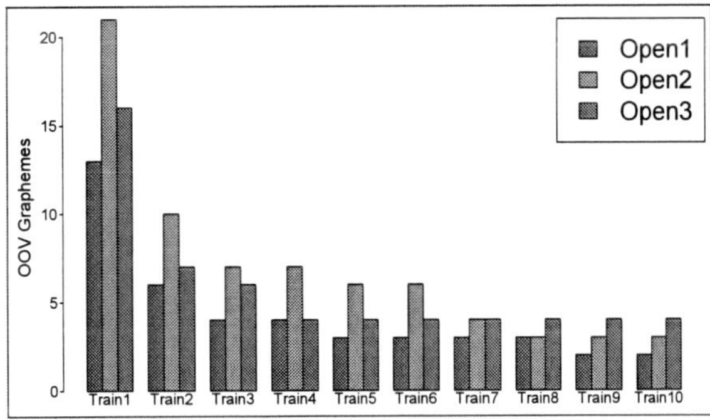

Figure 3: OOV graphemes over incremental training process

7 Conclusion and Future Work

The aim of this work is to show the relative performance of different machine learning techniques on Myanmar G2P conversion. Both automatic evaluation and manual evaluation showed that CRF, Phonetisaurus, SMT and RNN have their own unique advantages when applied to

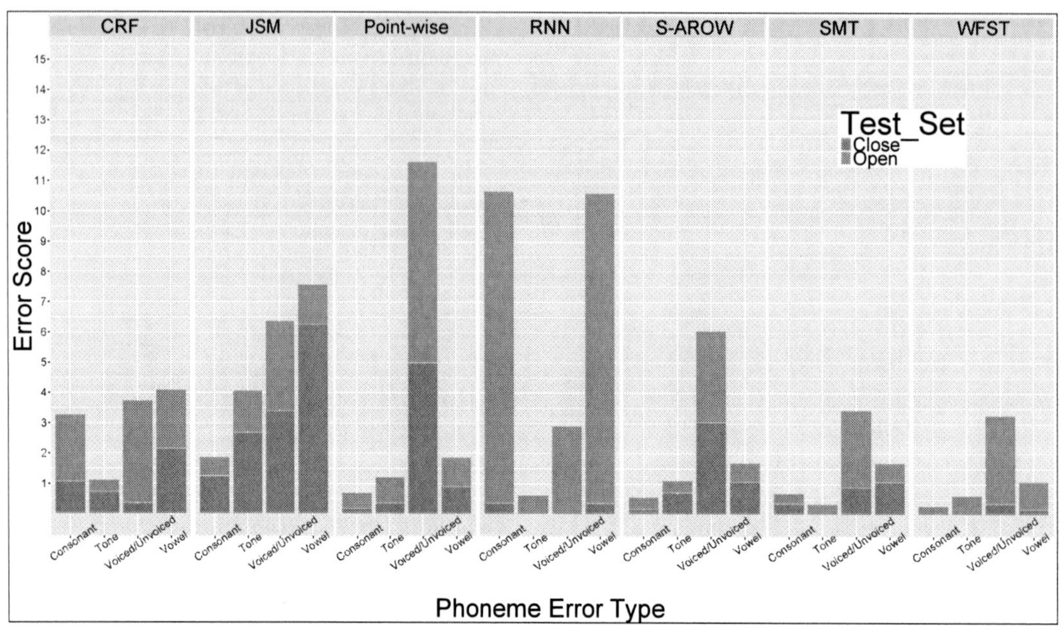

Figure 4: Average error scores of manual checking for G2P conversion methods

Myanmar pronunciation prediction. Although the manual evaluation was expensive, we believe it was necessary in order to analyse these approaches in depth. In summary, our main findings are that the CRF, Phonetisaurus, SMT approaches gave rise to the the lowest error rates on the most important features of Myanmar G2P conversion: voiced/unvoiced, vowel patterns and tone. We plan to find out the performance of these approaches on sentence level since Myanmar pronunciation highly depends on the context.

Acknowledgements

The authors would like to thank Dr. Andrew Finch, Multilingual Translation Lab., Advanced Speech Translation Research and Development Promotion Center, National Institute of Information and Communications Technology (NICT), Japan for valuable comments.

References

Dzmitry Bahdanau, Kyunghyun Cho, and Yoshua Bengio. 2014. Neural machine translation by jointly learning to align and translate. *CoRR*, abs/1409.0473.

Maximilian Bisani and Hermann Ney. 2008. Joint-sequence models for grapheme-to-phoneme conversion. *Speech Commun.*, 50(5):434–451, May.

Stanley F. Chen and Joshua Goodman. 1996. An empirical study of smoothing techniques for language modeling. In *Proceedings of the 34th Annual Meeting of the ACL*, pages 310–318. Santa Cruz, California, June.

Kyunghyun Cho, Bart van Merrienboer, Çaglar Gülçehre, Fethi Bougares, Holger Schwenk, and Yoshua Bengio. 2014. Learning phrase representations using RNN encoder-decoder for statistical machine translation. *CoRR*, abs/1406.1078.

Koby Crammer and Yoram Singer. 2003. Ultraconservative online algorithms for multiclass problems. *J. Mach. Learn. Res.*, 3:951–991, March.

Koby Crammer, Alex Kulesza, and Mark Dredze. 2013. Adaptive regularization of weight vectors. *Machine Learning*, 91(2):155–187.

R.I. Damper, Y. Marchand, M.J. Adamson, and K. Gustafson. 1999. A comparison of letter-to-sound conversion techniques for english text-to-speech synthesis.

Marelie Davel and Olga Martirosian. 2009. Pronunciation dictionary development in resource-scarce environments. In *in Proc. Interspeech*, pages 2851–2854.

Mark Dredze, Koby Crammer, and Fernando Pereira. 2008. Confidence-weighted linear classification. In *Proceedings of the 25th International Conference on Machine Learning*, ICML '08, pages 264–271, New York, NY, USA. ACM.

Ei Phyu Phyu Soe. 2013. Grapheme–to–phoneme conversion for myanmar language. In *The 11th International Conference on Computer Applications (ICCA2013)*, pages 195–200, Yangon, Myanmar, Feb.

Sepp Hochreiter and Jürgen Schmidhuber. 1997. Long short-term memory. *Neural Comput.*, 9(8):1735–1780, November.

Panagiota Karanasou and Lori Lamel. 2011. Automatic generation of a pronunciation dictionary with rich variation coverage using smt methods. In *Proceedings of the 12th International Conference on Computational Linguistics and Intelligent Text Processing - Volume Part II*, CICLing'11, pages 506–517, Berlin, Heidelberg. Springer-Verlag.

Philipp Koehn, Franz Josef Och, , and Daniel Marcu. 2003a. Statistical phrase-based translation. In *In Proceedings of the Human Language Technology Conference*, Edmonton, Canada.

Philipp Koehn, Franz Josef Och, and Daniel Marcu. 2003b. Statistical phrase-based translation. In *HLT-NAACL*.

Philipp Koehn, Hieu Hoang, Alexandra Birch, Chris Callison-Burch, Marcello Federico, Nicola Bertoldi, Brooke Cowan, Wade Shen, Christine Moran, Richard Zens, Chris Dyer, Ondřej Bojar, Alexandra Constantin, and Evan Herbst. 2007. Moses: Open source toolkit for statistical machine translation. In *Proceedings of the 45th Annual Meeting of the ACL on Interactive Poster and Demonstration Sessions*, ACL '07, pages 177–180, Stroudsburg, PA, USA. Association for Computational Linguistics.

Keigo Kubo, Sakriani Sakti, Graham Neubig, Tomoki Toda, and Satoshi Nakamura. 2014. Structured adaptive regularization of weight vectors for a robust grapheme-to-phoneme conversion model. *IEICE Transactions on Information and Systems*, E97-D(6):1468–1476, June.

John D. Lafferty, Andrew McCallum, and Fernando C. N. Pereira. 2001. Conditional random fields: Probabilistic models for segmenting and labeling sequence data. In *Proceedings of the Eighteenth International Conference on Machine Learning*, ICML '01, pages 282–289, San Francisco, CA, USA. Morgan Kaufmann Publishers Inc.

Antoine Laurent, Paul Deléglise, and Sylvain Meignier. 2009. Grapheme to phoneme conversion using an smt system. In *INTERSPEECH*, pages 708–711. ISCA.

San Lwin. 1993. *Myanmar - English Dictionary*. Department of the Myanmar Language Commission, Ministry of Education, Union of Myanmar.

Tohru Nagano, Shinsuke Mori, and Masafumi Nishimura. 2005. A stochastic approach to phoneme and accent estimation. In *INTERSPEECH 2005 - Eurospeech, 9th European Conference on Speech Communication and Technology, Lisbon, Portugal, September 4-8, 2005*, pages 3293–3296. ISCA.

Graham Neubig and Shinsuke Mori. 2010. Word-based partial annotation for efficient corpus construction. In *The seventh international conference on Language Resources and Evaluation (LREC 2010)*, pages 2723–2727, Malta, May.

Josef R. Novak, Paul R. Dixon, Nobuaki Minematsu, Keikichi Hirose, Chiori Hori, and Hideki Kashioka. Improving wfst-based g2p conversion with alignment constraints and rnnlm n-best rescoring.

Josef R. Novak, Nobuaki Minematsu, and Keikichi Hirose. 2012. Wfst-based grapheme-to-phoneme conversion: Open source tools for alignment, model-building and decoding. In *Proceedings of the 10th International Workshop on Finite State Methods and Natural Language Processing, FSMNLP 2012, Donostia-San Sebastiían, Spain, July 23-25, 2012*, pages 45–49.

Franz Josef Och and Daniel Marcu. 2003. Statistical phrase-based translation. pages 127–133.

F. J. Och and H. Ney. 2000. Improved statistical alignment models. In *ACL00*, pages 440–447, Hong Kong, China.

Franz J. Och. 2003. Minimum error rate training for statistical machine translation. In *Proceedings of the 41st Meeting of the Association for Computational Linguistics (ACL 2003)*, Sapporo, Japan.

Naoaki Okazaki. 2007. Crfsuite: a fast implementation of conditional random fields (crfs).

Eric Ringger, Peter McClanahan, Robbie Haertel, George Busby, Marc Carmen, James Carroll, Kevin Seppi, and Deryle Lonsdale. 2007. Active learning for part-of-speech tagging: Accelerating corpus annotation. In *Proceedings of the Linguistic Annotation Workshop*, LAW '07, pages 101–108, Stroudsburg, PA, USA. Association for Computational Linguistics.

Tim Schlippe. 2014. *Rapid Generation of Pronunciation Dictionaries for new Domains and Languages*. Ph.D. thesis, Uni Karlsruhe.

Lucia Specia. 2011. Tutorial, fundamental and new approaches to statistical machine translation. In *International Conference Recent Advances in Natural Language Processing*.

Andreas Stolcke. 2002. SRILM - An Extensible Language Modeling Toolkit. In *Proceedings of the International Conference on Spoken Language Processing*, volume 2, pages 901–904, Denver.

Christoph Tillmann. 2004. A unigram orientation model for statistical machine translation. In *Proceedings of HLT-NAACL 2004: Short Papers*, HLT-NAACL-Short '04, pages 101–104, Stroudsburg, PA, USA. Association for Computational Linguistics.

Seiya Tokui, Kenta Oono, Shohei Hido, and Justin Clayton. 2015. Chainer: a next-generation open source framework for deep learning. In *Proceedings of Workshop on Machine Learning Systems (LearningSys) in The Twenty-ninth Annual Conference on Neural Information Processing Systems (NIPS)*.

Yuta Tsuboi, Hisashi Kashima, Hiroki Oda, Shinsuke Mori, and Yuji Matsumoto. 2008. Training conditional random fields using incomplete annotations. In *Proceedings of the 22Nd International Conference on Computational Linguistics - Volume 1*, COLING '08, pages 897–904, Stroudsburg, PA, USA. Association for Computational Linguistics.

Ye Kyaw Thu, Win Pa Pa, Finch Andrew, Aye Mya Hlaing, Hay Mar Soe Naing, Sumita Eiichiro, and Hori Chiori. 2015a. Syllable pronunciation features for myanmar grapheme to phoneme conversion. In *The 13th International Conference on Computer Applications (ICCA2015)*, pages 161–167, Yangon, Myanmar, Feb.

Ye Kyaw Thu, Win Pa Pa, Finch Andrew, Ni Jinfu, Sumita Eiichiro, and Hori Chiori. 2015b. The application of phrase based statistical machine translation techniques to myanmar grapheme to phoneme conversion. In *The Pacific Association for Computational Linguistics Conference (PACLING2016)*, pages 170–176, Legian, Bali, Indonesia, May.

Character-Aware Neural Networks for Arabic Named Entity Recognition for Social Media

Mourad Gridach
High Institute of Technology
Ibn Zohr University - Agadir
`m.gridach@uiz.ac.ma`

Abstract

Named Entity Recognition (NER) is the task of classifying or labelling atomic elements in the text into categories such as Person, Location or Organisation. For Arabic language, recognizing named entities is a challenging task because of the complexity and the unique characteristics of this language. In addition, most of the previous work focuses on Modern Standard Arabic (MSA), however, recognizing named entities in social media is becoming more interesting these days. Dialectal Arabic (DA) and MSA are both used in social media, which is deemed as another challenging task. Most state-of-the-art Arabic NER systems count heavily on hand-crafted engineering features and lexicons which is time consuming. In this paper, we introduce a novel neural network architecture which benefits both from character- and word-level representations automatically, by using combination of bidirectional Long Short-Term Memory (LSTM) and Conditional Random Field (CRF), eliminating the need for most feature engineering. Moreover, our model relies on unsupervised word representations learned from unannotated corpora. Experimental results demonstrate that our model achieves state-of-the-art performance on publicly available benchmark for Arabic NER for social media and surpassing the previous system by a large margin.

1 Introduction

Named Entity Recognition (NER) is the task of tagging, labeling or identifying atomic items in the text with predefined set of named entity categories such as Person, Location, Organization, etc. from large corpora (Nadeau and Sekine, 2007) . Recently, named entity recognition has gained an important role in Natural Language Processing (NLP) because it can have an impact on other NLP applications. In Question Answering (QA), Ferrndez (2007) showed that using NER system in their QA model improves its performance and questions contain 85% Named Entities. Toda (2005) showed that adding NER system in their Text Clustering system enhanced its performance and allowed them to outperform the existing state-of-the-art system. Babych (2003) clarified that using named entity recognition in Machine Translation (MT) can help the system to improve the translation task. Thompson (1997) prompted that using NER improve Information Retrieval (IR) performance. In addition, NER could be used in various NLP systems to improve their performance such as semantic parsers, part of speech taggers, document and news searching.

Current state-of-the-art systems perform very well on recognizing Arabic named entities such as Person, Location, or Organization (Shaalan and Oudah, 2014) for MSA texts. However, there is relatively less interest on recognizing named entities in social media like Twitter, movies, TV shows. In this paper, we focus on recognizing Arabic named entities in Twitter. Lately, Arabic language was the fastest growing language on Twitter, and in 2012, it was the 6th most used language on Twitter (Semiocast, 2012). This rapid increase in online social media has encouraged researchers in many fields to analyze its content for many purposes such as opinion mining, event detection, and others. Since NER plays a vital role in many NLP applications, any of these applications focused on dealing with Twitter content,

Proceedings of the 6th Workshop on South and Southeast Asian Natural Language Processing,
pages 23–32, Osaka, Japan, December 11-17 2016.

needs to use NER system to improve its performance and deals with Twitter specific challenges. As consequences, Arabic is very complex language compared to European languages. On the one hand, it has both complex and rich morphology as well as ambiguity. On the other hand, there are no capital letters and Arabic texts are written without diacritics. Therefore, building Arabic NLP applications and especially NER is very intriguing.

Most of Arabic NER systems use three approaches: rule-based, machine learning and hybrid approaches. In this paper, we use Deep Neural Networks (DNN) because they are extremely powerful machine learning models that have attained great success in vast applications such as image classification (He et al., 2015) and speech recognition (Hinton et al., 2012). Furthermore, DNNs can achieve state-of-the-art in many NLP applications for instance Machine Translation (Cho et al., 2014; Sutskever et al., 2014) and sentiment analysis (Socher et al., 2013; dosSantos and Gatti, 2014). These powerful models can use backpropagation algorithm for training (Rumelhart et al., 1986).

In order to process variable length input, recurrent neural networks (RNNs) are the best solution (Goller and Kuchler, 1996). In recent years, RNNs are widely used and achieved state-of-the-art in several NLP tasks such as language modeling (Mikolov et al., 2011), machine translation (Cho et al., 2014) and speech recognition (Graves, 2013). We use Long Short-Term Memory (LSTM), which is one kind of RNNs with complex cells (Hochreiter and Schmidhuber, 1997). With its forget gate, LSTM allows highly non-trivial long-distance dependencies to be easily learned.

For sequential labeling tasks, it has been shown that using a bi-directional LSTM model is preferred to LSTM model because it can capture infinite amount of context on both sides for a sentence by eliminating the main problem of limited context in feed-forward neural networks (Graves et al., 2013). In fact, to build a system for Arabic NER for social media, we propose a model based on bidirectional LSTM networks with Conditional Random Field (CRF) layer on the top of the networks.

Most of the existing Arabic NER systems rely on handcrafted engineering features which is time consuming and the use of large gazetteers to improve the accuracy. In this paper, we investigate the impact of using character-level and word embedding features as inputs for bidirectional LSTM network with CRF on the top of the networks as contextual feature on Arabic NER performance for social media. Experimental results show that we are able to obtain state-of-the-art performance on Twitter dataset without using any large gazetteers and lots of handcrafted engineering features.

The main contributions of this paper are the following:

- Study the impact of bidirectional LSTM on sequence tagging like NER on Arabic Twitter texts;

- The effectiveness of using character-level for morphologically rich languages (Arabic as an example) and also show that using word representations improve the system performance;

- Investigate the use of CRF on the top of bidirectional LSTM to capture contextual features in Arabic Twitter texts;

- We get state-of-the-art results and outperform the existing systems on publicly available dataset.

2 Models

In this section, we provide a brief description of the models used in this paper. We begin by presenting the main neural network used: LSTMs and bidirectional LSTMs. Without further ado, CRF will be presented. Finally, we investigate the combination of bidirectional LSTMs and CRF.

2.1 LSTM Networks

Recurrent neural networks (RNNs) are an extension of a conventional feed-forward neural network. They are remarkably general models for sequence processing tasks. RNNs can handle the variable-length sequence using a recurrent hidden unit state whose activation at each time step is dependent on that of the previous one. However, standard RNNs suffer from the problem of vanishing gradients when it comes to long sequences. More recently, (Hochreiter and Schmidhuber, 1997) propose "Long Short-Term Memory" (LSTM) networks to solve this problem. LSTM can learn to bridge minimal time lags for

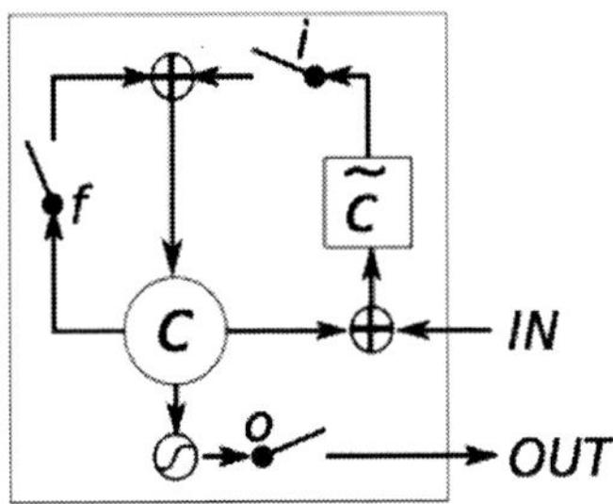

Figure 1: Long Short-Term Memory unit

more than 1000 discrete time steps (Hochreiter and Schmidhuber, 1997). Since then, many researchers in the field came with some minor changes to the original LSTM unit. In this paper, we follow the implementation of LSTM as used in (Graves, 2013). LSTM unit is different from RNNs unit, which simply computes a weighted sum of the input signal and applies a nonlinear activation function. Each LSTM unit maintains a memory cell c_t^j at each time t. The output h_t^j, or the activation, of the j-th LSTM unit is then computed as follow:

$$h_t^j = o_t^j \tanh(c_t^j) \tag{1}$$

where o_t^j is an *output gate* that modulates the amount of memory content exposure. The output gate o_t^j is then computed using the following equation:

$$o_t^j = \sigma(W_o x_t + U_o h_{t-1} + V_o c_t)^j \tag{2}$$

where σ is a logistic sigmoid function. V_o is a diagonal matrix. c_t^j is the memory cell updated by partially forgetting the existing memory and adding a new memory content $\tilde{c}_t^j$:

$$c_t^j = f_t^j c_{t-1}^j + i_t^j \tilde{c}_t^j \tag{3}$$

This new memory cell is computed using the following equation:

$$\tilde{c}_t^j = \tanh(W_c x_t + U_c h_{t-1})^j \tag{4}$$

f_t^j is called the *forget gate*, when its output value is close to zero, the network will effectively forget whatever value it was remembering. i_t^j is called the *input gate*, when its output value is close to zero, this value will be blocked from entering into the next layer. These two gates are computed using the following equations:

$$f_t^j = \sigma(W_f x_t + U_f h_{t-1} + V_f c_{t-1})^j \tag{5}$$

$$i_t^j = \sigma(W_i x_t + U_i h_{t-1} + V_i c_{t-1})^j \tag{6}$$

It should be noted that V_f and V_i are diagonal matrices. Figure 1 illustrates the graphical representation of LSTM unit.

It would rather be noted that there is a remarkable difference between standard recurrent unit and LSTM unit where the first unit overwrites its content at each time-step, while the second unit has the ability to decide whether to keep the existing memory by using these gates. As a result, LSTM unit can learn important features from input sequence by easily carrying this feature over long distance.

2.2 Bidirectional LSTM Networks

One shortcoming of standard LSTMs is that they are only able to make use of previous context. So, in sequence tagging like NER task, for a given time step, we can have access to both past features (using forward states) and future features (using backward states). To solve this problem, we use bidirectional

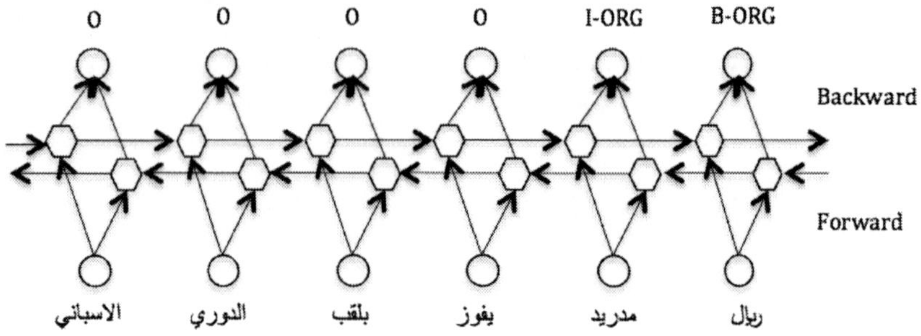

Figure 2: Bidirectional LSTM neural network

LSTMs. These models can process data in both directions where the output layer receives results from the two separate hidden layers. Figure 2 shows a graphical illustration of bidirectional LSTMs with the Arabic sentence "ريال مدريد يفوز بلقب الدوري الاسباني" which means "Real Madrid won the Spanish league title". For a given sentence $(x_1, x_2,...,x_n)$ in Twitter dataset containing n words, we compute two representations: the left context of the sentence at every word t denoted by $\overrightarrow{h}_t$ and the right context of the sentence denoted by $\overleftarrow{h}_t$ by using a second LSTM reading the same sentence in the opposite direction (we note that Arabic texts are written from right to left on the contrary to European languages). Every LSTM network has its own parameters. By using this model, we represent every word in a sentence by concatenating its right and left context representations $h_t = [\overrightarrow{h}_t; \overleftarrow{h}_t]$. These LSTMs networks are trained using backpropagation through time (BPTT) (Boden, 2002).

2.3 Bidirectional LSTM with CRF

We describe our final model, which combines bidirectional LSTM and CRF model. A state transition matrix is used for CRF layer as parameters. To predict the current tag, we use this transition matrix, which represents the past and future tags. We denote this transition matrix by $M_{i,j}$ representing the transition score from the i-th tag to the j-th tag. Given a sentence X = $(x_1, x_2,..., x_n)$, we denote $N([S]_1^T)_{i,t}$ to be the matrix of scores output by the bidirectional LSTM network for the sentence $[S]_1^T$ and the i-th tag at the t-th word. The score for a sentence $[S]_1^T$ along with a sequence of tags $[i]_1^T$ is given by the sum of the transition scores and the scores from the bidirectional LSTM network:

$$s([S]_1^T, [i]_1^T) = \sum_{t=1}^{T}(M_{[i]_{t-1},[i]_t} + N([S]_1^T)_{[i]_t,t}) \tag{7}$$

We use dynamic programming to compute $M_{i,j}$ and optimal tag sequences for inference (Lafferty et al., 2001). Finally, we use a softmax function over all possible tag sequences to get probabilities for the sequence $[i]_1^T$:

$$p(y|[S]_1^T) = \frac{e^{s([S]_1^T,[i]_1^T)}}{\sum_{\tilde{c}\in I_s} e^{s([S]_1^T,\tilde{c})}} \tag{8}$$

where I_s represents all possible tag sequences for a given sentence $[S]_1^T$. We note that in this paper, we use the IOB format (Inside, Outside, Beginning), which was the standard representation in the Twitter dataset (Darwish, 2013). During training, we maximize the log-probability $\log(p(y|[S]_1^T))$ of the correct tag sequence:

$$\log(p(y|[S]_1^T)) = \log(\frac{e^{s([S]_1^T,[i]_1^T)}}{\sum_{\tilde{c}\in I_s} e^{s([S]_1^T,\tilde{c})}})$$
$$= s([S]_1^T, [i]_1^T) - \log(\sum_{\tilde{c}\in I_s} e^{s([S]_1^T,\tilde{c})}) \tag{9}$$

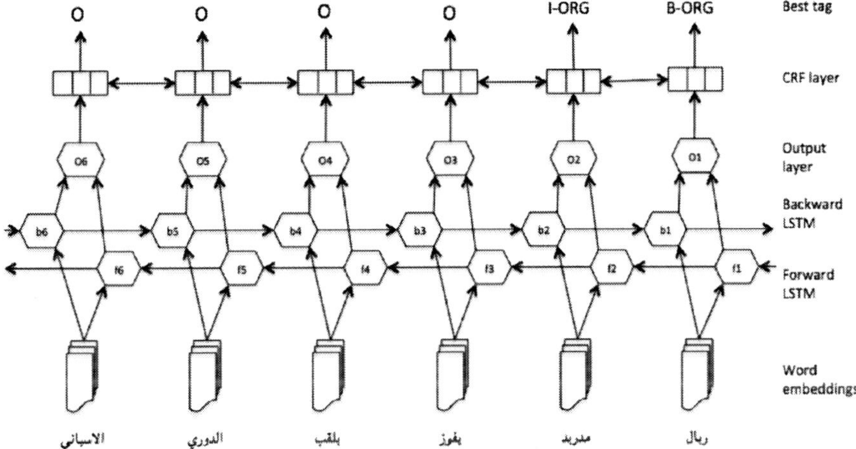

Figure 3: Word embeddings are fed to a bidirectional LSTM where f_j, b_j respectively represent the forward and backward of the word j. O_j represents the concatenation of the previous two vectors resulting in a representation of word j in its context.

3   Training Procedure

The architecture of our model is shown in Figure 3. For each sentence, we initialised our word vectors with pretrained word embeddings (Zahran et al., 2015) (see section 4.2 for more details). The input to the bidirectional LSTM network is the sequence of word embeddings for a given sentence S. Hence, every word in a sentence gets its left and right representation from the bidirectional LSTM. Then, we concatenate these two representations and linearly projected onto another layer whose size is equal to the number of distinct NER tags. As explained before, CRF layer is used on the top of the bidirectional LSTM in order to capture contextual features in the form of neighboring named entity recognition tags. As a result, we get predictions for each word in a sentence.

From equation 7, the model parameters are the parameters of the bidirectional LSTM obtained from the matrix $N([S]_1^T)_{i,t}$, the parameters obtained from the transition matrix of bigram scores $M_{i,j}$ and word embeddings. To train our models, we use Stochastic Gradient Descent (SGD). In each epoch, we divide the training dataset into mini-batches and process one batch at a time. Each mini-batch contains a number of sentences in the training data which is defined by the parameters of mini-batch size. More details will be discussed in the experimental results section.

4   Inputs for the Model

In this section, we explain the inputs to our model. We begin by presenting the character-based model of words used in this paper and how it could be useful especially for morphological rich languages like Arabic. Thus, we present word embeddings used to initialise our word vectors.

4.1   Character-based models of words

It has been shown that using character-level can help to improve the performance of models in many NLP applications. It is viewed as new paradigm in NLP applications using deep neural networks. It is widely used in Neural Machine Translation (NMT) and recent work show that adding character-level features improve the translation results for many languages (Luong and Manning, 2016; Ling et al., 2015; Chung et al., 2016). Hence, character-based approaches have also been applied to other tasks in natural language processing such as document classification (Xiao and Cho, 2016), language modeling (Kim et al., 2015; Ling et al., 2015) and parsing (Ballesteros et al., 2015). For NER, character-level was not extremely used to build models that deal with sequence tagging task. It was used in the context of text classification for

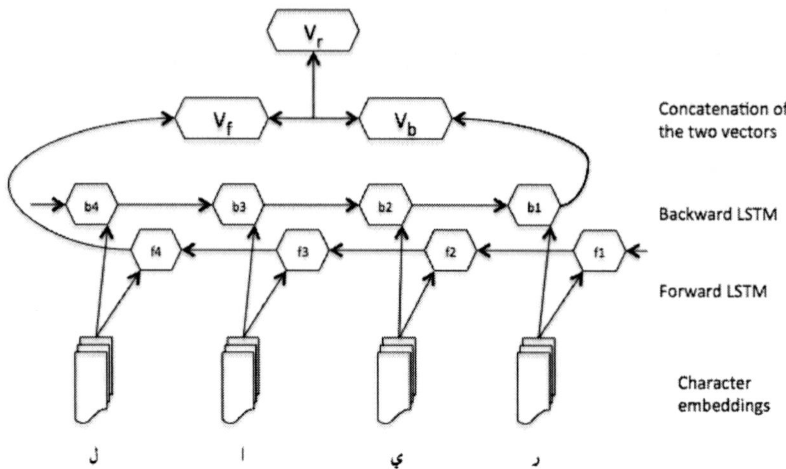

Figure 4: The character embeddings of the Arabic word "ريال" (real) using a bidirectional LSTMs. The final vector V_r is the result of concatenating the vector embedding V_f which represents the forward pass and the vector embedding V_b which represents the backward pass

learning representations of words from their characters (Zhang et al., 2015). As far as we know, we are the first to use character-level representations to build a system for Arabic NER for social media.

Arabic language belongs to the category of languages that has rich morphology. It is also an agglutinative language where some words could mean an entire sentence in English. Most of the Arabic words are constructed using: prefix (es) + stem + suffix (es), thus, it exhibits large vocabulary sizes and relatively high out-of-vocabulary (OOV) rates on the word level. Regardless, word-level embeddings generalize poorly to rarely seen or unseen words and therefore, can significantly impair the performance for high OOV rates. (Luong et al., 2013) proposed another approach based on morphemes as the sub-word unit to improve generalization. Compared to morphemes, characters have the advantage of being directly available from the original text and do not need complex pre-processing steps which makes character-based approach more robust to use in order to improve system performance.

Therefore, to add character-level features in our model, we modify the architecture of our system presented in Figure 3. A graphical illustration of the new architecture is depicted in Figure 4. We use bidirectional LSTMs to compute character-based vector embeddings of Arabic words. Hence, each character is represented with an LSTM cell. We read words character by character from right to left to compute the first vector embedding (V_f). We employ the same process to compute the second vector embeddings (V_b) where we start from the last character. Finally, we concatenate the first and second vectors to get the final representation of the word based on its characters (V_r). This representation is then concatenated with a word-level representation from a word lookup-table. This lookup-table was initialized using word2vec (see the next section).

4.2 Pretrained Word Embeddings

Word representations derived from unlabeled text have proven useful for many NLP tasks, such as part-of-speech (POS) tagging (Huang et al., 2014), named entity recognition (Collobert et al., 2011), chunking (Turian et al., 2010) and parsing (Bansal et al., 2014). In large corpora, names appear in regular contexts which will be fruitful for most of the sequence tagging tasks: like NER. So that, we initialize our word vectors with pretrained word embeddings. (Soricut and Och, 2015) show that using word embeddings can encode morphological information and may provide additional information to the character-based word embeddings.

Purposefully, to test the performance of pretrained word embeddings, we performed two experiments

Embedding	Dimension	F1 Score
Random Initialisation	100	75.22
Glove	100	83.25
Word2vec	100	**85.71**

Table 1: Results with different choice of word embeddings.

	Tokens	PER	LOC	ORG
Twitter-Train	55k	788	713	449
Twitter-Test	26k	464	587	316

Table 2: Twitter Evaluation data statistics.

with different sets of publicly available word embeddings and compare the results with a random sampling method to initialize our model. Table 1 shows the results obtained using the two different word embeddings as well as the randomly sample one. According to the results in Table 1, we got a significant improvements using pretrained word embeddings contrasted to the one using random embeddings. This is consistent with results reported by previous work (Collobert et al., 2011; Chiu and Nichols, 2015; Huang et al., 2015). We state that Arabic pretrained word embeddings for both word2vec and Glove models used in the experiments are publicly available and developed by (Zahran et al., 2015). From the two different embeddings, Word2vec achieves the best results, about 2.46 points in F1 score better than Glove embeddings and 10.49 points in F1 score better than random initialization. In the rest of the paper, we initiliaze our word vectors with pretrained word embeddings using word2vec model.

5 Evaluation

Evaluation was performed on the Twitter dataset developed by (Darwish, 2013). Table 2 gives an overview of this dataset. Before training starts, we split the dataset into sentences by replacing "." and "," by spaces. Every digit in the dataset is replaced by zero.

5.1 Twitter Dataset

We use the training and test datasets developed by (Darwish, 2013) in order to test our model. This dataset was tagged with three types of named entities: location, person and organisation. The training dataset contains tweets randomly selected from the period of May 3-12, 2012. The testing data contains tweets that were randomly selected between November 23, 2011 and November 27, 2011. We mention that these two datasets were annotated using the Linguistics Data Consortium ACE tagging guidelines. As we will see in the experimental results, this dataset was used in (Darwish and Gao, 2014) and (Zirikly and Diab, 2015) for testing.

5.2 Hyperparameters Details

We train our model using backpropagation through time (BBTT) algorithm to update parameters. We use mini-batch stochastic gradient descent (SGD) with a fixed learning rate. We explored more sophisticated optimization algorithms such as momentum, RMSProp (Hinton et al., 2012), Adam (Kingma and Ba, 14) and Adadelta (Zeiler, 2012). Even if some of these methods are considerably used in computer vision

Model	Precision	Recall	F1
B-LSTM	80.95	57.63	67.33
B-LSTM + char	74.07	67.80	70.80
B-LSTM + char + word emb	89.58	72.88	80.37
B-LSTM + char + word emb + CRF	90.57	81.36	**85.71**

Table 3: Twitter dataset results with our models

Model	Precision	Recall	F1
Zirikly and Diab	81.7	46.9	59.59
Darwish and Gao	76.8	56.6	65.20
Our system	**90.57**	**81.36**	**85.71**

Table 4: Comparison of our system with two other models on Twitter dataset

and show better results, our experiments demonstrate that these methods converge very fast than SGD, but none of them perform better than SGD. We use an embedding dimension of 100. For the hidden dimension of our character bidirectional LSTMs, we use 25 for each one. The final dimension of our character-based representation of words is 50.

6 Experimental Results and Discussions

We run many experiments representing the combination of different models and architectures to understand their influence on Arabic NER system for social media. We explored the impact of using CRF as contextual features, pretrained word embeddings and character-level embeddings. Table 3 shows the different results. Experiments show that the marvelous improvement in the overall system performance was observed with the use of pretrained word embeddings (indicated by "word emb" in Table 3) which gives us an improvement by 9.57 points in F1 score. Adding CRF layer provides us an improvement of 5.34 points in F1 score. Using character-level embeddings (indicated by "char" in Table 3) improve our system performance by 3.47 points in F1 score.

We compare our system with two other models. The best score reported on this task was obtained by (Darwish and Gao, 2014). Their system uses large gazetteers, and a semi-supervised method. They got 65.2 points in F1 score. The same Twitter dataset was used by (Zirikly and Diab, 2015) to test their model, which used a lot of handcrafted engineering features and gazetteers. They obtained F1 score of 59.59. Our model outperforms these two models without using any large gazetteers, and with the use of minimal features combined with bidirectional LSTMs. Table 4 shows our results on Arabic NER for social media in comparison with these two systems.

On the one hand, as far as we know, we are the first to explore the impact of character-level embeddings, pretrained word embeddings and contextual features (CRF) to develop a system for Arabic NER for social media. Using character-level embeddings allow our model to learn interesting morphological and orthographic features instead of hand-engineering them. On the other hand, we are the first to use Arabic pretrained word embeddings developed by (Zahran et al., 2015) to initialize our word vectors for Arabic NER for social media and explore their impact on our system performance.

7 Conclusion

In this paper, we have shown that our neural networks model, which uses bidirectional LSTMs, character-level embeddings, pretrained word embeddings, CRF on the top of the neural networks achieves state-of-the-art results in building an Arabic named entity recognition system for social media and surpassing the previous state-of-the-art system by a large margin without the use of any large gazetteer and lots of hand-engineering features.

Given the inflectional and derivational aspect of Arabic language which leads to a language with complex morphological rules, the intuition behind these results lies in incorporating both pretrained word and character-level embeddings, which allow our system to learn interesting morphological features without hand-engineering them. In addition, using CRF as contextual features was another key success for our system.

References

Bogdan Babych and Anthony Hartley. 2003. *Improving Machine Translation Quality with Automatic Named Entity Recognition, Proceedings of EACL,*

Miguel Ballesteros, Chris Dyer, and Noah A. Smith. 2015. *Improved transition-based dependency parsing by modeling characters instead of words with LSTMs*, Proceedings of EMNLP, Lisbon. Association for Computational Linguistics.

Mohit Bansal Kevin Gimpel, and Karen Livescu. 2014. *Tailoring continuous word representations for dependency parsing*, Proceedings of ACL, Baltimore. Association for Computational Linguistics.

Mikael Boden. 2002. A guide to recurrent neural networks and backpropagation, *Technical report*.

Jason PC Chiu and Eric Nichols. 2015. Named entity recognition with bidirectional lstm-cnns, *arXiv preprint arXiv:1511.08308*

Kyunghyun Cho, Bart van Merrienboer, Caglar Gulcehre, Fethi Bougares, Holger Schwenk, and Yoshua Bengio. 2014. *Learning phrase representations using RNN encoder-decoder for statistical machine translation*, Proceedings of EMNLP, Doha. Association for Computational Linguistics.

Junyoung Chung, Kyunghyun Cho, and Yoshua Bengio. 2016. *A Character-level Decoder without Explicit Segmentation for Neural Machine Translation*, Proceedings of ACL, Berlin. Association for Computational Linguistics

Ronan Collobert, Jason Weston, Léon Bottou, Michael Karlen, Koran Kavukcuoglu, and Pavel Kuksa. 2011. Natural Language Processing (Almost) from Scratch, *Journal of Machine Learning Research,*12(1):2493- 2537.

Kareem Darwish. 2013. *Named entity recognition using cross-lingual resources: Arabic as an example*, Proceedings of ACL, Sofia, Bulgaria. Association for Computational Linguistics.

Kareem Darwish and Wei Gao. 2014. *Simple effective microblog named entity recognition: Arabic as an example*, Proceedings of the Ninth International Conference on Language Resources and Evaluation, Reykjavik, Iceland.

Cìcero dos Santos and Maìra Gatti. 2014. *Deep convolutional neural networks for sentiment analysis of short texts*, Proceedings of COLING 2014, the 25th International Conference on Computational Linguistics. Technical Papers, Dublin, Ireland Association for Computational Linguistics.

Sergio Ferrndez, Antonio Toral, scar Ferrndez, Antonio Ferrndez, and Rafael Muoz. 2007. *Applying wikipedias multilingual knowledge to crosslingual question answering*, Zoubida Kedad, Nadira Lammari, Elisabeth Mtais, Farid Meziane, and Yacine Rezgui, editors, Reykjavik, Iceland. Springer.

Christoh Goller and Andreas Kuchler. 1996. *Learning task-dependent distributed representations by backpropagation through structure*, Proceedings of the International Conference on Neural Networks,

Alex Graves and Jürgen Schmidhuber. 2005. *Framewise phoneme classification with bidirectional LSTM networks*, Proceedings of IJCNN.

Alex Graves. 2013. Generating sequences with recurrent neural networks, *arXiv preprint*

Geoffrey Hinton, Nitish Srivastava, and Kevin Swersky. 2012. *Coursera, Lecture 6e: rmsprop: divide the gradient by a running average of its recent magnitude*, Neural Networks for Machine Learning,

Sepp Hochreiter and Jürgen Schmidhuber. 1997. Long short-term memory, *Neural Computation*, 9(8):1735–1780.

Kaiming He, Xiangyu Zhang, Shaoqing Ren, and Jian Sun. 2015. Deep Residual Learning for Image Recognition, *arXiv preprint*

Fei Huang, Arun Ahuja, Doug Downey, Yi Yang, Yuhong Guo, and Alexander Yates. 2014. Learning representations for weakly supervised natural language processing tasks, *Computational Linguistics*, 40(1).

Zhiheng Huang, Wei Xu, and Kai Yu. 2015. Bidirectional lstm-crf models for sequence tagging, *arXiv preprint arXiv:1508.01991*

Jun'ichi Kazama and Kentaro Torisawa. 2007. *Exploiting Wikipedia as external knowledge for named entity recognition*, Proceedings of EMNLP - CoNLL, Prague, Czech Republic. Association for Computational Linguistics.

Yoon Kim, Yacine Jernite, David Sontag, and Alexander M. Rush. 2015. Character-aware neural language models, *CoRR, abs/1508.06615*

Diederik Kingma and Jimmy Ba. 2014. Adam: A method for stochastic optimization, *arXiv preprint arXiv:1412.6980*.

John Lafferty, Andrew McCallum, and Fernando CN Pereira. 2001. *Conditional random fields: Probabilistic models for segmenting and labeling sequence data, Proceedings of ICML*.

Wang Ling, Tiago Luıs, Luıs Marujo, Ramon F. Astudillo, Silvio Amir, Chris Dyer, Alan W. Black, and Isabel Trancoso. 2015. *Finding function in form: Compositional character models for open vocabulary word representation*, Proceedings of EMNLP - CoNLL, Lisbon, Portugal. Association for Computational Linguistics.

Minh-Thang Luong, Richard Socher, and Christopher D. Manning. 2013. *Better Word Representations with Recursive Neural Networks for Morphology, Proceedings of CoNLL*, Sofia, Bulgaria. Association for Computational Linguistics.

Minh-Thang Luong and Christopher D. Manning. 2016. *Achieving Open Vocabulary Neural Machine Translation with Hybrid Word-Character Models, Proceedings of ACL*, Berlin, Germany. Association for Computational Linguistics.

Tomàš Mikolov, Stefan Kombrink, Lucàš Burget, Jan Cernocký, and Sanjeev Khudanpur. 2011. *Extensions of recurrent neural network language model*, Proceedings of ICASSP.

Tomàš Mikolov, Ilya Sutskever, Kai Chen, Greg Corrado, and Jeffrey Dean. 2013. *Distributed representations of words and phrases and their compositionality*, Proceedings of NIPS.

David Nadeau and Satoshi Sekine. 2007. A survey of named entity recognition and classification, *Journal of Linguisticae Investigationes*, 30(1).

David E. Rumelhart, Geoffrey E. Hinton, and Ronald J. Williams 1986. *Learning Internal Representations by Error Propagation*, Symposium on Parallel and Distributed Processing.

Semiocast. 2012. *Geolocation analysis of Twitter accounts and tweets by Semiocast.*

Khaled Shaalan and Mai Oudah. 2014. A hybrid approach to Arabic named entity recognition, *Journal of Information Science*, 40(1):67–87.

Richard Socher, Alex Perelygin, Jean Y. Wu, Jason Chuang, Christopher D. Manning, Andrew Y. Ng, and Christopher Potts. 2013. *Recursive deep models for semantic compositionality over a sentiment treebank*, Proceedings of EMNLP, Seattle, USA. Association for Computational Linguistics.

Radu Soricut and Franz Och. 2015. *Unsupervised Morphology Induction Using Word Embeddings*, Proceedings of the NAACL-HLT, Denver, Colorado. Association for Computational Linguistics.

Ilya Sutskever, Orion Vinyals, and Quoc V. Le. 2014. *Sequence to sequence learning with neural networks*, Proceedings of NIPS, Montreal, Canada.

Paul Thompson and Christopher C. Dozier. 1997. *Name searching and information retrieval*, Proceedings of EMNLP, Association for Computational Linguistics.

Hiroyuki Toda and Ryoji Kataoka. 2005. *A Search Result Clustering Method using Informatively Named Entities*, Proceedings of the 7th annual ACM international workshop on Web information and data management (WIDM), ACM Press.

Joseph Turian, Lev-Arie Ratinov, and Yoshua Bengio 2010. *Word representations: A simple and general method for semi-supervised learning*, Proceedings of ACL, Uppsala, Sweden. Association for Computational Linguistics.

Yijun Xiao and Kyunghyun Cho 2016. Efficient character-level document classification by combining convolution and recurrent layers, *arXiv preprint arXiv:1602.00367*

Mohamed A. Zahran, Ahmed Magooda, Ashraf Y. Mahgoub, Hazem Raafat, Mohsen Rashwan, and Amir Atyia. 2015. *Word Representations in Vector Space and their Applications for Arabic*, the Proceedings of CICLing, Cairo, Egypt. Springer.

Matthew D. Zeiler 2012. ADADELTA: an adaptive learning rate method, *CoRR, abs/1212.5701*

Xiang Zhang, Junbo Zhao, and Yann LeCun 2015. *Character-level convolutional networks for text classification*, the Proceedings of NIPS, Montreal, Canada.

Ayah Zirikly and Mona Diab. 2015. *Named Entity Recognition for Arabic Social Media*, Proceedings of the NAACL-HLT, Denver, Colorado. Association for Computational Linguistics.

Development of a Bengali parser by cross-lingual transfer from Hindi

Ayan Das, Agnivo Saha, Sudeshna Sarkar
Department of Computer Science and Engineering
Indian Institute of Technology, Kharagpur, WB, India
ayan.das@cse.iitkgp.ernet.in
agnivo.saha@gmail.com
sudeshna@cse.iitkgp.ernet.in

Abstract

In recent years there has been a lot of interest in cross-lingual parsing for developing treebanks for languages with small or no annotated treebanks. In this paper, we explore the development of a cross-lingual transfer parser from Hindi to Bengali using a Hindi parser and a Hindi-Bengali parallel corpus. A parser is trained and applied to the Hindi sentences of the parallel corpus and the parse trees are projected to construct probable parse trees of the corresponding Bengali sentences. Only about 14% of these trees are complete (transferred trees contain all the target sentence words) and they are used to construct a Bengali parser. We relax the criteria of completeness to consider well-formed trees (43% of the trees) leading to an improvement. We note that the words often do not have a one-to-one mapping in the two languages but considering sentences at the chunk-level results in better correspondence between the two languages. Based on this we present a method to use chunking as a preprocessing step and do the transfer on the chunk trees. We find that about 72% of the projected parse trees of Bengali are now well-formed. The resultant parser achieves significant improvement in both Unlabeled Attachment Score (UAS) as well as Labeled Attachment Score (LAS) over the baseline word-level transferred parser.

1 Introduction

Parsing is a very important component of natural language processing. Machine learning techniques have been applied to produce highly accurate parsers for natural languages given collections of annotated parse trees called treebanks. However, creating treebank for a language involves a great deal of manual effort and treebanks do not exist for a large number of the world's languages and good quality parser learning requires a large treebank.

In recent years there have been some interesting work on developing dependency parsers where in the absence of treebanks, cross-lingual parsing has been used to develop a parser in a Target Language (TL) taking advantage of an existing parser or a treebank in a different source language (SL). Some of these systems use a parallel corpus to improve the quality of transfer parsers along with some other resources.

Though Bengali is the seventh most spoken language in the world, resources available for NLP in Bengali are scant. A small treebank consisting of about 1300 parse trees was made available for the participants of ICON 2009 (http://www.icon2009.in/) tool contest on parsing in Bengali in which 150 sentences were used for testing. We wish to explore the efficacy of cross-lingual parser transfer in Indian languages by applying it on the Hindi-Bengali language pair. Though a lot of experiments in cross-lingual parsing have been carried out in European languages, no work has been reported in Indian language pairs.

Hindi and Bengali belong to the same family of Indo-Aryan languages and share certain basic syntactic similarities. Both have the SOV sentence structure. However, there are several differences in the morphological structure of the words and phrases between these two languages.

In this paper, we refer to a transferred tree as a "complete" tree if it is connected, projective, has root aligned to the root word of the source tree and contains all the words in the target sentence. If the tree

Proceedings of the 6th Workshop on South and Southeast Asian Natural Language Processing,
pages 33–43, Osaka, Japan, December 11-17 2016.

has size greater than one, satisfies all other conditions of a complete tree but does not contain all the target sentence words then it is called a "well-formed" tree. Naturally, the number of well-formed trees is much larger than the number of complete trees and it has been found that a parser trained using the well-formed trees is slightly more accurate than the parsers trained using complete trees.

We also show that due to the high-level syntactic similarities between between the Hindi and Bengali, a phrase-level transfer results in more number of well-formed parse trees (72% of the projected parse trees) than by word-level transfer (43% of the projected parse trees). The increase in number of trees also helps in developing a better parser in TL.

Though it is challenging to develop a full parser for a language, developing a shallow parser or chunker is relatively straightforward and can be done using simple rule-based or statistical methods. We use the chunkers for Bengali and Hindi along with projection of Hindi parse trees to develop a Bengali parser by phrase-level transfer. The resulting parsers improves Unlabeled Attachment Score (UAS) from 67 to 80 and Labeled Attachment Score (LAS) from 47 to 62 compared to the word level parser.

2   Related work

In this section we present the major approaches to cross-lingual syntactic transfer proposed in the literature.

Direct Transfer - Delexicalized parsing   Direct transfer method learns a parser in SL and applies it to TL. A direct transfer model cannot make use of lexical features or address difference in word order. Delexicalized parsing proposed by Zeman and Resnik (2008) involves supervised training of a parser model in on a SL treebank without using any lexical features and then applying the model directly to parse sentences in TL. This was applied to Danish-Swedish pair. Søgaard (2011) used a similar method for several different language pairs and found that performance varied widely (F1-score : 50%-75%) depending upon the similarity of the language pairs. Täckström et al. (2012) used cross-lingual word clusters obtained from a large unlabelled corpora as additional features in their delexicalized parser. Naseem et al. (2012) proposed a method for multilingual learning to languages that exhibit significant differences from existing resource-rich languages which selectively learns the features relevant for a target language and ties the model parameters accordingly. Täckström et al. (2013) improved performance of delexicalized parser by incorporating selective sharing of model parameters based on typological information.

Distributed Representation   Distributed representation of words as dense vector can be used to capture cross-lingual lexical information and can be augmented with delexicalized parsers. Bilingual dictionaries may be used to transfer lexical features. Xiao and Guo (2014) learnt language-independent word representations to address cross-lingual dependency parsing. Duong et al. (2015) followed a similar approach where the vectors for both the languages are learnt using a skipgram-like method in which the system was trained to predict the POS tags of the context words instead of the words themselves.

Annotation projection   Cross-lingual parser transfer by annotation projection use parallel data and project parse trees in SL to TL through word alignment. But most translations are not word-to-word and only partial alignments can be obtained in many cases. Hwa et al. (2005) proposed a set of projection heuristics that make it possible to project any dependency structure through given word alignments to a target language sentence. McDonald et al. (2011) proposed a method where a delexicalized direct transfer parser trained in SL was used to parse some TL sentences which were in turn used to seed a parser in TL. The target language parser so trained was used as a lexicalized parser in the space of the target language sentences. Ma and Xia (2014) built a dependency parser by maximizing the likelihood on parallel data and the confidence on unlabeled target language data.

Rasooli and Collins (2015) proposed a method to induce dependency parser in TL using a dependency parser in SL and a parallel corpus. The transferred trees that consist of a subset of the words in the target language sentence are expanded into full trees using a decoding technique. Lacroix et al. (2016) proposed a simple alignment scheme for cross-lingual annotation projection but their performance is lower than that of Rasooli and Collins (2015).

Treebank translation   Tiedemann et al. (2014) and Tiedemann (2015) proposed methods for treebank translation. They used a SMT system to obtain the phrase tables and word alignment information from the parallel corpus and used some heuristics to translate the SL treebank to a treebank of TL. They have shown that direct projection works quite well for some languages and significantly outperforms the direct delexicalized transfer model.

Parsing in Hindi and Bengali language: Bharati and Sangal (1993) and Bharati et al. (2002) are some of the first notable works on parsing of Indian languages. Nivre (2005) and Nivre (2009) have developed supervised parsers for Indian languages such as Hindi and Bengali. Some of the work in Indian language parsing use a chunk as unit instead of a word. Bharati et al. (2009) and Bharati et al. (2009) have proposed a two-stage constraint-based approach where they first try to extract the intra-chunk dependencies and resolve the inter-chunk dependencies in the second stage. Ambati et al. (2010) used disjoint sets of dependency relations and performed the intra-chunk parsing and inter-chunk parsing separately. Some of the major works on parsing in Bengali language appeared in ICON 2009 (http://www.icon2009.in/). The highest UAS and LAS for Bengali were 90.32 and 84.29 respectively.

3   Objective

We aim is to explore cross-lingual transfer parser development for Indian languages. For most Indian languages very little annotated resources are available. No annotated treebank is available in the open source for Bengali, though a 1300 sentence treebank was made available to participants of ICON 2009 tool contest. We explore methods for transfer parsing from Hindi to Bengali due to our familiarity with the languages and the Bengali language resources available with us. However we expect that this will be indicative of the type of performance between other language pairs belonging to the same family. We use a Hindi dependency treebank and a parallel Hindi-Bengali corpus to build the Bengali dependency parser by annotation projection.

We explore methods for transfer from Hindi to Bengali. Fully transferred projective trees have been found to be most useful to train a parser in the target language (Lacroix et al., 2016). To increase the amount of training data we wish to explore relaxations of this requirement so that more transferred trees can be used without negatively impacting the quality. We also wish to explore the use of other linguistic resources to improve the quality of the transferred trees.

4   Resources used

For our experiments, we used the Hindi HDTB treebank (ltrc.iiit.ac.in/treebank_H2014/) and the UDEP treebank (http://universaldependencies.org/). The HDTB treebank consists of 18637 parse trees and the Hindi UDEP treebank consists of 15870 parse trees divided into training, development and testsets. In HDTB and UDEP treebanks, Anncorra (Sharma et al., 2007) and universal dependency (McDonald et al., 2013) tagsets are used to tag the parse trees respectively. For our experiments, we used the neural network based parser (Saha and Sarkar, 2016).

The initial Hindi and Bengali word embeddings were obtained by running word2vec (Mikolov et al., 2013) on Hindi Wikipedia dump corpus and FIRE 2011 (http://www.isical.ac.in/ clia/2011/) corpus respectively.

For chunking we used the chunker developed at our institute. For testing we used the testset of 150 parse trees annotated using tagset similar to Anncorra tagset. This set of Bengali trees is the testset of the Bengali treebank used in ICON2009 (http://www.icon2009.in/) contest to train parsers for various Indian languages. The original dataset contains partially labeled parse trees with only inter-chunk dependency relations and chunk information of each sentence. We completed each parse tree by manually tagging the intra-chunk dependencies using the chunk information. We used these full trees for our experiments.

5   Proposed Method

We explore cross-lingual parser transfer by annotation projection from Hindi to Bengali by making use of a Hindi-Bengali parallel corpus. We first developed a system that does word level annotation projection as described below.

5.1 Word level annotation projection based transfer

We use word level annotation projection to project the dependencies of the parsed Hindi sentences via the aligned parallel corpus to create a Bengali treebank on which the Bengali parser can be trained.

Word alignment of parallel corpus The parallel corpora $C_{HB} = \{(h^{(i)}, b^{(i)})\}$, where $h^{(i)}$ is a Hindi sentence and $b^{(i)}$ is the corresponding Bengali sentence, contains m parallel sentence pairs. The sentences in the parallel data were aligned in both directions using the GIZA++ tool and combined using the intersection heuristic which selects only $1 : 1$ alignment links. The intersect heuristic was chosen to avoid aligning a word with multiple words which might result in the formation of cycles and multiple links in the parse trees during the transfer. It results in more accurate but less number of alignments resulting in non-alignment of some Bengali words.

Annotation projection The Hindi treebank (HTB) comprise of n trees $\{(h^{(i)}, \text{tree}(h^{(i)}))\}$ where $h^{(i)}$ is a Hindi sentence and $\text{tree}(h^{(i)})$ is the corresponding parse tree. Algorithm 1 outlines the steps for training the Bengali parser by word-level annotation projection method. We used the following criteria to select

---

Algorithm 1: Training the Bengali parser by word-level annotation projection method

---

input : Hindi treebank HTB, Hindi-Bengali parallel corpus C_{HB}
output: Bengali parser trained using transferred Bengali treebank

1 Use GIZA++ alignment tool on C_{HB} to get word-aligned sentences. For $(h^{(i)}, b^{(i)})$ get the alignment $A^{(i)} = \{(x, y)\}$, where word $h_x^{(i)}$ is aligned to word $b_y^{(i)}$.
2 Train a parser using the HTB to get *hindiparser*
3 Initialize: Bengali treebank (BTB) = NULL
4 **for** *each Hindi sentence $h^{(i)}$ in C_{HB}* **do**
5   Parse (h_i) using *hindiparser*.
    `/* Project tree(`$h^{(i)}$`) on `$b^{(i)}$` using `$A^{(i)}$` to get dep(`$b^{(i)}$`)        */`
6      $\text{dep}(b^{(i)})$ = `Project(`tree($h^{(i)}$)`,`$b^{(i)}$`,`$A^{(i)}$`)`
    `/* Check if dep(`$b^{(i)}$`) corresponds to a well-formed tree for `$b^{(i)}$`  */`
7   If there is exactly one ROOT **AND** $\text{dep}(b^{(i)})$ forms a well-formed connected tree **AND** it is projective **AND** all words $\in b^{(i)}$ appear in $dep(b^{(i)})$
8   Add $\text{dep}(b^{(i)})$ to BTB
9 **end**
10 Train a parser using BTB to get a Bengali parser *benparser*
11 **Procedure** `Project(`*tree($h^{(i)}$)*$, b^{(i)}, A^{(i)}$`)`
12      $\text{dep}(b^{(i)})$ = NULL
13   **for** *each dependency (head, modifier) in tree($h^{(i)}$)* **do**
14   **if** $\exists w_1 : \text{(head, } w_1) \in A(i)$ ***AND*** $\exists w_2 : \text{(modifier, } w_2) \in A(i)$ ***AND*** $w_1 \neq w_2$ **then**
15   Add (w_1, w_2) to $\text{dep}(b^{(i)})$
16   **end**
17   **end**
18   **return** $\text{dep}(b^{(i)})$

---

complete trees:

1. The ROOT of the target tree must be mapped to the ROOT of the source tree.

2. The transferred dependency set must form a connected projective tree.

3. Every word in the Bengali sentence appears in the tree.

We find that large number of trees were eliminated due to incomplete transfer because some of the Bengali words in these sentences did not get aligned to any Hindi word. We then relax the requirement of complete trees by removing the requirement of complete trees by replacing the criterion 3 by the criterion that size of tree must be greater than 1 and making the corresponding change in Algorithm 1 to obtain the well-formed trees.

Well-formed parse trees were obtained for $21,554$ Bengali sentences, out of which 7018 were complete when HDTB treebank was used to train the Hindi parser. The percentage of fully transferred trees largely depends upon the syntactic similarities of the languages which is evident from the fact that during English to German transfer, only 2.4% of the trees were fully transferred (Rasooli and Collins, 2015).

Rasooli and Collins (2015) have shown that the inclusion of partial and incomplete trees degrades performance of the parser. In English to German parsing, the German parser trained using 18000 full trees gave an accuracy of 85.8% and a parser model trained on 968000 transferred parse trees comprising of a mixture of full and partial trees gave an accuracy of 74%. They considered trees where a subset of words forms a projective tree or a span of k words appear as modifiers. However, we observed that inclusion of well-formed partial trees (according to our criteria) along with the fully transferred trees results in increase in UAS from 66% to 67.4%. The results are shown in Table 2.

5.2 Motivation for chunk-level transfer

We hypothesize that the number of transferred trees can be increased if we can address the problem of difference in phrase structure of the two languages. The example in Section 5.2 shows how the chunk-level transfer can address the problem on non-alignment of some words due to difference in phrase structure. Thus, chunk-level transfer may significantly increase the number of transferred well-formed trees. In Table 1, we show some examples of Hindi and Bengali phrases that bring out the difference in the structure of phrases in the two languages, which means that one to one mapping between words is often not possible.

English phrase	Hindi phrase	Bengali phrase
is eating	khA rAhA hAy (eat being is)	khAchchhe (eating)
died	mare (died)	mArA jay (death happened)
due to earthquake	bhukAmp ke dwArA (earthquake of by)	bhumikamper fale (earthquake-of result)

Table 1: Example phrases with English, Hindi and Bengali equivalents

English sentence (E_1): "Several people got stuck due to landslide on way to KedarnAth".
Hindi sentence (H_1): "KedArnAth ke rAste mein bhuskhalan ke kAran bahut se log fAnse"
Bengali sentence (B_1): "KedArnAther pathe dhaser kArane bahu lok Atke pade"

The following example illustrates the word-level and chunk-level transfer of the parse tree of H_1 to the parse tree of B_1. Both H_1 and B_1 have the same meaning as that of E_1.

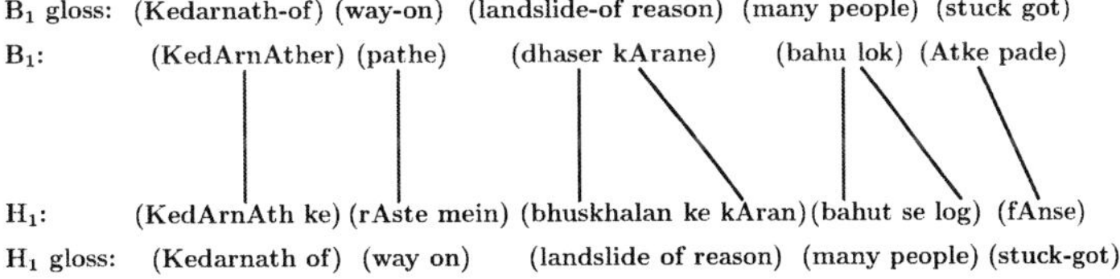

Figure 1: Word alignment between B_1 and H_1

Figure 2 shows the parse trees for B_1 and H_1, and the Bengali parse tree formed after transfer via word alignment. Note that the dependencies "Atke → pade" was not obtained in the projected tree since the

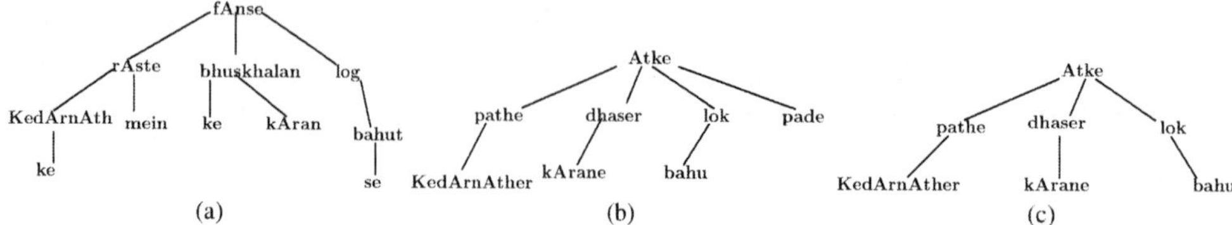

(a)   (b)   (c)

Figure 2: (a) Parse tree of H_1 (b) Parse tree of B_1 (c) Transferred Bengali word-level tree.

words "pade" was not aligned to any Hindi word. However, this problem can be eliminated by chunk-level transfer as shown below. Figure 3 shows the chunk alignment of B_1 and H_1. Each parenthesized

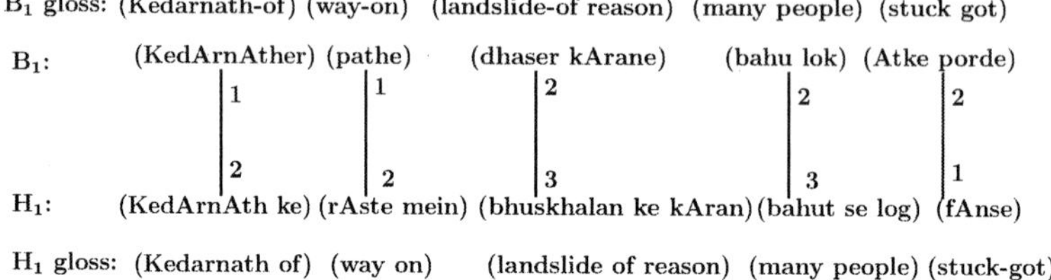

Figure 3: Chunk-level mapping between B_1 and H_1

set of words indicates a chunk. The numbers corresponding to each chunk indicate the number of words in each chunk. Figure 4a and Figure 4b show the chunk-level trees which contain only the inter-chunk

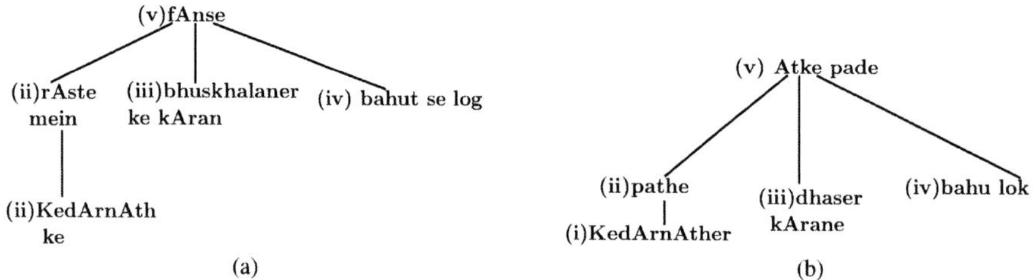

(a)   (b)

Figure 4: (a) Chunk-level parse tree of H_1 (b) Chunk-level parse tree of B_1

links. Figure 5a shows the chunk-head tree of B_1 obtained by chunk level transfer. Figure 5b shows the

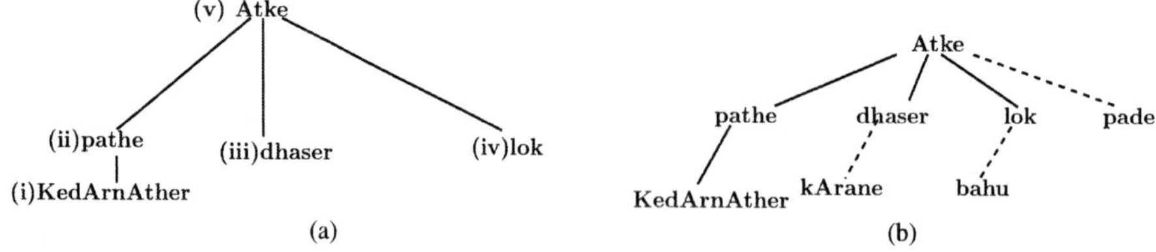

(a)   (b)

Figure 5: (a) Bengali chunk head parse tree before expansion (b) The same tree after expansion

expanded chunk-head tree containing all the words. This shows that chunk-level transfer may alleviate the problem arising due to non-alignment of some words.

5.3   Chunk-based annotation projection method

In this section we discuss the method for creating a Bengali transfer parser by our approach of chunking based cross-lingual parser transfer using annotation projection. The method is described in Algorithm 2. In step 7 of Algorithm 2 we map Hindi chunk-level trees to Bengali chunk-level trees. Note that the basic algorithm for converting the chunk-level Hindi trees to chunk-level Bengali trees using the chunk

Algorithm 2: Bengali chunk-level parser by chunk-level annotation projection method

input : Hindi treebank, word alignment of Hindi-Bengali parallel corpus
output: Bengali chunk-level parser

1 **Chunk Alignment**: Obtain chunk-alignment of the Hindi-Bengali parallel sentences (C_{HB}) from the corresponding word alignment by Procedure `ChunkAlign` $\forall$ sentence pairs $(h^{(i)}, b^{(i)}) \in C_{HB}$

2 Convert the parse trees $\{ht^{(i)}\}$ of the Hindi sentences in C_{HB} to Hindi chunk-level parse trees $\{hct^{(i)}\}$ by collapsing the chunks using the following heuristics applied to each dependency.

3 **begin**

4   If both head and modifier are chunk head, replace them by the corresponding chunk identifiers.

5   If head and modifier belongs to same chunk, ignore the dependency.

6 **end**

7 Transfer Hindi chunk-level parse trees $\{hct^{(i)}\}$ to Bengali chunk-level parse trees $\{bct^{(i)}\}$ using chunk alignment obtained in Step 1.

8 Replace the Bengali chunk identifiers in each Bengali chunk tree by the corresponding chunk heads for all trees in $\{bct^{(i)}\}$.

9 Train the Bengali parser using chunk-head trees in $\{bct^{(i)}\}$ to get the Bengali chunk-level parser.

10 **Procedure** `ChunkAlign` (*Sentence pair (h, b), set of Hindi chunks (hcset) and set of Bengali chunks (bcset), word alignment* $\mathbf{a}^w = \{(x, y)\}$)

11   **for** *each Hindi chunk hc_i in hcset* **do**

12   Initialize: 1. Set of Bengali chunks to which hc_i is aligned $map(hc_i) = \{\}$

13   2. Chunk alignment ($\mathbf{a}^c$) of (h, b)

14   **for** *each word w_h in hc_i* **do**

15   **if** *w_h aligned to a Bengali word (w_b) i.e. $(w_h, w_b) \in \mathbf{a}^w$* **then**

16   Add the Bengali chunk (bc) containing w_b to $map(hc_i)$

17   **end**

18   **end**

19   **if** *all words in hc_i aligned to words in a single Bengali chunk (bc_j)* **then**

20   Add (hc_i, bc_j) to $\mathbf{a}^c$

21   **else if** *words in hc_i are aligned to multiple Bengali chunks* **then**

22   Find the chunk head $head(hc_i)$

23   **if** *$head(hc_i)$ aligned to a Bengali chunk bc* **then**

24   Add (hc_i, bc) to $\mathbf{a}^c$

25   **else**

26   No map for hc_i

27   **end**

28   **end**

29   return $\mathbf{a}^c$

alignment is same as in word-level transfer (Algorithm 1) except that chunk-level transfer uses the chunk alignment instead of the word alignment and the chunk-level trees are transferred instead of the word-level trees. From the chunk level trees we obtain the chunk-head trees by replacing the chunk identifiers with the corresponding chunk heads in step 8 of Algorithm 2. In step 9 of Algorithm 2 the chunk-head trees are used to train a chunk-level parser.

The final parser comprises of two parts, a) a chunk-level parser and b) a chunk expander. The chunk-expander uses a set of rules for intra-chunk expansion. For expanding the chunks we used the rules proposed by Kosaraju et al. (2012) as well as some additional rules. At first, the chunk-level parser is used parse the chunk-head test trees and then the chunk-expander is used to complete the intra-chunk dependency relations.

5.4 Experimental results

We performed the experiments separately using two different treebanks, HDTB and UDEP. We did not mix the two treebanks because they use different dependency relation tagset and a substantial number of sentences are common between the two treebanks. We report only the unlabeled attachment score (UAS) for our experiments when the Hindi parser used to parse the Hindi sentences of the parallel sentences was trained using the UDEP treebank because the Hindi treebank (UDEP) is tagged with Universal Dependency tagset which is different from that of the Bengali testset of 150 parse trees. We report both UAS and LAS for our experiments when the HDTB treebank was used because the tagset used in ICON and HDTB have some similarity.

Table 2 summarizes the results of the word-level and chunk-level transfer parser for the two treebanks. We observe that the number of well-formed trees obtained by chunk-level transfer have increased significantly over word-level transfer. The drop in number of complete trees in chunk-level transfer is due to the disagreement of the chunker outputs of the two languages.

It is seen that considering well-formed trees along with complete trees results in slight improvement in result and the chunk-level annotation projection method performs significantly better than the word-level annotation projection-based method for both the datasets used to train the initial Hindi parser.

Treebank used for training Hindi parser	Method	Complete trees			Well-formed trees		
		Number of trees	UAS	LAS	Number of trees	UAS	LAS
HDTB	Word-level transfer	7018	65.7	44.7	21554	67.4	47.2
	Chunk-level transfer	6679	79.3	60.1	36196	**80.6**	**62.1**
UDEP	Word-level transfer	7882	60.2	-	26827	61.0	-
	Chunk-level transfer	7061	79.1	-	37323	**79.4**	-

Table 2: Comparison of UAS and LAS of chunk-level transfer parser with word-level transfer parser when Hindi parser trained using HDTB and UDEP treebanks.

Table 3: Comparison of errors for the most frequent dependency tags. The entries of column 3 to 6 indicates the number of dependencies bearing the corresponding tags in the gold data that actually appear in the parsed trees and the accuracy (in %). Rows 2-10 (k1 to k7t) are inter-chunk dependencies and Rows 11-15 (rsym to lwg_neg) are intra-chunk dependencies

	Actual Count of dependency relations	Word-level transfer (UD)		Chunk-level transfer followed by expansion (UD)		Word-level transfer (HDTB)		Chunk-level transfer followed by expansion (HDTB)	
k1 (doer/agent/subject)	166	122	(73.5)	128	(77.1)	119	(71.7)	129	(77.7)
main (root)	150	84	(56.4)	104	(69.8)	101	(67.3)	108	(72.5)
k2 (object)	131	98	(74.8)	102	(77.9)	98	(74.8)	103	(78.6)
vmod (Verb modifier)	111	68	(61.3)	74	(66.7)	83	(74.8)	87	(78.4)
r6 (possessive)	82	49	(59.8)	45	(54.9)	51	(62.2)	38	(46.3)
pof (part of)	59	54	(91.5)	58	(98.3)	57	(96.6)	59	(100)
k7p (Location in place)	50	32	(64.0)	41	(82.0)	33	(66.0)	37	(74.0)
ccof (conjunction of)	47	2	(4.25)	2	(4.26)	15	(31.9)	14	(29.8)
k7t (Location in time)	40	26	(65.0)	26	(65.0)	25	(62.5)	29	(72.5)
rsym (punctuation)	249	119	(47.8)	241	(98.4)	154	(61.8)	242	(98.8)
nmod_adj (adjectival noun modifier)	79	74	(93.7)	79	(100)	76	(96.2)	79	(100)
lwg_vaux (auxiliary verb)	54	43	(79.6)	54	(100)	52	(96.3)	54	(100)
lwg_rp (particle)	23	4	(17.4)	19	(82.6)	8	(34.8)	21	(91.3)
lwg_neg (negation)	22	6	(27.3)	21	(95.4)	3	(13.6)	22	(100)

Rasooli and Collins (2015) incrementally increased the number of full trees by completing the partial trees using a trained arc-eager parser model. The accuracy of the English to German transfer parser model increased from 70.6% to 74.32% as completed full parse trees were incrementally added to the set. Compared to the above result our method results in an increase in UAS from 67.4 to 80.6 and 61.0 to 79.4 for HDTB and UDEP respectively.

6 Error analysis

We analyzed the errors in dependency relations of the parse trees obtained by parsing the test sentences based on the number of dependency relations in the gold data that actually appear in the trees parsed by our parser. Table 3 summarizes the accuracies of the most frequent inter-chunk and intra-chunk dependency tags. We observe that the parser trained using the HDTB treebank identifies the "conjunct of" dependencies more accurately than the parser trained using UDEP treebank due to difference in annotation scheme of Anncorra and UDEP. However, the overall performance of the transferred parsers on the "ccof" relations is poor. We need to investigate further on this issue. The possessive/genitive (r6) dependencies are better identified by word-level transferred parser. For the proper identification of possessive/genitive relations the inflectional informations are essential which can be obtained from the modifiers. In case of chunk-level transfer, we are using embeddings and features of the chunk-head only, which may not be sufficient to capture the necessary information. We also observe that the rule-based expansion of chunks helps to identify the intra-chunk relations more accurately than by word-level transfer.

From the data we observed that disagreement between the Hindi and Bengali chunkers, disagreement between Hindi chunker and parser outputs and error in word alignment are some of the major sources of error resulting in multiple links, cycles, partial trees and non-projectivity. We shall give a detailed discussion of the errors in an extended version of the paper.

7 Conclusion

This work is a basic exercise on the development of a Bengali parser without using any Bengali treebank. We have shown that a Bengali parser of fair accuracy can be developed by cross-lingual transfer from Hindi language using a Hindi treebank and a Hindi-Bengali parallel corpus. We have also shown that chunk-level transfer parser outperforms the word-level transfer parser in terms of both UAS and LAS and it increases the number of transferred well-formed trees on two different datasets.

References

Bharat Ram Ambati, Samar Husain, Sambhav Jain, Dipti Misra Sharma, and Rajeev Sangal. 2010. Two methods to incorporate 'local morphosyntactic' features in hindi dependency parsing. In *Proceedings of the NAACL HLT 2010 First Workshop on Statistical Parsing of Morphologically-Rich Languages*, pages 22–30, Los Angeles, CA, USA, June. Association for Computational Linguistics.

Akshar Bharati and Rajeev Sangal. 1993. Parsing free word order languages in the paninian framework. In *Proceedings of the 31st Annual Meeting on Association for Computational Linguistics*, ACL '93, pages 105–111, Stroudsburg, PA, USA. Association for Computational Linguistics.

Akshar Bharati, Rajeev Sangal, and T Papi Reddy. 2002. A constraint based parser using integer programming. *Proc. of ICON*.

Akshar Bharati, Samar Husain, Meher Vijay, Kalyan Deepak, Dipti Misra Sharma, and Rajeev Sangal. 2009. Constraint based hybrid approach to parsing indian languages. In *Proceedings of the 23rd PACLIC*, pages 614–621, Hong Kong, December. City University of Hong Kong.

Long Duong, Trevor Cohn, Steven Bird, and Paul Cook. 2015. Cross-lingual transfer for unsupervised dependency parsing without parallel data. In *Proceedings of the Nineteenth Conference on Computational Natural Language Learning*, pages 113–122, Beijing, China, July. Association for Computational Linguistics.

Rebecca Hwa, Philip Resnik, Amy Weinberg, Clara Cabezas, and Okan Kolak. 2005. Bootstrapping parsers via syntactic projection across parallel texts. *Natural Language Engineering*, 11:11–311.

Prudhvi Kosaraju, Bharat Ram Ambati, Samar Husain, Dipti Misra Sharma, and Rajeev Sangal. 2012. Intra-chunk dependency annotation : Expanding hindi inter-chunk annotated treebank. In *Proceedings of the Sixth Linguistic Annotation Workshop*, pages 49–56, Jeju, Republic of Korea, July. Association for Computational Linguistics.

Ophélie Lacroix, Lauriane Aufrant, Guillaume Wisniewski, and François Yvon. 2016. Frustratingly easy cross-lingual transfer for transition-based dependency parsing. In *Proceedings of the 2016 Conference of the North American Chapter of the Association for Computational Linguistics: Human Language Technologies*, pages 1058–1063, San Diego, California, June. Association for Computational Linguistics.

Xuezhe Ma and Fei Xia. 2014. Unsupervised dependency parsing with transferring distribution via parallel guidance and entropy regularization. In *Proceedings of the 52nd Annual Meeting of the Association for Computational Linguistics (Volume 1: Long Papers)*, pages 1337–1348, Baltimore, Maryland, June. Association for Computational Linguistics.

Ryan McDonald, Slav Petrov, and Keith Hall. 2011. Multi-source transfer of delexicalized dependency parsers. In *Proceedings of the Conference on Empirical Methods in Natural Language Processing*, EMNLP '11, pages 62–72, Stroudsburg, PA, USA. Association for Computational Linguistics.

Ryan McDonald, Joakim Nivre, Yvonne Quirmbach-Brundage, Yoav Goldberg, Dipanjan Das, Kuzman Ganchev, Keith Hall, Slav Petrov, Hao Zhang, Oscar Täckström, Claudia Bedini, Núria Bertomeu Castelló, and Jungmee Lee. 2013. Universal dependency annotation for multilingual parsing. In *Proceedings of the 51st Annual Meeting of the Association for Computational Linguistics (Volume 2: Short Papers)*, pages 92–97, Sofia, Bulgaria, August. Association for Computational Linguistics.

Tomas Mikolov, Ilya Sutskever, Kai Chen, Greg S Corrado, and Jeff Dean. 2013. Distributed representations of words and phrases and their compositionality. In C. J. C. Burges, L. Bottou, M. Welling, Z. Ghahramani, and K. Q. Weinberger, editors, *Advances in Neural Information Processing Systems 26*, pages 3111–3119. Curran Associates, Inc.

Tahira Naseem, Regina Barzilay, and Amir Globerson. 2012. Selective sharing for multilingual dependency parsing. In *Proceedings of the 50th Annual Meeting of the Association for Computational Linguistics: Long Papers - Volume 1*, ACL '12, pages 629–637, Stroudsburg, PA, USA. Association for Computational Linguistics.

Joakim Nivre. 2005. Dependency grammar and dependency parsing. Technical report, Vxj University.

Joakim Nivre. 2009. Parsing indian languages with MaltParser. In *Proceedings of the ICON09 NLP Tools Contest: Indian Language Dependency Parsing*, pages 12–18.

Mohammad Sadegh Rasooli and Michael Collins. 2015. Density-driven cross-lingual transfer of dependency parsers. In *Proceedings of the 2015 Conference on Empirical Methods in Natural Language Processing*, pages 328–338, Lisbon, Portugal, September. Association for Computational Linguistics.

Agnivo Saha and Sudeshna Sarkar. 2016. Enhancing neural network based dependency parsing using morphological information for hindi. In *17th International Conference on Intelligent Text Processing and Computational Linguistics (CICLing)*, Konya, Turkey, April. Springer.

D.M. Sharma, Sangal R., L. Bai, R. Begam, and K. Ramakrishnamacharyulu. 2007. Anncorra : Treebanks for indian languages, annotation guidelines (manuscript).

Anders Søgaard. 2011. Data point selection for cross-language adaptation of dependency parsers.

Oscar Täckström, Ryan McDonald, and Jakob Uszkoreit. 2012. Cross-lingual word clusters for direct transfer of linguistic structure. In *Proceedings of the 2012 Conference of the North American Chapter of the Association for Computational Linguistics: Human Language Technologies*, NAACL HLT '12, pages 477–487, Stroudsburg, PA, USA. Association for Computational Linguistics.

Oscar Täckström, Ryan T. McDonald, and Joakim Nivre. 2013. Target language adaptation of discriminative transfer parsers. In *Human Language Technologies: Conference of the North American Chapter of the Association of Computational Linguistics, Proceedings, June 9-14, 2013, Westin Peachtree Plaza Hotel, Atlanta, Georgia, USA*, pages 1061–1071.

Jörg Tiedemann, Željko Agić, and Joakim Nivre. 2014. Treebank translation for cross-lingual parser induction. In *Proceedings of the Eighteenth Conference on Computational Natural Language Learning*, pages 130–140, Ann Arbor, Michigan, June. Association for Computational Linguistics.

Jörg Tiedemann. 2015. Improving the cross-lingual projection of syntactic dependencies. In *Proceedings of the 20th Nordic Conference of Computational Linguistics (NODALIDA 2015)*, pages 191–199, Vilnius, Lithuania, May. Linköping University Electronic Press, Sweden.

Min Xiao and Yuhong Guo. 2014. Distributed word representation learning for cross-lingual dependency parsing. In *Proceedings of the Conference on Natural Language Learning (CoNLL)*.

D. Zeman and Philip Resnik. 2008. Cross-language parser adaptation between related languages. *NLP for Less Privileged Languages*, pages 35 – 35, 2008///.

Sinhala Short Sentence Similarity Measures using Corpus-Based Similarity for Short Answer Grading

JCS Kadupitiya, Surangika Ranathunga, Gihan Dias
Department of Computer Science and Engineering
University of Moratuwa, Katubedda 10400
Sri Lanka
{jcskadupitiya.16,surangika,gihan}@cse.mrt.ac.lk

Abstract

Currently, corpus based-similarity, string-based similarity, and knowledge-based similarity techniques are used to compare short phrases. However, no work has been conducted on the similarity of phrases in Sinhala language. In this paper, we present a hybrid methodology to compute the similarity between two Sinhala sentences using a Semantic Similarity Measurement technique (corpus-based similarity measurement plus knowledge-based similarity measurement) that makes use of word order information. Since Sinhala WordNet is still under construction, we used lexical resources in performing this semantic similarity calculation. Evaluation using 4000 sentence pairs yielded an average MSE of **0.145** and a Pearson correlation factor of **0.832**.

1   Introduction

There has been no research conducted for measuring similarity between short sentences written in Sinhala, an official language of Sri Lanka, which is currently used by a population of over 16 million.
 Several unsupervised techniques are used for short sentence similarity calculations. These unsupervised approaches can be categorized in to four basic classes: corpus-based, knowledge-based, string-based, and other similarity measures (e.g. those that consider word order and word length). Corpus-based similarity determines the similarity between two sentences/texts according to information gained from a corpus. Knowledge-based similarity measures are based on identifying the degree of similarity between words using information derived from semantic networks (e.g. WordNet) or lexical resources. Corpus-based and knowledge-based measures are also referred to as semantic similarity measures (Li, 2006). String-based similarity measures operate on string sequences and character composition. This technique can be further divided in to character-based similarity measures and term-based similarity measures. Even though each of these techniques could be directly used to calculate the similarity of two given sentences, much previous research work combined two or more approaches to form hybrid similarity measuring techniques to gain a higher accuracy (Li, 2006; Zhao, 2014). The most popular hybrid techniques include corpus based similarity calculations, and knowledge based similarity calculations that use WordNet for Word Sense Disambiguation (WSD). For English, the most promising results were given by the latter. The former technique does not require special Natural Language processing (NLP) tools other than a corpus. In contrast, the latter requires many NLP resources such as part of speech (POS) taggers, lexical databases, word lists, and corpora in addition to WordNet. However, as an under-resourced language, development of many of these basic resources for Sinhala is still at inception stage (Welgama, 2011; Weerasinghe, 2013).

This research focuses on finding the best possible NLP technique(s) for similarity calculation between short Sinhala phrases by utilising existing unsupervised techniques for English. Constrained by the available resources, we experimented with two hybrid techniques: semantic similarity measures that make use of word order information as presented by Li et. al's (2006), and semantic similarity measures that make use of word length information as presented by Zhao (2014). Both these hybrid similarity measures make use of corpus based and knowledge based approaches plus a basic lexical database, and

Proceedings of the 6th Workshop on South and Southeast Asian Natural Language Processing,
pages 44–53, Osaka, Japan, December 11-17 2016.

domain-specific word glossaries. Best results were given for the first approach that made use of word order information. The rest of the paper is organized as follows. Section 2 discusses previous work on short sentence similarity in general. Section 3 provides the methodology whereas section 4 describes the results and discussion. Conclusion and limitations of the current implementation, and suggestions for future work are given in sections 5 and 6, respectively.

2   Related work

Techniques for short sentence similarity measurement can be broadly categorised into two groups as unsupervised and supervised approaches. In this section, we only discuss unsupervised techniques, as this is what is employed in our research. However, we mention in passing that most of the methodologies used in supervised approaches require WordNet, morphological analyser, and/or a POS tagger to generate the features (Mohler, 2011; Alves, Bestgen, Biçici and, Zhao 2014), whereas most of the unsupervised approaches do not require these resources. Moreover, as reported by some researchers, unsupervised techniques have performed well than supervised approaches in some situations (Marelli, 2014).

As mentioned earlier, previous research focused on combining two or more unsupervised approaches to form a hybrid similarity measuring technique to gain a higher accuracy.

Gomaa (2012) employed thirteen well-known algorithms (Damerau-Levenshtein, Jaro, Jaro–Winkler, N-gram, Cosine Similarity, etc.) to calculate the similarity score between two short English sentences. Six of these algorithms are character-based and the other seven are term-based measures. For the corpus based similarity measures they have used Latent Semantic Analysis (LSA) and Explicit Semantic Analysis (ESA). Gomaa (2012) claims that the best results are given when N-gram was combined with LSA.

A research focused on similarity calculation for Hindi language employs knowledge-based similarity approaches using WordNet and String-Based approaches (Tayal, 2014). They claim that semantic similarity calculation can be applied for any Indic language such as Hindi, Marathi. Sinhala also belongs to this branch of the language tree.

Mohler et. al (2009) has done a comprehensive evaluation of different knowledge-based and corpus-based measures for the task of short answer grading using both corpus-based algorithms and knowledge-based algorithms. Their techniques make use of WordNet hierarchy and Wikipedia corpus. They conducted comparative evaluations using eight knowledge-based measures of semantic similarity (shortest path, Leacock and Chodorow(1998), Lesk(1986), Wu & Palmer (1994), Resnik (1995), Lin (1998), Jiang & Conrath (1997), Hirst and St-Onge, (1998)), and two corpus-based measures (LSA and ESA) . Out of all these techniques, the best results were given for the LSA approach.

A research done by Li et. al's (2006) focused on sentence similarity measurement based on a hybrid approach by combining semantic similarity measures (knowledge and corpus based similarity measures) and, word order based similarity measures. It presents an algorithm that takes account of semantic information and word order information implied in the sentences. The semantic similarity of two sentences is calculated using information from the WordNet and from the corpus statistics using Brown corpus. In this approach, a sentence is considered as a sequence of words, each of which carries useful information about the meaning. The words and their combined structure make a sentence to convey a particular meaning. When comparing all the possible unsupervised techniques for English short sentence similarity, Li's (2006) method has given the most accurate results.

Recent research work done by Zhao (2014) has focused on a combined unsupervised approach using knowledge based similarity measures (8 similarity measures based on WordNet : Wu & Palmer (Wu and Palmer, 1994), Resnik (Resnik, 1995), etc) and word length based similarity measurements (8 similarity measures, which are further described in section 3.3). They have combined knowledge based feature vector and length measure vector for their final similarity calculation. This has outperformed author's supervised approach for the similarity calculation task.

3   Methodology

As described in the literature review, most of the unsupervised techniques do not require much NLP resources, and the techniques are language independent to a great extent. Moreover, unsupervised techniques have given comparable, or even better results than supervised approaches in some cases. Due to these facts, we decided to follow an unsupervised approach in this research.

We identified that Li's (2006) methodology has given the best results among other research for semantic similarity based techniques we referred to ((Gomaa, 2012) and (Mohler, 2011)). This approach focuses on combining semantic similarity measures (knowledge-based and, corpus based similarity measures) and word order based similarity measures to form a hybrid approach. In the absence of Sinhala WordNet, we modified Li's (2006) knowledge-based similarity measures to use the Sinhala lexical resources we created considering similar word sets. We also modified his corpus based similarity calculation methodology to consider statistical information taken from Sinhala word glossaries. Other than this, Li's (2006) methodology is language-independent.

Following Zhao (2014), we also tried combining semantic similarity calculation with word length based similarity measures, however, this did not outperform our previous approach.

3.1 Data Preparation

In the Semeval-2014 task 1[1], a dataset called SICK was built using the 8K ImageFlickr[2] data set (Marelli, 2014). The SICK data set consists of about 10,000 English sentence pairs, each sentence pair was annotated for relatedness and entailment by means of crowdsourcing techniques. Similar to the approach followed for data set preparation in this task, we selected 500 images from this dataset and asked five participants to describe each image using one short Sinhala sentence. Thereby we collected 2500 short Sinhala sentences. We randomly formed 5000 sentence pairs from these 2500 sentences. Finally, we employed another three persons to manually annotate these pairs with a score from 0 to 5 (with 0 being completely dissimilar and 5 being exactly similar). Table 1 shows example sentence pairs with different degrees of semantic relatedness; gold relatedness scores are expressed on a 6-point rating scale. For the final evaluation, these scores (between 0-5) were normalized to form a similarity score that lies between 0 and 1.

Relatedness score	Example Sentence Pair
3.34	A : මිනිසෙකු වාහනයක් අලුත් වැඩියා කරයි (A man repairs a vehicle)[3] B : මිනිසෙක් ඔසවා ඇති මෝටර් රථයක් සෝදමින් සිටියි (A man is washing a motor car, which is lifted)
2.34	A : මිනිසෙක් යතුරු පැදියක් ධාවනය කරයි (A man rides a motorcycle) B : යතුරු පැදි ධාවකයෙක් දකුණට වංගුවක හැරෙයි (A motorcycle rider takes a right turn at a bend)
3.67	A : තරගයක ක්‍රීඩකයෝ තිදෙනෙක් ගුවනේ ඇති පන්දුව ග්‍රහණය කරගැනීමට පොර කති (In a game, three players are competing to grab the ball that is in the air) B : පාපන්දු ක්‍රීඩකයෙක් තවත් ක්‍රීඩකයෙකුගෙන් පන්දුව ලබා ගැනීමට උත්සහ කරයි (A Football player tries to get the ball from another player)
0.00	A : ක්‍රීඩකයෙක් අශ්වයාගේ පිටින් වැටෙයි (A player falls from a horseback) B : බේස්බෝල් ක්‍රීඩකයෙක් කලු පිත්තක් අතින් අල්ලාගෙන සිටියි (A baseball player is holding a black bat by the hand)

Table 1: Example sentence pairs with their gold relatedness scores (on 6-point rating scale).

3.2 Sinhala Lexical Database and Domain Specific Glossaries

Almost all the knowledge-based techniques reviewed in section 2 employ WordNet for calculating semantic similarity between short sentences (Li, 2006; Mohler, 2009; Tayal, 2014; Zhao, 2014). However, WordNet for Sinhala[4] is still under construction (Welgama, 2011; Wijesiri, 2014). Thus we opted to use a Sinhala lexical database, as approaches that employed lexical databases have also given performance results similar to those employed WordNet (Corley, 2005). Accordingly, we created a Sinhala lexical database consisting of 195781 words and 30564 synsets using online dictionaries (English-Sinhala). This lexical resource is created in such a way that all the words similar in meaning share a unique identification number. Using our lexical resource, we were able to check whether two Sinhala words are

---

[1] http://alt.qcri.org/semeval2014/task1/

[2] http://nlp.cs.illinois.edu/HockenmaierGroup/data.html

[3] Each Sinhala sentence was manually translated to English by the author, so that a wider audience can understand.

[4] http://ucsc.cmb.ac.lk/ltrl/?page=panl10n_p2&lang=en

similar or dissimilar, but we are unable to get partial relatedness values as given by WordNet synsets. We also used domain specific word glossaries from the Department of Official Languages[5], Sri Lanka. These glossaries[6] are for 22 domains such as education, statistics, physics, mathematics, sports, and linguistics.

3.3 Semantic Similarity Calculation using Word Order Information

Fig. 1 shows the procedure for calculating the semantic similarity between two candidate sentences using the technique presented by Li et. al's (2006). In this approach, a vector is dynamically formed in the form of a Bag of Word vector (BoW vector) considering the occurrence of unique words in the two sentences. For both sentences (S_1 and S_2), raw vectors (v_1 and v_2) are derived with the help of the lexical resources. Each entry in the raw vector corresponds to a word in the BoW, so the dimension of the vectors equals the number of unique words in the two sentences. When creating the raw vectors, we consider two cases: if word appears in the sentence, corresponding element of the vector is set to 1, if word does not appear in the sentence, lexical resources are used to check whether a similar word is there. If it is there, corresponding element of the vector is set to 1 and if it is not there, vector element is set to 0. Then v_1 and v_2 are further processed to form two semantic vectors (V_1 and V_2). Here, since every word in a sentence differently contributes to the meaning of the whole sentence according to the domain in which we compare the similarity, a weight is introduced to the words. This weight is introduced as the TF-IDF (term frequency-inverse document frequency) value for the particular word considering relevant domain specific glossary vs. other available glossaries. Sports domain glossary is selected as specific glossary as our dataset was created using mostly sports images. Semantic similarity between two sentences ($S_{1,2}$) is defined as the cosine coefficient between the two vectors V_1 and V_2.

As in other comparable Indic languages (e.g. Hindi), stop words in Sinhala sentences also carry very important information about the semantic similarity (Tayal, 2014). Because of that, we chose not to remove stop words.

Now consider the below sentences, S_1 and S_2.

S_1 : මිනිසෙකු බල්ලෙකු මතට සතුටින් පනී (A man happily jumps onto a dog)
S_2 : බල්ලෙකු මිනිසෙකු මතට සතුටින් පනී (A dog happily jumps onto a man)

If the two sentences (S_1 and S_2) contain the same set of words, any method based on the BoW model will give a decision that S_1 and S_2 are exactly the same.

However, it is clear to a human eye that S_1 and S_2 are not same. The dissimilarity between S_1 and S_2 is due to the word order. Therefore, the similarity calculation method for sentence comparison should consider the impact of word order as well.

The right hand side of Fig. 1 shows the procedure for calculating the word order similarity between two candidate sentences. For the sentence pair S_1 and S_2, the joint word set ($S = S_1 U S_2$) can be formed as:

S : { මිනිසෙකු, බල්ලෙකු, මතට, සතුටින්, පනී } (a man, a dog, onto, happily, jumps)

If we assign a unique index number for each word in S_1 and S_2, we can form two word order vectors (r_1 and r_2). The index number is simply the order number in which the word appears in the sentences. For an example, the index number is 2 for "බල්ලෙකු (a dog)" in S_1 and index number is 1 for "බල්ලෙකු (a dog)" in S_2 . If a particular word is not present in a sentence, we look for similar words using the lexical database. By applying the procedure on S_1 and S_2, the word order vectors (r_1 and r_2) can be

$$r_1 : \{ 1\ 2\ 3\ 4\ 5 \}$$
$$r_2 : \{ 2\ 1\ 3\ 4\ 5 \}$$

obtained:

---

[5] http://www.languagesdept.gov.lk

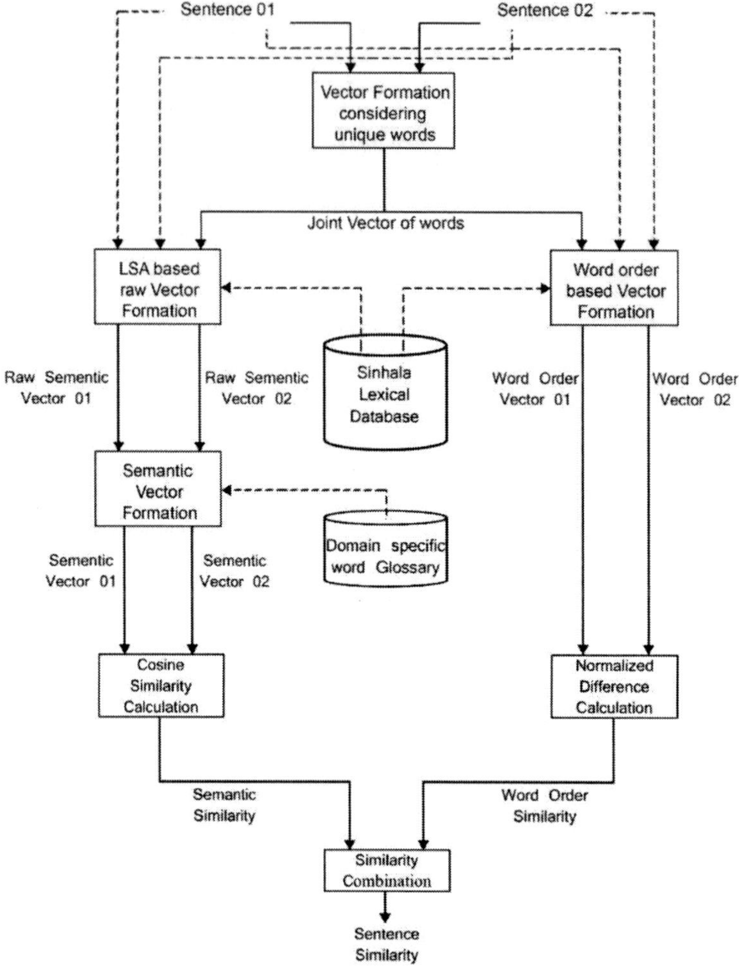

Fig. 1 Overview of the similarity calculation process

Therefore, a word order vector is a basic structure of information of words for a sentence. The task is to measure how similar the word order is. Therefore, we determined the word order similarity (S_r) by the normalized difference of word order as in equation (1). According to Li et. al's (2006), this metric is the best one for indicating the word order in terms of word sequence and location in a sentence.

$$S_r = 1 - \frac{|r_1 - r_2|}{|r_1 + r_2|} \quad (1)$$

In par with Li et. al's (2006), semantic similarity measure is calculated using corpus-based and knowledge-based similarity measures with the aid of the lexical database and domain specific glossaries, respectively. Relationship between the words is represented by word order based similarity measures. Therefore, combination of these two measures represents both semantic and syntactic information about the short sentences, respectively. Previous researchers have combined many different similarity features using simple weighted average mechanisms (Gomaa, 2012; Mohler, 2011; Li, 2006). Li et. al (2006) combined semantic similarity measures and word order based similarity measures considering only a single weight. Since our approach also requires a single weighted feature combining equation, we adapted Li et. al's (2006) feature combining equation and thus the overall similarity can be calculated as in equations (2) and (3),

$$Sim(S_1, S_2) = T_{val}.S_{1,2} + (1 - T_{val}).S_r \qquad (2)$$

$$Sim(S_1, S_2) = T_{val}.\frac{V_1.V_2}{|V_1|.|V_2|} + (1 - T_{val}).\frac{|r_1 - r_2|}{|r_1 + r_2|} \qquad (3)$$

where $T_{val} > 0$ decides the relative contributions of semantic and word order information to the overall similarity computation. Since syntax plays a subordinate role for semantic processing of text, T_{val} should be a value greater than 0.5, i.e. $T_{val} \in (0.5, 1]$. We can tune this parameter to any specific domain with minimum effort. For example, when it comes to automatic grading, S_1 would be a student answer sentence and S_2 would be a model answer sentence.

Semantic Similarity Calculation using Word Length Information

When considering the similarity of sentences, word length features also play an important role (Zhao, 2014). For any given two sentences S_1 and S_2, length features record the length information using the following eight measurement functions given in Table 2 as proposed by Zhao (2014). Since these features are language independent, we could directly use them in the context of Sinhala. We created two length vectors (l_1 and l_2) for the sentences S_1 and S_2. Considering these eight length features, we calculated the cosine similarity between the two vectors to form the word length based similarity measures.

Feature	Description
$|S_1|$	Number of non-repeated words in sentence S_1.
$|S_2|$	Number of non-repeated words in sentence S_2.
$|S_1 - S_2|$	Number of unmatched words found in S_1 but not in S_2
$|S_2 - S_1|$	Number of unmatched words found in S_2 but not in S_1
$|S_1 \cup S_2|$	Set size of non-repeated words found in either S_1 or S_2
$|S_1 \cap S_2|$	Set size of shared words found in both S_1 and S_2.
$\dfrac{|S_1 - S_2|}{S_1}$	Normalized number of unmatched words found in S_1 but not in S_2
$\dfrac{|S_2 - S_1|}{S_2}$	Normalized number of unmatched words found in S_2 but not in S_1

Table 2: Eight length features used in the similarity calculation approach.

Similar to the previous technique, we combined this word length based similarity value ($L_{1,2}$) with the semantic similarity value calculated earlier using a single weight by replacing S_r in equation 2 with $L_{1,2}$. So word length feature based similarity value can be calculated as in equation (4).

$$Sim(S_1, S_2) = T_{val}.\frac{V_1.V_2}{|V_1|.|V_2|} + (1 - T_{val}).\frac{l_1.l_2}{|l_1|.|l_2|} \qquad (4)$$

4 Results and Discussion

Due to space limitations, we only report the results for the hybrid similarity calculation that combined semantic similarity measures with word order based similarity measures, as it gave us the best results.

The hybrid similarity measurement technique discussed in Section 3.3 requires one parameter to be determined before use: the factor T_{val} for weighting the significance between semantic information and syntactic information. Using 1000 sentence pairs, we tuned T_{val} parameter to be 0.87. For the rest of the sentence pairs (4000), we calculated similarity values using our algorithm and compared the results against manually annotated similarity scores. Table 3 shows a comparison of similarities between randomly selected sentence pairs from the 4000 sentence pairs. Even though there are few variations, it can be clearly seen that the two similarity values always represent the same meaning about the sentences and the similarities in Table 3 are fairly consistent with human intuition.

In par with previous research (Bestgen, Biçici, Gupta and Zhao, 2014), we evaluated our results using Pearson (r) and Spearman (ρ) correlation factors along with average Mean Square Error (MSE) for the 4000 sentence pairs. Fig. 2 shows the performance comparison with different values for T_{val}. According to the experimental results, the optimum T_{val} is 0.87 (for English this value is 0.75, for Li et. al's (2006)), results in the lowest average MSE of 0.145. When we compared results reported in previous work done on the SICK dataset (ECNU (Zhao, 2014), CECL ALL (Bestgen, 2014), RTM-DCU (Biçici, 2014), and UoW (Gupta, 2014)), the lowest reported average MSE is 0.325 (Marelli, 2014) whereas our approach gave average MSE of 0.145. We also compared the correlation factors: for the Pearson correlation factor the maximum they could get was 0.828 (Marelli, 2014) whereas our system gave 0.832, and for the Spearman correlation factor they obtained maximum of 0.772 (Marelli, 2014) when our system gave 0.798.

Sentence Pair	Manually Annotated Score	System Generated Score
A: මිනිසෙකු වාහනයක් අලුත් වැඩියා කරයි (A man is repairing a vehicle) B: මිනිසෙකු මෝටර් රථයක් අලුත් වැඩියා කරයි (A man is repairing a motor car)	0.87	0.75
A: සුනඛයෙක් ඉදිරිය බලාගෙන සිටියි (A dog is looking ahead) B: බල්ලෙකු තණකොළ අතරින් වේගයෙන් දුවයි (A dog is running fast across the grass)	0.23	0.20
A: කුරුල්ලෙකු ජලය මතුපිට සිට පියාසර කිරීමට උත්සාහ කරයි (A bird is trying to fly from the surface of the water) B: පක්ෂියෙක් ගංගාවකට උඩින් පියාසර කරයි (A bird is flying over a river)	0.60	0.53
A: මුවෙක් වැටක් මතින් පනියි (A deer is jumping over a fence) B: මුවෙක් කම්බි වැටක් උඩින් පනියි (A deer is jumping over a wired fence)	1.00	0.85
A: නිල් පැහැති ඇඳුමක් ඇඳ සිටින ටෙනිස් ක්‍රීඩකයා තම ජයග්‍රහණය සමරයි (The tennis player in a blue suit is celebrating his victory) B: ක්‍රීඩකයෙක් පිත්ත ඔසවා ගෙන සතුටින් සිටියි (A player is holding up the bat happily)	0.35	0.29

Table 3: Comparison of similarities between randomly selected sentence pairs

It can be seen that word order similarity calculation has a less impact $((1 - T_{val}) = 0.13)$ on the final similarity calculation, when compared with English. This is due to the inflection (inflexion) nature of Sinhala. For an example, let's consider the sentence pair S_3 and S_4: the joint word set $(S = S_3 U S_4)$ for English and Sinhala are {the, man, gives, book, to, child} and {මිනිසා (the man), ළමයාට (to the child), පොත (the book), දෙයි (give), ළමයා (the child), මිනිසාට (to the man)}, respectively. When we form joint vectors for both sentences, it will be exactly similar for the two English sentences, whereas it would be different for the two Sinhala sentences. Here, in English, 'to child' is written as one word 'ළමයාට' in

S_3 : මිනිසා ළමයාට පොත දෙයි (The man gives the book to the child)
S_4 : ළමයා මිනිසාට පොත දෙයි (The child gives the book to child)

Sinhala, where 'ළමයා' gets inflated into 'ළමයාට' using the dative case.

The high accuracy of the results may be due to the following reasons: when expressing the same idea, the average word count is high for English than Sinhala due to the high agglutinative behaviour in Sinhala (e.g. "to the honourable president" can be written in one word in Sinhala as "ජනාධිපතිතුමාට"). For the 2500 sentences that we created for Sinhala, the average word count per sentence is 6.694 and for the SICK English dataset used in SemEval 2014, the average word count per sentence is 9.683. Because of this, when we form the semantic vector, we have more information about a single idea using a small number of words. Secondly our lexical resource was created in a way that words similar in meaning are in the same category.

We should also admit that it is not very reasonable to compare the results against that for English, however there is no other way to emphasise our results.

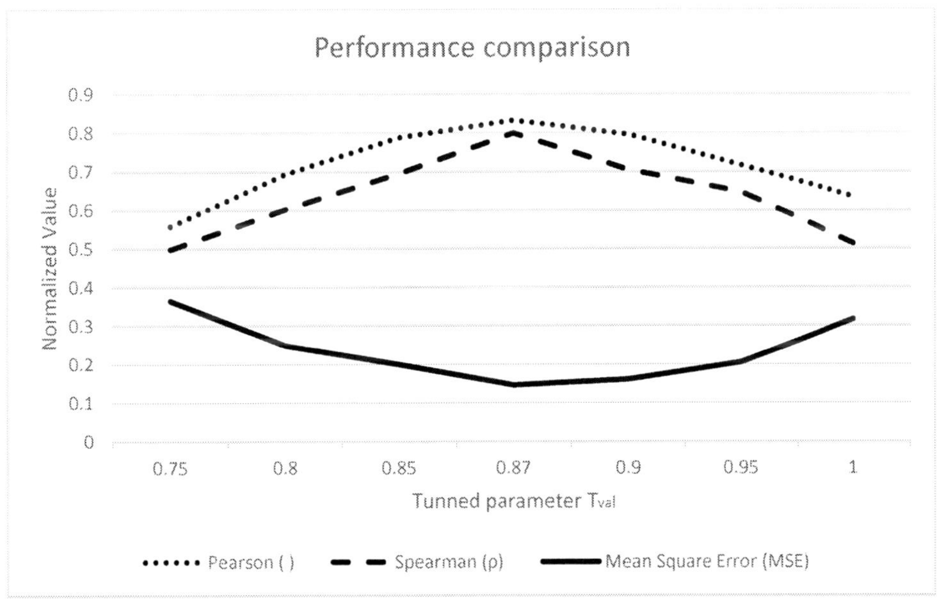

Fig. 2 Graphical representation of performance comparison with different T_{val}

5   Conclusion

We presented the first-ever research on short sentence similarity calculation for Sinhala language. This was carried out using an unsupervised approach based on a hybrid technique, which used semantic similarity measures and word order information. This approach could be implemented because it does not require any complex NLP lexical resources. Therefore, for an under-resourced language such as Sinhala, this is the most suitable way to compare short sentences. Since this technique is largely language independent, the algorithms used for English could be used for Sinhala with only minor modifications.

We found a higher accuracy than what was reported for a comparable dataset for English. Despite the simplicity of the approach used, this result could be partly due to the less average word count in Sinhala short sentences when compared with the same for English short sentences. The best results were given when weight for the word order similarity is 0.13 $(1 - T_{val})$. Therefore, we can conclude that the word order contribution to short sentence similarity is less for Sinhala, due to the inflection (inflexion) nature of Sinhala.

6   Limitations & Future work

Our lexical database is limited to one to one mappings of similar words, and it does not contain partial similarity values as we have in WordNet. Therefore, our lexical resource should be improved to increase the accuracy of the implemented methodology. Even though our lexical resource consists of multi-words, we do not consider multi-word lookups while creating the semantic vector, which is yet another limitation to be addressed in future research. In order to improve the accuracy furthermore, we plan to test more features for sentence comparison. We also have plans to improve the algorithm to disambiguate word sense using the surrounding words to give contextual information. We also plan to explore different types of short text answers from different domains with varying number of topics in order to prove the generality of our solution.

Acknowledgment

This research is funded by the DL4D 2016 research grant and Prof. V K Samaranayake research grant. The authors would like to thank the typists and annotators for their contribution to the research.

References

Alves, A. O., Ferrugento, A., Lourenço, M., & Rodrigues, F. (2014). Asap: Automatic semantic alignment for phrases. SemEval 2014, 104.

Bestgen, Y. (2014). CECL: a new baseline and a non-compositional approach for the Sick benchmark. Proceedings of SemEval 2014: The 8th International Workshop on Semantic Evaluation (pp. 160-165). Association for Computational Linguistics.

Biçici, E., & Way, A. (2014). RTM-DCU: Referential translation machines for semantic similarity. Proceedings of SemEval 2014: The 8th International Workshop on Semantic Evaluation (pp. 487-496). Association for Computational Linguistics.

Budanitsky, A., & Hirst, G. (2001, June). Semantic distance in WordNet: An experimental, application-oriented evaluation of five measures. In Workshop on WordNet and Other Lexical Resources (Vol. 2, pp. 2-2).

Corley, C., & Mihalcea, R. (2005, June). Measuring the semantic similarity of texts. In Proceedings of the ACL workshop on empirical modelling of semantic equivalence and entailment (pp. 13-18). Association for Computational Linguistics.

Gomaa, W. H., & Fahmy, A. A. (2012). Short answer grading using string similarity and corpus-based similarity. International Journal of Advanced Computer Science and Applications (IJACSA), 3(11).

Gupta, R., Bechara, H., El Maarouf, I., & Orasan, C. (2014, August). UoW: NLP techniques developed at the University of Wolverhampton for Semantic Similarity and Textual Entailment. In proceedings of the 8th International Workshop on Semantic Evaluation (SemEval'14) (pp. 785-789).

Hale, M. M. (1998). A comparison of WordNet and Roget's taxonomy for measuring semantic similarity. arXiv preprint cmp-lg/9809003.

Hirst G. and St-Onge D., (1998). Lexical chains as representations of contexts for the detection and correction of malaproprisms, The MIT Press.

Jayasuriya, M., & Weerasinghe, A. R. (2013, December). Learning a stochastic part of speech tagger for sinhala. In Advances in ICT for Emerging Regions (ICTer), 2013 International Conference on (pp. 137-143). IEEE.

Jiang, J. J., & Conrath, D. W. (1997). Semantic similarity based on corpus statistics and lexical taxonomy. In Proceedings of the International Conference on Research in Computational Linguistics. arXiv preprint cmp-lg/9709008.

Leacock C. and Chodorow M. (1998). Combining local context and WordNet sense similarity for word sense identification. In WordNet, an Electronic Lexical Database, the MIT Press.

Lesk, M. (1986, June). Automatic sense disambiguation using machine readable dictionaries: how to tell a pine cone from an ice cream cone. In Proceedings of the 5th annual international conference on Systems documentation (pp. 24-26). ACM.

Li, Y., McLean, D., Bandar, Z. A., O'shea, J. D., & Crockett, K. (2006). Sentence similarity based on semantic nets and corpus statistics. IEEE transactions on knowledge and data engineering, 18(8), 1138-1150.

Lin D. (1998, July). An information-theoretic definition of similarity. In Proceedings of the 15th International Conference on Machine Learning, Madison, WI (Vol. 98, pp. 296-304).

Marelli, M., Bentivogli, L., Baroni, M., Bernardi, R., Menini, S., & Zamparelli, R. (2014). Semeval-2014 task 1: Evaluation of compositional distributional semantic models on full sentences through semantic relatedness and textual entailment. SemEval-2014.

Mohler, M., & Mihalcea, R. (2009, March). Text-to-text semantic similarity for automatic short answer grading. In Proceedings of the 12th Conference of the European Chapter of the Association for Computational Linguistics (pp. 567-575). Association for Computational Linguistics.

Mohler, M., Bunescu, R., & Mihalcea, R. (2011, June). Learning to grade short answer questions using semantic similarity measures and dependency graph alignments. In Proceedings of the 49th Annual Meeting of the Association for Computational Linguistics: Human Language Technologies-Volume 1 (pp. 752-762). Association for Computational Linguistics.

Resnik P. (1995). Using information content to evaluate semantic similarity. In Proceedings of the 14th International Joint Conference on Artificial Intelligence. arXiv preprint cmp-lg/9511007.

Tayal, M. A., Raghuwanshi, M. M., & Malik, L. (2014). Word net based Method for Determining Semantic Sentence Similarity through various Word Senses. Proceedings of the First Joint Conference on Lexical and Computational Semantics.

Welgama, V., Herath, D. L., Liyanage, C., Udalamatta, N., Weerasinghe, R., & Jayawardana, T. (2011). Towards a sinhala wordnet. In *Proceedings of the Conference on Human Language Technology for Development.*

Wijesiri, M. Gallage, B. Gunathilaka, M. Lakjeewa, D. Wimalasuriya, G. Dias, R. Paranavithana, N. de Silva (2014). Building a WordNet for Sinhala. In Proceedings of the Seventh Global WordNet Conference, 2014, 100-108.

Wu Z. and Palmer M. (1994). Verb semantics and lexical selection. In Proceedings of the 32nd Annual Meeting of the Association for Computational Linguistics, Las Cruces, New Mexico.

Zhao, J., Zhu, T. T., & Lan, M. (2014). Ecnu: One stone two birds: Ensemble of heterogenous measures for semantic relatedness and textual entailment. Proceedings of the SemEval, 271-277.

Enriching Source for English-to-Urdu Machine Translation

Bushra Jawaid and **Amir Kamran** and **Ondřej Bojar**
Charles University in Prague, Faculty of Mathematics and Physics
Institute of Formal and Applied Linguistics
Malostranské nám. 25, Praha 1, CZ-118 00, Czech Republic
{jawaid,kamran,bojar}@ufal.mff.cuni.cz

Abstract

This paper focuses on the generation of case markers for free word order languages that use case markers as phrasal clitics for marking the relationship between the dependent-noun and its head. The generation of such clitics becomes essential task especially when translating from fixed word order languages where syntactic relations are identified by the positions of the dependent-nouns. To address the problem of missing markers on source-side, artificial markers are added in source to improve alignments with its target counterparts. Up to 1 BLEU point increase is observed over the baseline on different test sets for English-to-Urdu.

1 Introduction

Phrase-based statistical machine translation (SMT) systems encounter many challenges when translating from morphologically poor to morphologically rich languages. One main challenge is the correct identification of the grammatical structure of a sentence when the required information lies outside the phrasal boundaries. In fixed word order languages such as English, syntactic structure of a sentence follows a fixed subject-verb-object (SVO) pattern; hence, it omits the need of marking the grammatical roles of words. On the contrary, in free word order languages syntactic roles are either embedded as noun inflections or added as a separate token before or after the head noun. In either case, the generation of morphologically complex language becomes difficult task for SMT systems.

In Urdu, a separate token is added after head noun to identify the case such as nominative, accusative, dative etc. The existence of separate case markers not only introduces errors in alignment due to missing source counterparts but it also directly effects the selection of noun forms, which can either be "oblique" if followed by a case marker or "direct" otherwise.

Several approaches have been explored for the enrichment of the source corpus while dealing with the agreement phenomenon on target side. This work focuses on pre-processing the source corpus by adding pseudo-words that can improve alignments with their target counterparts. The experiments are carried out on the phrase-based English-to-Urdu SMT, a language pair that exemplifies the lack of information on source side for the generation of case markers on the target side.

Proceedings of the 6th Workshop on South and Southeast Asian Natural Language Processing,
pages 54–63, Osaka, Japan, December 11-17 2016.

2 Related Work

Several attempts have been made for the integration of the linguistics information to the existing phrase-based SMT systems. Few models that pre-process source corpus for dealing with the agreement phenomenon on target side are discussed below:

The method of source pseudo-words insertion to generate the target words is not novel. We build upon the work of Kamran (2011) who exploited the use of pseudo-words for generating the target case markers for the English-Urdu language pair. Kamran (2011) used preliminary set of linguistic rules to add case markers for subject, object, indirect object and additionally for verb auxiliaries. We refine the oversimplified linguistic rules for adding pseudo-words by first identifying the various syntactic and morphological features such as transitivity and animacy.

Avramidis and Koehn (2008) model case agreement phenomenon for English-to-Greek by adding case information as factor on source side. This approach uses source CFG parses to identify the grammatical roles of words, whereas we use the dependency parses. Also, due to the fact that Greek noun inflections depend on their role, information is added in the form of factors, whereas we use the single-factored setup with the assumption that pseudo-words will play a role in the selection of the correct noun forms.

Goldwater and McClosky (2005) aim at overcoming the data sparseness issue by increasing the similarity between languages using source morphological analysis for Czech-to-English MT. In this approach, the source input is first lemmatized and then extra tokens are added for the information that is stripped off during the lemmatization process, such as for negation words.

Birch et al. (2007) have shown the use of Combinatorial Categorial Grammar (CCG) supertags on source sentence, for German-to-English translation, in an attempt to capture the syntactic structure of the source language in factored SMT models. Recently, Dungarwal et al. (2014) have used CCG supertags as an additional factor on source for English-to-Hindi SMT system.

3 Enriching Source

3.1 Stanford Parser

Stanford parser[1] is a toolkit that contains java implementation for both probabilistic context-free grammar (PCFG) and dependency parsers. The dependency parser extracts the typed dependency parse (de Marneffe et al., 2006) using the phrase structure parse of the sentence. Typed dependencies – such as subject, direct object etc – represent the grammatical relations between the individual words. The Stanford dependencies are represented as triplets consist of the name of the dependency relation, the dependent and the governor (also known as the "head").

The Stanford CoreNLP framework[2] (Manning et al., 2014) is used for applying the NLP pipeline on the input sentence. The framework uses "annotators" for linguistic processing of input text. We use following annotators to process a sentence: tokenize, ssplit, pos, lemma, ner, parse and dcoref. Additionally, we set splitting of sentence (ssplit) to one sentence per input and tokenization is restricted to white space only.

---

[1] http://nlp.stanford.edu/software/lex-parser.shtml
[2] http://nlp.stanford.edu/software/corenlp.shtml

Stanford CoreNLP provides the dependency parse in three graphical representations: basic, collapsed and cc-processed (collapsed and propagated) dependencies. The collapsed and cc-processed dependencies are used to extract the typed dependencies. Example 1 shows the Stanford's collapsed typed dependencies[3] where each triplet begins with the name of a dependency relation followed by the head and the dependent consecutively.

(1) My dog also likes eating sausage.

poss(dog-2, My-1)   nsubj(likes-4, dog-2)   advmod(likes-4, also-3)   root(ROOT-0, likes-4)
xcomp(likes-4, eating-5)   dobj(eating-5, sausage-6)

3.2 Case Markers

There are seven cases in Urdu that are morphologically realized by seven markers (Butt and King, 2004). Table 1 shows the list of cases with their respective markers and grammatical functions, adapted from Butt and King (2004).

Case	Marker	Grammatical Function
Nominative	ϕ	subj/obj
Ergative	ne	subj
Accusative	ko	obj
Dative	ko	subj/ind. obj
Instrumental	se	subj/obl/adjunct
Genitive	k-	subj/specifier
Locative	mẽ/par/tak/ϕ	obl/adjunct

Table 1: Case Markers in Urdu

Absence of marker with subject or object roles marks the nominative case, while accusative and dative share the marker "ko". Due to the fact that nominative lacks the marker, we only add pseudo-words for ergative, accusative and dative markers. Rest of the three cases are not considered in this work.

4 Common Settings

For the training of our translation system, the standard training pipeline of Moses is used along with the GIZA++ (Och and Ney, 2000) alignment toolkit and a 5-gram SRILM language model (Stolcke, 2002). The source texts were processed using the Treex platform (Popel and Žabokrtský, 2010)[4], which included tokenization and lemmatization.

The target side of the corpus is tokenized using a simple tokenization script[5] by Dan Zeman and it is lemmatized using the Urdu Shallow Parser[6] developed by Language Technologies Research Center of IIIT Hyderabad.

The alignments are learnt from the lemmatized version of the corpus. For the rest of the SMT pipeline, word forms (i.e. no morphological decomposition) in their true case (i.e. names capitalized but sentence starts lowercased) are used. The lexicalized word-based reordering model (Koehn et al., 2005) is trained using *msd* orientation in both forward and backward direction, with model conditioned on both the source and the target languages (msd-bidirectional-fe).

---

[3] http://nlp.stanford.edu:8080/parser/index.jsp
[4] http://ufal.mff.cuni.cz/treex/
[5] The tokenization script can be downloaded from: http://hdl.handle.net/11858/00-097C-0000-0023-65A9-5
[6] http://ltrc.iiit.ac.in/showfile.php?filename=downloads/shallow_parser.php

The parallel and monolingual data is summarized in Table 2. The parallel data reported in
Jawaid et al. (2014a) (called "ALL") is used for training, development and test with the similar
data splits. Jawaid et al. (2014b) released large plain and annotated Urdu monolingual data
from mix of several domains. The plain text monolingual data is used to build the language
model.

	Dataset	Sents (en/ur)	Tokens (en/ur)
	Train	74.9k	1.5M/1.7M
Parallel	Dev	2K	41.5K/45.2K
	Test	2K	41.8K/45.6K
Mono	-	5.4M	95.4M

Table 2: Summary of training data.

Final BLEU scores (Papineni et al., 2002) are reported on the test set called "PTEST" in the
following and also on the three independent official test sets briefly explained by Jawaid et al.
(2014a).

5 Experiments

The experiments are conducted with the insertion of pseudo-words on the un-preordered source
side as well as after preordering the source corpus. For preordering of the English corpus, we
use the transformation module of Jawaid and Zeman (2011) that utilizes the Stanford PCFG
parse trees to first parse the input sentences and afterwards applies the hand-written rules to
transform the English sentences to closely match the syntactic structure of Urdu sentences.

For preordered system with pseudo-words, the pseudo-words are added to the input that also
contains the index of each word as an additional information. After generating the case markers,
words are printed in the order of the reordered indexes together with pseudo-words.

In the following section, the Stanford dependencies that are used to generate the pseudo-words
as well as the process of generating the case markers are briefly explained.

5.1 Case Marker Generation

Table 1 shows that ergative, accusative and dative cases take the roles of either subject, object
or indirect object. Stanford dependency parser identifies these roles as: nominal subject (nsubj),
direct object (dobj) and indirect object (iobj). The name of the dependencies are used to add the
respective pseudo-words. Ergative and accusative cases take the nsubj and dobj pseudo-words
respectively, whereas for dative case iobj marker is used to mark both subjects and indirect
objects. We only use passive subjects (nsubjpass) for marking the subject role of the dative
case. Only those relations are contemplated that hold verb as a governor of a relation unless
stated explicitly.

5.1.1 Ergative Case

In Urdu, noun represents ergative case for transitive head verbs with perfective aspect. If verbs
are tagged with "VBD" or "VBN" tags[7], they are considered as perfective, whereas verb take
the transitivity feature if it also hold dobj relation. There are cases where transitivity feature
requires to deal with few exceptions.

---

[7]https://www.ling.upenn.edu/courses/Fall_2003/ling001/penn_treebank_pos.html

In case of a missing dobj dependency of a head verb, verb is marked transitive if followed by a prepositional phrase[8].

Exception is also made for intransitive verbs or verbs with missing objects that contain the clausal complement (ccomp) relation with other verbs. In ccomp relations the internal subject of a dependent of ccomp relation acts as an object of a governor that qualifies the nsubj dependency relation to take the transitivity attribute.

Perfective attribute is ignored for question sentences in past indefinite tense where head noun of nsubj relation is tagged with either "VBP" or "VB".

If a subject of a relation is Wh-determiner then the case marking process is only followed for "which", "who" or "that" determiners. We don't add erg marker if cardinals are dependent of a nsubj relation and also if auxiliary verbs are governor of a relation.

The dependency relation of reduced non-finite verbal modifier (vmod) is also used for marking the ergative case of nouns. In vmod relation, dependent modifies the meaning of a governor that can either be a verb or a noun. We only deal with cases where noun is a governor of relation and its also not a dependent of dobj, iobj or nsubjpass relations. Rest of the checks for adding an erg marker are similar to the way we deal with nusbj relation. vmod relations are used only after looking at few training examples but they need to be further investigated.

5.1.2 Accusative Case

The assignment of a dobj marker for an accusative case is not always straight forward. Butt and King (2004) show examples where "ko" alternates with null marker of nominative on direct objects.

(2) Nadya has driven a car

nādyh ne   *gāṛī*   *člāī*   *he*

Nadya=Erg car=Nom drive=perfective be=present

nādyh ne   *gāṛī ko*   *člāyā*   *he*

Nadya=Erg car=Acc drive=perfective be=present

To avoid the complexity, we do not add markers for "inanimate" objects. "dobj" marker is added for accusative cases that satisfy following conditions: governing verb is transitive, it does not contain the iobj relation and the dependent of dobj relation is "animate" object.

Similar to the ergative case, there are few exception for checking the transitivity of verb before adding the dobj marker. If the head verb has missing nsubj and iobj relation then we search for prepositional clausal modifier (prepc) and conjunct (conj) dependency relations that contains head verb either as a governor or a dependent. If binding of head verb is found in any of prepc or conj relation then dependent noun is marked as accusative and get the dobj marker.

5.1.3 Dative Case

"iobj" marker is added for all iobj dependencies without any constraints and exceptions.

---

[8]we ignore following prepositions for transitivity check: in, into, of, on, by, from, since, until, behind, between, beyond, but, with, near, inside, after, at, before, within, without, under, underneath, up, upon, opposite.

For nsubjpass relations transitivity and perfective features are validated before adding iobj marker. Verb of a nusbjpass relation is attributed transitive if it either contains direct object or prepositional phrase following the verb. Similar to the ergative case, perfective aspect of verb is verified using VBD and VBN POS tags.

5.2 Markers Positioning

The placement of pseudo-words play crucial role due to the word order differences in English-Urdu language pair. We look for conj, appos, dep and prep_of dependencies of the nouns before adding the erg marker and only conj dependency incase of obj marker, if these dependencies exist then markers are added only with the dependents of these dependencies. Example 3 shows the movement of erg marker from head of prep_of dependency to the dependent of a relation, whereas Example 4 shows the deletion of obj marker from the head of conj relation when both governor and dependent are acting as an object.

(3) Before: The savagery **erg** of the attack has shocked the government and observers.

   After: The savagery of the attack **erg** has shocked the government and observers.

(4) Before: Prime Minister Gilani erg brought his penchant for consensus politics to bear upon the problem recently by bringing together top federal **obj** and provincial leaders **obj** for a two-day conference to develop consensus.

   After: Prime Minister Gilani erg brought his penchant for consensus politics to bear upon the problem recently by bringing together top federal and provincial leaders **obj** for a two-day conference to develop consensus.

With preordered source corpus, we don't reposition markers of prep_of dependency because they are automatically repositioned after reordering the source corpus.

5.3 Results

Table 3 shows the source preordering and psuedo-words insertion results on all four test sets. Baseline results of phrase-based and hierarchical systems are also reported from Jawaid et al. (2014a) to see the relative gain in BLEU scores. All results reported in Table 3 were tested with MultEval[9] for statistical significance of the improvement over the baseline. Based on 3 independent MERT runs of both the baseline and the experiment in question, • marks the 100% confidence on improvement over the baseline. Similarly, † and ‡ marks 96% and 90% confidence and * shows 80% confidence on gain in systems performance over the baseline setup.

The preordering of source corpus, PBR system, brings minimum 1 point (on PTEST) to maximum 2.8 point (on CLE) gain in BLEU scores. The phrase-based system with case markers (PBC) bring 0.6 to 1 point increase in BLEU on all independent test sets except PTEST that did not gain any improvements over the baseline with the additional pseudo-words in source corpus. On the other hand, hierarchical system with pseudo-words also shows minimum 0.2 (again on PTEST) to maximum 1 point gain in BLEU on all test sets. CLE shows maximum performance gain in all setups due to the availability of multiple reference translations.

---

[9] https://github.com/jhclark/multeval

	PTEST	CLE	IPC	NIST2008
	1 refs	3 ref	1 ref	1 ref
Phrase-based Baseline (PB)	19.3	18.2	15.8	15.0
With-Markers (PBC)	‡ 19.3	• 19.1	• 16.5	• 15.6
Preordered (PBR)	• 20.1	• 21.0	• 17.9	• 16.5
Preordered-with-Markers (PBCR)	• 20.5	• 21.1	• 18.8	• 16.7
PBCR without definite article	• 20.7	• 21.3	• 18.6	• 17.1
Hierarchical Baseline	21.4	19.4	18.7	16.7
With-Markers	† 21.6	• 20.4	* 19.0	• 17.1

Table 3: Results of Phrase-based and Hierarchical MT with and without case markers.

We also report results of phrase-based system together with preordered source corpus and added case markers (PBCR) to achieve the maximum performance gain in terms of BLEU. Over the PBR system, this system brings approximately 1 point gain on IPC to minimum 0.1 increase on CLE test set. The PBCR system did not bring significant improvements on all test sets (except IPC) compared to PBR system. It is not evident from the results, whether PBCR system has performed better than hierarchical system with case markers or vice versa. Even though, except PTEST, results of PBCR system always exceed (remain same for NIST test set) the hierarchical baseline results.

Figure 1 shows the impact of average source phrase length used during decoding on BLEU scores for all four phrase-based systems. The results verify that the systems perform better when the longer source phrases are matched during decoding. Figure 1 also shows the significance of preordering the source corpus that allows the MT engine to extract the longer matching phrases.

In Table 4, alignment statistics of baseline setup and our best performing phrase-based system (PBCR) is provided. In base-

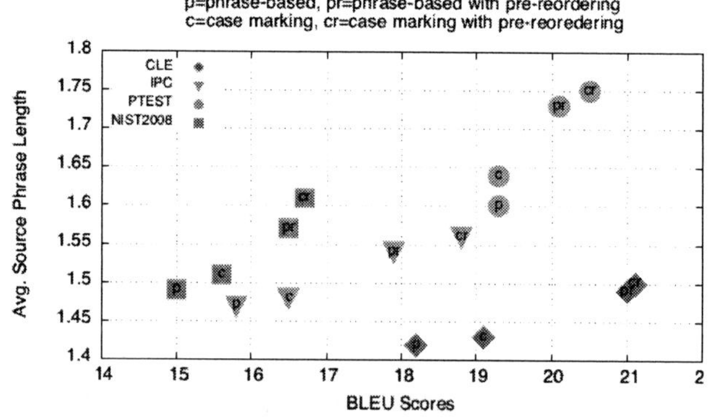

Figure 1: Plot of BLEU vs average source phrase length of each experimental setting indicated in "p", "pr", "c" and "cr" for all four test sets.

line system, case marker 'nay' gets mostly aligned to auxiliary 'have', followed by alignments with verbs and definite article. Interestingly, 'nay' remains unaligned 2.7K times out of 23K occurrences in reference. Furthermore, 'ko' aligns to 'the' most of the time, followed by alignments with prepositions. Out of 25K total occurrences, it remains unaligned 4.3K times.

In PBCR system, the statistics of most frequent alignment pairs change drastically for both markers. 'nay' gets aligned to 'erg' marker on source side 16K times, whereas the unaligned count reduces by 48.5%. The 'erg' marker remains unaligned around 6.6K times, which suggests that there might be an over generation of the 'erg' marker. This speculation can be confirmed from the total number of 'erg' occurrences in source text that are 3.8K times more than its target counterpart. The stats of 'ko' marker does not show the same amount of improvement as 'nay'. Out of 25K 'obj' markers only 5K aligned to 'ko' and out of 1.3K 'iobj' markers only 380 aligned to 'ko'. The count of unaligned 'ko' markers only reduced by 10.6% compare to the baseline unaligned frequency. Even though, compared to the baseline setup, alignment count of 'ko' with definite article reduces by 35% but still 3K 'ko' markers aligned with the definite article. Our initial hypothesis was that due to the unavailability of the definite article in Urdu, the alignment between 'ko' and 'obj' was not learnt properly. To investigate this issue, we stripped off definite article from the source side and then re-ran the PBCR system. The result of this system is also reported in Table 3; small gains in terms of BLEU is observed on most test sets over the PBCR system but unfortunately improvements in alignment count of 'obj' and 'ko' markers are not up to the expectations, instead alignment count of 'the-ko' pair shifts to the unaligned 'ko' count, raising it to 5.3K. It is hard to predict why the large number of 'obj' markers remain unaligned; by looking at the total count of 'obj' marker in source, it can not be attributed to the over generation problem. Perhaps, it is added to the places where there was no matching marker on the target side exists. One simple solution would be (only for training) to add the 'obj' or 'iobj' marker in source when there exists at least one occurrence of 'ko' marker on target side. This way, it is possible to avoid the addition of the marker to unwanted places. The in-depth analysis of 'ko' is needed to investigate this issue further.

Markers	erg		نے|ne		obj		iobj		کو|ko	
Count in Refer.	–		23,747		–		–		25,095	
Count in Source	27,574		–		25,238		1341		–	
Baseline system	–	–	5588	have	–	–	–	–	6147	the
	–	–	4046	say	–	–	–	–	5348	to
	–	–	2727	unalign	–	–	–	–	4379	unalign
	–	–	2696	the	–	–	–	–	895	on
	–	–	456	do	–	–	–	–	500	as
PBCR system	16,664	نے(ne)	16,664	erg	7904	unalign	380	کو(ko)	5382	obj
	6676	unalign	1404	unalign	5788	کا(ka)	360	unalign	3915	unalign
	492	کو(ko)	1043	the	5382	کو(ko)	69	انہیں(*)	3700	to
	406	میں(meñ)	641	say	1760	سے(se)	26	تمہیں(*)	2979	the
	356	سے(se)	624	by	855	پر(per)	23	سے(se)	953	on

Table 4: Most frequent word alignments for source artificial markers and target case markers in training corpus for baseline and PBCR experiments.

6 Conclusion

The approach of introducing artificial source marking for phrasal clitics in Urdu (target side) shows significant improvements over baseline (PB vs PBC) except for one test set i.e., PTEST. In order to encounter target-side reordering problems, experiments are also carried out with preordered source sentences together with artificial markers. Due to the fact that reordering helps phrasal SMT to match longer phrases, it eventually helps to produce missing case markers due to longer matches. Hence, less improvements have been observed between PBR and PBRC

---

* انہیں = inheñ, تمہیں = tūmheñ

systems with one exception being the IPC test set that shows significant gain over PBR system. The problem of over-generation of markers might have caused the inconsistent improvements over different test sets; however, it is still an open question and needs further investigation.

Acknowledgments

This work was supported by European Union's innovation programme under grant agreement no. 645452 (QT21).

References

Eleftherios Avramidis and Philipp Koehn. 2008. Enriching morphologically poor languages for statistical machine translation. In *Proceedings of ACL-08: HLT*, pages 763–770, Columbus, Ohio, June. Association for Computational Linguistics.

Alexandra Birch, Miles Osborne, and Philipp Koehn. 2007. CCG Supertags in Factored Statistical Machine Translation. In *Proceedings of the Second Workshop on Statistical Machine Translation*, pages 9–16, Prague, Czech Republic, June. Association for Computational Linguistics.

Miriam Butt and Tracy Holloway King. 2004. The status of case. In *Clause structure in South Asian languages*, pages 153–198. Springer Netherlands.

Marie-Catherine de Marneffe, Bill MacCartney, and Christopher D. Manning. 2006. Generating typed dependency parses from phrase structure parses. In *Proceedings of Language Resources and Evaluation (LREC)*, pages 449–454.

Piyush Dungarwal, Rajen Chatterjee, Abhijit Mishra, Anoop Kunchukuttan, Ritesh Shah, and Pushpak Bhattacharyya. 2014. The iit bombay hindi-english translation system at wmt 2014. In *Proceedings of the Ninth Workshop on Statistical Machine Translation*, pages 90–96, Baltimore, Maryland, USA, June. Association for Computational Linguistics.

Sharon Goldwater and David McClosky. 2005. Improving statistical mt through morphological analysis. In *Proceedings of the Conference on Human Language Technology and Empirical Methods in Natural Language Processing*, HLT '05, pages 676–683, Stroudsburg, PA, USA. Association for Computational Linguistics.

Bushra Jawaid and Daniel Zeman. 2011. Word-order issues in english-to-urdu statistical machine translation. *The Prague Bulletin of Mathematical Linguistics*, (95):87–106.

Bushra Jawaid, Amir Kamran, and Ondřej Bojar. 2014a. English to urdu statistical machine translation: Establishing a baseline. pages 1–6, Dublin, Ireland. Dublin City University, Dublin City University.

Bushra Jawaid, Amir Kamran, and Ondřej Bojar. 2014b. A tagged corpus and a tagger for urdu. In Nicoletta Calzolari, Khalid Choukri, Thierry Declerck, Hrafn Loftsson, Bente Maegaard, and Joseph Mariani, editors, *Proceedings of the 9th International Conference on Language Resources and Evaluation (LREC 2014)*, pages 2938–2943, Reykjavík, Iceland. European Language Resources Association.

Amir Kamran. 2011. Hybrid Machine Translation Approaches for Low-Resource Languages. Master's thesis, UFAL, Prague, September.

Philipp Koehn, Amittai Axelrod, Alexandra B. Mayne, Chris Callison-Burch, Miles Osborne, and David Talbot. 2005. Edinburgh System Description for the 2005 IWSLT Speech Translation Evaluation. In *Proceedings of International Workshop on Spoken Language Translation*.

Christopher D. Manning, Mihai Surdeanu, John Bauer, Jenny Finkel, Steven J. Bethard, and David McClosky. 2014. The Stanford CoreNLP natural language processing toolkit. In *Proceedings of 52nd Annual Meeting of the Association for Computational Linguistics: System Demonstrations*, pages 55–60, Baltimore, Maryland, June. Association for Computational Linguistics.

Franz Josef Och and Hermann Ney. 2000. A Comparison of Alignment Models for Statistical Machine Translation. In *Proceedings of the 17th conference on Computational linguistics*, pages 1086–1090. Association for Computational Linguistics.

Kishore Papineni, Salim Roukos, Todd Ward, and Wei-Jing Zhu. 2002. BLEU: a Method for Automatic Evaluation of Machine Translation. In *ACL 2002, Proceedings of the 40th Annual Meeting of the Association for Computational Linguistics*, pages 311–318, Philadelphia, Pennsylvania.

Martin Popel and Zdeněk Žabokrtský. 2010. TectoMT: Modular NLP Framework. In Hrafn Loftsson, Eirikur Rögnvaldsson, and Sigrun Helgadottir, editors, *Lecture Notes in Artificial Intelligence, Proceedings of the 7th International Conference on Advances in Natural Language Processing (IceTAL 2010)*, volume 6233 of *Lecture Notes in Computer Science*, pages 293–304, Berlin / Heidelberg. Iceland Centre for Language Technology (ICLT), Springer.

Andreas Stolcke. 2002. Srilm - an extensible language modeling toolkit. In *In Proceedings of the 7th International Conference on Spoken Language Processing (ICSLP) 2002*, pages 901–904.

The IMAGACT4ALL Ontology of Animated Images: Implications for Theoretical and Machine Translation of Action Verbs from English-Indian Languages

Pitambar Behera*, Sharmin Muzaffar[1], Atul Ku. Ojha[2] & Girish Nath Jha[3]
*[3]Centre for Linguistics, [23]SCSS & [1]Dept. of Linguistics
*[23]Jawaharlal Nehru University & [1]Aligarh Muslim University
New Delhi & Aligarh, India
`[pitambarbehera2, sharmin.muzaffar, shashwatup9k, girishjha]@gmail.com`

Abstract

Action verbs are one of the frequently occurring linguistic elements in any given natural language as the speakers use them during every linguistic intercourse. However, each language expresses action verbs in its own inherently unique manner by categorization. One verb can refer to several interpretations of actions and one action can be expressed by more than one verb. The inter-language and intra-language variations create ambiguity for the translation of languages from the source language to target language with respect to action verbs. IMAGACT is a corpus-based ontological platform of action verbs translated from prototypic animated images explained in English and Italian as meta-languages. In this paper, we are presenting the issues and challenges in translating action verbs of Indian languages as target and English as source language by observing the animated images. Among the ten Indian languages which have been annotated so far on the platform are Sanskrit, Hindi, Urdu, Odia (Oriya), Bengali, Manipuri, Tamil, Assamese, Magahi and Marathi. Out of them, Manipuri belongs to the Sino-Tibetan, Tamil comes off the Dravidian and the rest owe their genesis to the Indo-Aryan language family. One of the issues is that the one-word morphological English verbs are translated into most of the Indian languages as verbs having more than one-word form; for instance as in the case of conjunct, compound, serial verbs and so on. We are further presenting a cross-lingual comparison of action verbs among Indian languages. In addition, we are also dealing with the issues in disambiguating animated images by the L1 native speakers using competence-based judgements and the theoretical and machine translation implications they bear.

1   Introduction

IMAGACT (see fig. 1) is a multilingual infrastructure for representing the lexical encoding of around 1017 English and Italian action verbs in the first release (Moneglia et al., 2014b). It is a visual ontology of 3d prototypic animated action images of verbs broadly categorized into nine macro-level categories: facial expressions, actions referring to the body, movement, modification of the object, deterioration of an object, force on an object, change of location, setting relation among objects and actions in the inter-subjective space (Moneglia et al., 2014b; Panunzi et al., 2014; Moneglia et al., 2014a). Since action verbs deal with spontaneous speech of real pragmatic contexts, they occur frequently in any speech corpus (Moneglia et al., 2012; Moneglia and Panunzi, 2007). In the second release i.e. IMAGACT4ALL, the competence-based extensions have been extended to incorporate any natural language. Research has already been conducted as to how to make use of the IMAGACT data as an e-learning platform for various languages (Moneglia et al., 2013). Moneglia et al., (2014a) have also explained the annotation of Sanskrit, Hindi and Bengali, the very first Indian languages that have been annotated on the platform. The issues and challenges regarding annotating Urdu action verbs on the said platform have also been discussed in detail by Muzaffar et al, (2016). The theoretical implications have been provided by the research by Panunzi et al., (2014) in which they have discussed about the translation of action verbs from the dictionary of images. The Natural Language Processing (NLP) aspect has been provided by the research conducted by Moneglia (2011) wherein he has pointed out the fact that the variations in action verbs across languages have not been captured by any platform so far and are largely unknown,

Proceedings of the 6th Workshop on South and Southeast Asian Natural Language Processing,
pages 64–73, Osaka, Japan, December 11-17 2016.

but the IMAGACT platform brings out those variations for linguistic disambiguation purposes in Machine Translation (MT).

Figure 1. IMAGACT4ALL Log-in Platform

On this platform, the metalanguages considered for translation of animated actions are English and Italian and later extended to Spanish and Chinese. As reported by Muzaffar et al. (2016), the number (521) of verbs from Italian-English annotated is 515 and translated is 473. Out of the total 550, annotated and translated verbs from English-Italian are 546 and 497 respectively. So far as Italian is concerned, Italian-Chinese out of total 521 verbs, 430 have been annotated and 156 have been translated. In addition, the annotated and translated verbs are 30 and 22 respectively out of 550 verbs from English-Chinese. As far as the Indian languages are concerned, (see fig. 2) Odia, Manipuri and Tamil have 110 number of annotated verbs each and Magahi and Urdu have 100 each respectively. Hindi, Bengali, Sanskrit and Assamese have 149, 210, 256 and 662 annotated verbs respectively whereas Marathi is at the initial stage of incorporation.

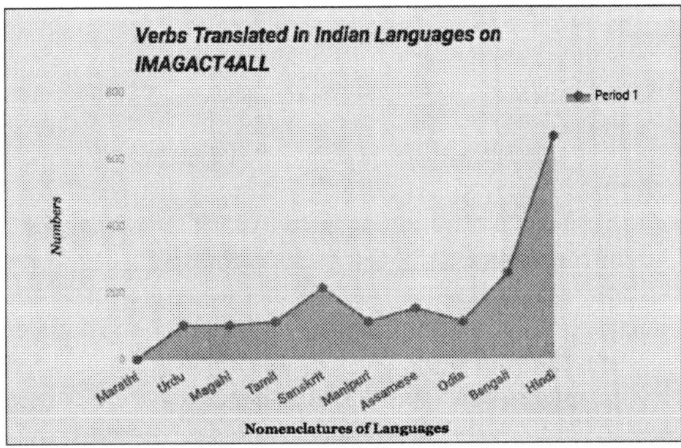

Figure 2. Translated Verb Distribution from English-Indian Languages on the IMAGACT4ALL Platform[2]

1.1 Process of Translation

The process of translation can be comprehended from the very architecture (see fig. 3) of the IMAGACT Platform. The platform contains an ontology of action verbs that are quite frequent in any natural language. Some of the most universally frequent action verbs have been selected for incorporation into the web-based interface. All the actions have been initially annotated in English and Italian as meta-languages. Later, in the IMAGACT4ALL platform the verbs have been extended to Spanish and Chinese. Based on the actions, the verbs have been visually animated and linked by the BabelNet Project[3] for the avoidance of semantic under-determinacy. The gallery of images has been divided into nine macro-level

---

[2] As adapted from Jha et al., 2016
[3] http://babelnet.org/

categories to incorporate all the action types. While interpreting the animations for translation purposes the decoder can refer to the annotations in the meta-languages. The decoder must be either a native speaker or an L1 speaker of target language (TL) as all the possible interpretations of the verb have to be captured in the respective TL. He must know any of the meta-languages to appreciate the animation. Finally, the output has to be annotated in any natural TL text considering especially the verbs and their valences. One thing an annotator has to keep in account is that he/she is to annotate the verbs in the present imperfective participle form. The arguments of the verbs especially the nomenclature for the human agent has to be specified as according to the commonly occurring named entities of the given output language.

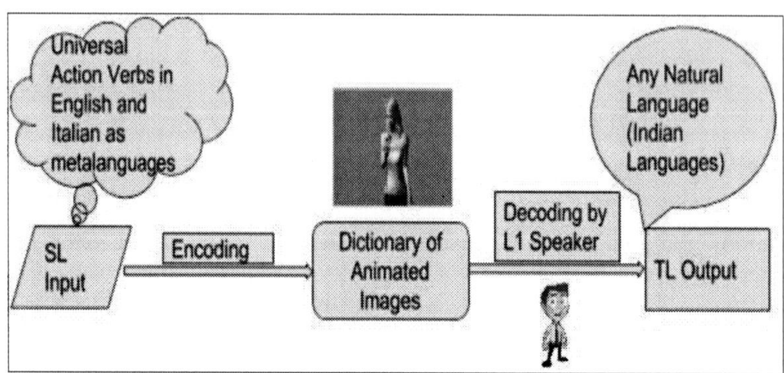

Figure 3. The Architecture of the Translation on the IMAGACT4ALL Platform

For the time being, the process of translation is semi-automated which can be fully automated applying Finite State Automata, applying bilingual corpora of dictionary or any other Machine Learning technique. In this paper, the source language (SL) input considered as the meta-language is English and the TL outputs are in ten Indian languages: Sanskrit, Hindi, Urdu, Odia, Bengali, Manipuri, Tamil, Assamese, Magahi and Marathi. In the following instance (see fig. 4), SL input has been provided in English and Italian and the TL outputs are in ten Indian languages. The input animated image suggests that a lady is hanging her head. Therefore, the input sentence is "Mary hangs her head" which has been translated into Sanskrit as "latA mUrdhAm avanamati/ latayA avashIryate/latA avamUrdhayati", Hindi as "SitA sar jhukAti hai", Urdu as "AfarIna sara jhukAti hai", Odia as "banitA tA muNDaku nuA.Muchi/jhulAuachi", Bengali as "latA mAthA jho.MkAcche/nAmAcche/noyAcche", Manipuri as "Meri makok nonthai", Tamil as "mEri tan talaiyai kIzhE to~ga pOTTaa/~niRkiRaaL", Assamese as "meriYe mura dapiYAiche" and into Magahi as "sitavA muMDI gota ke baiThala halai". So far as the lexical verbal variation is concerned, English has captured two variations as 'hang' and 'drop'. On the other hand, Odia, Bangla and Sanskrit have captured three variations each. Tamil has captured two variations and the rest have annotated one verbal variation each.

2   Typological Features of Verbs in Indian Languages

In South-Asian languages such as Sanskrit, Hindi, Urdu, Odia, Bengali, Manipuri, Tamil, Assamese, Magahi and Marathi and many others, verbs referring to specific actions pose serious problems for NLP and other linguistic tasks. Action verbs that occur spontaneously in day-to-day communication are highly ambiguous in nature from the semantic perspective and consequently cause disambiguation complexities that are really relevant and applicable to Language Technologies (LT) like MT and NLP (Muzaffar et al., 2016).

The Indian languages considered so far for annotation on the IMAGACT4ALL include three language families from the Indian sub-continent region: The Sino-Tibetan, The Dravidian and the Indo-Aryan (IA). Hindi, Sanskrit, Marathi and Magahi use Devanagari script. Assamese and Bengali use Bengali while Manipuri uses both Bengali and Meithei. Odia, Tamil use their own independent scripts whereas Urdu uses Perso-Arabic.

With regard to the typological features, Indian languages have both subject-verb agreement and object-verb agreement. Intransitive dative subject is also one of the typological features used by almost all the Indian languages irrespective of their families. Complex predicates (V+V, N+V & JJ+V constructions) (Subbārāo, 2008 & 2012) are used for expressing a single verb translation in English. Similarly, a large number of verbs owes their genesis from Sanskrit which can be observed from lexicon, grammar and literature of the given language under consideration. Besides, Indian languages have also borrowed words from English, Portuguese and French (Jha et al., 2016).

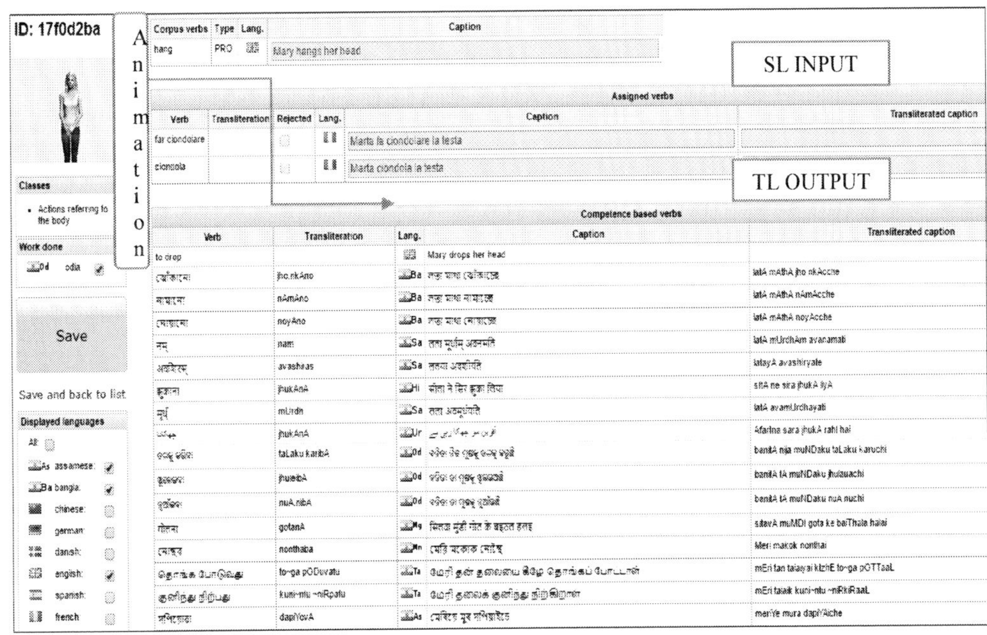

Figure 4. A Translated Specimen on the IMAGACT4ALL Platform

2.1 Subject and Object Verb Agreement

In Indian languages verbs agree with both the subject and the object; provided some conditions are fulfilled. On one hand, in Hindi (Jha et al., 2014), Urdu (Muzaffar et al., 2015; Muzaffar & Behera, 2014) and Marathi, the oblique (both ergative and non-nominative) sentences generally have object-verb agreement while the ergative marker does not entail to the object-verb agreement in Assamese[4]. The rest of the languages (non-ergative) like Sanskrit, Odia (Jha et al., 2014; Behera, 2015; Ojha et al., 2015), Bengali, Magahi (Atreya et al., 2014), Manipuri and Tamil have non-nominative subjects where verbs agree with the object. Below are some of the sentences of subject-verb agreement in imperfective participle and progressive aspect.

For instance,

(1) (Hindi) rAMa   TopI ko khU.MTI pe laTakA-tA hai
    Ram-3.MSG.NOM. hat PP hook   PP hang-3MSG.IMPFV. is-PRS.
    "Ram hangs the hat on the hook."

(2) (Assamese) meriYe posTAra-khana matak-Aiche
    Marry-3.FSG.ERG poster-CL   roll-3.SG.PROG.PRS.
    "Marry is rolling up the poster."

(3) (Magahi) citThIa   nai likh-ala   jA hai
    Letter-3.FSG.NOM   not write-PASS go is-PRS.
    'Letter is not being written.' (Atreya et al., 2014)

(4) (Odia) dishArI Chabiku Abaddha karuaChi

---

[4] Ergativity is non-functional in terms of agreement in Assamese.

Dishari-3.FSG.NOM picture surround do-3.SG.PROG.PRS.
"Dishari is surrounding/wrapping the picture."
(5) (Manipuri) imA-na   haujika cAk thong-li.
my mother-3.FSG.NOM. now meals cook-3.SG.PROG.PRS
"My mother is cooking meals now." (Manjulakshi and Devi, 2013)

2.2   Present Imperfective Participle

In Indian languages the imperfective participles are formed with the addition of inflected phonemes and morphemes (IA languages and Sino-Tibetan) and agglutinated morphemes (Dravidian). In most of the Eastern IA languages, the verbal string for the imperfective participle is one inflected string. For languages like Hindi, Urdu, Magahi and Marathi the string consists of two verbs (main + auxiliary). For Tamil, it is of one string which includes the agglutinated morphemes for PN and TAM features. In the instance below, for Tamil the agglutinated morpheme /ya/ is suggestive of the number, tense and aspect. Similarly, in Odia the /e/ phoneme is referent to the number, tense and aspect. In Hindi and Urdu, the root verb /pa.Dh/ takes /tA/ verbal suffix to express person, number, gender and aspect.

(6) (Tamil) nAna velai cey-ya
I-1.SG.NOM. the work do-SG.PRS.IMPFV.
"I do the work."
(7) (Odia) sItA tAraku mo.De
Sita-3.FSG.NOM wire-ACC bend-SG.PRS.IMPFV
"Sita bends the wire."
(8) (Hindi-Urdu) rAhula kitAba pa.Dha-tA hai
Rahul-3.MSG.NOM. book   read-3.MSG.IMPFV is-PRS
"Rahul is reading the book."
(9) (Magahi) gItA apanAra laikabAna para dhiyAna deba haI
Geeta   her children   attention on give-IMPFV be-PRS.
"Geeta pays attention to her children." (Rakesh and Kumar, 2013)

2.3   Complex Predicates

Complex predicates (Subbārāo, 2008, 2012) are one of the interesting phenomena in Indian languages. They encapsulate both the compound and conjunct verbs. The compound verbs are those which comprise of a main verb (compound) or a nominal/adjectival component (conjunct) followed by an auxiliary having the function of an 'intensifier, explicator, operator or vector' (Masica, 1993). According to him and Abbi (1991), the auxiliaries are so called because they explicate the meaning of the complete action bearing the TAM and concord markers.

(10) (Hindi-Urdu) (Muzaffar et al., 2015 & Muzaffar et al., 2016)
Compound (V+ V) /KhA liyA/, /mAra DAlanA/, /de denA/, /to.Da diyA/ etc.
Conjunct (N/JJ + N) /BharosA karanA/, /pariwartana karanA/, /Khusha honA/, /mazabUr honA/ etc.
(11) (Magahi) (Rakesh and Kumar, 2013)
Compound
rAma Chata se gira gelal (fell down)
"Ram fell down from the roof."
Conjunct
okAr GharwA hama kala sAfa karale (cleaned) haliAI
I cleaned his/her room yesterday."
(12) (Odia) (Jha et al., 2014)
Compound /mAri debA/, /hasi uThibA/, rAgI jibA/, /uThi pa.DibA/ etc.
Conjunct /BharasA karibA/, /duKhI hebA/, /nAca karibA/, /Bhadra hebA/, /saPhA hebA/ etc.

2.4   Dative Subjects

The dative subject (Subbārāo, 2008 & 2012) or the non-nominative subject or the Indirect Construction[5] is the experiencer rather than the nominative or ergative agent in Indian languages. One of the NPs

---

[5] Masica uses 'indirect construction' as a term derived from the traditional description.

which is the main candidate for the syntactic role subject gets the dative case. In Bengali, Assamese and Oriya it is also marked by the genitive case in most of the circumstances (Masica, 1993). But from the instance exemplified in the following example (14), it is quite evident that Odia does not apply genitives for expressing dative subject experiencer. Therefore, they should not be confused with each other. According to Masica (1993), 'experience' includes (a) the physical conditions and sensations like feeling cold, feeling sleepy, feeling hungry or thirsty etc., (b) psychological or mental states like liking and perceiving, (c) wanting or needing (d) obligation or compulsion (e) having kinship relations and (f) external circumstances or events that are not controlled by dative subjects.

    (13) (Hindi-Urdu) muJha-ko miThAIAM pasanda haiM
        I-DAT   sweets-3.FSG.   like-3.PL.IMPFV.PRS
        "I like sweets."

    (14) (Odia) mote bhoka   lAg-u-Chi
        I-DAT hunger-3.SG.NOM feel-3.SG.PROG.PRS
        "I am feeling hungry."

    (15) (Bengali) amAr triSnA peyeChile (Masica, 1993)
        I-GEN thirst-3.SG.NOM drink- 3.SG.PRFV.PST
        "I was thirsty."

    (16) (Assamese) mora bhoka lAgisil (Masica, 1993)
        I-GEN hunger-3.SG.NOM feel-3.SG.PRFV.PST
        "I was hungry." Or "I felt hungry."

3   Challenges in Translation of Verbs

When an annotator annotates the verbs observing the dictionary of animated images, they are confronted with some barriers. The barriers are owing to the fact that issues such as ambiguously annotated illustrations, verbal polysemy, affordances, valence and thereby semantic discrepancy persist. Although much care has been taken into account to avoid the semantic discrepancy on the platform, there is still a place for ambiguity. Some of the nomenclatures have been taken from the paper by Muzaffar et al., (2016).

3.1   Ambiguity in Visual Illustrations

When the images themselves are equivocal, ambiguous and misleading they are included in this category. In other words, owing to the fact that the action verbs are wrongly encoded as 3d animations, the L1 annotators are confronted with ambiguity issues which thereby paves the way for disambiguation challenges. If one observes the figure no. 4 above and the below images, the English verbal lemma of which is 'to hang' or 'to drop' has been interpreted with deviant annotations in the SL English. Because hanging, waving and dropping of head bear several semantic, pragmatic and discourse consequences. Therefore, the annotations in Indian languages vary and sometimes they get deviant. Analogously, the instances exemplified in the following section point to the fact that verbs like rotate, spin and turn (refer to section 3.2) have invariably been annotated for all the actions. One can observe that both the images are annotated as 'to hang' and 'to incline' in English that have further been annotated as the Hindi cognates of 'jhukAnA' in other Indian languages. Therefore, in most of the Indian languages the distinction between 'to tilt' and 'to hang' the head is clearly marked.

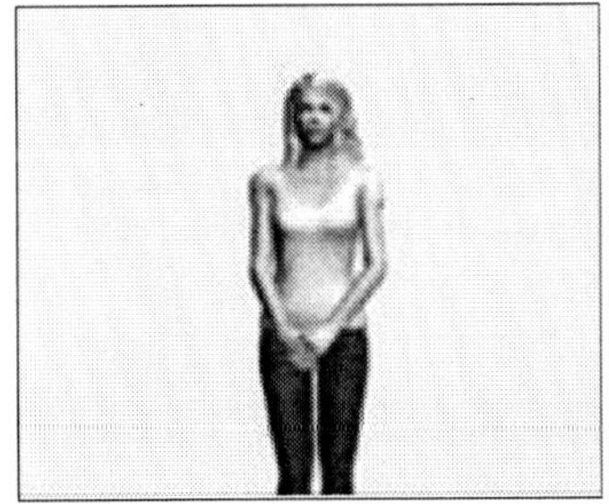

Figure 5. Illustrations for 'to hang'

3.2 Verbal Polysemy and Semantic Discrepancy

When one visual illustration of action refers to more than one verb and several animated actions refer to one verbal string they are categorized under this category. This issue behaves as a bottleneck so far as the annotation of actions is concerned for annotators. The verb 'to turn' with the id number 51ad2030 has been interpreted by Indian L1 speakers differently. In Sanskrit, the number of variations (for e.g. arda, shuka, narda, cala, gacha etc.) has amounted to thirty which is due to the over-interpretation and over-generalization by the annotators. The other languages that have captured variations are Hindi (mu.DanA, ghumanA), Urdu (mu.DanA and ghUmanA), Odia (ghuribA, bulibA) and Bengali (ghorA, pherA) with two variations each. The ambiguity arises as all the illustrations suggest a single verbal lemma 'to spin' or 'to rotate' or 'to turn' which is also quite evident from the languages of the Indian counterpart. It is further quite evident in the Italian language itself where 'girare' has been translated from the infinitive 'to turn'.

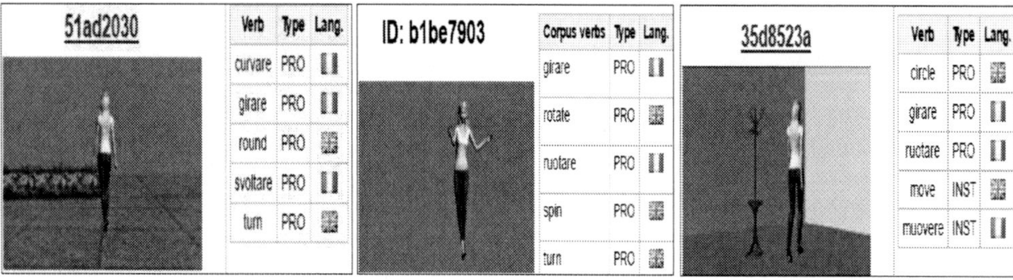

Figure 6. Images for 'to turn'

In all the images illustrated in the following, the sense of 'wiping' has been captured. Thus a single verb 'to wipe' has been used to refer to a series of actions that more or less are equivalent from the perspective of their meaning.

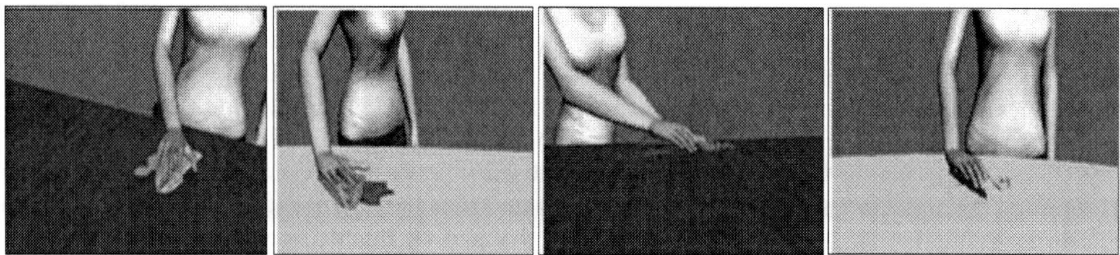

Figure 7. Illustrations for 'to clean'

Similarly, all these below images suggest the English verb 'to roll' or 'roll up' that have been translated differently by Indian languages (as in Hindi-Urdu lu.DhakAnA for the first two images (left-right), mo.DanA for the next two images and ghumAnA for the final two images.

Figure 8. Illustrations for 'to roll'

3.3 Affordances

Results demonstrate the fact that pragmatic information (affordances) is more relevant than semantic information in assigning the appropriate interpretation to sentences. The theory of affordances establishes a co-relation between the action and the perception by the annotator (De Felice, 2014). Taking into consideration the affordances like the shape and size of the objects, facial expressions, actions referring to the body, movement, modification of the object, deterioration of an object, force on an object, change of location, setting relation among objects and actions in the intersubjective space (Moneglia et al., 2014b; Panunzi et al., 2014; Moneglia et al., 2014a), verbs can be annotated exactly and all the action images have been categorized on this basis.

On the basis of grasping the shape and size of the objects, grasping has been divided into four major categories (De Felice, 2014): one hand grasp, both hand grasp, grasp with part and grasp with instrument. The first category includes grasping the objects whose size and shape must not exceed two-three fingers as two fingers will be needed to hold them by bending (for example, holding a lighter, a pen etc.). The following category represents grasping the objects not necessarily on the basis of size and shape as it may expand in the case of holding a baby with both the hands. The third category includes the grasping of the objects the size of which exceeding the hand size; as for instance holding a suitcase or any human being. The final division discusses the grasping of the objects that are handled with another recipient. For instance, when we talk of a fluid (water, oil) or solid (ice cubes) substance it is obvious and suggestive of the fact that we are taking assistance of some other instrument. Thus, we are taking the help of a glass (of beers or cubes) or bowl (of milk) as instruments for carrying them. Therefore, an annotator needs to take into account both the semantic and pragmatic knowledge while translating.

3.4 Factors of Verb Selection Preferences

All the actions on the IMAGACT4ALL platform can broadly be categorized into two action types: transitive and intransitive considering the semantic aspect of the language and the valence the verb takes as arguments. Furthermore, the transitive verbs can be classified as mono-transitive and di-transitive verbs. There are several action illustrations that are intransitive and hence one needs to consider the argument of the verb as its forms are dependent on the transitivity of the sentence; especially in Indian languages here.

The verb 'to roll' in the exemplary animations has to be annotated taking into consideration the arguments of the verb. Although there is no change of the verbal string (rolling) of the English annotation, the very information of causation is encoded in the verbal string in Indian languages. So, the annotations for the same string in Hindi-Urdu become 'lu.DhakanA' (intransitive) and 'lu.DhakAnA' (transitive). In Odia 'roll' becomes (ga.Duachi and ga.DAuachi), Sanskrit (ghurNati & ghurNayati), and Assamese (ghurigaiche & ghurAidiche)[6].

---

[6] The rest of the examples in Odia, Sanskrit and Assamese follow the same chronological order (intransitive & transitive) as in Hindi-Urdu.

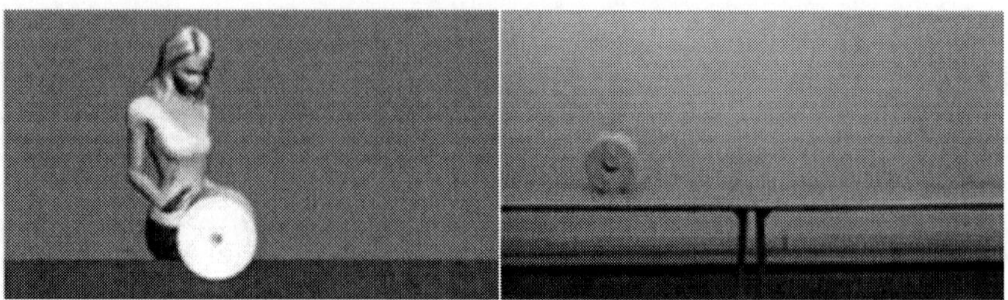

Figure 9. Illustrations for 'to roll' on a Surface

4 Scope and Implications for Theoretical and Machine Translation

The IMAGACT platform generates a huge amount of new horizons of knowledge for Lexicography, Language Typology and Translation Theory (Moneglia, 2011) in linguistics. So far as the theoretical translation is concerned, it bears an enormous amount of consequences as the L1 translator or decoder directly involves in the process of translation. Since the input is provided in both the orthographic annotation and 3d prototypic animated images, there should not be any divergence or discrepancy with respect to translating SL text into the TL. In spite of the encoded text in both the forms there still has some room for ambiguity. All the ambiguities pertaining to both processing of the translation and their interpretations have been provided from different perspectives in the present paper.

With regard to Machine Translation, there are a few points that are noteworthy to be made here. The IMAGACT platform has been a repository of verbs and their animated images. The repository of verbs can be made automated from translating SL text to TL text. This will facilitate the process of automatic translation of verbs without the assistance from the native speaker. Consequently, we are certain that this will provide efficient results as the annotation concerns only present imperfective participle finite verbs. Furthermore, the platform can also be made Text-speech and Speech-text translation among languages belonging to various families. In doing so, the bilingual dictionary of verbs (Panunzi et al., 2014) can play a significant role when we reach at level with fair number of verbal annotation. Although prototypic scenes are not computable objects the verbal database can be exploited to disambiguate which will pave the way for new generation computational tools for MT (Moneglia, 2011). Therefore, this will definitely be quite beneficial for disambiguating action verbs as no any other platform exists which is solely dedicated to action verbs and their translations.

5 Conclusion

In the very introductory section, we have discussed about the IMAGACT platform, the languages that have been annotated so far and the architecture of the process of translation. In the following section, the typological features pertaining to verbs in Indian languages have been discussed in detail. The features such as subject-verb agreement, the present imperfective participle, complex predicates and dative subjects have been provided due emphasis on inter-familial and intra-familial contrast with English and other Indian languages. The third section throws much light on the challenges such as ambiguity in visual illustrations, verbal polysemy and semantic discrepancy, affordances and factors of verb selection preferences. The final section lays emphasis on making the platform an automatic translator of verbs using the annotated bilingual dictionary of verbs.

Acknowledgements

We acknowledge the IMAGACT team in the University of Florence for developing the multilingual platform.

References

Anvita Abbi. 1991. Semantics of Explicator Compound Verbs. In *South Asian Languages, Language Sciences*, *13:2*, 161-180.
Atanu Saha & Bipasha Patgiri. 2013. Ergativity in Axomiya. *Language in India*, *13*(12).

Atul Ku. Ojha, Pitambar Behera, Srishti Singh, and Girish N. Jha. 2015. Training and Evaluation of POS Taggers in Indo-Aryan Languages: A Case of Hindi, Odia and Bhojpuri. In *Language Technology Conference-2016*.

Alessandro Panunzi, Irene De Felice, Lorenzo Gregori, Stefano Jacoviello, Monica Monachini, Massimo Moneglia, Valeria Quochi, and Irene Russo. 2014. Translating Action Verbs Using a Dictionary of Images: The IMAGACT Ontology. In *XVI EURALEX International Congress: The User in Focus*, pages 1163-1170.

Colin P. Masica. 1993. *The Indo-Aryan Languages*. Cambridge University Press.

Girish N. Jha, Lars Hellan, Dorothee Beermann, Srishti Singh, Pitambar Behera, and Esha Banerjee. 2014. Indian languages on the TypeCraft platform–the case of Hindi and Odia. In *WILDRE-2, LREC-2014*.

Girish N. Jha, Atul Ku. Ojha, Sharmin Muzaffar, and Pitambar Behera. 2016. Indo Aryan languages on IMAGACT. In *the IMAGACT Panel*, MODELACT Conference on *"Action, Language and Cognition"*, CNR, Rome.

Irene De Felice. 2014. «Possibilities for Action» in Language: Affordances and Verbal Polysemy. *Italian Journal of Cognitive Sciences* 1: 179-191.

Kārumūri V. Subbārāo. 2008. Typological characteristics of South Asian languages. *Language in South Asia*, pages 49-78.

Kārumūri V. Subbārāo. 2012. *South Asian languages: A syntactic typology*. Cambridge University Press.

Lata Atreya, Rajesh Kumar, and Smriti Singh. 2014. Passives in Magahi. *IOSR*, 19(4), pages 47-53.

Lorenzo Gregory, Andrea Amelio Ravelli, and Alessandro Panunzi. 2016. Enriching BabelNet verbal entities with videos: a linking experiment with the IMAGACT ontology of action. In *the Luxembourg BabelNet Workshop*, 2-3 March 2016, Luxembourg.

Massimo Moneglia and Alessandro Panunzi. 2007. Action Predicates and the Ontology of Action across Spoken Language Corpora. The Basic Issue of the SEMACT Project. In M. Alcántara, T. Declerck, In International Workshop on the Semantic Representation of Spoken Language (SRSL7). Salamanca: Universidad de Salamanca, pages 51-58.

Massimo Moneglia. 2011. Natural Language Ontology of Action: A Gap with Huge Consequences for Natural Language Understanding and Machine Translation. In *Language and Technology Conference*, pages 379-395, Springer International Publishing.

Massimo Moneglia, Gloria Gagliardi, Alessandro Panunzi, Francesca Frontini, Irene Russo, and Monica Monachini. 2012. IMAGACT: Deriving an Action Ontology from Spoken Corpora. In *Eighth Joint ACL-ISO Workshop on Interoperable Semantic Annotation (isa-8)*, pages 42-47.

Massimo Moneglia, Alessandro Panunzi, Gloria Gagliardi, Monica Monachini, Irene Russo, Irene De Felice, Fahad Khan, and Francesca Frontini. 2013. IMAGACT E-learning Platform for Basic Action Types. In *6th International Conference ICT for Language Learning*, pages 85-90.

Massimo Moneglia, Susan W. Brown, Aniruddha Kar, Anand Kumar, Atul Kumar Ojha, Heliana Mello, Niharika, Girish Nath Jha, Bhaskar Ray, and Annu Sharma. 2014a. Mapping Indian Languages onto the IMAGACT Visual Ontology of Action. In *WILDRE-2*, pages 51-55.

Massimo Moneglia, Susan W. Brown, Francesca Frontini, Gloria Gagliardi, Fahad Khan, Monica Monachini, and Alessandro Panunzi. 2014b. The IMAGACT Visual Ontology: An Extendable Multilingual Infrastructure for the representation of lexical encoding of Action. In *LREC-2014*, pages 3425-3432.

Nilu Rakesh & Rajesh Kumar. 2013. Agreement in Magahi Complex Predicate. *International Journal of Linguistics*, 5(1), 176.

Pitambar Behera. 2015. *Odia Parts of Speech Tagging Corpora: Suitability of Statistical Models*. M.Phil. Dissertation, Jawaharlal Nehru University (JNU), New Delhi, India.

Pitambar Behera. 2016. Evaluation of SVM-based Automatic Parts of Speech Tagger for Odia. In *WILDRE-3, LREC-2016*.

Sharmin Muzaffar, Pitambar Behera. 2014. Error Analysis of the Urdu Verb Markers: A Comparative Study on Google and Bing Machine Translation Platforms, *Aligarh Journal of Linguistics* (ISSN- 2249-1511), 4 (1-2), pages 199-208.

Sharmin Muzaffar, Pitambar Behera, Girish Nath Jha, Lars Hellan, and Dorothee Beermann. 2015. The TypeCraft Natural Language Database: Annotating and Incorporating Urdu. *Indian Journal of Science and Technology*, 8(27).

Sharmin Muzaffar, Pitambar Behera, and Girish Nath Jha. 2016. Issues and Challenges in Annotating Urdu Action Verbs on the IMAGACT4ALL Platform. In *LREC-2016*, pages 1446-1451.

Sharmin Muzaffar, Pitambar Behera, and Girish Nath Jha. 2016. A Pāninian Framework for Analyzing Case Marker Errors in English-Urdu Machine Translation. *Procedia Computer Science (Elsevier)*, 96, 502-510.

Crowdsourcing-based Annotation of Emotions
in Filipino and English Tweets

Fermin Roberto G. Lapitan[1]   **Riza Batista-Navarro**[1,2]   **Eliezer A. Albacea**[1]

[1]Institute of Computer Science, University of the Philippines Los Baños, Philippines
[2]School of Computer Science, University of Manchester, United Kingdom
{fglapitan,eaalbacea}@up.edu.ph, riza.batista@manchester.ac.uk

Abstract

The automatic analysis of emotions conveyed in social media content, e.g., tweets, has many beneficial applications. In the Philippines, one of the most disaster-prone countries in the world, such methods could potentially enable first responders to make timely decisions despite the risk of data deluge. However, recognising emotions expressed in Philippine-generated tweets, which are mostly written in Filipino, English or a mix of both, is a non-trivial task. In order to facilitate the development of natural language processing (NLP) methods that will automate such type of analysis, we have built a corpus of tweets whose predominant emotions have been manually annotated by means of crowdsourcing. Defining measures ensuring that only high-quality annotations were retained, we have produced a gold standard corpus of 1,146 emotion-labelled Filipino and English tweets. We validate the value of this manually produced resource by demonstrating that an automatic emotion-prediction method based on the use of a publicly available word-emotion association lexicon was unable to reproduce the labels assigned via crowdsourcing. While we are planning to make a few extensions to the corpus in the near future, its current version has been made publicly available in order to foster the development of emotion analysis methods based on advanced Filipino and English NLP.

1   Introduction

Social media platforms are integral to the lives of Filipinos. In terms of time spent on using social media, Filipinos currently rank first, with an average of 3.7 hours of usage per day (Kemp, 2016). Social media penetration is at 47% of the population which means that almost half of 102 million Filipinos have social media access. Among the most commonly used social media platforms, Twitter ranks sixth with 16% of Filipinos on social media using it. As of May 2016, there are 7.56 million active Twitter users in the Philippines, making it the world's tenth country with the most number of Twitter users.

The Philippines is known not only for being the social media capital (Cameron, 2016), but also for being one of the world's five most natural disaster-prone countries (Esplanada, 2015). Each year, around twenty typhoons enter the Philippine Area of Responsibility (PAR), of which eight to nine make landfall. Aside from typhoons, earthquakes and volcanic eruptions also occur frequently as the country is located within the Pacific Ring of Fire. The local and national government have utilised social media as a means for communicating with citizens during times of disaster. For example, Project NOAH (Lagmay, 2012) of the Philippine Atmospheric Geophysical and Astronomical Services Administration (PAGASA) has created a dedicated Twitter account for announcing weather updates via tweets. Some heads of municipalities and provinces post announcements, e.g., those pertaining to suspension of classes or work, on Facebook and Twitter. Meanwhile, ordinary citizens tweet about traffic situations, current conditions in their local area, as well as share how they feel as these events unfold. Tweets circulating during disasters can thus aid responders obtain meaningful feedback on the current situation in particular areas as well as assess the emotional states of those affected.

Proceedings of the 6th Workshop on South and Southeast Asian Natural Language Processing,
pages 74–82, Osaka, Japan, December 11-17 2016.

Emotions conveyed in tweets could inform decisions pertinent to disaster risk reduction and management (DRRM). However, such decisions often need to be made urgently. This poses a challenge considering the large volume of tweets that Filipinos generate especially in the event of natural disasters. Automating the identification of emotions in tweets is therefore beneficial, potentially leading to more efficient and timely decision-making. Nevertheless this is considered a difficult natural language processing (NLP) task primarily due to the noisy textual content of tweets. With a 140-character limit per tweet, Twitter users often compact their messages with the use of ungrammatical sentence fragments, intentionally misspelled words and abbreviations. Furthermore, often very little contextual information is expressed in tweets, with each one typically containing only a few words. In the Philippines, another complication arises from the fact that tweets are expressed in either of the country's two official languages: Filipino (the official name for Tagalog) or English, or even in a mix of both (i.e., "Taglish"). As Filipino is a low-resourced language, not many dictionaries and corpora that could potentially support Filipino NLP are available.

In order to support the development of advanced automatic methods for recognising emotions in tweets generated in the Philippines, we constructed an emotion-annotated corpus of 1,146 disaster-relevant tweets from the country. It consists of Filipino and English tweets which were annotated according to the eight primary emotions identified by Plutchik: anger, anticipation, joy, sadness, trust, surprise, disgust and fear (Plutchik, 2001). In this work, we demonstrate how crowdsourcing facilitated the efficient collection of human-supplied annotations, and describe our measures for ensuring that data quality and reliability were not compromised. A discussion of our results is then presented followed by an analysis that emphasises the value of our newly developed corpus in the context of supporting the development of Filipino and English NLP methods for emotion identification.

2   Related work

Sentiment analysis, the automatic classification of pieces of text according to positive, negative or neutral sentiment, has been an active area of NLP research (Pang and Lee, 2008). Some efforts have however further addressed finer-grained classification, in which the specific emotion conveyed by a piece of text is identified. Strapparava and Mihalcea (2007) built a corpus of news titles (i.e., headlines) extracted from news web sites and classified them according to six predefined emotions (Anger, Disgust, Fear, Joy, Sadness, and Surprise) and valence (Positive or Negative). A web interface was developed, allowing annotators to use slider widgets in assigning values between 0 and 100, to indicate how much any of the six emotions of interest is conveyed in each of 1,250 headlines. Six annotators carried out the task, guided by sample annotated headlines including ones expressing multiple emotions. The resulting corpus, split into development and test sets (containing 250 and 1,000 headlines respectively), was employed as gold standard data in the Affective Text shared task of the SemEval 2007 Workshop.

Microblogs generated by social media have also attracted active research on sentiment and emotion analysis. Wen and Wan (2014) sought to classify Chinese microblog texts into one of eight emotion categories (i.e., Anger, Disgust, Fear, Happiness, Like, Sadness, Surprise and None). To support the development of their methods, they constructed a data set consisting of 13,252 sentences from 4,000 microblog texts sourced from Sina Weibo, a popular Chinese microblogging site. Similarly, De Leon and Estuar (2013) aimed to automatically analyse emotions in social media posts, specifically in tweets generated in the Philippines which are mostly written in Filipino or English. To this end, they gathered hundreds of thousands of tweets in both languages, during some of the country's most prominent disasters. While the resulting data set is undoubtedly a valuable resource, it does not contain any manually produced annotations and thus cannot serve as a gold standard for the development or evaluation of NLP methods.

Indeed, manually labelling emotions in a huge number of tweets is a daunting effort. If done in the traditional manner, i.e., by a small team of human annotators, the task can quickly turn into a burden, potentially leading to the generation of inconsistent annotations. Crowdsourcing, the process of soliciting judgements from contributors (crowds) over the internet, lends itself well to the task of analysing emotions expressed in text. Mohammad and Turney (2013) used Amazon's crowdsourcing platform,

Mechanical Turk[1], to build EmoLex, a lexical resource capturing associations between words and any of Plutchik's eight primary emotions. However, given the risk of attracting underperforming annotators, a few issues with quality control arose, which the proponents attempted to address by keeping annotation instructions simple and easy to understand.

In this study, we cast the analysis of emotions in social media content as a crowdsourcing-based task. We employed the CrowdFlower platform[2], allowing us to define measures for ensuring that high-quality annotations on tweets are produced. As a result, we have constructed the first gold standard emotion-annotated corpus of Filipino and English tweets, which can facilitate the development of advanced NLP methods for emotion analysis.

3 Methods

In this section, we present details on how the annotation of emotions in Filipino and English tweets was carried out. We first describe the data preparation methods employed and then proceed to a discussion of our annotation schema. Finally, we focus on the design and configuration of the task in our chosen crowdsouring platform.

3.1 Data preparation

Upon request, we obtained a corpus of 660,000 tweets from the Ateneo de Manila University's Social Computing Science Laboratory who provided us with the data set in compliance with Twitter's terms and conditions[3]. That is, the original data set was exported to a spreadsheet format which was split into smaller spreadsheets with 50,000 tweets each, provided to us on a one-spreadsheet-per-day basis over a total of 14 days. These tweets were gathered from the 7th to the 9th of August 2012 during which the Philippines' largest island, Luzon, was hit by heavy southwest monsoon rain (locally known as "habagat"). We first randomly selected 2300 tweets from the whole set. Two automatic pre-processing steps were then carried out on these tweets, namely, duplicate removal and language detection (using Google Spreadsheets'detectlanguage detectlanguage function). As our interest is in obtaining annotations on Filipino and English tweets, with the intention to acquire more for the former—given that it is lower-resourced, we finally included 778 Filipino and 570 English tweets in our selection, for a total of 1,348 tweets.

3.2 Definition of emotion classification schema and guidelines

In defining our schema for classifying tweets according to emotion, we adopted the eight primary types identified by Robert Plutchik: Anger, Anticipation, Joy, Sadness, Trust, Surprise, Disgust and Fear (Plutchik, 2001). His wheel of emotions, shown in Figure 1, illustrates how other emotions are just varying intensities of the eight primary ones, or derived through combinations. For example, Ecstasy is a more intense feeling of Joy while Serenity is its less intense variant. Love, on the other hand, is Joy and Trust combined. Apart from the eight emotion types, an additional category Other was included in the classification scheme to account for tweets which are judged as not expressing any emotion.

In order to elucidate the specifications of our task, we formulated a few guidelines. Firstly, only one of the nine categories mentioned above can be assigned to any given tweet; in cases where multiple emotions are conveyed, annotators were asked to select the emotion that is most strongly expressed. Where the identified emotion (e.g., Contempt) falls between two primary emotions (e.g., Anger and Disgust), the annotator should use his/her best judgement to select the emotion which is more strongly conveyed. Emoticons contained in tweets can be considered as valid indicators of predominant emotions. Finally, we define Other as a catch-all category; when a tweet does not express any emotion or if it was written in an unfamiliar language, this category should be selected. Sufficient examples were provided to illustrate each of these guidelines.

---

[1] https://www.mturk.com/mturk/welcome

[2] https://www.crowdflower.com

[3] https://dev.twitter.com/overview/terms/agreement-and-policy

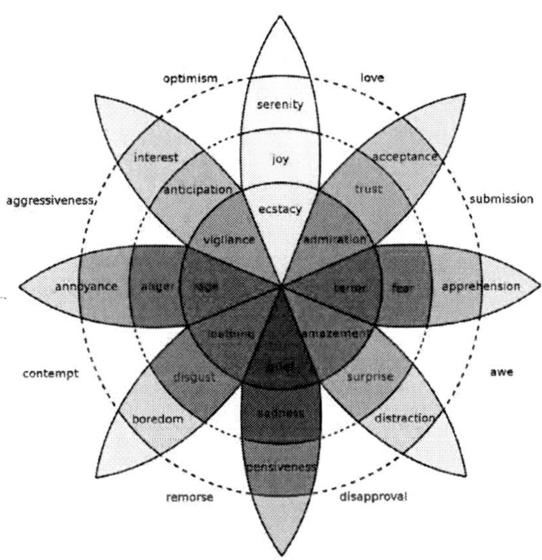

Figure 1: Plutchik's Wheel of Emotions

3.3 Crowdsourcing platform configuration

In implementing our annotation task, two of the most popular crowdsourcing platforms, Amazon Mechanical Turk (AMT) and CrowdFlower, were considered and compared to each other in terms of supporting functionalities. We eventually selected CrowdFlower as our platform due to its in-built measures for ensuring that only high-quality judgements are collected. For instance, it allows for the incorporation of hidden test questions (with corresponding gold standard answers) that could help distinguish hasty annotators from those who are more serious about the task. In this way, only the more conscientious annotators can proceed with the task and contribute their judgements, thus helping us to automatically eliminate ones performing at a low level of accuracy.

After signing up for a trial account in CrowdFlower, we created a task (termed as "job") and uploaded our data set of 1348 tweets in the form of a spreadsheet. For the purpose of presenting the data to the annotators in a more intuitive manner, a user-interactive web-based form was designed using the CrowdFlower Markup Language (CML). This resulted in the interface depicted in Figure 2, which presented each tweet as well as the nine possible emotion types that an annotator can choose from (Anger, Anticipation, Joy, Sadness, Trust, Surprise, Disgust, Fear and Other) in the form of radio buttons. In order to make the choices more graphical, corresponding illustrative icons were also displayed. Only five tweets (termed in CrowdFlower as "rows") per page were presented to the annotator at a time, together with the guidelines described above.

Various measures were taken to ensure that only high-quality annotations have been included in our corpus. Firstly, we configured the job to require that each row is assigned independent judgements from at least three different annotators, thus enabling us to assess the level of inter-annotator agreement for each tweet. Furthermore, we took advantage of CrowdFlower's functionality for including hidden test questions in order to disallow annotators who were performing at a low accuracy, to proceed with the task. To this end, we randomly selected a small set of 50 tweets and manually categorised each of them according to our scheme. Out of these, 28 tweets representative of the emotion types of interest were handpicked as hidden test questions which were interspersed with the rest of the tweets. In defining these test questions, we were allowed by CrowdFlower to specify multiple gold standard answers, e.g., in cases where determining a tweet's conveyed emotion is not straightforward, i.e., where more than one emotion type could potentially apply. Judgements from annotators eliminated based on our test questions (i.e.,

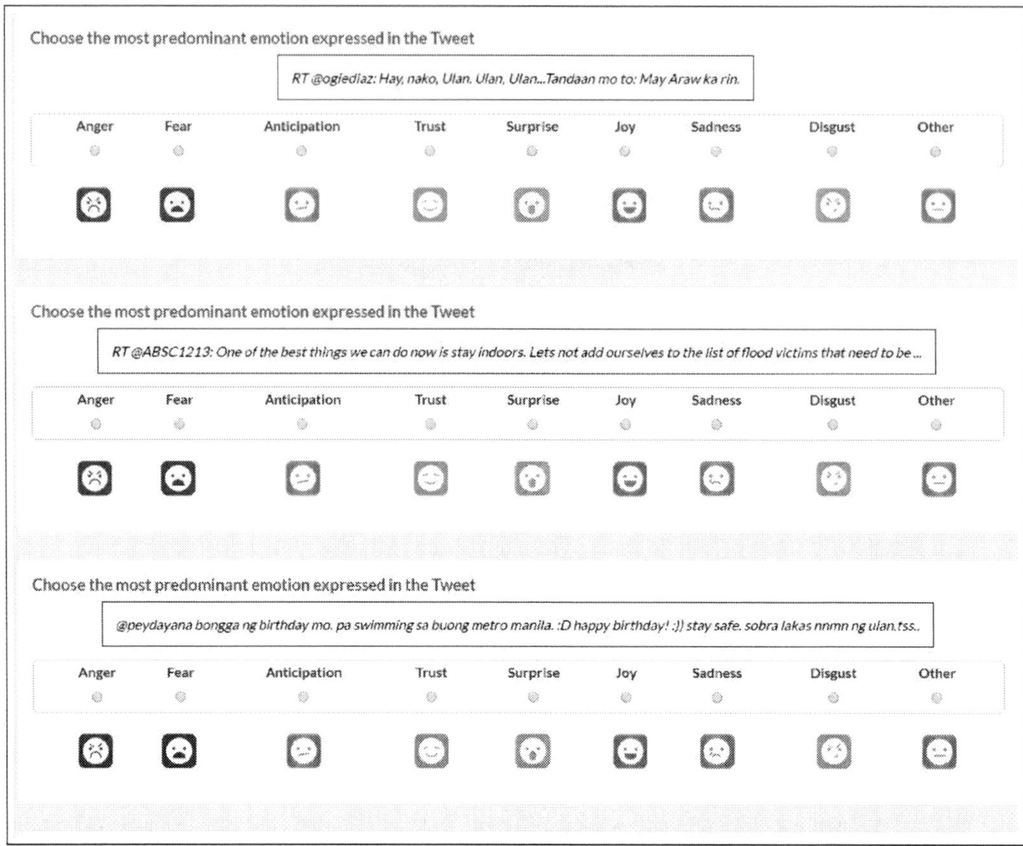

Figure 2: Interface for the annotation of emotions in tweets

those whose accuracy was computed to be less than 70%) were automatically marked by CrowdFlower as untrusted.

In CrowdFlower, task proponents are allowed to specify which performance measure determines task completion. On the one hand, choosing optimal speed (performance = 1) defines the job as complete once the required number of judgements has been obtained, regardless of whether they come from trusted or non-trusted contributors. Choosing optimal quality (performance = 3), on the other hand, makes the job accessible to only the platform's handful of most trusted contributors, thus potentially taking a longer time to obtain the required number of judgements. For our task, we opted for a compromise between speed and quality (performance = 2), thus allowing us to obtain judgements in a timely manner without sacrificing quality.

Whilst our task is aimed at gathering annotations on Filipino tweets, CrowdFlower does not as yet offer a Filipino language crowd, in the same way that it does for Spanish, French, German, Italian, Hindi, Arabic, Indonesian, Turkish, Italian, Russian, Vietnamese and Chinese (Josephy, 2014). As a workaround, to maximise the exposure of our task to Filipino speakers, we configured our job's geographical location settings to specify that only contributors from the Philippines are allowed to access the job. However, before launching the job officially, we first gathered feedback on the task from invited contributors (termed in CrowdFlower as "internal workforce"). After making changes according to their suggested revisions on the web-based form and wording of the guidelines, we finally launched our first CrowdFlower job to external contributors with the maximum allowed 999 rows. Upon its completion, we launched a similarly configured second job, this time with the remaining 349 unannotated tweets. While the first job took 26 hours to complete, the second one finished in less than six hours.

Emotion type	Filipino	English	Overall
Anger	67 (10.36%)	11 (2.20%)	78 (6.81%)
Anticipation	37 (5.72%)	14 (2.81%)	51 (4.45%)
Disgust	20 (3.09%)	3 (0.60%)	23 (2.01%)
Fear	20 (3.09%)	5 (1.00%)	25 (2.18%)
Joy	165 (25.50%)	43 (8.62%)	208 (18.15%)
Sadness	72 (11.13%)	22 (4.41%)	94 (8.20%)
Surprise	10 (1.55%)	7 (1.40%)	17 (1.48%)
Trust	33 (5.10%)	20 (4.01%)	53 (4.62%)
other	223 (34.47%)	374 (74.95%)	597 (52.09%)
TOTAL	647 (100.00%)	499 (100.00%)	1146 (100.00%)

Table 1: Distribution of Filipino and English tweets according to emotion

Emotion type	With consensus from 3 annotators	With consensus from 2 annotators	Overall
Anger	19 (28.36%)	48 (71.64%)	67
Anticipation	8 (21.62%)	29 (78.38%)	37
Disgust	5 (25.00%)	15 (75.00%)	20
Fear	5 (25.00%)	15 (75.00%)	20
Joy	94 (56.97%)	71 (43.03%)	165
Sadness	39 (54.17%)	33 (45.83%)	72
Surprise	2 (20.00%)	8 (80.00%)	10
Trust	9 (27.27%)	24 (72.73%)	33
other	95 (42.60%)	128 (57.40%)	223
TOTAL	276 (42.66%)	371 (57.34%)	647

Table 2: Inter-annotator agreement on Filipino tweets

4 Results and analysis

A total of 1,348 tweets were manually assigned emotion labels according to the methods described above. However, only judgements on which at least two annotators agreed were retained in order to keep the annotations in our corpus reliable and of high quality. Specifically, an annotated tweet was included in our corpus only if at least two out of three contributors labelled it with the same emotion type. Upon applying this filter, 202 annotations were discarded, leaving a total of 1,146 annotated tweets in our corpus, of which 647 are in Filipino and 499 are in English. Table 1 presents the distribution of these tweets according to the emotion labels assigned to them.

Overall, more than half (52.09%) of the tweets were categorised under the catch-all type Other, many of which were labelled as such for not conveying any emotion, e.g., containing only informative news or announcements. The distribution of such emotion-empty tweets is different though, when the number of annotations is analysed while taking into account the tweets' language. While most of the English tweets (74.95%) do not express any emotion, in the case of Filipino tweets, majority do convey some emotion (with emotion-empty ones accounting for only 34.47% of the total). This pattern is consistent with previously reported findings that Filipinos tend to tweet in the Filipino language when expressing their feelings, whereas English is mostly used for sharing news and announcements (De Leon and Estuar, 2013). The predominant emotion in both Filipino and English tweets is Joy, having a relative frequency of 25.50% and 18.15%, respectively. For both sets of tweets, the emotion which is least observed is Surprise, which comprises only 1.48% of the tweets.

To aid in our analysis of inter-annotator agreement on the crowdsourced judgements, we compared the number of Filipino tweets that were annotated with perfect agreement (i.e., obtaining consensus from all contributors) against those with majority agreement (i.e., with consensus from only two out of three

Emotion type	With consensus from 3 annotators	With consensus from 2 annotators	Overall
Anger	4 (36.36%)	7 (63.64%)	11
Anticipation	0 (0.00%)	14 (100.00%)	14
Disgust	0 (0.00%)	3 (100.00%)	3
Fear	1 (20.00%)	4 (80.00%)	5
Joy	20 (46.51%)	23 (53.49%)	43
Sadness	12 (54.55%)	10 (45.45%)	22
Surprise	2 (28.57%)	5 (71.43%)	7
Trust	5 (25.00%)	15 (75.00%)	20
Other	243 (64.97%)	131 (35.03%)	374
TOTAL	287 (57.52%)	212 (42.48%)	499

Table 3: Inter-annotator agreement on English tweets

contributors), shown in Table 2. It can be observed that out of the eight primary emotions, Joy and Sadness are the two categories that contributors have assigned to Filipino tweets with perfect agreement more often than not, i.e., at the rates of 56.97% and 54.17%, respectively. In contrast, perfect agreement was much more difficult to obtain in the case of other emotion categories. For instance, 80% and 78.38% of the tweets assigned the labels of Surprise and Anticipation, respectively, were placed under these categories based on majority agreement. Meanwhile, based on inter-annotator agreement on English tweets (Table 3), it can be observed that perfect agreement is difficult to achieve on tweets categorised under Anticipation and Disgust, with all of such annotations resulting from majority agreement only. As in the case with Filipino tweets, many of the English tweets under Joy and Sadness (46.51% and 54.55%, respectively) were obtained based on perfect agreement.

The lack of perfect agreement on many of the annotations indicate that the task of categorising Philippine-generated tweets according to the emotion they convey is non-trivial. This thus confirms our motivation for undertaking this manual annotation task: that the complex language used in tweets necessitates the development of more language resources and advanced NLP methods. To further verify that currently available off-the-shelf tools and resources are not sufficient for accurately categorising tweets according to emotion, we attempted to automatically reproduce the labels manually assigned to our corpus' Filipino and English tweets by leveraging existing resources. Specifically, we made use of the Hashtag Emotion Lexicon (Mohammad, 2012), a dictionary of 16,862 words frequently appearing in tweets[4]. In this resource, the association of each word with any of Plutchik's eight primary emotions is specified using a real-valued score, with bigger values indicating stronger associations. We thus predicted the predominant emotion in each of our corpus' 1,146 tweets by matching words against this lexicon. This allowed us to calculate a cumulative score for each of the eight emotions per tweet; based on this, we took the highest scoring emotion as the tweet's predominant emotion. The predictions obtained in this manner were then compared against the emotion labels manually assigned to the tweets through crowdsourcing. Shown in Table 4 are the results per emotion category in terms of precision, recall and F-score. Overall, a very low F-score of 13.18% was obtained, although for the Joy and Surprise categories, individual F-scores are higher, i.e., 32.77% and 16.00%, respectively. There are, however, categories (e.g., Anticipation and Disgust) for which no correct predictions were obtained. These findings confirm that further language resources, e.g., gold standard corpora such as the one being proposed in this work, need to be built in order to support the development of accurate methods for identifying emotions in Filipino and English tweets.

---

[4]http://saifmohammad.com/WebPages/lexicons.html

Emotion type	True positives	False positives	False negatives	Precision	Recall	F-score
Anger	7	30	71	18.92%	8.97%	12.17%
Anticipation	0	126	51	0.00%	0.00%	0.00%
Disgust	0	42	23	0.00%	0.00%	0.00%
Fear	5	164	20	2.96%	20.00%	5.15%
Joy	106	333	102	24.15%	50.96%	32.77%
Sadness	7	76	87	8.43%	7.45%	7.91%
Surprise	4	29	13	12.12%	23.53%	16.00%
Trust	14	186	39	7.00%	26.42%	11.07%

Table 4: Performance of lexicon-based prediction of emotions against crowdsourced annotations

5 Future work and Conclusions

Through croudsourcing, we were able to build an emotion-annotated corpus of 1,146 disaster-relevant tweets from the Philippines. Our results demonstrate that with appropriate measures for quality control, crowdsourcing can indeed facilitate the efficient collection of emotion-annotated Filipino and English tweets. This was evidenced by the short turnaround time and satisfactory level of inter-annotator agreement on the obtained annotations. We investigated if the human-provided emotion labels of our tweets can be automatically predicted based on a publicly available word-association lexicon. Results from this experiment were not favourable, thus confirming the need for language resources that can facilitate the development of automatic emotion detection methods which obtain better accuracy. One of our immediate future steps involves increasing the number of emotion-annotated tweets in our corpus, especially for categories which currently have low frequencies, e.g., Surprise, Disgust, Fear. Nevertheless, we have made the current version of our newly constructed resource, the EMOTERA (Emotion-annotated Tweets for Disaster Risk Assessment) Corpus, available to the NLP community (`http://tinyurl.com/emoteracorpus`).

Acknowledgements

We thank all of our reviewers for their invaluable feedback. We are also grateful to the Ateneo de Manila University's Social Computing Science Laboratory, headed by Dr. Regina Estuar, for sharing their collection of tweets with us. Furthermore, the first author acknowledges the funders of his PhD studies: the Accelerated Science and Technology Human Resource Development Program (ASTHRDP) of the Philippines' Department of Science and Technology-Science Education Institute (DOST-SEI).

References

[Cameron2016] Nathan Cameron. 2016. The Social Media Capital of the World. Online: `http://www.godinternational.org/god-intl-blog/2016/7/the-social-media-capital-of-the-world`. Accessed: 2016-09-20.

[De Leon and Estuar2013] Marlene M. De Leon and Ma. Regina E. Estuar. 2013. Disaster Emotions: A Bilingual Sentiment and Affect Analysis of Disaster Tweets. In *Proceedings of the 2013 Annual International Conference on Computer Games and Multimedia*, page 70.

[Esplanada2015] Jerry Esplanada. 2015. PH on UN list of top 5 disaster-prone areas. Online: `http://globalnation.inquirer.net/132796/ph-on-un-list-of-top-5-disaster-prone-areas`. Accessed: 2016-09-20.

[Josephy2014] Tatiana Josephy. 2014. CrowdFlower Now Offering Twelve Language Crowds. Online: `https://www.crowdflower.com/crowdflower-now-offering-twelve-language-skill-groups/`. Accessed: 2016-09-20.

[Kemp2016] Simon Kemp. 2016. Digital in 2016. Online: `http://wearesocial.com/uk/special-reports/digital-in-2016`. Accessed: 2016-09-20.

[Lagmay2012] AMF Lagmay. 2012. Disseminating near-real time hazards information and flood maps in the philippines through web-gis. *Project NOAH Open File Reports*, 1:21–36.

[Mohammad and Turney2013] Saif M Mohammad and Peter D Turney. 2013. Crowdsourcing a word-emotion association lexicon. *Computational Intelligence*, 29(3):436–465.

[Mohammad2012] Saif Mohammad. 2012. #Emotional Tweets. In *Proceedings of the Sixth International Workshop on Semantic Evaluation (SemEval 2012)*, pages 246–255, Montréal, Canada, 7-8 June. Association for Computational Linguistics.

[Pang and Lee2008] Bo Pang and Lillian Lee. 2008. Opinion mining and sentiment analysis. *Foundations and trends in information retrieval*, 2(1-2):1–135.

[Plutchik2001] Robert Plutchik. 2001. The Nature of Emotions. *American Scientist*, 89(4):344–350.

[Strapparava and Mihalcea2007] Carlo Strapparava and Rada Mihalcea. 2007. SemEval-2007 Task 14: Affective text. In *Proceedings of the 4th International Workshop on Semantic Evaluations*, pages 70–74. Association for Computational Linguistics.

[Wen and Wan2014] Shiyang Wen and Xiaojun Wan. 2014. Emotion Classification in Microblog Texts Using Class Sequential Rules. In *AAAI*, pages 187–193.

Temporal Information Extraction in Clinical Domain (TIECA)

K.K.Shujeevan
UCSC
No 35, Reid Avenue, Colombo - 07,
Sri Lanka
`kkshujeevan@gmail.com`

W.V.Welgama
A.R.Weerasinghe
University of Colombo School of Computing
No 35, Reid Avenue, Colombo - 07,
Sri Lanka
`wvw@ucsc.cmb.ac.lk`

Abstract

In the present context, there are many records available in textual format that offers a means to share knowledge and valuable information which are in most of the scenarios temporally bound. It is not straightforward to access the information which are relevant to a specific time frame without identifying the time, event information along with their relation in any form of documentation. The importance of temporality is especially crucial in the medical domain where the records of a patient are varying with age, medication and surgeries.

Most of the existing approaches for information extraction are of limited use due to its limited applicability in the medical domain in an elaborate manner. TIECA aims to provide an efficient approach comparing the performance of rule based and machine learning approaches, along with a clear analysis elaborating the rationale behind the variation of the evaluation criteria values for extracting temporal content within medical text. Successful results were achieved by evaluating the proposed method using data obtained from Mayo Clinic. These experiments show state of the art promising results, proving that the proposed approach suits information extraction within the medical domain.

KeywordsRule Based; Machine Learning; Temporal Information; Information Extraction; Time; Event; Relation Identification.

1 Introduction

Time provides a substrate for the human management of perception and action. As a pervasive element of human life, time is a primary element that allows us to observe, describe and reason about what surrounds us in the world . As a cognitive and linguistic component for describing changes which happen through the occurrence of events, processes, and actions, time provides a way to record, order and measure the duration of such occurrences . The nature of time is critical to our ability to communicate plans, stories and change. Further, much of the information and many of the assertions made in a text are bounded in time.

Information Extraction is the process of automatic extraction of structured information such as entities, relationships between entities, and attributes describing entities from unstructured sources. This enables much richer forms of queries on the abundant unstructured sources than possible with keyword searches alone.

Within the biomedical community there has been a long standing interest in temporal reasoning. The interest led to the automatic extraction and interpretation of temporal information from medical texts, which includes electronic discharge summaries, patient case summaries etc. In the perspective of medical researchers making effective use of gathered temporal information from the above mentioned narratives in terms of temporality is considered important.

Proceedings of the 6th Workshop on South and Southeast Asian Natural Language Processing,
pages 83–92, Osaka, Japan, December 11-17 2016.

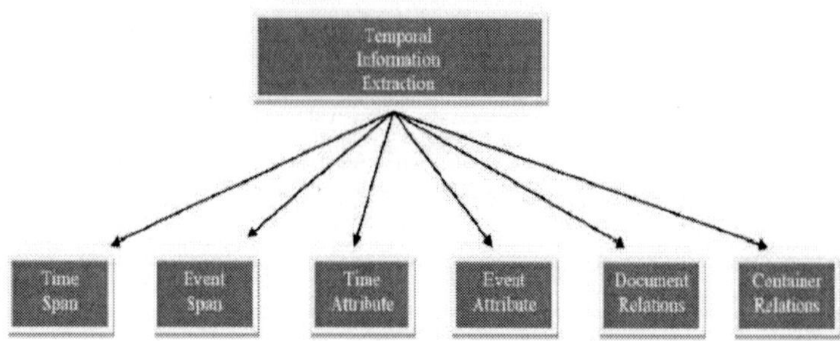

Figure 1: Sub tasks of the implemented system

TIECA consisted of six subtasks related to these core concepts: TIMEX3 span (TS) and attribute (TA) classification, EVENT span (ES) and attribute (EA) classification, document creation time (DR) and narrative container (CR) relations as depicted in Figure 1. The Colon cancer patient data set of the Mayo Clinic provided in SemEval 2016 was used. We attempted to provide a solution to all six subtasks through this research, with the aim of benchmarking existing tools and methods on this corpus for further development of semantic processing of clinical notes. A system was developed through this research using both rule based and machine learning techniques. In this paper, we describe our system, its results, and an error analysis for the identified subtasks.

This paper is organized as follows. The next section explains some of the background which will be followed by the related works in Section 3. The methodology used to produce the TIECA model provided in Section 4 Experimental results are presented in Section 5. Section 6 gives the Discussion followed by Conclusion in Section 7 and future work are given in the last section.

2   Background

For successful temporal modelling, three core concepts need to be defined: *temporal expressions* (**TIMEX3**), denoting time references like dates; events (**EVENT**), denoting salient occurrences; and temporal relations (**TLINK**) denoting order (e.g. before, after) between an event and / or TIMEX3.

2.1   Time Extraction

Time related information in text is often expressed using a phrase that precisely describes a point or duration. Sometimes these points reference an absolute unambiguous time (anchored via e.g. a calendar), which is of great help when trying to map events from a discourse to a timeline. It is also often that case that such phrases explicitly state an interval's length. Since they are so explicit, these phrases are used when temporality is critical.

Under this definition, we considers only "proper interval" (an interval where the start point is before the end point.) as the intervals; that is, no minimum atomic duration is recognized, and there is no quantization of time into chronons. Rather, temporal entities are described by infinitesimal points that bound them.

In the context of our research a "temporal expression", or timex, is any expression that denotes a moment, interval or other temporal region without having to rely upon an event. Each interval is composed of two points between which it obtains. For example, *24th August 1997*, *two weeks* and *now* are all temporal expressions; after the storm is not. Time can belong to any one of the following classes, namely, *Absolute, Deictic, Anaphoric, Duration, Set, Pre Post Expressions* and *Quantifiers*.

2.2   Event Extraction

The term *Event*, has many definitions in the real world but in the context of our research Events are considered as a cover term for situations that happen or occur. *Events* can be punctual or last for a period of time. Events may also be those predicates describing states or circumstances in which something obtains or holds true.

Events do not have to be real and observable for them to be annotated in a given text. Unreal events, such as those in a fictional or modal context should be included in a temporal annotation of a document. Description of future events or of things subordinated into the conditional world of an if condition (for example) are still events, and ought to be processed as such.

An event can belong to any of the following types, namely, *Aspectual, Intentional Actions, Occurrences, Perception, Reporting, Evidential* or *State*.

2.3 Relation Extraction

In the context of our research interval algebra which describes a relation are considered to be those that define types of relation between intervals and a set of axioms for operating with these relations; an interval has a start and an end point. Some temporal logic use points instead of intervals. For interval logic, a point event may be represented by an interval whose start and end occur simultaneously; a proper interval is an interval where the end occurs after the start . Temporal logic deal with reasoning about the relations that hold between intervals.

In our research context the DR consist of four class categories: *before, after, overlap* and *before / overlap* which describes the overall relationship. The CR, focuses on the contains class to recognize whether an event or time mentioned within the document consists or is contained by another.

3 Related Work

3.1 Annotation Standard and Guidelines

TimeML is an expressive language for temporal information annotation, designed to connect the processes of temporal analysis of a text with a representation and formal meaning of time. It is a specification language for event and temporal expressions in natural language text able to capture distinct phenomena in temporal markup, to anchor events to temporally denoting expressions, and to order relative event expressions.

The development of temporal annotation standards and corpora has a long history. Of note is the TimeBank corpus which contains 183 news articles annotated with temporal information, events, times and temporal links between events and times. This corpus was developed in multiple iterations, and prior analyses of the annotated data and the annotation standard aided the evolution of both. For example, Boguraev and Ando presented an extensive analysis of the TimeBank reference corpus in terms of development support of TimeML-compliant analytics, which helped advance the state of the art in temporal annotation. Indeed, iterative application of an annotation standard and examination of the resulting annotated data are critical steps in the MATTER development cycle, used for construction annotation standards [8].

3.2 Rule Based Systems

HeidelTime which is a multilingual, cross-domain temporal tagger initiated at the Database Systems Research Group at Heidelberg University. It extracts temporal expressions from the documents and normalizes them according to the TIMEX3 annotation standards. HeidelTime distinguishes between narrative-style documents and news-style documents (e.g., Wikipedia articles) in all languages. Also in addition, English colloquial (e.g., Tweets and SMS) and scientific articles (e.g., clinical trails) are supported.

MedTime is temporal information extraction system for clinical narratives. It was developed as a part of EVENT/TIMEX3 track of the 2012 i2b2 clinical temporal relations challenge. MedTime uses hybrid system which uses cascaded rule-based and Machine Learning Techniques to extract Event and Time Expressions. It also normalizes extracted Time Expressions. Temporal Tagging was done by incorporating Heideltime temporal tagger. Rule specific to clinical discharge summaries were added to existing rule set.

3.3 Machine Learning systems

Maximum entropy model, unlike HMM, are discriminative model. Given a set of features and training data, the model directly learns the weight for discriminative features for classification. In Maximum entropy models, objective is to maximize the entropy of the data, so as to generalize as much as possible for the training data. ATT System used big windows and rich syntactic and semantic features for the TempEval time expression and event segmentation and classification tasks.

4 Methodology

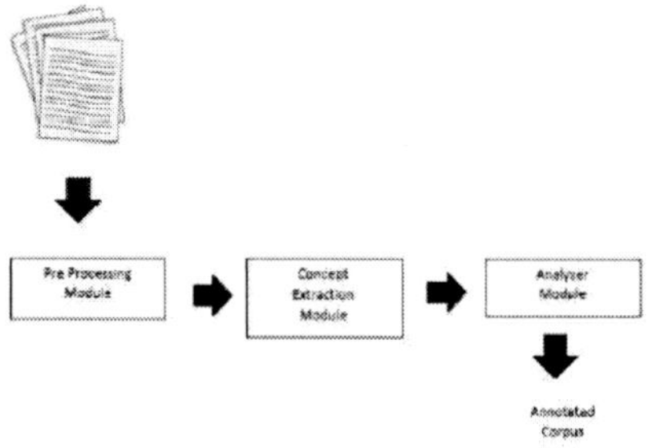

Figure 2: Design Overview

The TIECA system consisted of the main components as depicted in Figure 2, while the processes listed below were carried out to achieve the desired objective.

4.1 Data Cleaning

The data obtained from Mayo Clinic had documents consisting of different types of documents with a variety of encoding. Due to the differences in encoding some of the content could not be processed due to dirty data. As a result the data had to be cleaned initially before subjecting them to use within the research.

Table 1: Corpus Information

	Train	Test
Documents	293	147
EVENTS	38890	20974
TIMEX 3s	3833	2078
TLINKS with TYPE = CONTAINS	11176	6173

A python script was written to filter the clean data within the corpus which would be utilized for the research while the other dirty data were discarded. Finally, the corpus for training consisted of 293 reports for the purpose of training while there were 147 reports for the purposes of testing as shown in Table 1.

4.2 Preprocessing of the Corpus

Most of the time natural language sentences used as inputs for sentiment analysis, likely to contain malformed and incomplete text because of the less restricted, free format nature users were given at the time of generating the content. In order to prepare the data for further process, each sentence has to be normalized using some simple filters. Word boundaries: white space and punctuations are handled such that removing them will not affect the features of sentences, ex: Ph.D., Mr. is kept unchanged. The preprocessing was conducted by a module developed in python using NLTK (Natural Language Tool Kit).

4.3 Concept Extraction

Decomposition of natural language sentences into concepts is a focal task of any information extraction system. This module is responsible for extracting a set of concepts, known as a bag of concepts from sentence given as the input. First the sentence is decomposed into clauses. A general assumption during clause separation is that, if a piece of text contains a preposition or subordinating conjunction, the words preceding these function words are interpreted not as events but as objects. Then each clause is processed to generate verb and noun chunks using shallow parsing or natural language chunking and part-of-speech (POS) tagger. Once lexical categories are identified, single word (unigram) and multiword (bigram or trigram) concepts are formulated by checking for pre-defined set.

4.4 Analyzer Module for Time

The time module will be split into two components which focus on rule based and machine learning approaches. The rule based approach was developed using General Architecture for Text Engineering (GATE), where different rules were developed for identifying words relevant to each class within TS and capturing the TA after making the prior classification. A pipeline needs to be built for the tasks of TS and TA using SVM classifier for the machine learning approach with parameters being set manually via grid search for the machine learning approach. Separate classifiers needs to be built for each of the Time Attribute type using simple lexical features. The lexical features considered within this context are the token itself in full and without its ending (2 characters), part of speech tag, numeric type, capital type, lower case, surrounding tokens and gazetteer information based partly on an adapted version of Heidel Time.

Each token will be classified as either B (Begin), I (Inside), O (Out) using BIO chunking mechanism. For identifying TA values a slightly different context window size and information pertaining to the gazetteer need to be employed.

4.5 Analyzer Module for Event

Event module will utilize a SVM based approach for the purposes of identifying spanning events along with discovering the attributes of the components. From the comprehensive literature review it had been made clear that this produces comparatively better results in comparison to other proven techniques available.

SVM are supervised learning models with associated learning algorithms that analyze data and recognize patterns, used for classification and regression analysis. Given a set of training input bag-of-concepts, each marked as belonging to one of two polarity categories, an SVM training algorithm builds a model that assigns test bag-of- concepts into one category, making it a non-probabilistic binary linear classifier. An SVM model is a representation of the examples as points in space, mapped so that the examples of the separate categories are divided by a clear gap that is as wide as possible. New bag-of-concept examples are then mapped into that same space and predicted to belong to a polarity category based on which side of the gap they fall on.

4.6 Analyzer Module for Relations

The relation classification endeavor consisted of two sub components namely, DR and narrative CR. Previous phases involved identifying the event mentioned in the document and the associated time frames along with the document time, which needs to be used as the basis of input in determining the relationship between the components.

Token level features needs to be used for each of the sentences found within the provided text corpus. From the output which will be thus obtained will undergo an extraction procedure in terms of the following features: binary feature (which indicated if the token position in terms of if it is the first token in the provided sentence), the token lemma and the normalization forms, its associated type of token (word / punctuation / symbol / number / contraction) and whether if it was tagged as any of the semantic types which have been already identified (medical , procedure, anatomical site, sign/symptom, disease / disorder and concept). Another feature indicating whether the token was part of an event mention, a time mention or none of those, will be extracted from the initial predictions (phase 1) or the gold annotation (phase 2).

A CRF tool (CRF++) will be used for the DR identification using the aforementioned features along with a window of +5 or -5 tokens for each feature as contextual feature. For the CR identification an integrated approach incorporating both rule based and machine learning techniques is considered as a possible potential solution. The search space for the provided scenarios will be limited to three event or time mentions in the ascending sequential order from the text to classify CR between the identified two mentions. CRF++ can be used for the machine learning part with the same token features as identified for DR. If the two adjacent mentions were located in separate sentences those type of sentences will be merged together to form one sentence.

For the rule based section GATE or Moonstone could be utilized. Moonstone can be placed in the pipeline along with the before identified predictions for the purpose of recognizing potential instances of the contains relation, using the below two rules:

1. *If a DATE annotation initiates a sentence, and an EVENT annotation occurs anywhere in the following three sentences, with no intervening DATE mention, then infer a CR between the two.*

2. *If two EVENT annotations appear within a sentence, and one appears commonly as the first argument in the training annotations denoting the contains relation, and the second commonly appears as the second contains argument in the training annotations, then infer a CR between the two.*

In the final stage both machine learning and rule based techniques needs to be integrated after three runs. The first run (V1) will be entirely based on the Machine Learning solution. In the second run (V2) the mentions extracted from the rule based system will be added along with V1 search space. In the third run (V3), initially start with the mentions from the rule based system and add random pairs from the first run maintaining the constraint that maximum 3 nearest mentions are included along with the rule based feature.

5 Experiments

For the purpose of the research all the data belonging to the above three different types were analyzed together in the training and evaluation phase due to the fact that the time related information(words) with respect to the six classes are used in a similar format as a result of the English grammar and sentence structure. As a result there was no need to consider them separately for the purpose of the research.

5.1 Rule Based

The rules of the system were derived following the principles mentioned in Heidel Time [9] by developing individual rules for the sub tasks and afterwards combining them to obtain the a collaborative procedure. For each sub-task there were instances when more than one rule was required for the purpose of identifying the relevant detail for the extraction of the words.

Initially two different corpuses were formulated in GATE namely, training and testing corpus. After creating empty corpus and naming it as the training corpus the 293 documents were added to it for the purpose of running the tests on the training data, a similar procedure was done for the testing data set as well. When the rule based system was developed to extract the time related information for the six different classes there were scenarios in which more than one rule was required for the purpose identifying the appropriate class and attribute of the identified element. The variations in linguistics nature of English language and its different forms of applications in general scenarios require different rules to be utilized for certain types of classes.

The rules were written in JAPE format, where there were individual files consisting of rules to identify the elements belonging to each of the relevant class. There were rules written in GROOVY to identify the attributes of the identified elements in terms of their values.

Table 2: Performance results of rule based approach

	Precision	Recall	F1-Score
Span	0.752	0.675	0.711
Class	0.741	0.662	0.699

The scores obtained for each is as shown in Table 2 in terms of precision, recall and f1-score. From the table it was evident that the rule based system performed well in identifying the span of the temporal words comparatively more than that of identifying the appropriate class of the identified elements. The training data was analyzed in many ways and different types of rules were developed but after a certain degree the rules proved to be inappropriate for the testing set, as a result they were discarded.

5.2 Machine Learning

The features and their relative values were extracted with the aid of Natural Language Tool Kit (NLTK) and Pandas libraries. After identifying the features and extracting them, the features were ranked by its relative significance for the purposes of TIECA research. The feature selection was conducted using Waikato Environment for Knowledge Analysis (WEKA).

In the context of machine learning there are scenarios where certain features act as noise or there may be presence of redundant features which hinder the performance of the entire system as a whole. The reason is that the complexity within the system increases when there are a lot of features which the system uses to identify the temporal information as a result run time tends to increase with not much significant improvement in productivity.

The selected features out of the identified features were namely, the token itself, capital type (e.g. all in upper case, mixed case, lower case), stripped token (the two last characters, e.g. decades - decad), POS tag, numeric type (e.g. digit, alphanumeric), surrounding tokens (from 5 to 2 preceding and subsequent tokens, but never more than 5 and never less than 2.) and time-specific gazeteer which was used as a feature (whether or not the token was in the gazeteer).

Table 3: Performance results of machine learning approach

	Precision	Recall	F1-Score
Span	0.752	0.675	0.711
Class	0.741	0.662	0.699

The machine learning solution performed comparatively better than the rule based system and produced a much better result in terms of precision, recall and f1-score as depicted in Table 3. When more features were incorporated into the machine learning based solution it produced better results for training but the relative performance on the testing set began to drop due to overfitting.

6 Discussion

The machine learning solution produced scores in terms of the identified surpassing similar systems. The rule based approach developed using GATE had a low scores compared to that of the machine learning approach. In order to understand why the TIECA system achieved comparatively low Precision with the Clinical TempEval results, an extensive analysis was performed on the manually annotated time expressions provided for that task.

6.1 Analysis of Span and Class

Table 4: Timex class and span inconsistencies

Kind of Expressions	Annotation Agreements	Annotation Disagreements	Found Expressions
Periods of the day	38	51	107
Temporal granularity as frequency	11	44	80
Explicit times	18	26	445
DATE modified to DURATION	35	60	95
DURATION from explicit DATEs	11	8	19
TOTAL	113	189	746

When comparing the guidelines against the manually annotated corpus some inconsistencies can be observed concerning the span and the class feature of a timex. A degree of error can be expected to be seen in any manually annotated corpus; however, similar divergences could be found to be occurring repeatedly. Table 4 summarizes all the expression types which were analyzed, detailing the number of annotation agreements and disagreements, as well as the total number of expressions found in the corpus.

Explicit times of the day should be annotated as a timex of class TIME (TimeML guideline). This should be the case even if such expressions appear isolated in the text (e.g., 1:33 pm) or within a more complex expression together with a date (e.g., 04-Oct-2010 09:44). Less than 10% of the expressions denoting time were manually annotated. Of these, almost 60% represent annotation disagreements as a timex of class DATE instead of TIME.

THYME Guidelines state that words like since, during and until preceding a timex of class DATE should modify the timex class to DURATION. However, in almost 65% of such modified timexes, we found that this rule was not followed, and that the timex was presented as a DATE.

Additionally, in the same section, one can find that two dates can be used to construct a DURATION timex (e.g., December 2009 through March 2010). However, because each one represents a single point in time, they should both be separately annotated as DATE rather than DURATION.

6.2 Non Markable Expressions

Table 5: Non-markable time expressions

Expressions	Annotation Disagreements	Found Expressions
Words "Date/Time"	63	359
Non-quantifiable durations	43	185
Prepositions as triggers	130	1248
TOTAL	**236**	**1792**

The guidelines are clear about a diverse set of non-markable expressions. The TIDES Guidelines have a specific section to describe what should not be annotated as a timex, including prepositions and subordinating conjunctions, specific duration and frequency expressions, and proper names. Table 5 lists time expressions found in the provided corpus that are non-markable expressions according to the guidelines.

There is no reference in the guidelines to annotating the words Date and Time as a timex when they are not part of a more complex expression, as such isolated words cannot be normalized. In expressions like Date/Time=Mar 3, 2010, it is expected that Mar 3, 2010 should be annotated as a DATE, but not the words Date and Time as time expressions of class DATE and TIME respectively. We found 359 occurrences of such words in 217 different documents, from which 63 of them were incorrectly annotated as DATE and TIME (17.5%).

Non-quantifiable durations are not markable, as they refer to some vague duration (interval) of time, including expressions like duration, for a long time, some time, and an appropriate amount of time. On the other hand, temporal expressions denoting imprecise amount of time should be annotated as a timex (e.g., many days, few hours). We found 185 non-quantifiable duration expressions, from which 43 were incorrectly annotated as a timex with class DURATION (almost 25% of disagreement).

Prepositions which introduce noun phrases are never triggers for time expressions and they can never appear as the syntactic head of an annotated expression. In around 10% of those kind of expressions found in the corpus, time expressions were incorrectly annotated including the head preposition (in, on, at, during, after, since, until). Some examples include until July, on Monday, in the last year.

6.3 Frequent Expressions

Table 6: Frequent Expressions

Expressions	Manually Annotated	Found Expressions
DATE: present reference	372	836
DATE: past reference	52	117
DATE: explicit years	55	91
DURATION: precise and imprecise	22	114
SET: times and frequency	20	1087
SET: frequency	0	216
SETs: 999 /min	114	266
TOTAL	635	2727

We observed that some expressions tend to appear more often than others in the Clinical TempEval datasets. Most of these are a timex of class SET. A SET is defined (section 4.2.6 of THYME Guidelines) as an expression which comprises a quantifier (optional) and an interval to represent a frequency (mandatory). Three times weekly, monthly and 1/day are considered as a SET, but not twice which is considered as a QUANTIFIER. We selected a set of the most significant expressions, in terms of the number of occurrences, in order to compare the number of manually annotated expressions against the number of expressions which we found within the text.

Table 6 shows how many times each expression was manually annotated and how many times we found it within the corpus (number of found occurrences). Considering all of the selected expressions for this analysis, only 23.3% of such expressions were manually annotated. Considering only SET expressions, the percentage of manually annotated expression is even lower (8.5%).

Annotation guidelines should clearly state the full set of rules defining what should or should not be annotated, and how. For THYME, the annotators had to piece together several guidelines to figure out what to annotate. This is a potential source of error. Training in the use of multiple sets of guidelines could be considered as an alternative.

In creating the THYME gold standard, multiple annotators and an adjudication process were used. A potential source of error with this approach is that where all annotators have a low recall and adjudication focuses only on resolving disputes, the resulting recall can be no greater than the union of the two. This casts doubt on the veracity of inter-annotator agreement as an indicator of the accuracy of annotation of a corpus.

This last point raises the potential merit of using a high recall rule-based system to prepare a corpus, creating annotations for review by human annotators. Some constructs and guidelines can be represented by simple, unambiguous rules, and where this is the case, the rules will most likely outperform the human annotator in terms of recall. We feel that in such high recall cases, the disadvantage of the approach, that there tends to be a poor correction of missing spans, would be outweighed by the increased number of annotations found.

6.4   Quantifiers

A special type of timex of class QUANTIFIER was introduced in the THYME Annotation Guidelines. These are used to identify expressions such as twice, four times, and three incidents which represent the number of occurrences of an EVENT. However, the THYME Guidelines do not make it clear whether or not the words that identify the event itself should be part of the timex span.

In order to understand the way in which QUANTIFIERs and associated EVENTs should be annotated, we examined their occurrence in the Clinical TempEval corpus. We listed all non-numerical words that we found either (a) annotated as part of the QUANTIFIER span or (b) immediately after the QUANTI-FIER span. Our reasoning was that these represented the repeated EVENT.

We compared the number of manually annotated QUANTIFIERs associated with these EVENTs in the reference corpus, with the number of all QUANTIFIERs that we could find, where they were related to the same kind of EVENT. For example, if the reference corpus included a QUANTIFIER annotation for twice in the expression twice before colonoscopy, then we looked for all occurrences of QUANTIFIER expressions associated with colonoscopy. Only 11.6% of the QUANTIFIERs that we found were manually annotated in reference the corpus. A questionnaire was distributed among 20 participants which provided results that helped us to further validate the findings which we were able to conclude.

7 Conclusion

Present day, Web 2.0 and other online textual records offers a great means to share knowledge, which may be useful to various kinds of people with the constraint of temporal validity. Most of the existing approaches have been unable to provide a wholistic solution for this concern. TIECA focuses on providing solution for the problem of temporal information extraction within the medical domain, since it is the area in which temporality of data is vital for life critical scenarios.

This research proposed a novel approach that encompasses a rule based and machine learning approach to solve the problem of temporal information extraction primarily within the medical domain. One of the major contributions of this research is the rules used within the system and the classification methodology used to identify the temporal words along with their attribute.

It was observed that the proposed TIECA methodology was always few steps ahead of the benchmarked systems on all the experimentations. Very promising results in terms of precision, recall and F1-score are visible with the system developed through this research. Successful results were achieved in the latter stages of the research due to fine tuning the system without overfitting to the training data. This experiment shows well ahead results, proving that the proposed method is very adequate for the context of the medical domain.

The task of adapting annotation of temporal semantics to clinical notes is a challenging and significant task. Within this research a detailed results of a principled analysis of expert manual annotations of temporal expressions in the THYME schema over a corpus of clinical notes. In multiple categories discrepancies between annotations and the guidelines were found. The spans or temporal expressions were in some instances incorrect. Ambiguities remained regarding the correct identification of the Timex class, as also happened in TimeML. Wording in the guidelines was sometimes misinterpreted leading to non markable timexes being annotated. TimeML confusion appeared around the annotation of complex. SET type timexes and their quantifiers. This data driven analysis and its findings should help to guide future temporal annotation efforts in the clinical domain.

8 Future Works

Construction of multilingual temporal information extraction with the aid of appropriate lexical resources as well as taggers and parsers (i.e., POS taggers). The research was conducted taking into consideration a medical domain, in the future branching this work to other domains as well which rely on temporal validity. Enforcing a text quality filter for the purpose of filtering incomplete and misspelled words.

Acknowledgements

The authors would like to thank Mayo Clinic and the 2016 Clinical TempEval challenge organizers for granting access to the clinical corpus. In addition special thanks will go to Dr. Saatviga Sudhar and Dr. Dinusha Ushanth for their continuous support in assisting me to resolve the ambiguities and issues that were encountered in the path of finishing this research.

References

Caselli T. 2009. *Time, Events and Temporal Relations: an Emphirical Model for Temporal Processing of Italian Texts*, Ph. D. thesis. University of Pisa, Pisa, Italy.

Bartak, R., R. Morris, and K. Venable. 2013. *An Introduction to Constraint-Based Temporal Reasoning*, Synthesis Lectures on Artificial Intelligence and Machine Learning. Morgan & Claypool.

Naushad UzZaman, Hector Llorens, Leon Derczynski, James Allen, Marc Verhagen, and James Pustejovsky. 2013. Atlanta, Georgia, USA, June.

J. R. Hobbs and F. Pan. "An ontology of time for the semantic web. 2004. Alternation. *ACM Transactions on Asian Language Information Processing (TALIP)*, pages 66-85.

Hsinchun Chen Yu-Kai Lin and Randall A Brown. 2013. *Medtime: A temporal information extraction system for clinical narratives*. Journal of biomedical informatics, pages 20-28,

Sentiment Analysis of Tweets in Three Indian Languages

Shanta Phani
Information Technology
IIEST, Shibpur
Howrah 711103, West Bengal, India
shantaphani@gmail.com

Shibamouli Lahiri
Computer Science and Engineering
University of Michigan
Ann Arbor, MI 48109
lahiri@umich.edu

Arindam Biswas
Information Technology
IIEST, Shibpur
Howrah 711103, West Bengal, India
abiswas@it.becs.ac.in

Abstract

In this paper, we describe the results of sentiment analysis on tweets in three Indian languages –
Bengali, Hindi, and Tamil. We used the recently released SAIL dataset (Patra et al., 2015), and
obtained state-of-the-art results in all three languages. Our features are simple, robust, scalable,
and language-independent. Further, we show that these simple features provide better results
than more complex and language-specific features, in two separate classification tasks. Detailed
feature analysis and error analysis have been reported, along with learning curves for Hindi and
Bengali.

1 Introduction

Sentiment Analysis (also known as *Opinion Mining*) refers to the problem of identifying the dominant
sentiment in a given piece of text. The sentiment is usually modeled as a categorical variable with three
values: positive, negative, and neutral. With the proliferation of social media data such as blogs, news
articles and comments on them, YouTube comments, Amazon product reviews and Yelp reviews, online
forum discussions, tweets, Facebook posts, and emails, we face an ever-increasing need to process this
information and distill the evaluative sentiment present in these pieces of text, so that we can better
identify and analyze the minds of the people – usually in order to make better policy decisions, be it in
business or government.

Sentiment Analysis in Twitter data is relatively recent (we discuss relevant related work in Section
2), and sentiment analysis of tweets in Indian languages is more recent still. It was only last year, for
example, that a sizable corpus of sentiment-annotated tweets was released as part of the SAIL task (Patra
et al., 2015) in three different Indian languages – Bengali, Hindi, and Tamil.

In this paper, we have two goals:

1. Can we beat the performance of the systems that participated in the SAIL task?

2. Can we do so using a set of features that are simple, robust, scalable, and language-independent?

Note that language-independence is critical for Indian languages, because India has hundreds of languages,[1] and most of them are resource-poor.[2] Robustness and Scalability, on the other hand, are necessary to combat the exponential increase in content in Indian languages. At this point, it is useful to
point out that the dominant categories of features used so far in sentiment analysis of Indian languages
fail in at least one of the four criteria (Table 1). Syntax does not scale because we still do not have
dependency parsers for Indian languages. WordNet is not robust (and does not scale) because it needs
continuous improvement, hand-curation, regular maintenance, and management. Besides, its coverage is
small. In this paper, we design a set of features that meet all four criteria, and still achieve state-of-the-art
performance.

---

[1]https://en.wikipedia.org/wiki/Languages_of_India

[2]With more data, we can use deep learning for sentiment analysis (Zhang et al., 2015) for Indian languages, but we are not
quite there yet. Indian languages still do not have sufficient annotated data for training convolutional neural networks.

Proceedings of the 6th Workshop on South and Southeast Asian Natural Language Processing,
pages 93–102, Osaka, Japan, December 11-17 2016.

	Simplicity	Robustness	Scalability	Language-independence
Syntax	FAIL	SO-SO	FAIL	FAIL
WordNet	OK	FAIL	FAIL	FAIL
N-grams	OK	OK	OK	OK
Surface	OK	OK	OK	OK

Table 1: Features used in sentiment analysis of Indian languages. First two rows are used in existing research, whereas we focus on the last two rows. WordNet refers esp. to SentiWordNet (Baccianella et al., 2010; Das and Bandyopadhyay, 2010).

The rest of this paper is organized as follows. We discuss relevant literature in Section 2. Section 3 gives details on the SAIL task, especially the data, task description, and our adaptation of it. We also describe our features, classifiers, and experimental methodology in this section. Section 4 provides experimental evaluation, along with feature ranking, error analysis, learning curves, and important insights. We conclude in Section 5, outlining our contributions, limitations, and directions for future research. Relevant terminology is introduced as and when they first appear in the paper.

2   Related Work

The overall task of sentiment analysis has been described in the books by Liu (2015), and Pang and Lee (2008). Essentially, the task is modeled as a three-way classification where a piece of text must be given one of the labels – positive, negative, or neutral. Sometimes the task is formulated as a regression problem, where a continuous output is desired. More details can be found in the surveys by Feldman (2013), and Montoyo et al. (2012).

The task of Twitter Sentiment Analysis is relatively recent. One of the first studies (Go et al., 2009) looked into this problem as a *query-driven classification* task. Using emoticons as (noisy) labels, authors achieved an accuracy above 80%. Subsequently, Pak and Paroubek (2010) created a corpus of 300,000 tweets (balanced between positive, negative and neutral classes) by querying happy and sad emoticons, and newswire tweets. The authors analyzed the relationship between POS tags and sentiment label of a tweet. A classification framework was then designed to investigate the relationships between training set size and test F-score, accuracy and negation words, accuracy and n-gram size, and salience vs. entropy.

Kouloumpis et al. (2011) showed that part-of-speech features are not very useful for Twitter sentiment analysis, whereas Agarwal et al. (2011) reported that POS-specific prior polarity features and tree kernels result in a 4% increase in accuracy over state-of-the-art. Zhang et al. (2011) performed Twitter sentiment analysis at the *entity level*, and Wang et al. (2012) reported a real-time system for Twitter sentiment analysis of US Presidential elections.

A. R. et al. (2012) reported the first study in cross-lingual sentiment analysis for Indian languages, where they showed that using WordNet senses as features can successfully bridge the language gap, achieving an accuracy improvement of 14%-15% over an approach that uses a bilingual dictionary. Sharma et al. (2014) reported a survey of sentiment analysis in Hindi, and Pandey and Govilkar (2015) proposed a system for sentiment analysis of Hindi movie reviews using Hindi SentiWordNet. Patra et al. (2015) reported the SAIL task, and the data released as part of it. Six teams submitted their systems. One of the best-performing systems is reported in (Kumar et al., 2015) that used distributional thesauri and sentence-level co-occurrences to expand Indian sentiment lexicons. They achieved an accuracy of 43.2% and 49.68% for the constrained submissions for Bengali and Hindi, respectively. A second system, reported in (Sarkar and Chakraborty, 2015) achieved constrained accuracy of 41.2% and 50.75% for Bengali and Hindi, respectively, using Multinomial Naive Bayes classifier. Finally, Akhtar et al. (2016) created an annotated dataset for aspect-based sentiment analysis in Hindi, consisting of Hindi product reviews crawled from multiple websites. The authors obtained an average F-score of 41.07% for aspect term extraction, and an accuracy of 54.05% for sentiment classification.

	Training data			Development data		
	Positive	Negative	Neutral	Positive	Negative	Neutral
Bengali	277	354	368	24	29	0
Hindi	168	559	495	18	19	19
Tamil	387	316	400	–	–	–

Table 2: Statistics of the SAIL dataset that we used. Each number represents the number of tweets in the corresponding category. Note that the values reported here may slightly differ from those reported in (Patra et al., 2015), because some tweets have been deleted by their authors.

3   Task Description

The SAIL task (Patra et al., 2015) released a set of sentiment-annotated tweets in three languages – Hindi, Bengali, and Tamil. The statistics are shown in Table 2. Each tweet was human-annotated as positive, negative, or neutral. Training data was released for all three languages, whereas development data was available for only two languages – Hindi and Bengali. We did not have access to the test data for any of the languages, so we performed our experiments only on training and development data.

The SAIL task defined two types of submission – *constrained* and *unconstrained*. In the constrained submission, participants were only allowed to use the corpora released as part of the task, and the Indian SentiWordNet from Das and Bandyopadhyay (2010). In the unconstrained submission, participants were additionally allowed to use any external resources such as POS-taggers, named entity recognizers, parsers, and additional data. Participants were requested to report the external resources they used.

At the end of the task, it was observed that constrained systems performed better than unconstrained ones (please see Table 3 of (Patra et al., 2015)). We therefore chose to work with the constrained version of the task. We ran two types of classification experiments: (1) **2-class classification:** positive and negative tweets only; (2) **3-class classification:** positive, negative, and neutral tweets. As mentioned before, we did not have access to the test data, so we performed stratified 10-fold cross-validation on the training data, chose the best model (features + classifier) from the cross-validation experiments, retrained the model on whole training data, and tested it on the development data. Final accuracy values are thus reported on the development data. Note that Tamil did not have a development dataset, so for Tamil we only report accuracy values from 10-fold cross-validation.

We experimented with four categories of features: (1) **Word n-grams** (n = 1, 2, 3) with and without stop words.[3], (2) **Character n-grams** (n = 1, 2, 3) with and without space characters and punctuation symbols, (3) **Surface features** (described later), and (4) **SentiWordNet features** (Das and Bandyopadhyay, 2010) (described later).

Note that the first three categories of features meet the simplicity, scalability, robustness, and language-independence criteria outlined in Section 1 (Table 1). For the word and character n-gram features, we experimented with three representations: binary (presence/absence), term frequency (tf), and tfidf. For the surface features, we used twelve of them, as follows: (1) Number of words in the tweet, (2) Number of characters in the tweet, (3) Number of hashtags in the tweet, (4) Number of English-character segments in the tweet, (5) Average English segment length in words, (6) Average English segment length in characters, (7) Number of "@" symbols in the tweet, (8) Number of "RT @" symbols in the tweet (*retweets*), (9) Number of "http:/" in the tweet (*hyperlinks*), (10) Number of punctuation characters in the tweet, (11) Number of punctuation characters, without leading and trailing periods, (12) Type-token ratio of the tweet (number of unique words divided by number of words).

Most of the surface features are derived from a manual inspection of the training data. For the SentiWordNet features, we constructed a vocabulary from all unique words given in the SentiWordNet files released by Das and Bandyopadhyay (2010). Then we used the following encoding: Positive word: +5,

---

[3]We used the Bengali and Hindi stop word lists available from http://fire.irsi.res.in/fire/static/resources, and combined them with the stop word lists available from https://github.com/6/stopwords-json. Tamil does not have a stop word list available online, so for Tamil we used all words.

Figure 1: Feature ranking for Bengali, Hindi, and Tamil. Top 20 features are shown in each case.

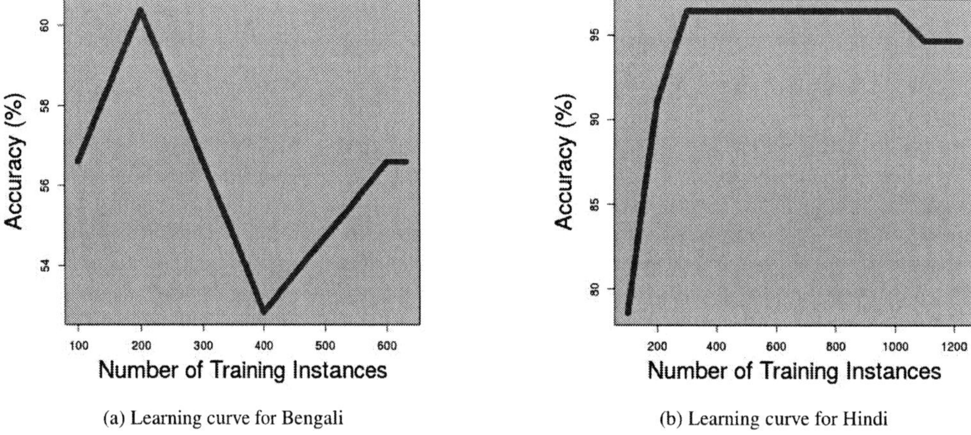

(a) Learning curve for Bengali

(b) Learning curve for Hindi

Figure 2: Learning curves for Bengali and Hindi. Y-axis is the % Accuracy on the **development set**.

Neutral word: +4, Negative word: +3, Ambiguous word: +2, and added up the scores for each unique word. So for example, if the word "ABCD" appears twice as positive and once as neutral, then its score will be $2 \times 5 + 4 = 14$. With these scores as our vocabulary, we experimented with three representations – binary, tf, and tfidf – as features. Note that SentiWordNet does not meet all the criteria outlined in Table 1. However, we still used it to compare other features with SentiWordNet, and see how it performs.

We used six different classifiers from the scikit-learn package (Pedregosa et al., 2011) with default parameter settings: **Multinomial Naive Bayes** (NB), **Logistic Regression** (LR), **Decision Tree** (DT), **Random Forest** (RF), **SVM SVC** (SV), and **SVM Linear SVC** (LS). In the next section, we will see how the combinations of different features and classifiers perform. Classifiers are written as "NB", "LR", etc.

4 Results

We show the results for 2-class classification in Table 3, and the results for 3-class classification in Table 4. Results from term frequency (tf) and tfidf representations have been omitted due to space restrictions;

Feature Representation	Feature Category	Feature Type	NB	LR	DT	RF	SV	LS
Bengali	Surface features		51.66	53.88	48.81	50.87	52.61	49.29
Binary (Presence/Absence)	SentiWordNet		56.1	56.1	56.1	56.1	56.1	56.1
	Word unigrams	AW	67.67	64.03	59.75	59.75	56.1	64.03
		NS	65.61	62.28	56.89	60.22	56.1	62.28
		OS	56.26	56.89	55.94	56.74	56.1	56.89
	Word bigrams	AW	60.86	58.64	55.47	59.27	56.1	57.53
		NS	57.21	58.95	51.51	58.64	56.1	57.69
		OS	56.42	55.78	55.78	55.47	56.1	54.83
	Word trigrams	AW	57.37	59.43	51.19	53.25	56.1	58.95
		NS	56.26	59.43	53.09	53.09	56.1	58.95
		OS	56.1	56.1	55.94	56.1	56.1	56.1
	Character unigrams	AC	55.78	57.05	50.55	56.89	55.63	57.69
		SS	55.78	56.89	49.92	56.58	55.47	57.37
		PP	53.88	56.42	49.6	56.42	56.74	56.58
		SP	53.88	56.58	52.3	54.83	56.74	56.58
	Character bigrams	AC	51.82	53.09	53.88	58.16	56.1	51.66
		SS	51.19	52.93	55.78	56.89	56.1	52.3
		PP	52.46	53.41	54.04	58.8	56.1	54.2
		SP	52.14	54.52	58.8	59.75	56.1	54.68
	Character trigrams	AC	54.04	56.1	53.57	58.16	56.1	53.72
		SS	50.55	52.14	49.45	55.47	56.1	51.98
		PP	52.77	55.47	53.72	60.38	56.1	52.61
		SP	52.3	51.51	54.68	58.32	56.1	50.71
Hindi	Surface features		64.79	75.79	66.99	75.1	78.4	65.75
Binary (Presence/Absence)	SentiWordNet		76.89	76.89	76.89	76.89	76.89	76.89
	Word unigrams	AW	78.68	81.57	76.62	79.92	76.89	80.61
		NS	73.04	80.33	75.93	79.78	76.89	79.78
		OS	73.59	74.97	67.68	76.89	76.89	71.53
	Word bigrams	AW	35.49	78.82	77.17	78.82	76.89	79.23
		NS	29.57	78.95	78.68	78.95	76.89	78.82
		OS	67.26	78.4	58.46	66.99	76.89	68.5
	Word trigrams	AW	28.2	78.68	78.54	78.82	76.89	78.82
		NS	30.4	78.68	78.82	78.82	76.89	78.95
		OS	46.22	78.4	77.44	75.93	76.89	76.48
	Character unigrams	AC	69.74	75.52	68.09	78.27	76.89	74.42
		SS	69.88	75.52	68.5	77.99	76.89	74.42
		PP	69.46	75.93	68.5	78.13	76.89	75.38
		SP	69.46	75.93	67.4	77.99	76.89	75.38
	Character bigrams	AC	75.24	76.48	71.11	78.82	76.89	70.29
		SS	75.1	75.24	69.19	78.13	76.89	71.11
		PP	74.42	77.17	70.84	78.95	76.89	73.18
		SP	74.83	75.93	69.88	78.4	76.89	72.21
	Character trigrams	AC	76.2	74.83	73.45	79.23	76.89	71.25
		SS	76.07	75.38	74.55	79.23	76.89	70.7
		PP	75.93	75.24	71.66	79.37	76.89	70.84
		SP	76.34	75.79	74.0	78.95	76.89	68.5
Tamil	Surface features		53.06	56.47	50.64	54.48	54.34	51.92
Binary (Presence/Absence)	SentiWordNet		55.05	55.05	55.05	55.05	55.05	55.05
	Word unigrams	AW	62.16	60.17	56.76	57.61	55.05	59.46
	Word bigrams	AW	49.36	56.9	56.19	56.76	55.05	55.76
	Word trigrams	AW	44.95	57.04	56.76	56.9	55.05	57.18
	Character unigrams	AC	57.89	58.04	49.22	57.18	57.47	58.46
		SS	57.89	58.04	50.64	57.61	57.61	58.46
		PP	57.04	55.48	50.36	55.76	57.33	56.47
		SP	56.76	55.76	51.64	57.04	57.18	56.61
	Character bigrams	AC	58.32	57.18	53.49	59.89	55.05	52.35
		SS	59.46	57.04	49.93	59.17	55.05	53.63
		PP	55.48	54.62	52.49	59.74	55.05	54.91
		SP	55.76	55.33	53.91	59.89	55.05	55.62
	Character trigrams	AC	56.9	55.05	54.05	60.31	55.05	52.2
		SS	58.32	57.75	55.76	59.89	55.05	56.47
		PP	56.05	53.34	53.77	59.6	55.05	52.06
		SP	56.33	56.05	55.62	57.04	55.05	54.34

Table 3: % accuracy of 2-class classification for three languages on 10-fold cross-validation on the training data. AW = all words, NS = all words except stop words, OS = only stop words. AC = all characters, SS = all characters except space, PP = all characters except punctuation, SP = all characters except space and punctuation. Rightmost six columns are classifiers, as indicated at the end of Section 3.

Feature Representation	Feature Category	Feature Type	NB	LR	DT	RF	SV	LS
Bengali	Surface features		34.43	42.64	34.93	38.14	39.44	36.44
Binary (Presence/Absence)	SentiWordNet		36.84	36.84	36.84	36.84	36.84	36.84
	Word unigrams	AW	47.65	51.25	47.75	48.05	36.84	50.05
		NS	46.95	49.85	44.14	49.35	36.84	50.15
		OS	37.74	39.54	39.84	39.84	37.74	39.24
	Word bigrams	AW	45.45	48.55	44.74	46.05	36.84	48.15
		NS	43.84	47.45	44.04	45.75	36.84	47.55
		OS	36.14	36.04	37.64	38.14	36.84	35.44
	Word trigrams	AW	42.34	46.35	43.84	44.54	36.84	46.35
		NS	42.04	45.95	42.74	44.14	36.84	45.35
		OS	35.44	36.84	36.04	36.04	36.84	36.24
	Character unigrams	AC	39.14	43.34	38.14	45.95	40.24	43.54
		SS	39.24	43.44	38.04	44.84	40.24	43.34
		PP	36.74	41.34	39.54	43.14	40.04	41.54
		SP	36.84	41.14	39.34	43.34	40.04	41.54
	Character bigrams	AC	37.24	39.24	40.04	43.44	36.84	40.54
		SS	38.04	38.74	37.14	44.14	36.84	38.44
		PP	37.24	39.44	39.34	44.14	36.84	39.94
		SP	36.54	39.84	38.84	44.34	36.84	37.44
	Character trigrams	AC	38.24	41.04	39.14	44.44	36.84	40.94
		SS	36.94	39.44	35.74	45.25	36.84	37.04
		PP	36.84	38.34	37.34	47.75	36.84	37.84
		SP	37.64	38.04	41.54	44.94	36.84	36.14
Hindi	Surface features		41.82	48.2	43.86	45.99	46.4	33.47
Binary (Presence/Absence)	SentiWordNet		45.74	45.74	45.74	45.74	45.74	45.74
	Word unigrams	AW	54.83	55.32	49.92	56.38	45.74	56.38
		NS	51.55	54.75	48.85	52.13	45.74	55.48
		OS	46.24	50.25	42.06	47.87	45.66	49.51
	Word bigrams	AW	25.2	52.45	48.28	47.95	45.74	52.86
		NS	21.19	46.07	43.45	47.71	45.74	46.64
		OS	44.68	50.49	46.15	48.12	45.74	47.3
	Word trigrams	AW	19.23	47.05	45.5	45.74	45.74	45.91
		NS	22.75	47.71	43.7	44.27	45.74	44.35
		OS	33.72	47.22	43.7	45.42	45.74	46.15
	Character unigrams	AC	45.25	50.98	42.39	51.31	49.59	50.82
		SS	45.17	50.98	43.13	52.45	49.59	50.82
		PP	45.25	49.26	43.37	50.41	49.75	48.61
		SP	45.01	49.18	41.0	51.47	49.84	48.61
	Character bigrams	AC	46.24	50.08	43.21	52.54	45.74	45.99
		SS	47.71	49.51	43.45	51.72	45.74	46.56
		PP	45.99	50.9	45.66	53.19	45.74	46.15
		SP	46.07	51.39	42.55	52.05	45.74	49.26
	Character trigrams	AC	48.04	47.38	45.17	53.03	45.74	45.5
		SS	47.38	47.05	43.86	52.29	45.74	46.64
		PP	48.2	48.2	42.31	53.11	45.74	45.42
		SP	46.89	49.02	44.84	51.8	45.74	46.15
Tamil	Surface features		39.08	43.52	34.27	37.17	39.17	36.9
Binary (Presence/Absence)	SentiWordNet		36.26	36.26	36.26	36.26	36.26	36.26
	Word unigrams	AW	40.71	39.53	39.26	42.07	36.26	38.8
	Word bigrams	AW	36.08	40.25	38.08	39.26	36.26	40.34
	Word trigrams	AW	30.92	37.99	37.35	37.99	36.26	38.17
	Character unigrams	AC	43.52	40.98	36.08	43.16	43.25	40.71
		SS	43.52	41.07	36.9	44.15	43.34	40.34
		PP	43.25	41.25	39.98	41.07	43.16	40.62
		SP	43.43	41.25	39.44	39.89	43.06	40.34
	Character bigrams	AC	42.25	41.34	39.89	43.61	36.26	37.81
		SS	41.7	41.34	37.81	44.24	36.26	39.44
		PP	39.17	39.08	39.98	42.52	36.26	38.89
		SP	39.44	40.07	37.81	41.61	36.26	40.16
	Character trigrams	AC	39.26	38.8	37.53	43.34	36.26	35.63
		SS	39.89	41.98	37.53	43.16	36.26	39.89
		PP	38.44	39.26	37.99	40.89	36.26	38.53
		SP	38.62	40.98	35.9	41.98	36.26	38.89

Table 4: % accuracy of 3-class classification for three languages on 10-fold cross-validation on the training data. AW = all words, NS = all words except stop words, OS = only stop words. AC = all characters, SS = all characters except space, PP = all characters except punctuation, SP = all characters except space and punctuation. Rightmost six columns are classifiers, as indicated at the end of Section 3.

প্রত্যেককে মৃত্যুর স্বাদ আস্বাদন করতে হবে। আমি তোমাদেরকে মন্দ ও ভাল দ্বারা পরীক্ষা করে থাকি এবং আমারই কাছে... http://t.co/ObQrprZHEr

(a) Bengali Negative example confused as Positive

কয়েকটি ক্ষেত্রে অগ্রগতি হলেও জাতিসংঘের বেঁধে দেয়া উন্নয়ন লক্ষ্যমাত্রা পূরণে দাতাদের কাছ থেকে প্রতিশ্রুত অর্থ... http://t.co/uALjZDzh8H

(b) Bengali Positive example confused as Negative

@SrBachchan जगत है चलायमान, बहती नदी के समान, पार कर जाओ इसे तैरकर, इस पर बना नहीं सकते घर।। ~HRB http://t.co/zvzYWbfyyw

(c) Hindi Neutral example confused as Negative

दीपिका तो लाजबाब

(d) Hindi Positive example confused as Neutral

Figure 3: Error cases for Bengali and Hindi.

however, they are qualitatively similar to the binary feature representation.[4] There are several observations to be made from Tables 3 and 4. The first observation is that overall, Hindi has the highest accuracy values, followed by Tamil, followed by Bengali. This indicates that sentiment classification in Bengali is the most difficult, followed by Tamil and Hindi. Later, we will perform error analysis to see which cases are the most difficult. Note further that we did not have access to a Tamil stop word list, hence the absence of "OS" and "NS" types for Tamil. Another interesting observation is that the accuracy values from 2-class classification are substantially higher – cell for cell – than those from 3-class classification. This shows that the 2-class classification task is substantially easier than the 3-class classification task.

Surface features performed very well in this task, which is a surprising finding. It shows that a handful of manually chosen features can go a long way when the features are inspired by the data. Feature ranking by importance showed that tweet length in words and characters, and the number of punctuation symbols were the most important features in this category. SentiWordNet features performed comparably to surface features; however, their performance was not affected by the classifier used or the feature representation (binary/tf/tfidf). We believe that the reason this happened is because SentiWordNets are highly language-specific, and any feature representation would perform equivalently good (or bad) depending on what language we are dealing with, not what classifiers we have at our disposal.

The best performance numbers came from word and character n-grams, thereby showing beyond doubt that simple, robust, scalable, and language-independent features outperform complex, fragile, cumbersome, and language-dependent features. The best-performing feature-classifier combinations are as follows:[5]

- **Bengali, 2-class:** Word unigrams, no stop words, tfidf, NB classifier (67.83%).
- **Bengali, 3-class:** Word unigrams, all words including stop words, binary, LR classifier (51.25%).
- **Hindi, 2-class:** Word unigrams, all words including stop words, binary, LR classifier (81.57%).
- **Hindi, 3-class:** Word unigrams, all words including stop words, tf, LR classifier (56.96%).
- **Tamil, 2-class:** Word unigrams, all words including stop words, binary, NB classifier (62.16%).
- **Tamil, 3-class:** Character unigrams, all characters, tf, RF classifier (45.24%).

Note that our best 3-class accuracy values are better than the best reported accuracy values in (Patra et al., 2015). We obtained 51.25% for Bengali compared to 43.2%, 56.96% for Hindi compared to 55.67%, and 45.24% for Tamil compared to 39.28% – in the constrained version of the task. With the best combinations, we went ahead and trained them on the *whole* training data, and tested the models on the *development data* made available for Hindi and Bengali. For Hindi, we used the 3-class model because the development data had 3 classes, whereas for Bengali we used the 2-class model, because Bengali development data did not have any samples from the "neutral" class. We obtained 94.64% accuracy on the Hindi development data (which widely beats the 55.67% reported in (Patra et al., 2015)), and 56.6%

[4]All results are available in the supplementary PDF at `http://web.eecs.umich.edu/~lahiri/WSSANLP_supplement.pdf`.

[5]For full results, please see the supplement at `http://web.eecs.umich.edu/~lahiri/WSSANLP_supplement.pdf`.

accuracy on the Bengali development data (which also handily beats the 43.2% reported by Patra et al. (2015)) – showing again the importance of simple, robust, scalable, and language-independent features.

One question that arises at this point, is: *which features are the most important* in these top-performing models? We ranked the features by their importance in the training data, and show them in Figure 1. Note that each ranking has at least one English segment – which shows that English words can be important in discriminating between sentiment classes. Note further that the Bengali words are more abstract, such as "freedom", "people", "wish", and "judges", with only one positive word – "joy" – in the end. Hindi words, on the other hand, are more direct: "auspicious", "development", "God", "help", "apology", "grace", "victory", "change", and "hearty". We believe that the reason this happened is the data collection process. The Bengali tweets that were collected reflect a more *general* view, whereas Hindi tweets reflect a more *personal* view.

Another question that arises, is: *how sensitive is the development accuracy on the size of the training data?* In other words, if we varied the training set size, how would the development accuracy change? To answer this question, we varied the number of training samples for Hindi and Bengali from 100 to the maximum – in steps of 100, trained the best-performing model on this *reduced* training set, and tested the resulting model on the development set. This gave us two *learning curves*, as shown in Figure 2. First, note that the model *overfits* beyond a certain number of training instances, and the development accuracy drops beyond this point. Second, we do not need all training instances to obtain optimal development accuracy. For Bengali, the optimum comes at 200 training instances (60.38% accuracy), whereas for Hindi, the optimum comes at 300 instances (96.43% accuracy).

The last question that we investigated, is: *what are the error cases that our best-performing models did not get right?* Do they have any specific properties that make them hard to classify? To answer this question, we looked into the cases our models misclassified on the *development set* for Hindi and Bengali. Hindi had only three cases misclassified out of 56, and Bengali had 23 cases misclassified out of 53. We show four examples in Figure 3 that have been misclassified with relatively high confidence. Among these cases, Figure 3d is a case where the classifier truly misclassified a positive example as a neutral one. However, Figure 3c's neutral-ness is debatable, because it is describing a somewhat negative and pessimistic aphorism on the transience of life. Similarly, the example shown in Figure 3b is not uniformly positive, because it starts to describe a set of financial impediments to the successful implementation of some of the policy recommendations by the United Nations. Also, Figure 3a's dominant sentiment is negative, but it begins to provide a sense of hope, faith, and enlightenment towards the end. These examples show that although our best classifiers are not perfect, they misclassified examples that are truly *hard* to classify, and in fact may even be hard to classify by a human being.

5   Conclusion

In this paper, we performed tweet sentiment analysis of three Indian languages – Bengali, Hindi, and Tamil. We experimented with a set of simple, robust, scalable, and language-independent features, and showed that they achieve performance superior to the state-of-the-art, and also superior to language-specific features. We performed detailed error analysis, and found out that in most cases, our models were performing well, and they only got confused when the sample was truly confusing – perhaps even to a human being. We performed feature importance ranking to identify words that were relevant to the task of sentiment classification in three different languages, and showed the variations thereof. We also showed how the development accuracy changed in response to the size of the training data. Our limitations include: not having access to the test data, and the stop word list for Tamil. However, our results demonstrably overcame these limitations. Future research should look into collecting more sentiment-annotated tweets to get a better handle on the underlying psychological phenomena of *opinion* and *subjectivity*, and using existing NLP tools in Bengali, Hindi, and Tamil to see how they perform in this very interesting, but also challenging task.

References

Balamurali A. R., Aditya Joshi, and Pushpak Bhattacharyya. 2012. Cross-Lingual Sentiment Analysis for Indian Languages using Linked WordNets. In *Proceedings of COLING 2012: Posters*, pages 73–82, Mumbai, India, December. The COLING 2012 Organizing Committee.

Apoorv Agarwal, Boyi Xie, Ilia Vovsha, Owen Rambow, and Rebecca Passonneau. 2011. Sentiment Analysis of Twitter Data. In *Proceedings of the Workshop on Languages in Social Media*, LSM '11, pages 30–38, Stroudsburg, PA, USA. Association for Computational Linguistics.

Md Shad Akhtar, Asif Ekbal, and Pushpak Bhattacharyya. 2016. Aspect based Sentiment Analysis in Hindi: Resource Creation and Evaluation. In Nicoletta Calzolari (Conference Chair), Khalid Choukri, Thierry Declerck, Sara Goggi, Marko Grobelnik, Bente Maegaard, Joseph Mariani, Helene Mazo, Asuncion Moreno, Jan Odijk, and Stelios Piperidis, editors, *Proceedings of the Tenth International Conference on Language Resources and Evaluation (LREC 2016)*, Paris, France, may. European Language Resources Association (ELRA).

Stefano Baccianella, Andrea Esuli, and Fabrizio Sebastiani. 2010. SentiWordNet 3.0: An Enhanced Lexical Resource for Sentiment Analysis and Opinion Mining. In Nicoletta Calzolari (Conference Chair), Khalid Choukri, Bente Maegaard, Joseph Mariani, Jan Odijk, Stelios Piperidis, Mike Rosner, and Daniel Tapias, editors, *Proceedings of the Seventh conference on International Language Resources and Evaluation (LREC'10)*, Valletta, Malta, may. European Language Resources Association (ELRA).

Amitava Das and Sivaji Bandyopadhyay. 2010. SentiWordNet for Indian Languages. In *Proceedings of the Eighth Workshop on Asian Language Resouces*, pages 56–63, Beijing, China, August. Coling 2010 Organizing Committee.

Ronen Feldman. 2013. Techniques and Applications for Sentiment Analysis. *Commun. ACM*, 56(4):82–89, April.

Alec Go, Richa Bhayani, and Lei Huang. 2009. Twitter Sentiment Classification using Distant Supervision. Technical report, Stanford University.

Efthymios Kouloumpis, Theresa Wilson, and Johanna Moore. 2011. Twitter Sentiment Analysis: The Good the Bad and the OMG!

Ayush Kumar, Sarah Kohail, Asif Ekbal, and Chris Biemann. 2015. IIT-TUDA: System for Sentiment Analysis in Indian Languages using Lexical Acquisition. In *Proceedings of the Third International Conference on Mining Intelligence and Knowledge Exploration - Volume 9468*, MIKE 2015, pages 684–693, New York, NY, USA. Springer-Verlag New York, Inc.

Bing Liu. 2015. *Sentiment Analysis: Mining Opinions, Sentiments, and Emotions*. Cambridge University Press.

Andrés Montoyo, Patricio Martínez-Barco, and Alexandra Balahur. 2012. Subjectivity and sentiment analysis: An overview of the current state of the area and envisaged developments. *Decision Support Systems*, 53(4):675 – 679. 1) Computational Approaches to Subjectivity and Sentiment Analysis 2) Service Science in Information Systems Research : Special Issue on {PACIS} 2010.

Alexander Pak and Patrick Paroubek. 2010. Twitter as a Corpus for Sentiment Analysis and Opinion Mining. In Nicoletta Calzolari (Conference Chair), Khalid Choukri, Bente Maegaard, Joseph Mariani, Jan Odijk, Stelios Piperidis, Mike Rosner, and Daniel Tapias, editors, *Proceedings of the Seventh conference on International Language Resources and Evaluation (LREC'10)*, Valletta, Malta, may. European Language Resources Association (ELRA).

Pooja Pandey and Sharvari Govilkar. 2015. A Framework for Sentiment Analysis in Hindi using HSWN. *International Journal of Computer Applications*, 119(19):23–26, June.

Bo Pang and Lillian Lee. 2008. Opinion mining and sentiment analysis. *Foundations and Trends in Information Retrieval*, 2(1-2):1–135, January.

Braja Gopal Patra, Dipankar Das, Amitava Das, and Rajendra Prasath, 2015. *Shared Task on Sentiment Analysis in Indian Languages (SAIL) Tweets - An Overview*, pages 650–655. Springer International Publishing, Cham.

Fabian Pedregosa, Gaël Varoquaux, Alexandre Gramfort, Vincent Michel, Bertrand Thirion, Olivier Grisel, Mathieu Blondel, Peter Prettenhofer, Ron Weiss, Vincent Dubourg, Jake Vanderplas, Alexandre Passos, David Cournapeau, Matthieu Brucher, Matthieu Perrot, and Édouard Duchesnay. 2011. Scikit-learn: Machine Learning in Python. *Journal of Machine Learning Research*, 12:2825–2830.

Kamal Sarkar and Saikat Chakraborty, 2015. *A Sentiment Analysis System for Indian Language Tweets*, pages 694–702. Springer International Publishing, Cham.

Richa Sharma, Shweta Nigam, and Rekha Jain. 2014. Opinion Mining In Hindi Language: A Survey. *CoRR*, abs/1404.4935.

Hao Wang, Dogan Can, Abe Kazemzadeh, François Bar, and Shrikanth Narayanan. 2012. A System for Real-time Twitter Sentiment Analysis of 2012 U.S. Presidential Election Cycle. In *Proceedings of the ACL 2012 System Demonstrations*, pages 115–120, Jeju Island, Korea, July. Association for Computational Linguistics.

Lei Zhang, Riddhiman Ghosh, Mohamed Dekhil, Meichun Hsu, and Bing Liu, 2011. *Combining Lexicon-based and Learning-based Methods for Twitter Sentiment Analysis*. 89 edition, June.

Xiang Zhang, Junbo Zhao, and Yann LeCun. 2015. Character-level Convolutional Networks for Text Classification. In C. Cortes, N. D. Lawrence, D. D. Lee, M. Sugiyama, and R. Garnett, editors, *Advances in Neural Information Processing Systems 28*, pages 649–657. Curran Associates, Inc.

Dealing with Linguistic Divergences in English-Bhojpuri Machine Translation

Pitambar Behera[*], Neha Maurya[1] & Vandana Pandey[2]

[*]Centre for Linguistics & [12]Dept. of Linguistics

[*]Jawaharlal Nehru University & [12]Banaras Hindu University

New Delhi, Banaras India

[pitambarbehera2, neha.mourya8, vandanapandey732]@gmail.com

Abstract

In Machine Translation, divergence is one of the major barriers which plays a deciding role in determining the efficiency of the system at hand. Translation divergences originate when there is structural discrepancies between the input and the output languages. It can be of various types based on the issues we are addressing to such as linguistic, cultural, communicative and so on. Owing to the fact that two languages owe their origin to different language families, linguistic divergences emerge. The present study attempts at categorizing different types of linguistic divergences: the lexical-semantic and syntactic. In addition, it also helps identify and resolve the divergent linguistic features between English as source language and Bhojpuri as target language pair. Dorr's theoretical framework (1994, 1994a) has been followed in the classification and resolution procedure. Furthermore, so far as the methodology is concerned, we have adhered to the Dorr's Lexical Conceptual Structure for the resolution of divergences. This research will prove to be beneficial for developing efficient MT systems if the mentioned factors are incorporated considering the inherent structural constraints between source and target languages.

1 Overview

The terminology 'divergence' refers to the concept of structural or 'parametric variation' between a source language (SL) and a target language (TL) pair in Machine Translation (MT). In other words, it emerges when the decoded output content lacks 'well-formedness' because of the inherent linguistic constraints. According to Dorr (1993), "translation divergence arises when the natural translation of one language into another results in a very different form than that of the original." Therefore, it is pertinent for the identification of divergences as it facilitates and builds a blueprint towards the architectural design and implementation of MT platforms (Parameswari, 2015). So far, the availability of literature in divergence is meagre with regard to the less-resourced languages like Bhojpuri. In English-Indian languages, research on divergence has been conducted in around 9 languages: Sanskrit (Shukla et al., 2010), Hindi (Gupta & Chatterjee, 2003; Sinha & Thakur, 2005; Sinha & Thakur, 2005a), Urdu (Saboor & Khan, 2010; Muzaffar et al., 2016), Marathi (Dave et al., 2001; Kulkarni et al., 2013), Punjabi (Bhalla, 2014), Bengali (Das, 2013), Hindi-Nepali (Manger, 2014), Telugu (Ithagni, 2014), & Sindhi (Nainwani, 2015).

Dorr (1993) has classified various divergences broadly into two primary categories: syntactic and lexical-semantic. Dorr's classification of divergences is based on the Government and Binding framework as proposed and explained by (Chomsky, 1981; Jackendoff, 1990) of linguistic theory which attempts at capturing surface structure variations by deep structure. The deep structure provides a background as the universal structure which may possibly be applicable to all languages. Therefore, it can however be posited that both the classification and resolution of translation divergences are explained from the perspective of the universal grammar formalism.

1.1. The Areal Features of English and Bhojpuri

Bhojpuri belongs to the Indo-Aryan or Indian language family whereas English owes its origin to the Germanic family. There are a lot of incompatible, divergent and linguistically-grounded features pertaining to morphology, syntax and semantics (Muzaffar et al., 2016) between English and Bhojpuri.

Proceedings of the 6th Workshop on South and Southeast Asian Natural Language Processing,
pages 103–113, Osaka, Japan, December 11-17 2016.

Like most of the Indo-Aryan languages, Bhojpuri (Ojha et al., 2015; Singh, 2014; Singh, 2015; Singh, 2015a) is also a morphologically rich and non-configurational language, unlike English. In addition, English applies expletives, existential subjects and no verbal honorific agreement. Besides, Bhojpuri as a South Asian language has some atypical constructions: complex predicates, serial verb constructions, non-nominative subjects, conjunctive participle and so on (Subbārāo, 2008 & 2012).

2 Dorr's LCS for Dealing with Divergences

The Lexical Conceptual Structure (LCS)[2] is the semantic representation of predicate argument structures through decomposition of their features.

Give: [CAUSE (x, [GO (y, [TO (z)])])]

In the theoretical specification demonstrated above, the verb 'give' can be decomposed as having three predicates viz. CAUSE, GO, and TO, as per the intuition that a sentence i.e. 'Rohit gave Sita a pencil' means that Rohit (which equals to x) caused the pencil (=y) to go to Sita (=z). In other words, agent is Rohit, patient is the pencil and the beneficiary is Sita. Hence, the LCS theoretical specification can be fit into any natural language having this type of structural specifications. As a result, it becomes language independent in nature and the issue of divergences can be addressed applying this concept. Divergences can be approached from two points of views: syntax (the syntactic structure) and semantics (lexical semantics).

2.1 The Syntactic Structure

Constituents in the sentence are grouped on the basis of their relevance and position in the hierarchy. The convention applied in the bracketing is based partially on the Government and Binding theory with some modifications in notation for simplification of the concepts.

- CP: it is the complementizer phrase such as 'that' in English and 'kI' in Hindi which augments a subordinate clause in a sentence.
- IP: it stands for the inflectional phrase which encapsulates the auxiliaries (modal and be verbs) in English.
- Some other notation conventions are nominal phrase (NP or DP), verbal phrase (VP), prepositional phrase (PP), adverbial phrase (ADVP), adjectival phrase (ADJP) etc.

The instance "I came quickly" is considerable here. The structural representation of the given sentence syntactically is provided below.

[CP [IP [NP I]

    [VP [VP [V came] [ADV quickly]] [PP from [NP [DET the] [N market]]]]]]

[CP [IP [NP hama]

    [VP [PP [N bajaare] [PP se]] [VP [ADVP [ADV jaldiya] [PP se]] [V aagailI]]]]]]

In this above instantiated example, [V aagailI] is the syntactic head of the sentence whereas [NP hama] is the syntactic subject and [ADV jaldiya] is the adverb which makes an ADVP including an adposition [PP se] in Bhojpuri. On the other hand, English sentence contains [V came] as the head of the sentence, [NP I] as the subject and [ADV quickly] as the ADVP.

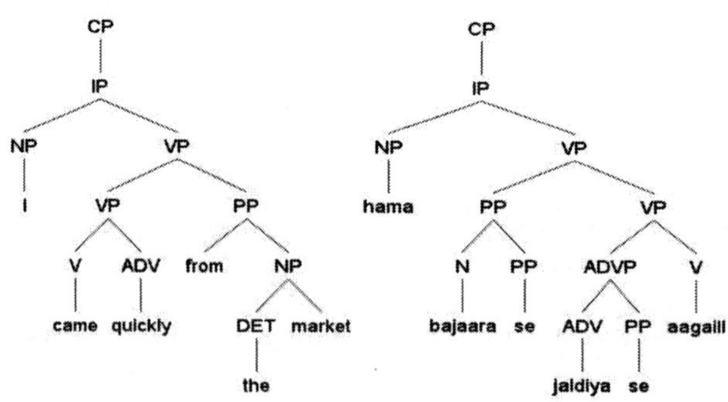

---

² For more basics on notation convention please refer to Dorr, 1994; Gupta and Chatterjee, 2003 and Muzaffar et al., 2016

2.2 The Lexical Semantics

The syntactic constituents are analyzed for providing an intermediate representation in a form known as the LCS. The LCS may be acquired with the unification of Root Lexical Conceptual Structure (RLCS) of the constituent words in the given sentence. It is a modified and adapted version of the representation as proposed by Jackendoff (1983, 1990) which conforms to the following form:

$$[_{T(X')} X' ([_{T(W')} W'], [_{T(Z'1)} Z'1]...[_{T(Z'n)} Z'n] [_{T(Q'1)} Q'1]...[_{T(Q'm)} Q'm])]$$

In addition, this representation is compositional with decompositional features, language independent in nature and provides a theoretical framework for the representation of a sentence with the help of semantics. The sentence "I came from the market quickly" is represented in the LCS as the following.

$$[_{Event} COME_{Loc}$$
$$([_{Thing} I],$$
$$[_{Path} FROM_{LOC} ([_{Position} AT_{LOC} [_{Thing} I] [_{Location} THE\ MARKET])])]$$
$$[_{manner} QUICKLY])]$$

Where COMELoc is the head of LCS, 'I' pronominal is the LCS subject, $FROM_{LOC}$ is the LCS object, QUICKLY is the LCS modifier. The Root Lexical Conceptual Structure (RLCS) is 'an uninstantiated LCS' (Dorr, 1994) which is associated with the definition of a word in the lexicon. For instance, the RLCS of the verb 'come' is as follows.

$$[_{Event} COME_{Loc}$$
$$([_{Thing} X],$$
$$[_{Path} FROM/TO_{Loc} ([_{Position} AT_{Loc} ([_{Thing} X], [_{Thing} Z])])])]$$

To get a composed (CLCS) we unify RLCSs for 'come' and 'I'. Generalized Linking Routine (GLR) correlates the constituent words of the syntactic representations to those of the LCS by the mappings as demonstrated in the following.

- ❏ V' ⇔ V ([GO_{Loc}] ⇔ [V came])
- ❏ S' ⇔ S ([RAHIM] ⇔ [NP I])
- ❏ O' ⇔ O ([TO_{LOC}] ⇔ [PP from ...])
- ❏ M' ⇔ M ([FAST] ⇔ [ADV quickly])

Lastly, the lexical-semantic items are related in a systematic manner to their corresponding syntactic categories by applying Canonical Syntactic Realization (CSR): For instance:

LCS Types	Syntactic Categories
Event, State	V (verb)
Thing	N (noun)
Property	Adj (adjective)
Path, Position	P (preposition)
Location, Time, manner, Intensifier and Purpose	ADV (adverbial)

Table. 1 The LCS Types and Notation Conventions

3 Categorization of Divergences

Dorr (1993) has classified various divergences broadly into two primary categories: syntactic and lexical-semantic. Furthermore, each of the classes has been sub-categorized and the corresponding instances have been drawn as in the following.

3.1 Syntactic Divergences

This set of divergences, which are based on the syntax of concerned languages, has been sub-categorized into seven lower-level types: constituent order, adjunction, preposition-stranding, movement, null-subject, dative subject and pleonastic. These are some of the universal parametric variations atypical to English as an SL and any natural language as the TL.

3.1.1 Constituent Order

This divergence pertains to the word-ordering of the concerned SL and TL languages. It emerges when there is mismatch between the word order patterns of SL and TL. On one hand, English is a configurational language which follows a rigid pattern (SVO) and is unmarked. On the other hand, Bhojpuri being an Indic language allows relatively free word order patterns viz. SOV (unmarked), SVO and OVS (marked). However, both the types of patterns are acceptable syntactically in Bhojpuri.

For instance,

The boys are playing Cricket.

laikana	*krikeTa*	*khela-taaDana.*
Boys.M.PL.3.NOM	cricket	play.PRS.PL.IPFV.M.
S	O	V

laikana	*khela-taaDana*	*krikeTa.*
Boys.M.PL.3.NOM	play.PRS.PL.IPFV.M.	cricket
S	V	O

krikeTa	*khela-taaDana*	*laikana.*
Cricket	play.PRS.PL.IPFV.M.	Boys.M.PL.3.NOM
O	V	S

3.1.2 Adjunction

Adjunction divergence concerns with the difference of mapping in complements (prepositional, non-finite verbal complements etc.) and adjuncts (prepositional phrases, participial constructions etc.) between two languages. In the English input sentence, the infinitival adjunction is translated as prepositional complement 'badanaama kare ke kosIs' in Bhojpuri.

He tried to defame me.

u	*hamake*	*badanaama kare ke kosIs kailasa*
he.NOM.SG.3.NHON	me.DAT	defame do of try do.PST.PRF.NHON.3

He came here after having food.

u	*khaanaa khaile*	*ke baada*	*ihaaN aayal.*
he.NOM.SG.3.NHON	food eat.PST.PRF.	after	here come.PST.PRF.NHON.3

3.1.3 Preposition-stranding

Preposition-stranding, otherwise called as P-stranding, is one of the syntactic constructions where the preposition occurs somewhere in the sentence (generally at the end) other than its canonical position; adjacent to its object. This construction is quite alien to most of the South-Asian languages which includes Bhojpuri. As a result parametric variation emerges between a pair of languages.

For instance,

Where are you coming from?

kahaaN tu	*aava-ta*	*hauaa se?*
where You.	come.PRS.	be.PROG.PRS.3. from

3.1.4 Movement

When we try to move certain constituents in English input sentence, they cannot be moved as freely as Bhojpuri. This accounts for the fact that Indian languages are relatively free so far as the process of scrambling is concerned. If we shuffle the word order of the following input sentence, it becomes grammatically acceptable but semantically not well-formed. Because 'the book' semantically cannot buy 'Ram'. In other words, the inanimate object cannot play the role of an animate subject which is logical.

For Example,

Ram purchased a book. *A book purchased Ram

raama ekhe/ekthe kitaaba kharidalana

Ram.NOM.PST.3.HON   a book   buy.PST.IPFV.3.HON

ekhe/ekthe   kitaaba   raama   kharidalana.

a   book   Ram.NOM.PST.3.HON   buy.PST.IPFV.3.HON

3.1.5 Null-subject

When the position of the subject is either left implicit or attributed by some pronouns such as 'there' in English it is called a null-subject. When there is a covert subject the agreement features are generally marked with the verb when there is S-V agreement. So, in the example mentioned below there is no equivalent translation for the existential 'there' in Bhojpuri. Consequently, this divergence crops up which proves to be a barrier in MT.

Example,

There was a lion in the forest.

jangala meN   ekhe baagha rahala.

Forest in.LOC a   tiger   be.PST.PRF.3.

3.1.6 Dative Subject

This construction is otherwise known as the non-nominative construction which is atypical to South Asian languages. The psychological predicates such as 'hunger', 'thirst' and so on are expressed with the addition of a dative subject postpositional marker in Indian languages (here 'ke').

I have fever.

ham-ke   bokhaara   hava/baa

I.DAT.SG.1.   fever   be.PRS.1.IPFV

3.1.7 Pleonastic

Pleonastic pronoun or dummy pronoun is a pronoun which lacks meaning and is used when the argument is irrelevant, non-existent or reduntant. In the input sentence, 'it' is considered to be impersonal semantically and intransitive syntactically. On the other hand, with the absence of the pleonastic subject, 'water' becomes the subject of the intransitive verb 'rain' /barasata/.

It is raining.

paanii barasata   hava

water   rain.PRS.PROG be.PRS.

3.2 The Lexical-Semantic Divergences

On the basis of lexical-semantics of the given languages, the lexical-semantic divergences have been sub-classified into seven sub-divisions: thematic, promotional, structural, inflational, conflational, categorial and lexical.

3.2.1 Thematic

This categorization is based on the principle of the thematic roles of the arguments of the verbs. For instance the role of the agent (Ham-ke DAT) is realized as the dative subject in Bhojpuri whereas the English counterpart has nominative case (I-NOM) marker on the agentive subject and accusative on the other argument. As a result owing to the fact that Bhojpuri allows an oblique subject where the object gets co-indexed with the verb which is not true so far as English is concerned.

I had fever.

ham-ke bokhaara rahala

I.DAT. fever   be.PST.

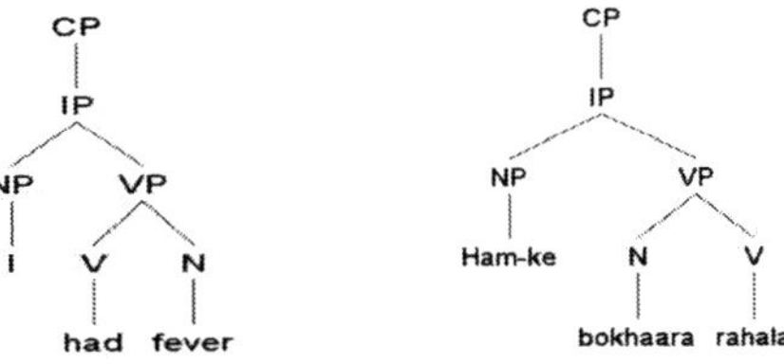

3.2.2 Promotional

This divergence occurs when one constituent in a given language having a lower position in the hierarchy gets promoted to a higher position in the target language. In this case, the category of adverb ('on' in English) which has a lower position (modifier of the verb) in the hierarchy gets promoted to the higher status of verb (chalata hava) in Bhojpuri counterpart.

The fan is on.

pankhaa   chalata   hava.
Fan   run.PROG   be.PRS

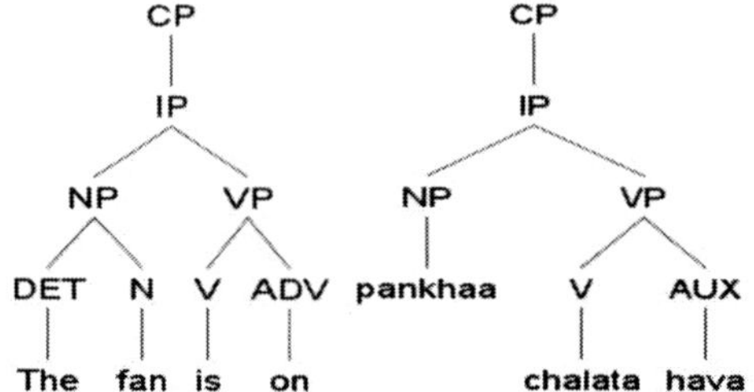

3.2.3 Structural

It occurs when there is difference between languages on the basis of structure or syntax. For instance, the nominal phrase argument in English is translated as the prepositional adjunct in the target language. This divergence generally originates when there is phrase-level parametric variations which becomes a barrier for MT. So, the NP, which is an argument of the verb 'face' in English, is translated as an adjunctive PP (musIbata kaa saamanaa) in Bhojpuri.

For instance,

I face difficulties.

hamke   musIbata   ka   saamanaa   kare(ke)   paDala.
I.DAT   difficulty   of   face   do   have.PST.PRF.

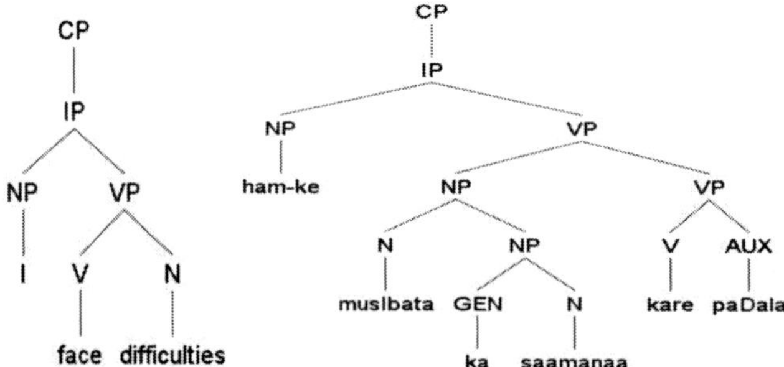

3.2.4 Inflational & Conflational

On one hand, when on linguistic element in SL is inflated as the realization of more than one element in the TL it is called as the inflational divergence. On the other hand, when two or more linguistic elements in SL are conflated to be realized as one word in TL it is known as conflational divergence. In the inflational example below, the SL 'suggested' gets realized in the TL as having two elements 'salaaha dehalana'. In the conflational instance, phrasal verb "looked for" gets translated in Bhojpuri as having only one word i.e. 'khojalasa'.

He suggested me on this matter.

u	*hamake*	*I*	*maamalaa*	*meN*	*salaaha*	*dehalana.*
he.NOM.3	me.DAT.OBJ.	this	matter	in.OBL	advise	give.PST.PRF.3

He looked for a room.

u	*ekhe*	*makaana*	*khojalasa*
he.NOM.3	a	house	search.PST.PRF.3

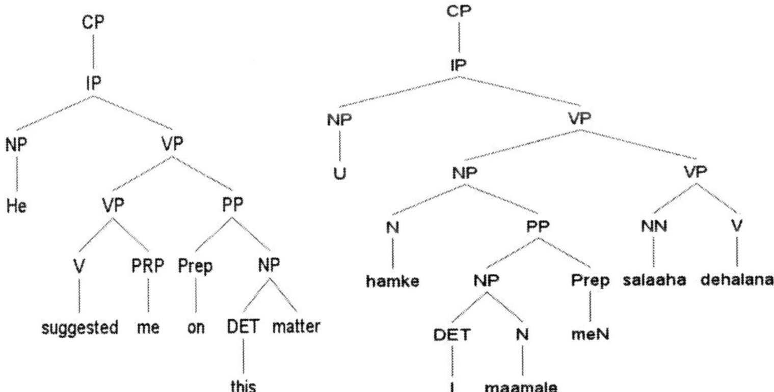

3.2.5 Categorial

When there is a change in the very grammatical category of a linguistic element in TL it is known as the categorial divergence. In the example instantiated below the predicative adjective 'hungry' in English gets translated as the nominal phrase in Bhojpuri. Thus there is a change in the parts of speech categories from adjective to noun.

I am hungry.

ham-ke	*bhukha*	*lagala*	*hava*
I.DAT.3	hunger	seem.PRF	be.PRS.

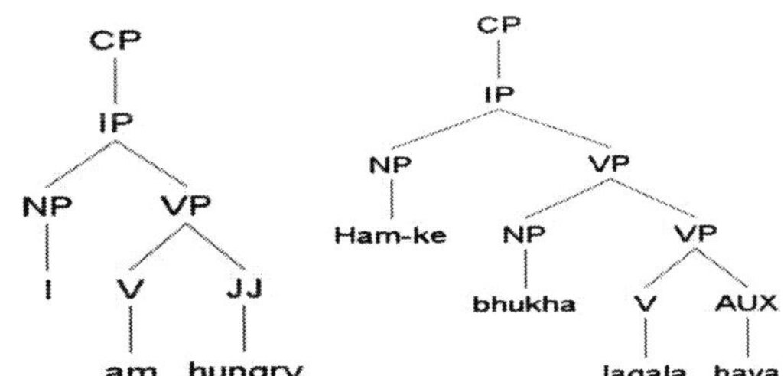

3.2.6 Lexical

This divergence occurs when two or more divergence types combine or because of the unavailability of the exact equivalent translation. Thus, in the following example, there is no equivalent translation for the expression 'see you' in Indian languages like Bhojpuri. There is fair amount of lexical divergences between a pair of languages that are responsible for creating divergence issues in MT.

See you!

phira   milala jaayIM
Again   meet   go.FUT.PL.1.IPFV

4 The Identification and Resolution Procedure

This section provides the systematic method for the identification and probable solution of the lexical-semantic divergences between English and Bhojpuri.

4.1 Thematic

This divergence emerges when the GLR invokes the following steps of relation (Dorr, 1990a).

Firstly, one needs to relate the syntactic object with the LCS subject $\Rightarrow$ O$'\Leftrightarrow$ S

Secondly, one needs to have the relation between the syntactic subject to the LCS object $\Rightarrow$ S$'\Leftrightarrow$ O

The syntactic structure and the corresponding CLCS are provided in the following.

[CP [IP [NP I] [VP [V had] [N fever]]]]

$\Leftrightarrow$ [$_\text{State}$ BEI$_\text{Ident}$ ([Thing I],

[$_\text{Position}$ AT$_\text{Ident}$ ([$_\text{Thing}$ I], [$_\text{Thing}$ FEVER])],

[$_\text{manner}$ SEVERELY])]

$\Leftrightarrow$ [CP [IP [NP Ham-ke] [VP [N bokhaara] [V rahala]]]]

In the above instantiated example, the subject gets the thematic roles of a nominative agentive subject in English and concedes the role of impersonal and non-agentive subject with dative case marker.

4.2 Promotional

In this divergence the GLR augments in the following manner.

On needs to consider the following steps:

1. One needs to relate the LCS verb with the syntactic object $\Rightarrow$ V$'\Leftrightarrow$ S
2. Promote the LCS modifier (adverb) position to the position of verb $\Rightarrow$ M$'\Leftrightarrow$ V

The syntactic structure and the respective CLCS are demonstrated below.

[CP [IP [NP [DET The] [N fan]] [VP [V is] [ADV on]]]]

$\Leftrightarrow$ [$_\text{State}$ BEI$_\text{Ident}$ ([$_\text{Thing}$ THE FAN],

[$_\text{Position}$ AT$_\text{Ident}$ ([$_\text{Thing}$ THE FAN],

[$_\text{manner}$ OFF])]

$\Leftrightarrow$ [CP [IP [NP pankhaa] [VP [V chalata] [AUX hava]]]]

4.3 Structural

This divergence is quite different from the above two types of divergences in so far as the alternation of the position of the constituents is concerned. But it changes the nature of the relation between various positions.

The syntactic structure and CLCS are provided below.

[CP [IP [NP I] [VP [V face] [N difficulties]]]]

⇔ [$_{Event}$ GO$_{Loc}$

    ([$_{Thing}$ I],

        [$_{Path}$ TO$_{Loc}$ ($_{Position}$ IN$_{Loc}$ ([$_{Thing}$ I], [$_{Thing}$ DIFFICULTIES])])])]

⇔ [CP [IP [NP ham-ke] [VP [NP [N musIbata] [NP [GEN kaa] [N saamanaa]]] [VP [V kare] [AUX paDala]]]]]

One of the arguments of the verb in English is translated as the prepositional phrase in Bhojpuri which creates complexity for automatic translation.

4.4 Inflational & Conflational

In the bracketing representation demonstrated following, it is quite obvious that the one-word token verbal element i.e. 'suggested' is translated as having two tokens i.e. "salaaha dehalana" in Bhojpuri and is a quintessential example of inflational divergence. It is completely based on the economy of usage of strings in both the concerned languages. When the economically inflated expressions in the SL are reduced to a conflated expression in the TL counterpart, it is called as conflational divergence. The syntactic structure and the CLCS are demonstrated in the following.

[CP [IP [NP He] [VP [VP [V suggested] [PRP me]] [PP [Prep on] [NP [DET this] matter]]]]]

⇔ [$_{Event}$ GO$_{Loc}$

    ([Thing HE],

        [$_{Path}$ TO$_{Loc}$ ($_{Position}$ IN$_{Loc}$ ([$_{Thing}$ HE], [$_{Thing}$ ME], ([$_{Thing}$ THE MATTER])])])])]

⇔ [CP [IP [NP U] [VP [NP [N hamke] [PP [NP [DET I] [N maamalaa]] [Prep meN]]] [VP [NN salaaha] [V dehalana]]]]]

4.5 Categorial

In this divergence, there is no identicality in the relationship between the syntactic category and the concerned lexical-semantic item.

[CP [IP [NP I] [VP [V am] [JJ hungry]]]]

⇔ [$_{State}$ BEI$_{Ident}$

    ([$_{Thing}$ I],[$_{Position}$ AT$_{Ident}$ ([$_{Thing}$ I], [$_{property}$ HUNGRY])]

⇔ [CP [IP [NP Ham-ke] [VP [NP bhukha] [VP [V lagala] [AUX hava]]]]]

In the examples mentioned above the divergence owes to the fact that adjectival parts of speech category in English is translated into a nominal category in Bhojpuri counterpart.

4.6 Lexical

This divergence is considered to be one of the by-products of any of the above-described combination of divergences. In addition, the unavailability of the proper translation in the target language is also encapsulated in this category.

[CP [IP [VP See] [NP [you]]]]

[CP [IP [VP [ADV Phira] [VP [V milala] [AUX [jaayIM]]]]]]

5 Conclusion

The successful implementation of any MT platform solely depends upon how well an instance of translation is retrieved from a plethora of data and modified to cater to the demand of the desired translation output. Although the heuristic linguistic rules are capable of dealing with several errors but are not sufficient for tackling the exceptional cases of linguistic divergences (Gupta & Chatterjee, 2003). Therefore, our rationale for dealing with the divergence patterns between English and Bhojpuri language pair is to bring out various types of divergent, incompatible or incongruent features.

In this study, we have focused light on classifying various divergences between English and Bhojpuri translations. The theoretical framework for classification is based on Dorr's classification of divergences from syntactic and lexical-semantic points of views. So far as the identification and resolution are concerned, we have adhered to the LCS schema. This analytical study on divergence between English and Bhojpuri language pair can prove to be fruitful for any IA language in general and less-resourced languages in particular to develop efficient and qualitative Machine Translation platforms.

References

Abdus Saboor & Mohammad Abid Khan. 2010. *Lexical-semantic divergence in Urdu-to-English example based Machine Translation.* 6th International Conference on Emerging Technologies (ICET), vol., no., 316, 320.

Atul Ku. Ojha, Pitambar Behera, Srishti Singh, and Girish N. Jha. 2015. Training and Evaluation of POS Taggers in Indo-Aryan Languages: A Case of Hindi, Odia and Bhojpuri. In *Language Technology Conference-2016.*

Bonnie J. Dorr. 1990b. Solving thematic divergence in Machine Translation. In *28th Annual Conference of the Association for Computational Linguistics,* 127-134: Pittsburg, PA University of Pittsburg.

Bonnie J. Dorr. 1993. *Machine Translation: A View from the Lexicon.* The MIT Press, Cambridge, Mass.

Bonnie J. Dorr. 1994. Classification of Machine Translation divergences and a proposed solution. *Computational Linguistics,* 20(4): 597-633.

Bonnie J. Dorr. 1994a. Machine translation divergences: A formal description and proposed solution. *Computational Linguistics, 20*(4), 597-633.

Deepa Gupta and Niladri Chatterjee. 2003. Identification of divergence for English to Hindi EBMT. In *MT Summit*-IX, 141-148.

Deepti Bhalla, Nisheeth Joshi, and Iti Mathur. 2014. Divergence Issues in English-Punjabi Machine Translation. *Language in India,* 14(10).

K. Parameswari. 2015. Development of Telugu-Tamil Transfer-Based Machine Translation system: With Special reference to Divergence Index. In *1st Deep Machine Translation Workshop,* 48-54.

K. M. Manger. 2014. Translation Divergences in Hindi-Nepali Machine Translation. *Language in India, 14*(5).

Kārumūri V. Subbārāo. 2008. Typological characteristics of South Asian languages. *Language in South Asia,* pages 49-78.

Kurumari V. Subbarao. 2012. *South Asian languages: A syntactic typology.* Cambridge University Press, England.

Niladri S. Das. 2013. Linguistic divergences in English to Bengali Translation. *International Journal of English Linguistics*; Vol. 3, No. 1; 2013.

Noam Chomsky. 1981. *Lectures on government and binding.* Dordrecht: Foris.

Pinkey Nainwani. 2015. *Challenges in Automatic Translations of Natural Languages- A Study of English-Sindhi Divergence.* Doctoral Dissertation, Centre for Linguistics, Jawaharlal Nehru University, New Delhi, India.

Preeti Shukla, Devanand Shukl, and Amba Kulkarni. 2010. Vibhakti divergence between Sanskrit and Hindi. In *Sanskrit Computational Linguistics.* Springer Berlin Heidelberg, 198-208.

Rai M. K Sinha & Anil Thakur. 2005. Translation Divergence in English-Hindi MT. In *EAMT Xth Annual Conference,* Budapest, Hungary.

Rai M. K Sinha & Anil Thakur. 2005a. Divergence Patterns in Machine Translation between Hindi and English. In *MT Summit X.* Phuket, Thailand, 12-16th September, 346-353.

Ray S. Jackendoff. 1983. *Semantics and Cognition.* MIT Press, Cambridge.

Ray S. Jackendoff. 1990. *Semantic Structures.* MIT Press, Cambridge.

S. B Kulkarni, P. D. Deshmukh, and K. V Kale. 2013. Syntactic and structural divergence in English-to-Marathi Machine Translation. *IEEE 2013 International Symposium on Computational and Business Intelligence,* August 24-26, 2013, New Delhi,191-194, (doi: 10.1109/ISCBI.2013.46).

Shachi Dave, Jignashu Parikh, and Pushpak Bhattacharya. 2001. Interlingua-based English-Hindi Machine Translation. *Journal of Machine Translation,* 16(4), 251-304. (http://dx.doi.org/10.1023/A:1021902704523.)

Srishti Singh and Esha Banerjee. 2014. Annotating Bhojpuri Corpus using BIS Scheme. In *Proceedings of 2nd Workshop on Indian Language Data: Resources and Evaluation (WILDRE-2), Ninth International Conference on Language Resources and Evaluation, LREC (2014),* Reykjavik, Iceland, May 26-31, 2014.

Srishti Singh. 2015. *Challenges in Automatic POS Tagging of Indian Languages- A Comparative Study of Hindi and Bhojpuri.* M. Phil. Dissertation. Jawaharlal Nehru University, New Delhi.

Srishti Singh and Girish N. Jha. 2015a. Statistical Tagger for Bhojpuri (employing Support Vector Machine). In *4th International Conference on Computing, Communication and Informatics (ICACCI, 2015).*

Sharmin Muzaffar, Pitambar Behera, and Girish N. Jha. 2016. Classification and Resolution of Linguistic Divergences in English-Urdu Machine Translation. In *WILDRE-3 (LREC-2016),* Portoroz, Slovenia.

Sharmin Muzaffar, Pitambar Behera, and Girish Nath Jha. 2016. A Pāniniān Framework for Analyzing Case Marker Errors in English-Urdu Machine Translation. *Procedia Computer Science (Elsevier)*, *96*, 502-510.

Venkanna Ithagani. (2014). Linguistic Convergence and Divergence in Telugu-Urdu Contact Situation: A Study with Special Reference to Telangana Dialect.

The development of a web corpus of Hindi language and corpus-based comparative studies to Japanese

Miki Nishioka
Osaka University
Osaka
Japan
dumas@lang.osaka-u.ac.jp

Shiro Akasegawa
Lago Language Institute
Shiga
Japan
lagoinst@gmail.com

Abstract

In this paper, we discuss our creation of a web corpus of spoken Hindi (COSH), one of the Indo-Aryan languages spoken mainly in the Indian subcontinent. We also point out notable problems we've encountered in the web corpus and the special concordancer. After observing the kind of technical problems we encountered, especially regarding annotation tagged by Shiva Reddy's tagger, we argue how they can be solved when using COSH for linguistic studies. Finally, we mention the kinds of linguistic research that we non-native speakers of Hindi can do using the corpus, especially in pragmatics and semantics, and from a comparative viewpoint to Japanese.

1   Introduction

Hindi-Urdu is a member of the Indo-Aryan language family widely distributed in Indian subcontinent. It is originally related the Indo-Iranian branch of the Indo-European language family. In contrast, Japanese is an East Asian language spoken mainly in Japan. Genealogically, geographically, and even historically, Japanese has no direct relation to Hindi-Urdu, with Japanese lacking the declension of nouns, pronouns, adjectives and verbs based on person, gender and number peculiar to the languages such as Hindi-Urdu. Nevertheless, morpho-syntactically and semantically, both languages have many common features, such as the word order of a simple sentence and a compound sentence (except a complex sentence). Other common features are: complex predicates (basically 'noun + light verb' as in H. *paRhaaii karnaa* vs. J. *benkyou suru* both for 'studying do'), noun modification with participles of a verb, nominalization with genitive particle *no* in Japanese, and *vaalaa* and genitive postposition *kaa* in Hindi, and verb-verb concatenation, that is, so-called 'compound verbs' (CV). These features are similar (analogical), but not homological: alike in appearance, and working similarly but not exactly the same. It is sometimes hard for us non-native speakers of Hindi-Urdu (hereafter simply 'Hindi') to understand nuances of meaning, since we lack intuition of the language.

To make up for lack of intuition, large-scale corpora will make useful tools for language study. In this paper, we will discuss how we created a web corpus of the Hindi language, and the kind of concordancer that we have developed. Based on these, we will give a few examples of comparative studies of Hindi and Japanese.

2   General methods for studying a foreign language; their pros and cons

Before introducing the corpus and the concordancer, we should discuss general methods for studying a foreign language. When studying a foreign language, meaning a non-native language, there are three basic methods for investigating linguistic phenomena:

    a. Finding a handful of native speakers of the target language and interviewing them about a linguistic topic.

Proceedings of the 6th Workshop on South and Southeast Asian Natural Language Processing,
pages 114–123, Osaka, Japan, December 11-17 2016.

b. Conducting a questionnaire about the topic and collecting results from a larger population.

c. Using a large corpus and collecting results from a much larger population automatically. This last method is useful for proving a linguistic phenomenon objectively.

Method a. is an orthodox and common way for linguists to study a foreign language. It is quite convenient, as finding a nearby native speaker of the target language is easy, especially nowadays. However, the number of results is too small to be scientifically valid. Method b. is used to make up for this lack of objectivity. It too is an orthodox way of investigating a target language. However, the number of results it yields is still small, and the results themselves tend to fluctuate depending on the pre-set questions and answers.

How about method c: using a large corpus? This method lets us easily collect results from a far larger population. It is one of the more promising ways to qualify results, eliminate subjectivity as much as possible for investigative purposes, and provide objectivity and reliability. However, it's not without its problems. Undeniably, a corpus still has some imbalance in genres of the language. In addition, it's difficult to build a large corpus in a short time. Furthermore, technical problems can arise, especially when tagging and annotating words in the corpus.

To maintain or increase the quality of results, we should bear in mind that each of the methods in itself is insufficient, since all have both strong and weak points. For example, method a. can produce imbalances in data based on the researcher's own personal experience of the language, unless the informant is well-trained in both the language and linguistic research. This kind of useful informant is rather rare. Thus, utilizing all three methods effectively is the key for future research, especially on non-native languages.

3   Development of a web-corpus and a concordancer

Since I keenly felt the need for a large-scale corpus for semantic or pragmatic research on Hindi, I have devoted considerable effort to building a web corpus, with the kind technical assistance of Shiro Akasegawa. A development version of this corpus will be open to the public in October, 2016. The present size of the corpus is 179,979,464 tokens. In preparing to build the corpus, we encountered several technical issues in dealing with Devanagari script online. These are described below.

3.1   Pre-treatment for building the Hindi web corpus

In the process of preparing the Hindi web corpus, we faced several problems. As we know, Hindi is not the only language to use Devanagari script: there are Nepali, Marathi, Maithili, Rajasthani, Bhojpuri, Sanskrit, and others. Thus, in our collecting of data in Devanagari script, some Nepali, Sanskrit, and Maithili data slipped in with them. Sanskrit is easy to tell apart, as its words tend to combine according to Sandhi rules, emphasizing a definite phonetic harmony. Other languages, however, look the same as Hindi, with a blank space to divide words. To weed these out, we took steps as below.

Judging whether a language was Hindi or not was done as follows:

a. We targeted Hindi, Nepali, Rajsthani, and Bhojpuri

b. We made a lexical list for each language, choosing 100 frequently-used lexicons. The list calculates the frequency of the lexicons as contained in corpora texts.

c. Using a random sampling technique, we prepared 637 text files of Bhojpuri, Maithili, Marathi, Nepali, Rajsthani, and Sanskrit, all of which are generally written in Devanagari script.

We checked whether the languages of the texts and each high-scoring language were the same. We found that language identification failed only in one Nepali case. The number of Nepali files was 27, of which 26 had a higher rate of Hindi lexicons than of Nepali lexicons. Only one file had the same rate of Hindi and Nepali lexicons (9%).

The determining criterion: analyzing these results, we found that all files with over **20%** frequency of Hindi lexicons were in Hindi. Therefore, we decided the criterion was valid, and used it to identify languages. Only files found to be acceptable based on this criterion were included in the eventual corpus.

file	nepali	word_count	ratio_hindi	ratio_nepali	results
00037538.txt	*	2277	3%	11%	napali
00062480.txt	*	2594	9%	9%	
00065110.txt	*	2350	1%	9%	napali
00112681.txt	*	2199	1%	6%	napali
00122140.txt	*	2365	2%	13%	napali
00125281.txt	*	2324	2%	8%	napali
00246808.txt	*	2325	1%	12%	napali
00255987.txt	*	2295	1%	9%	napali
00291093.txt	*	2355	2%	10%	napali
00397198.txt	*	2309	2%	9%	napali
00397218.txt	*	2276	1%	7%	napali
00502483.txt	*	2391	2%	8%	napali
00566962.txt	*	2198	1%	12%	napali
00732119.txt	*	1959	1%	8%	napali
00828334.txt	*	2229	0%	10%	napali
00888026.txt	*	2164	1%	9%	napali
00911584.txt	*	2395	2%	10%	napali
00991354.txt	*	2364	1%	6%	napali
01047956.txt	*	2327	2%	9%	napali
01060542.txt	*	2171	2%	9%	napali
01096439.txt	*	2275	1%	5%	napali
01096542.txt	*	2288	2%	7%	napali
01110078.txt	*	2230	2%	8%	napali
01113026.txt	*	2330	3%	8%	napali
01116002.txt	*	2492	1%	6%	napali
01119626.txt	*	2253	2%	7%	napali
01121133.txt	*	2568	1%	10%	napali

Table 1: A sample of the determining criterion

Another prominent problem we had to face was **duplicated data** found in the first raw web corpus. We divided the corpus files into sentence units, sorted them, and deleted the duplicates. From an initial 12,170,339 sentences, we ended up with 8,806,658 sentences, meaning 3,360,000 duplicates, or about 28% of all sentences.

Another problem is that we left out Hindi data in the Roman alphabet. The Internet features copious Hindi data in Roman alphabet, providing precious linguistic material in natural Hindi (which might also be called 'Urdu'). However, Hindi Romanization is vastly inconsistent, and since we found few if any established rules, we decided to exclude those data for the time being.

3.2   Annotation by a POS tagger

To annotate the Hindi data in our web corpus, we chose Shiva Reddy's POS tagger[1] implemented for Sketch Engine[2]. According to Reddy, this tagger achieves 91.31% accuracy, trained on a corpus of 30,409,730 tokens[3]. However, our web corpus consists of natural language, and tends to contain numerous new loanwords from other languages, written in Devanagari – which the tagger cannot tag properly. Moreover, typographic errors are commonplace on the Internet, because no fixed orthography has taken root among common people, unlike in Japanese. These errors should prevent the tagger from achieving 91.31% accuracy on tokens in our web corpus. The real accuracy in the web corpus should be lower.

Another big problem is Hindi itself. There are many homographs in Hindi. As Dalal et al (2007) have mentioned, these are longstanding problems in computational linguistics. There are some patterns of ambiguity. Some prominent ones are mentioned below.

Ambiguity of categories (POS)

---

[1] Available at http://sivareddy.in/downloads

[2] Hosted at https://www.sketchengine.co.uk/

[3] See Hindi Part of Speech (POS) Tagger, at https://bitbucket.org/sivareddyg/hindi-part-of-speech-tagger, accessed Aug 7, 2016.

A notable example of this type is the homograph *aam*. It has two meanings: an adjective [JJ] 'general' and a masculine noun [NN] 'mango'. However, the word order of a noun phrase is fixed: an adjective comes before a noun in Hindi. So it's easy to tell which is JJ and which is NN, especially on the basis of the trigram and the probability of the POS attached to the tagger. Thus, this example poses a rather minor problem.

Ambiguity of forms in the same POS category

What the tagger cannot distinguish easily is a homograph with various forms in the same POS category. One example is the verb *baiTh-naa*. The annotated part cited in Table 2 is *udaas baiTh-aa hai*. 'He is sitting sadly.'

surface form	lemma	tag	details[4]	POS	gender	number	person	case
उदास	उदास	NN	----	adj	any	any	any	any
बैठा	बैठा	VM	0	v	any	any	any	--
है	है	VAUX	है	v	any	sg	2	--

Table 2: Example of annotation by Shiva Reddy's tagger

Putting aside *udaas,* which here is annotated NN, *baiTh-aa,* the perfect participle form here consisting of a stem and a perfect participle or past [for both masculine and singular] suffix *–aa,* is annotated as VM [0], meaning a stem form – i.e., the form with no suffixes. In other words, it indicates a stem form of *baiThaa-naa*[5] or *biThaa-naa* 'to make someone sit', even though it should be the perfect participle *baiTh-aa,* which is derived from the verb intransitive *baiTh-naa.* This is true of such verb pairs as *ban-naa* 'to be made' (intransitive) vs. *banaa-naa* 'to make' (transitive), and *cal-naa* 'to move' (intransitive) vs. *calaa-naa* 'to move '(transitive). We have also found examples such as *samajh-naa* 'to understand' vs. *samjhaa-naa* 'to cause to understand', *sun-naa* 'to hear' vs. *sunaa-naa* 'to cause to hear', and *pahan-naa* 'to wear, to put on' vs. *pahanaa-naa* 'to cause to put on'.

Regarding homographs, we can provide a couple of more examples such as verbal nouns and a finite form of the same verb. The verb *khaa-naa* 'to eat' in the infinitive is identical to the verbal noun or noun *khaanaa* 'food' itself. However, in all of our randomly chosen samples, the tagger has distinguished the noun form from the infinitive form successfully. In addition, there are other representative verbal nouns with an *-ii* ending, such as *paRhaa-ii* 'studying', *sunaa-ii* 'hearing', and *dikhaa-ii* 'seeing'. However, *paRhaa-ii* is annotated as successfully as *khaanaa* 'food' above. The latter two forms are used in Noun + *de-naa* 'to give'/ *paR-naa* 'to fall'; that is, in so-called complex predicates. This might be the reason why the verbal nouns are annotated as VM, not NN.

Some complex tagging and POS details

In addition to the above, what we must point out is the complex tagging by the tagger. For example, regarding so-called complex predicates, the slots consist of | Slot 1 | + | Slot 2 |. Options for slot 1 are Noun, Adjective and Verb. Slot 2 is mostly filled with so-called light verbs. There are some primary light verbs, that is V2, such as *kar-naa* 'to do', *ho-naa* 'to be', *le-naa* 'to take', *de-naa* 'to give', etc. Of these V2s, when it comes to *de-naa* 'to give', we find that certain nouns such as *dhokhaa* 'deceit' and *udhaar* 'a loan, debt', as in *dhokhaa de-naa* 'to deceive' and *udhaar de-naa* 'to lend', respectively, are labelled as VM; while verbs for Slot 2 are VAUX.

Another thing to mention is that adjectives with *-aa* endings have separate masculine and feminine forms. Following, from top to bottom, is an example of the adjective बड़ा *baRaa* 'big' in the masculine (m) and singular (sg) form, which is the default or lemma form[6]; बड़े *baRe* in the masculine and singular plus the oblique case (o); and बड़ी *baRii* in the feminine (f) and either singular or plural, i.e., (any).

---

[4] Here suffixes like the infinitive –ना (*-naa*), imperfect participle –ता (*-taa*), and perfect participle -या (*-yaa*) are added in this column optionally.

[5] The suffix *aa* in the verb is added to make an intransitive verb into a transitive. The same applies hereafter.

[6] A lemma form, that is, an unmarked word in Hindi, is treated as a direct case (d), not in the oblique case (o).

surface form	lemma	tag	details	POS	gender	number	person	case
बड़ा	बडा	JJ	----	adj	m	sg	--	d
बड़े	बडा	JJ	----	adj	m	sg	--	o
बड़ी	बडी	JJ	----	adj	f	any	--	any

Table 3: A sample of annotation for adjective baRaa 'big'

As we see in Table 3, *baRe* in the second line is identical to *baRe* the masculine and plural form. However, the tagger tends to annotate *baRe* as the same form in the oblique case. In addition, lemma forms here are without ○ (*nuqtaa*), the dot under each character: बडा *baDaa* and बडी *baDii*. In any event, the lemma of *baDii* should basically be the same as that of *baDaa*, and yet the tagger keeps the feminine form for *baDii*. We have another example of *baRaa*, *baRe* and *baRii*, as shown in Table 4 below.

surface form	lemma	tag	details	POS	gender	number	person	case
बड़ा	बडा	XC	----	punc	--	--	--	--
बड़े	बडे	NN	----	punc	--	--	--	--
बड़ी	बडी	XC	----	punc	--	--	--	--

Table 4: Another sample of annotation for Adjective baRaa 'big'

The surface form and the lemma form in the first and third lines are the same as in Table 3. However, the word is tagged as (XC), that is, compound[7]. The second *baRe* is annotated as a noun (NN), though the POS is labeled as a punctuation. The lemma form is also *baDe*, which is different from the pattern of Table 3. A similar example of adjectives is अच्छा *acchaa* 'good'.

surface form	lemma	tag	details	POS	gender	number	person	case
अच्छा	अच्छा	JJ	----	adj	m	sg	--	d
अच्छे	अच्छे	JJ	----	adj	any	any	--	any
अच्छी	अच्छी	JJ	----	adj	f	any	--	any

Table 5: A sample of annotation for Adjective acchaa 'good'

Acchaa has three different lemma forms in the first place, अच्छा *acchaa*, अच्छे *acche*, अच्छी *acchii*, for (m) + (sg), (m) + (any), and (f) + (any), respectively. Although all lemma forms of *-aa* adjectives should be only *-aa* forms, they are tagged like this.

From what we've seen here, it is necessary for users to understand these facts, such as ambiguities and tagging problems, when searching certain words by lemma or by tag.

3.3   Pre-treatment for developing a concordancer

In order to release the web corpus, we planned to develop a special concordancer. Before developing it, we tried running a search using a Perl script, and found additional technical problems requiring attention. Of these, Unicode Devanagari character processing and its character codes was the most difficult to solve. There are two ways to type a character with a *nuqtaa* dot. We can type ड़ in two ways: as 0921 (ड) + 093C (○), i.e., *nuqtaa*; and as 095C (ड़). The problem is that when the tagger normalizes texts and identifies characters with the *nuqtaa*, it automatically deletes the *nuqtaa* from the characters –

---

[7] X is a variable of the type of compound. See Bharati et al (2006)

which forces users to search words without a *nuqtaa*: ex. पीड़ा → पीडा. This means that original texts would be missing and never reappear after being tagged. Moreover, if the characters remain as they are, without a *nuqtaa*, it can cause a problem when searching for words with a *nuqtaa*. To avoid this, we have devised the following:

(1) Text normalization 1: Concatenated character string → Combined character

   Ex. ड़ (095C) → ड़ (095C), ड़ (0921+093C) → ड़ (095C)

(2) Text normalization 2: Deleting the *nuqtaa* from concatenated strings too before tagging

As mentioned above, combined characters such as ड़ (095C) in original texts were being converted into characters without *nuqtaa*, such as ड (0921); as in पीडा (surface form, not lemma). Therefore, we added a pre-treatments to the general normalization process. Firstly, we kept the combined characters as they are, and converted the concatenated character strings into the combined characters – this in order to keep the original texts. Secondly, we deleted the *nuqtaa* from concatenated strings too before tagging - this because the tagger tends to delete *nuqtaa* only from combined characters, not from concatenated character strings. Technically, the tagger replaces, e.g., ड़ (095C) with ड (0921). We merged the outputs tagged by the tagger with the changed texts made in processes (1) and (2). An illustrative example follows.

surface form	lemma	tag	details	POS	gender	number	person	case
पीड़ा	पीडा	NN	0	n	f	sg	3	d

We can see *पीड़ा* in the surface form column. It contains the character ड़ (095C). This pre-treatment allowed us to do a uniform search by either the combined characters or concatenated characters at the level of surface forms, and to keep the original texts as they are.

3.4 Development of a specific concordancer for linguistic research

We developed a concordancer to run searches on COSH. This is a web application. A search request made by the user goes through a web framework called Django, and the search is done on a BlackLab server. The search result returns to Django and is displayed on the interface.

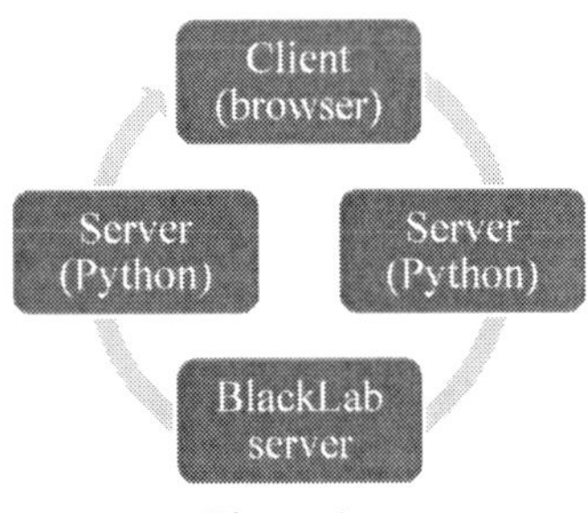

Figure 1

Every time we run a search on the COSH, the client browser requests it from the BlackLab server. Then the Python system we developed processes the search results on the server side, and eventually displays them on the browser, i.e., client side.

4   What kind of linguistic research can we do with the corpora and concordancer?

Although, to my knowledge, there have been few linguistic studies on Hindi-Urdu using a corpus thus far, it's possible to say that this kind of corpora enables even us non-native speakers, who lack intuition of the Hindi language, to do linguistic research on semantic and pragmatic levels. Here's an introduction of the kind of studies we can do using this corpus.

4.1   Verb (V1) + Verb (V2) concatenation

It is well known that Hindi has V1 (a main verb) + V2 (an auxiliary verb) device for adding nuances of lexical aspect or modality to the main verb. Masica (1991) labels meanings expressed by V2s as *Aktionsart,* a term derived from Germanic linguistics.

We can observe a rather similar device in Japanese. Of the V2s used in Japanese, the verb *shimau* 'PUT something AWAY' or 'finish' is frequently used to nuance the V1 in the *-te* form: a conjunctive participle quite similar to *jaa-naa* in Hindi. *Shimau* essentially adds a nuance of 'completeness' to the meaning of the V1, which relates to lexical aspect. The nuance of 'completeness' added by *shimau* is sometimes extended to a modality such as unconsciousness, non-intentionality, and even regret depending on the given context.

Even though they have different meanings respectively, both *jaa-naa* and *shimau* behave alike by adding nuance to a V1's meaning. Both of their nuances depend on the given context, which is a good reason to find out what *kinds* of nuance V2s can add to V1s. Technically, the biggest question from a viewpoint of universal grammar is what exactly the compound verbs are. However, this is a pragmatic issue that native speakers have little consciousness of, and thus is difficult to explain to non-native speakers. Since natives have already learnt how to use the target language unconsciously, we naturally find that different informants often explain different impressions for the nuance, which rather confuses non-native speakers.

What, then, can we non-native speakers do to understand what exactly the compound verbs are? One key method is an investigation of real behaviours of V2 intensively and collectively using a large-scale corpus. Specifically, we can check how frequently those V2s are used, in what context and environment, if there are any restrictions when using them, and in what genres they are most frequently used. These aspects are all noticed by non-native speakers, and not by native speakers who care little for them when using the language.

For example, we investigated restrictions on the co-occurrence in Hindi of the STEM form of the main verb plus the vector or auxiliary verb *jaa-naa* 'GO' together with negative markers, using a Hindi corpus (Nishioka 2015). On this point, Jagannathan (1981: 272-3) claims that the Hindi negative markers such as *nahiiN* do not occur with a 'coloring verb', i.e., a secondary verb (V2) in a verb-verb concatenation. Snell (2010: 290), possibly in support of this claim, explains that "compound verbs give a specific sense of the way in which a particular action is done. It therefore follows that a sentence that's negative or general won't use them; …"

How about Japanese, then? There are numerous studies on *hukugo-doshi*, i.e., compound verb(s). Many of these are limited to explanations to native speakers, except, e.g., Teramura (1984) and Himeno (1999). Recently, Kageyama (2013) began to provide a Compound Verb Lexicon[8]. However, before Nishioka (2013), there seems to have been no specific study using a large corpus[9] that tries to point out why V2s do not occur in negative sentences and to clarify the relation between V2s and negative sentences. This is natural, since this is a matter that non-native speakers easily find when learning the target language.

As we see, using corpora offers the following benefits: non-native speakers of the target language can check a linguistic phenomenon or fact of the target language as objectively and quantitatively as possible; and we can observe the phenomenon from various aspects as required, since COSH provides a context-reference function around the example we have searched.

---

[8] The site is available at http://vvlexicon.ninjal.ac.jp/en/.
[9] The BCCWJ corpus, provided by National Institute for Japanese Language and Linguistics (NINJAL).

4.2 Noun modification and nominalization

Both Hindi and Japanese are SOV and head-final languages, although from different language families. In Hindi, there are four ways of noun modification and nominalization. The most notable way is modifications of a relative clause or an appositive clause. The other three are genitive postposition *kaa* with the allomorphs *ke* and *kii; vaalaa* with the allomorphs *vale* and *vaalii*, depending on the number and gender of the following noun; and imperfect/perfect participles.

Japanese also has two ways of noun modification and nominalization. One is the genitive case particle *no* (*kaku-joshi* in traditional Japanese language study) also considered a 'quasi-nominal particle' (*juntai-joshi*, considered a functional subset of the *kaku-joshi*); and the other is imperfect/perfect participles. In particular, the particle *no* is said to have multiple functions. For example, Wrona (2012) has summarized the functions of *no* throughout the history of Japanese: Copula (Adnominal), Genitive, Subjective marker, Pronominal, Complementizer, Stance-marker 1, and Stance-marker 2.

In fact, the participial modification in Japanese basically corresponds to modification of a relative clause or participles in Hindi. However, regarding the Hindi connection of ⟨Noun 1⟩ and ⟨Noun 2⟩ (the latter being a head noun), there are two devices: *kaa* and *vaalaa*. As for the latter, Kellogg (1876: 252, 317) and Beams (1879: 238-9) explain that *vaalaa* was descended from the Sanskrit *paalaka* 'keeper, protector'. Etymologically, it appears to have been used for forming nouns of agency. Although there seem to be no studies on the historical development of the functions of *vaalaa*, it must have developed other functions subsequent to its original etymology. In any event, there is a possibility that these two devices share the respectively different functions of noun modification and even nominalization, as seen in Japanese.

Under the circumstances, what contribution might a large corpus such as COSH make to linguistic studies? With this corpus, we can observe instances of actual use, based on the word itself or combinations of other POS and the word. For example, we find certain noun phrases, such as *piine kaa paanii* [drink.INF.OBL GEN water] and *piine vaalaa paanii* [drink.INF.OBL *vaalaa* water], both of which mean 'water to drink'; or *chuTTii ke din* [holiday GEN din] and *chuTTii vale din* [holiday *vaalaa* day] 'on a holiday'. However, these seem to be used in slightly different contexts. We can also find other examples with GEN or with *vaalaa*. Large corpora like COSH allow us to do a search easily, and to see a context around the example. Moreover, we can search the corpora specifying a part of speech. The corpora allow us to set an infinitive oblique form [-*ne*] in the slot for ⟨Noun 1⟩, should we need to limit ourselves to examples with only infinitive forms in that slot.

5 Conclusion

While the use of large corpora is not yet popular in South Asian language research, it is possible to say that the spread such use can encourage us non-native speakers to investigate linguistic phenomena more deeply than before, especially from viewpoints of pragmatics and semantics – that is, to pursue usage-based studies. Although, as we've seen in section 3, we have some points to improve in text annotation in the corpus, COSH will provide powerful supporting evidence to compensate for lack of intuition of the target language in linguistic research by non-native speakers.

Although the scope of this paper did not permit us to include many supporting examples of the aspects of language research, we hope this corpus study will contribute to the pragmatic and semantic study of the Hindi language by non-native speakers.

Acknowledgment

This work was supported by grants-in-aid for scientific research (C) [JSPS KAKENHI: no. JP15K02517 and no. JP20520384] and a grant-in-aid for challenging exploratory research [JSPS KAKENHI: no. JP23652084].

Reference

Beams, John. (1879). *Comparative Grammar of the Modern Aryan Languages of India : to wit, Hindi, Panjabi, Sindhi, Gujarati, Marathi, Oriya and Bangali* (Reprinted by Cambridge University Press edition, Volume 3: The Verb). New York: Trübner, reprinted by Cambridge University Press, 2012.

Bharathi, Akshar, Sharma, Dipi Mishra, Bai, Lakshmi and Sangal, Rajeev (2006). "Ann Corra: Annotating Corpora Guidelines for POS and Chunk Annotation for Indian Languages", Language Technologies Research Center, International Institute of Information Technology, IIT Hyderabad, India.

Bharathi, Akshar and Mannem, Prashanth R. (2007). "Introduction to the Shallow Parsing Contest for South Asian Languages", Language Technologies Research Center, International Institute of Information Technology, Hyderabad, India 500032.

Dalal, Aniket, Nagaraj, Kumar, Sawant, Uma, Shelke, Sandeep, and Bhattacharyya, Pushpak. (2007). "Building Feature Rich POS Tagger for Morphologically Rich Languages: Experiences in Hindi". In *Proceedings of ICON*. Available from https://www.cse.iitb.ac.in/~pb/papers/icon07-Hindi-memm-postag.pdf

Himeno, Masako (1999). *Hukugou doushi no imi youhou to kouzou*. Tokyo: Hitsuji shobou.

Hook, Peter E. (1974). *The Compound Verb in Hindi.* Michigan: University of Michigan, Center for South and Southeast Asian Studies.

Ishikawa, Shinichiro, Maeda, Tadahiko, and Yamazaki, Makoto (eds.) (2010) *Gengo Kenkyuu no tame no Toukei Nyuumon.*Tokyo: Kuroshio shuppan.

Ishikawa, Shinichiro (2012) *Basic Corpus Gengogaku (A Basic Guide to Corpus Linguistics).* Tokyo: Hitsuji shobou.

Jagannaathan, V. R. (1981). *Prayog aur prayog.* Dillii: Oxford University Pres.

Kachru, Yamuna. (1980). *Aspects of Hindi Grammar.* New Delhi: Manohar.

—— (2006). *Hindi.* Amsterdam/Philadelphia: John Benjamins Pub Co.

Kellogg, H. Samuel. (1938). *A Grammar of the Hindi Language : in which are treated the High Hindí, Braj, and the Eastern Hindí of the Rámáyan of Tulsí Dás, also the colloquial dialects of Rájputáná, Kumáon, Avadh, Ríwá, Bhojpúr, Magadha, Maithila, etc., with copious philological note (the 3rd edition).* London: Kegan Paul, Trench, Trubner and Co.

Masica, Colin. P. (1976). *Defining a Linguistic Area: South Asia.* Chicago: University of Chicago Press.

—— (1991). *The Indo-Aryan Languages.* Cambridge: Cambridge University Press.

McGregor, R.S. (1995). *Outline of Hindi Grammar.* Oxford: Oxford University Press.

Nishioka, Miki. (2005). "Hindii-go no iwayu ru meishiku ni tsuite: zokkaku kouchishi '*kaa*' wo chuushin-ni", *Kyoto Sangyo University essays Humanities series vol.33.* Pp. 74-98. Kyoto: Kyoto Industrial University.

—— (2013). "Te-kei + *shimau* to hiteiji to no kyouki seigen to sono kankyou ni tsuite: Hindii-go to no taishougengogakuteki shiten kara (Co-occurrence Restrictions on the '-*te* Form + *shimau*' and Negation in Japanese: A Contrastive Analysis with Hindi)", *Matani ronshū vol.7.* Pp.47-73, Osaka: Nihongo Nihon Bunka Kyouiku Kenkyuukai.

—— (2014). "Co-occurrence restrictions on the '-*te* Form + *shimau*' and negation in Japanese: A contrastive analysis with Hindi", presented at XXVIIes Journées de Linguistique d' Asie Orientale. Abstract is available from http://crlao.ehess.fr/docannexe/file/1698/booklet.pdf.

—— (2016) "Functions of *jaanaa* as a V2 in Hindi: From Lexicalization to Grammaticalization", presented at 32nd South Asian Languages Analysis Roundtable (SALA-32). Abstract (pp.57-9) is available from http://media.wix.com/ugd/56a455_223031a3531f4b18b7ad857a6626cc7b.pdf

Nishioka, Miki and Akasegawa, Shiro (2015) "Restrictions on co-occurrence of 'STEM + *jaanaa*' and negation in Hindi: a contrastive analysis with '-*te* + *shimau*' in Japanese". In Book of Abstracts South Asian Languages Analysis Roundtable (SALA 31). Abstract (pp.51-3) is available from http://ucrel.lancs.ac.uk/sala-31/doc/ABSTRACTBOOK-maincontent.pdf

Noonan, Michael. (1997). "Versatile Nominalizations". Bybee, Joan, Haiman, John, Thompson, Sandra A. (eds.), *Essays on Language Function and Language Type: Dedicated to T. Givón.* Pp. 373-394. John Benjamins Publishing.

P.J, Antony and K.P., Sonam. (2011). "Part of Speech Tagging for Indian Languages: A Literature Survey". In *International Journal of Computer Applications (0975-8887)*, Volume 34, No.8, pp.22-9. http://citeseerx.ist.psu.edu/viewdoc/download?doi=10.1.1.259.1220&rep=rep1&type=pdf

Snell, Rupert (2010). *Teach Yourself Get Started in Hindi (Teach Yourself Beginner's Languages)*. 2nd Revised. Teach Yourself Books.

Teramura, Hideo. (1984). *Nihongo no syntax to imi*, vol II (11th edition). Tokyo: Kuroshio shuppan.

Wrona, Janick. (2012). "The Early History of no as a Nominaliser". Frellesvig, Bjarke, Kiaer, Jieun, Wrona, Janick (eds.), *Studies in Asian Linguistics (LSASL 78): Studies in Japanese and Korean Linguistics*, available from http://www.engl.polyu.edu.hk/research/nomz/pdf/WRONA_History_of_NO.pdf#search='The+Early+History+of+no+as+a+Nominaliser'). München: LINCOM.

Automatic Creation of a Sentence Aligned Sinhala-Tamil

Parallel Corpus

**Riyafa Abdul Hameed, Nadeeshani Pathirennehelage, Anusha Ihalapathirana,
Maryam Ziyad Mohamed, Surangika Ranathunga, Sanath Jayasena, Gihan Dias,
Sandareka Fernando**
Department of Computer Science and Engineering, University of Moratuwa, Sri Lanka

```
{riyafa.12,pnadeeshani.12,anusha.12,maryamzi.12,surangika,
       sanath,gihan,sandarekaf}@cse.mrt.ac.lk
```


Abstract

A sentence aligned parallel corpus is an important prerequisite in statistical machine translation. However, manual creation of such a parallel corpus is time consuming, and requires experts fluent in both languages. Automatic creation of a sentence aligned parallel corpus using parallel text is the solution to this problem. In this paper, we present the first ever empirical evaluation carried out to identify the best method to automatically create a sentence aligned Sinhala-Tamil parallel corpus. Annual reports from Sri Lankan government institutions were used as the parallel text for aligning. Despite both Sinhala and Tamil being under-resourced languages, we were able to achieve an F-score value of 0.791 using a hybrid approach that makes use of a bilingual dictionary.

1   Introduction

Sentence and word aligned parallel corpora are extensively used for statistical machine translation (Al-Onaizan et al., 1999; Callison-Burch, 2004) and in multilingual natural language processing (NLP) applications (Kaur and Kaur, 2012). In recent years, parallel corpora have become more widely available and serve as a source for data-driven NLP tasks for languages such as English and French (Hallebeek, 2000; Kaur and Kaur, 2012).

A parallel corpus is a collection of text in one or more languages with their translation into another language or languages that have been stored in a machine-readable format (Hallebeek, 2000). A parallel corpus can be aligned either at sentence level or word level. Sentence and word alignment of parallel corpus is the identification of the corresponding sentences and words (respectively) in both halves of the parallel text.

Sentence alignment could be of various combinations including one to one where one sentence maps to one sentence in the other corpus, one to many where one sentence maps to more than one sentences in the other corpus, many to many where many sentences map to many sentences in the other corpus or even one to zero where there is no mapping for a particular sentence in the other corpus.

For statistical machine translation, the more the number of parallel sentence pairs, the higher the quality of translation (Koehn, 2010). However, manual alignment of a large number of sentences is time consuming, and requires personnel fluent in both languages. Automatic sentence alignment of a parallel corpus is the widely accepted solution for this problem. Already many sentence alignment techniques have been implemented for some languages pairs such as English-French (Gale and Church, 1993; Brown et al., 1991; Chen, 1993; Braune and Fraser 2010; Lamraoui and Langlais, 2013), English-German (Gale and Church, 1993) English-Chinese (Wu, 1994; Chuang and Yeh, 2005)

Proceedings of the 6th Workshop on South and Southeast Asian Natural Language Processing,
pages 124–132, Osaka, Japan, December 11-17 2016.

and Hungarian-English (Varga et al., 2005; Tóth et al., 2008). However, none of these techniques have been evaluated for Sinhala and Tamil, the two official languages in Sri Lanka.

This paper presents the first ever study on automatically creating a sentence aligned parallel corpus for Sinhala and Tamil. Sinhala and Tamil are both under-resourced languages, and research implementing basic NLP tool such as POS taggers and morphological analysers is at its inception stage (Herath et al., 2004; Hettige and Karunananda, 2006; Anandan et al., 2002). Therefore, not all the aforementioned sentence alignment techniques are applicable in the context of Sinhala and Tamil. With this limitation in mind, an extensive literature study was carried out to identify the applicable sentence alignment techniques for Sinhala and Tamil. We implemented six such methods, and evaluated their performance using a corpus of 1300 sentences based on the precision, recall, and F-measure using annual reports of Sri Lankan government departments as the source text. The highest F-measure value of 0.791 was obtained for Varga et al.'s (2005) Hunalign method, the hybrid method that combined the use of a bilingual dictionary with the statistical method by Gale and Church (1993).

The rest of the paper is organized as follows. Section 2 identifies related work in this area. Section 3 describes how different techniques were employed in the alignment process, and section 4 presents the results for these techniques. Section 5 contains a discussion of these results while section 6 presents the conclusion and future work.

2   Related Work

Automatic sentence alignment techniques can be broadly categorized into three classes: statistical, linguistic, and hybrid methods. Statistical methods use quantitative measures (such as sentence size, sentence character number) to create an alignment relationship; linguistic methods use linguistic knowledge gained from sources such as morphological analyzers, bilingual dictionaries, and word list pairs, to relate sentences; hybrid methods combine the statistical and linguistic methods to achieve accurate statistical information (Simões, 2004).

2.1   Statistical Methods

Gale and Church (1993), and Brown et al. (1991) have introduced statistical methods for aligning sentences that have been successfully used for European languages, including English-French, English-German, English-Polish, English-Spanish (McEnery et al., 1997), English-Dutch and Dutch - French (Paulussen et al, 2013).

These methods have also been used with Non-European languages such as English - Chinese (McEnery and Oakes, 1996), Italian-Japanese (Zotti et al, 2014), English-Arabic (Alkahtani et al, 2015), and English-Malay (Yeong et al, 2016). The general idea of these methods is that the closer in length two sentences are, the more likely they align. Brown et al.'s (1991) method aligns sentences based on sentence length measured using word count. Here anchor points are used for alignment. Gale and Church use the number of characters as the length measure. While the parameters such as mean and variance for Gale and Church's (1993) method are considered language independent for European languages, tuning these for non-'European language pairs has improved results (Zotti et al, 2014).

Both these methods have given good accuracy in alignment; however they require some form of initial alignment or anchor points.

Method by Chuang and Yeh (2005) exploits the statistically ordered matching of punctuation marks in the two languages English and Chinese to achieve high accuracy in sentence alignment compared with using the length-based methods alone.

2.2   Linguistic Methods

Linguistic methods exploit the linguistic characteristics of the source and target languages such as morphology and sentence structure to improve the alignment process. However linguistic methods are not used independently but have been introduced in conjunction with statistical methods, forming hybrid methods as described in the next section.

2.3   Hybrid Methods

Statistical methods such as that of Brown et al., (1991), and Gale and Church (1991) require either corpus-dependent anchor points, or prior alignment of paragraphs to obtain better accuracy. Hybrid

125

methods make use of statistical as well as linguistic features of the sentences obtaining better accuracy in documents with or without these types of prior alignments. Hence hybrid methods are widely used to achieve higher accuracy in alignment. The methods by Wu (1994), Chen (1993), Moore (2002), Varga et al. (2005), Sennrich and Volk (2011), Lamraoui and Langlais (2013), Braune and Fraser (2010), Tóth et al. (2008) and Mújdricza-Maydt et al. (2013) are some of them.

The method used by Wu (1994) is a modification of Gale and Church's (1993) length-based statistical method for the task of aligning English with Chinese. It uses a bilingual external lexicon with lexicon cues to improve the alignment accuracy. Dynamic programming optimization has been used for the alignment of the lexicon extensions. However, the computation and memory costs grow linearly with the number of lexical cues.

The method by Chen (1993) is a word-correspondence-based model that gives a better accuracy than length based methods, however, it was reported to be much slower than the algorithms of Brown et al., (1991) and Gale and Church (1993).

Moore's (2002) method aligns the corpus using a modified version of Brown et al.'s (1991) sentence-length-based model in the first pass. It then uses the sentence pairs that were assigned the highest probability of alignment to train a modified version of IBM Translation Model 1 (one of the five translation models that assigns a probability to each of the possible word-by-word alignments—developed by Brown et al. (1993)). The corpus is realigned, augmenting the initial alignment model with IBM Model 1, to produce an alignment based both on sentence length and word correspondences. It uses a novel search-pruning technique to efficiently find the sentence pairs that will be aligned with the highest probability without the use of anchor points or larger previously aligned units like paragraphs or sections. This is an effective method that gets a relatively high performance especially in precision. Nonetheless, this method has the drawback that it usually gets a low recall especially when dealing with sparse data (Trieu et al., 2015).

Hunalign sentence alignment method by Varga et al. (2005) uses a hybrid algorithm based on a length-based method that makes use of a bilingual dictionary. The similarity score between a source and a target sentence consists of two major components, which are token-based score and length-based score. The token-based score depends on the number of shared words in the two sentences while the length-based alignment is based on the character count of the sentence.

Varga et al.'s (2005) method uses a dictionary-based crude translation model instead of a full IBM translation model as used by Moore (2002). This has the very important advantage that it can exploit a bilingual lexicon, if one is available, and tune it according to frequencies in the target corpus. Moore's (2002) method offers no such way to tune a pre-existing language model. Moreover, the focus of Moore's (2002) algorithm on one-to-one alignments is less than optimal, since excluding one-to-many and many-to-many alignments may result in losing substantial amounts of aligned material if the two languages have different sentence structuring conventions (Varga et al., 2005).

Bleualign sentence aligner by Sennrich and Volk (2011) is based on the BLEU (bilingual evaluation understudy) score, which is an algorithm for evaluating the quality of text that has been machine-translated from one natural language to another. Instead of computing an alignment between the source and target text directly, this technique bases its alignment search on a Machine Translation (MT) of the source text.

The YASA method by Lamraoui and Langlais (2013) also operates a two-step process through the parallel data. Cognates are first recognized in order to accomplish a first token-level alignment that (efficiently) delimits a fruitful search space. Then, sentence alignment is performed on this reduced search space. The speed of the YASA aligner and memory use is comparatively better than Moore's (2002) aligner (Lamraoui and Langlais, 2013).

Though the method by Braune and Fraser (2010) is four times slower than Moore's (2002) method, it supports one to many and many to one alignments as well. It uses an improved pruning method and in the second pass, the sentences are optimally aligned and merged. This method uses a two-step clustering approach in the second pass of the alignment.

The method by Tóth et al. (2008) exploits the fact that Named Entities cannot be ignored from any translation process, so a sentence and its translation equivalent contain the same Named Entities.

The method by Mújdricza-Maydt et al. (2013) uses a two-step process to align sentences. Machine alignments known as "wood standard" annotations, produced using state-of-the-art sentence aligners in a first step, are used in a second step, to train a discriminative learner. This combination of arbitrary amounts of machine aligned data and an expressive discriminative learner provides a boost in precision. All features used in the second step, with the exception of the POS agreement feature, are language-independent.

According to Gale and Church (1993) a considerably large parallel corpus having a small error percentage can be built without lexical constraints. According to the authors, lexical constraints might slow down the program and make it less useful in the first pass. Linguistic methods can produce better results if the performance of the system is not a concern. Hybrid methods such as that of Moore's (2002) that do not require particular knowledge about the corpus or the languages involved are faster as they tend to build the bilingual dictionary for aligning using the input to the aligner based on previous word-correspondence-based models.

Furthermore, results of some of the above methods such as Hunalign (Varga et al, 2005), Bleualign (Sennrich and Volk, 2011) and Gargantua (Braune and Fraser, 2010) could be improved by applying linguistic factors such as word forms, chunks and collocations (Navlea and Todiraşcu, 2010). Some have used morphologically processed (lemmatized and morphologically tagged) data and have used taggers (POS tagger) because it significantly increases the value of the data (Bojar et al, 2014).

2.4 Indic Languages

Automatic alignment of sentences has been attempted for few Indic language pairs from the South Asian subcontinent including Hindi-Urdu (Kaur and Kaur, 2012) and Hindi-Punjabi (Kumar and Goyal, 2010). This research used the method proposed by Gale and Church (1993) citing the close linguistic similarities between languages of these pairs, causing parallel sentences to be of similar lengths.

3 Methodology

3.1 Data Source

The parallel corpus used in aligning sentences is from annual reports published by different government departments in Sri Lanka. These government reports have been manually translated from Sinhala to Tamil by translators with different levels of experience in translation and Sinhala-Tamil competency. Thus the quality of the translations compared to other sources such as those from the Parliament of Sri Lanka is comparatively low with a considerable number of omissions and mistranslations.

These annual reports are in pdf format. Text was automatically extracted from the pdf documents, and converted to Unicode to ensure uniformity. The text thus obtained was segmented into sentences using a custom tokenization algorithm implemented specifically for Tamil and Sinhala.

Although there are some tokenizers for Sinhala[1] and Tamil, they could not be used for this purpose, since the abbreviations used in our input text are different from those in the existing tokenizers. Therefore we created a list of manually extracted abbreviations. Splitting documents into sentences was done by using delimiters such as " ., ? , ! ". Splitting into sentences using full stops is misleading at abbreviations, decimal digits, e-mails, URLs etc., because full stops at these places are not actual sentence boundaries. Therefore splitting into sentences at these points was avoided by means of regular expression checks. However issues such as omissions of punctuation marks result in the need for complex alignments (one to many, many to many).

For example[2] the following sentences in Sinhala specify five cities (Kuruwita, Rathnapura, Balangoda, Godakawela, Opanayake) followed by the sentence "The Active Committee representing the Operations Co-ordination Centers for Language Associations in Vavuniya was established".

(කුරුවිට,රත්නපුර,බලංගොඩ, ගොඩකවෙල, ඕපනායක).
වවුනියාව භාෂා සංගම් මෙහෙයුම් මධ්‍යස්ථාන ක්‍රියාකාරී කමිටුව ස්ථාපිත කරන ලදී.

However due to the omission of the period in the corresponding Tamil text, the above is identified as one single sentence in Tamil requiring the alignment to map one Tamil sentence to many Sinhala sentences.

(குருவிட்ட இரத்தினபுரி பலாங்கொடை கொடகவெல ஒபநாயக) வவுனியாவிலும் மாவட்ட மொழிச்சங்க செயற்பாட்டு குழு உருவாக்கப்பட்டது.

---

[1] https://github.com/madurangasiriwardena/corpus.sinhala.tools
[2] Text extracted from English, Sinhala and Tamil Annual Reports of a Government Department

The bilingual dictionary used for alignment was obtained from the trilingual dictionary[3] combined with the glossaries obtained from the Department of Official languages[4], Sri Lanka. The number of words in the lexicon obtained has around 90000 words, but it does not have all the commonly used words in the languages and mostly has the spoken forms of words in Sinhala, which are not used in the written official documents.

3.2 Sentence Alignment

Depending on the similarities and dissimilarities between the languages and the quality of the data source, different techniques discussed in section 2 have given different results for the alignment for different language pairs. For example, a method like that of Chuang and Yeh (2005) would work well for parallel text where punctuations are consistent, while that of Varga et al. (2005) would work better for languages that lack etymological relations. Thus the objective of this research is to experiment with these techniques for Sinhala-Tamil, and identify the best technique.

However, not all methods described in section 2 can be used in the context of Sinhala and Tamil. For example, methods by Tóth et al. (2008) and Mújdricza-Maydt et al. (2013) cannot be used because NER systems and comprehensive POS taggers are not fully developed for Sinhala (Dahanayaka and Weerasinghe, 2014; Manamini et al., 2016) and Tamil (Pandian et al., 2008; Vijayakrishna and Devi, 2008). Also methods that align using the punctuations in the two languages similar to that of Chuang and Yeh (2005) cannot be used in this case because when extracting text from pdf, some punctuations are lost, and also the translators of the original text have not been consistent with the use of punctuations.

Constrained by the available resources, we compared methods by Gale and Church (1993), Moore (2002), Varga et al. (2005), Braune and Fraser (2010), Lamraoui and Langlais (2013), and Sennrich and Volk (2011). These methods have shown promising results for languages that show close linguistic relationships, which is also the case with Sinhala and Tamil. These close linguistic relationships include similarities in word or sentence length, similarities in sentence structure and in languages that use the character set, similarities between words. Linguistic similarities between Sinhala and Tamil include word and sentence length similarities and sentence structure similarity with both Sinhala and Tamil following a Subject-Object-Verb structure.

The mean and variance for the number of Tamil characters per Sinhala was found and these values were used for the Gale and Church's (1993) method. Default values were used for the other methods during the evaluation.

For Moore's (2002) method, a bilingual word dictionary is built using the IBM Model 1. However, this dictionary may lack significant vocabulary when the input corpus contains sparse data, as pointed out by Trieu and Nguyen (2015). The output files from this method contain all the sentences from the input files that align 1-to-1 with probability greater than the "threshold" according to the statistical model computed by the aligner. For evaluation using this method we used a threshold of 0.8 instead of the default value of 0.5.

Around 1300 sentences were extracted from pdf files and were aligned using these methods. This corpus is publicly available[3] for the benefit of Sinhala and Tamil language computing. The same sentences were manually aligned with the help of a human translator. Then the automatically aligned sentences were compared with the manually aligned sentences to obtain the precision and recall values.

4 Evaluation

The evaluation for sentence alignment was done by using data that was manually aligned. The reason for this approach instead of getting the human translator to evaluate the automatically aligned sentences was to ensure that the manual evaluation was independent from the automatically produced output, as the automated alignments may influence the human aligner. Furthermore this approach also facilitated the comparison of the performance of multiple methods. Table 1 shows the precision, recall, and F-measure obtained for the six methods.

---

[3] http://www.trilingualdictionary.lk/
[4] http://www.languagesdept.gov.lk/

	Gale and Church (1993) (modified)	Varga et al.'s (2005) (Hunalign)	Sennrich and Volk's (2011) (BLEUalign)	Moore's (2002)	Braune and Fraser's (2010)	Lamraoui and Langlais's(YASA) (2013)
Precision	77.24%	**81.67%**	76.91%	94.56%	81.52%	80.62%
Recall	72.52%	**76.73%**	69.78%	67.56%	65.71%	76.53%
F-measure	74.8%	**79.1%**	73.2%	78.8%	72.8 %	78.5%

Table 1: Evaluation Results

5 Discussion

Most of the above methods (Gale and Church, 1993; Brown et al., 1991; Chen and S.F, 1993; Braune and Fraser, 2010) have been first used for English and French sentence alignment. Both these languages have many similarities, which include the sentence structure and the sentence length. The sentence structure of these languages is of the form subject-verb-object and the sentence length is quite close.

The same similarities can also be found in Sinhala and Tamil languages. Sinhala and Tamil languages have the same sentence structure, Subject-Object-Verb. Also the average sentence lengths of the two languages are quite close. Considering 700 sentences, average length of Sinhala is 113.76 and for Tamil it is 130.53. Therefore statistical methods have given good results in our case. The lexical components used in the hybrid methods suggested above are also language independent. Thus the hybrid methods are also applicable for Sinhala and Tamil.

We used Gale and Church (1993) method even though we could not align the paragraphs before aligning the sentences, due the dissimilarities among the text converted from pdfs. The length of Tamil sentences was comparatively higher than Sinhala sentences and the correlation between Sinhala and Tamil was comparatively low, hence we cannot consider mean and variance as language independent as suggested by Gale and Church (1993). Therefore we calculated the mean and variance for Sinhala and Tamil using 700 sentences. Gale and Church (1993) introduced 1 as mean and 6.8 as variance for English and French Languages. For Sinhala and Tamil, we figured out mean is 1.152 and variance is 1.860. Even after changing the parameters for Sinhala and Tamil in the Gale and Church (1993) method, we obtained a comparatively low precision because this method does not only look at one to one alignments but also one to zero, many to one, one to many or many to many alignments. Also according to Gale and Church (1993), in this method one to zero alignment is never handled correctly. Most misalignments arise due to one to zero, many to one to many or many to many alignments, resulting in methods that consider only one to one alignments to have better precision values. Given the nature of the source documents used in this research, there were a significant non one-to-one alignments and incorrect translations, which affected the precision value. However, as this method omits only a few sentences, it obtains high recall and F-Score than some of the other methods.

Since the text used for alignment in our case has considerably sparse data, the dictionary built in the Moore's (2002) method lacks significant vocabulary. Furthermore because of the fact that Moore's (2002) method only considers one to one alignment, the recall obtained by this method is very low while the precision is very high. In our case, even though there are alignments that are not one to one, the high precision of Moore's method has shown that it is possible to align a considerable number of sentences only by using one to one alignments. According to Moore (2002), in practice one to one alignments are the only alignments that are currently used for training machine translation systems.

The YASA aligner by Lamraoui and Langlais (2013) has proven to be robust to noise by having a good precision and recall for the parallel corpus of Sinhala and Tamil. Also the Braune and Fraser's (2010) method is known to work better especially for corpora where the sentences do not align one to one that often. However, our source text has a number of one to one alignments (as was proved by the alignment in Moore's (2002) method) along with other forms of alignments, which could be the reason for the low recall of this method.

Even though the method by Varga et al. (2005) has given the highest F-score, the results for this method could be improved using a better dictionary that includes all or most of the words that are used in the annual reports.

A factor significantly affecting the results of the alignment process was the quality of the source documents. Compared to other documents such as parliamentary documents, news articles and subtitles commonly used in evaluating alignment, the annual reports we considered were of comparatively less quality including significant omissions and inconsistencies and high complexity with significant many to one, one to many, and many to many alignments. The data set considered comprised of nearly 7% many to one, one to many or many to many alignments and nearly 15% one to zero or zero to one alignments indicating improper or incomplete translations.

6   Conclusion

We have addressed the problem of the lack of sentence aligned Sinhala-Tamil parallel corpus large enough to be useful in a multitude of natural language processing tasks. We have experimented with a number of alignment techniques developed for other language pairs, introducing necessary modifications for Sinhala and Tamil, where applicable.

The results generated have been satisfactory, indicating that better results could be obtained with more language resources such as morphological analyzers, POS taggers and named entity recognizers, which are currently not fully developed for Sinhala. This research is carried out as part of a major project to build a machine translation system between Sinhala and Tamil. POS taggers and named entity recognizers are being developed as part of this larger project. With the availability of these resources, methods utilizing these resources could also be introduced for Sinhala and Tamil in the near future, to obtain improved results.

Future work in improving the automatic generation of the Sinhala-Tamil parallel corpus includes experimenting with more techniques that have worked for other language pairs. The suitability of techniques that specifically use language resources such as POS taggers and morphological analysers could also be evaluated with the availability of such resources of better quality. Additionally the identified techniques could be evaluated with documents from different domains, whereas in this research evaluation has been done only with annual reports.

Acknowledgement

This research is part of a larger project at the Department of Computer Science and Engineering, University of Moratuwa, on developing a machine translation system for Sinhala and Tamil languages. We would like to extend our gratitude to the project team, and Mrs. Lalitha Peiris in particular, who did the manual translation of text. We would also like to thank the Department of Official Languages for providing us with the language resources.

References

Alkahtani, Saad, Wei Liu, and William J. Teahan. "A new hybrid metric for verifying parallel corpora of Arabic-English." *arXiv preprint arXiv:1502.03752* (2015).

Al-Onaizan, Yaser, Jan Curin, Michael Jahr, Kevin Knight, John Lafferty, Dan Melamed, Franz-Josef Och, David Purdy, Noah A. Smith, and David Yarowsky. "Statistical machine translation." In *Final Report, JHU Summer Workshop*, vol. 30. 1999.

Anandan, P., K. Saravanan, RanjaniParthasarathi, and T. V. Geetha."Morphological analyzer for Tamil."In *International Conference on Natural language Processing*. 2002.

Bojar, Ondrej, VojtechDiatka, PavelRychlý, PavelStranák, VítSuchomel, Ales Tamchyna, and Daniel Zeman. "HindEnCorp-Hindi-English and Hindi-only Corpus for Machine Translation." In *Language Resources and Evaluation Conference*, pp. 3550-3555. 2014.

Braune, Fabienne, and Alexander Fraser. "Improved unsupervised sentence alignment for symmetrical and asymmetrical parallel corpora." In *Proceedings of the 23rd International Conference on Computational Linguistics*, pp. 81-89.Association for Computational Linguistics, 2010.

Brown, Peter F., Jennifer C. Lai, and Robert L. Mercer."Aligning sentences in parallel corpora."In *Proceedings of the 29th annual meeting on Association for Computational Linguistics*, pp. 169-176.Association for Computational Linguistics, 1991.

Brown, Peter F., Vincent J. Della Pietra, Stephen A. Della Pietra, and Robert L. Mercer. "The mathematics of statistical machine translation: Parameter estimation." *Computational linguistics* 19, no. 2 (1993): 263-311.

Callison-Burch, Chris, David Talbot,and Miles Osborne. 2004. Statistical machine translation with word-and sentence-aligned parallel corpora. In Proceedings of the 42nd Annual Meeting on Association for Computational Linguistics, pages 176–183, Barcelona

Chen, Stanley F. "Aligning sentences in bilingual corpora using lexical information."In *Proceedings of the 31st annual meeting on Association for Computational Linguistics*, pp. 9-16.Association for Computational Linguistics, 1993.

Chuang, Thomas C., and Kevin C. Yeh."Aligning parallel bilingual corpora statistically with punctuation criteria."*Computational Linguistics and Chinese Language Processing* 10, no. 1 (2005): 95-122.

Dahanayaka, J. K., and A. R. Weerasinghe."Named entity recognition for Sinhala language."In *2014 International Conference on Advances in ICT for Emerging Regions (ICTer)*, pp. 215-220. IEEE, 2014.

Gale, William A., and Kenneth W. Church. "A program for aligning sentences in bilingual corpora." *Computational linguistics* 19, no. 1 (1993): 75-102.

Hallebeek, Jos. "English parallel corpora and applications." *Cuadernos de FilologiaInglesa* 9, no. 1 (2000).

Herath, DulipLakmal, and A. R. Weerasinghe. "A Stochastic Part of Speech Tagger for Sinhala." In *Proceedings of the 06th International Information Technology Conference*, pp. 27-28. 2004.

Hettige, Budditha, and Asoka S. Karunananda."A Morphological analyzer to enable English to Sinhala Machine Translation."In *2006 International Conference on Information and Automation*, pp. 21-26.IEEE, 2006.

Kaur, Mandeep and NavdeepKaur. 2012. "Development And Analysis Of Hindi-Urdu Parallel Corpus". *International Journal Of Computing And Corporate Research* 2 (6).

Koehn, Philipp. *Statistical machine translation.*Cambridge University Press, 2009.

Kumar, Pardeep, and Vishal Goyal."Development of Hindi-Punjabi Parallel Corpus Using Existing Hindi-Punjabi Machine Translation System and Using Sentence Alignments."*Development* 5, no. 9 (2010).

Lamraoui, F. and Langlais, P., 2013. Yet another fast, robust and open source sentence aligner. Ttime to reconsider sentence alignment. *XIV Machine Translation Summit.*

Manamini, S. A. P. M., A. F. Ahamed, R. A. E. C. Rajapakshe, G. H. A. Reemal, S. Jayasena, G. V. Dias, and S. Ranathunga. "Ananya-a Named-Entity-Recognition (NER) system for Sinhala language."In 2016 *Moratuwa Engineering Research Conference (MERCon)*, pp. 30-35.IEEE, 2016.

McEnery, Tony, Andrew Wilson, Fernando Sanchez-Leon, and Amalio Nieto-Serrano. "Multilingual resources for European languages: contributions of the CRATER project." *Literary and Linguistic Computing* 12, no. 4 (1997): 219-226.

McEnery, Tony, and Michael Oakes."Sentence and word alignment in the CRATER project."*Using corpora for language research* (1996): 211-231.

Moore, Robert C. "Fast and accurate sentence alignment of bilingual corpora."In *Conference of the Association for Machine Translation in the Americas*, pp. 135-144.Springer Berlin Heidelberg, 2002.

Mújdricza-Maydt, Éva, HuiqinKörkel-Qu, Stefan Riezler, and Sebastian Padó."High-precision sentence alignment by bootstrapping from wood standard annotations."*The Prague Bulletin of Mathematical Linguistics* 99 (2013): 5-16.

Navlea, Mirabela, and AmaliaTodiraşcu."Linguistic Resources for Factored Phrase-Based Statistical Machine Translation Systems." In *Proceedings of the Workshop on Exploitation of Multilingual Resources and Tools for Central and (South) Eastern European Languages, 7th International Conference on Language Resources and Evaluation*, pp. 41-48. 2010.

Pandian, S., Krishnan AravindPavithra, and T. Geetha. "Hybrid three-stage named entity recognizer for Tamil." *INFOS2008, March Cairo-Egypt. Available at: http://infos2008. fci. cu. edu. eg/infos/NLP_08_P045-052. pdf* (2008).

Paulussen, Hans, LieveMacken, Willy Vandeweghe, and Piet Desmet. "Dutch parallel corpus: A balanced parallel corpus for Dutch-English and Dutch-French." In *Essential Speech and language technology for Dutch*, pp. 185-199.Springer Berlin Heidelberg, 2013.

Thomas, Jenny, and Mick Short, eds. *Using corpora for language research*. London: Longman, 1996.

Sennrich, Rico, and Martin Volk."Iterative, MT-based sentence alignment of parallel texts."In *18th Nordic Conference of Computational Linguistics*. 2011.

Sim͂oes, Alberto Manuel Brand͂ao. 2004. Parallel corpora word alignment and applications. Master's thesis, Escola de Engenharia - Universidadedo Minho.

Tóth, Krisztina, RichárdFarkas, and AndrásKocsor."Sentence Alignment of Hungarian-English Parallel Corpora Using a Hybrid Algorithm."*ActaCybern.* 18, no. 3 (2008): 463-478.

Trieu, Long Hai, and Thai Phuong Nguyen."A New Feature to Improve Moore's Sentence Alignment Method."*VNU Journal of Science: Computer Science and Communication Engineering* 31, no. 1 (2015).

Varga, Dániel, LászlóNémeth, PéterHalácsy, AndrásKornai, Viktor Trón, and Viktor Nagy.Parallel corpora for medium density languages. In *Proceedings of the Recent Advances in Natural Language Processing 2005 conference*, pages 590–596, Borovets, Bulgaria, 2005.

Vijayakrishna, R., and SobhaLalitha Devi. "Domain Focused Named Entity Recognizer for Tamil Using Conditional Random Fields." In *International Joint Conference on Natural Language Processing*, pp. 59-66. 2008.

Wu, Dekai. "Aligning a parallel English-Chinese corpus statistically with lexical criteria."In *Proceedings of the 32nd annual meeting on Association for Computational Linguistics*, pp. 80-87.Association for Computational Linguistics, 1994.

Yeong, Yin-Lai, Tien-Ping Tan, and SitiKhaotijah Mohammad."Using Dictionary and Lemmatizer to Improve Low Resource English-Malay Statistical Machine Translation System."*Procedia Computer Science* 81 (2016): 243-249.

Zotti, Patrizia, and Riccardo Apolloni Yuji Matsumoto."Sentence Alignment of a Japanese-Italian Parallel Corpus.Towards a web-based Interface." *Available at: http://www.anlp.jp/proceedings/annual_meeting/2014/pdf_dir/P1-6.pdf* (2014).

Clustering-based Phonetic Projection in Mismatched Crowdsourcing Channels for Low-resourced ASR

Wenda Chen and **Mark Hasegawa-Johnson**
Beckman Institute
University of Illinois at Urbana-Champaign
USA
wchen113, jhasegaw@illinois.edu

Nancy F. Chen
Institute for Infocomm Research
A*STAR
Singapore
nfychen@i2r.a-star.edu.sg

Preethi Jyothi
Indian Institute of Technology Bombay
India
pjyothi@cse.iitb.ac.in

Lav R. Varshney
Beckman Institute
University of Illinois at Urbana-Champaign
USA
varshney@illinois.edu

Abstract

Acquiring labeled speech for low-resource languages is a difficult task in the absence of native speakers of the language. One solution to this problem involves collecting speech transcriptions from crowd workers who are foreign or non-native speakers of a given target language. From these mismatched transcriptions, one can derive probabilistic phone transcriptions that are defined over the set of all target language phones using a noisy channel model. This paper extends prior work on deriving probabilistic transcriptions (PTs) from mismatched transcriptions by 1) modelling multilingual channels and 2) introducing a clustering-based phonetic mapping technique to improve the quality of PTs. Mismatched crowdsourcing for multilingual channels has certain properties of projection mapping, e.g., it can be interpreted as a clustering based on singular value decomposition of the segment alignments. To this end, we explore the use of distinctive feature weights, lexical tone confusions, and a two-step clustering algorithm to learn projections of phoneme segments from mismatched multilingual transcriber languages to the target language. We evaluate our techniques using mismatched transcriptions for Cantonese speech acquired from native English and Mandarin speakers. We observe a 5–9% relative reduction in phone error rate for the predicted Cantonese phone transcriptions using our proposed techniques compared with the previous PT method.

1 Introduction

Mismatched crowdsourcing is a recently developed method of acquiring transcribed speech in low-resourced and zero-resourced languages (Jyothi et al., 2016). It makes use of cross-lingual perceptions from speakers of high-resourced languages (e.g. English, Mandarin, etc.) when native speakers are unavailable for the target language. When an utterance is perceived by listeners or transcribers who do not speak the utterance language, they may misperceive its phonemes; we model this misperception as a noisy communication channel. The annotator's orthography from his or her native language will introduce further variations due to randomness in the phoneme to grapheme conversion.

The result of mismatched crowdsourcing is a set of transcriptions in, say, English or Mandarin annotation orthography. These mismatched transcripts are aligned, filtered, and decoded, using a maximum a posteriori (MAP) decoder, to compute a distribution over phone sequences in the target language (referred to as a probabilistic transcript or PT) (Hasegawa-Johnson et al., 2016). More accurate PTs could be derived by modeling crowd workers with different native backgrounds separately and merging their

Proceedings of the 6th Workshop on South and Southeast Asian Natural Language Processing,
pages 133–141, Osaka, Japan, December 11-17 2016.

cross-lingual misperceptions, after estimating how the phonemes in the transcriber languages can be mapped to the phonemes in the target language.

This paper provides a novel approach for merging cross-lingual perceptions from more than one language channel without using any *a priori* knowledge of phone mappings between the transcriber languages and the target language. Section 2 describes the dataset used in this work. Section 3 explores how phonetic and tonal confusions in mismatched transcriptions relate to the distinctive features of phonemes in the transcriber languages. Section 4 describes a two-step clustering technique for our transcription prediction task using a bipartite graph. Section 5 shows our experimental results on Cantonese speech using mismatched transcriptions in English and Pinyin from native speakers of English and Mandarin, respectively.

2   Data Preparation and Description

The original multilingual mismatched crowdsourcing corpus is described in (Chen et al., 2016). We use mismatched transcriptions from native speakers of English and Mandarin corresponding to roughly one-hour of speech in Cantonese. A total of 3443 short utterances in Cantonese were each transcribed in Pinyin by six Mandarin speakers and 8130 Cantonese utterances were transcribed in English (using nonsense syllables) by ten English speakers. Native phonetic transcriptions were available for 813 Cantonese utterances. Table 2 shows the phonetic transcription of a sample Cantonese utterance, along with pairs of English and Pinyin mismatched transcriptions corresponding to this utterance. The original corpus in (Chen et al., 2016) also consisted of Vietnamese speech data which is not used in this work.

Cantonese (original with Babel Lexicon)		pin3 geung1 gan1 jyu6 le1
Cantonese transcribed in English	Transcriber number #1	hing kung gun chi
	Transcriber number #2	kin kup gun che
Cantonese transcribed in Mandarin	Transcriber number #1	pin3 geng2 gen1 ju3 le4
	Transcriber number #2	pin2 gong4 gen1 ju2 ne1

Table 1: *Sample utterance in Cantonese with mismatched transcriptions in English and Pinyin.*

Mandarin	p	p^h		k	k^h
English		p^h	b		k^h
Cantonese	p	p^h		k	k^h
Syllabic	-	-	-	-	-
Sonorant	-	-	-	-	-
Continuant	-	-	-	-	-
Labial	+	+	+	-	-

Table 2: *Example of Phoible Table for the Languages.*

Each annotator's error rate is estimated as the average string edit distance from his or her annotations to those of every other annotator using the same orthography as in (Jyothi et al., 2016). Between 2–6 Mandarin annotators and 2–6 English annotators with the lowest average pairwise string edit distance are selected for further analysis. (Section 5 compares results using 2, 3, or 6 annotators per annotation language). PTs are computed by aligning all the transcripts specific to a particular transcriber language i.e., the English and Mandarin transcripts are aligned separately to form two sets of PTs. The Mandarin

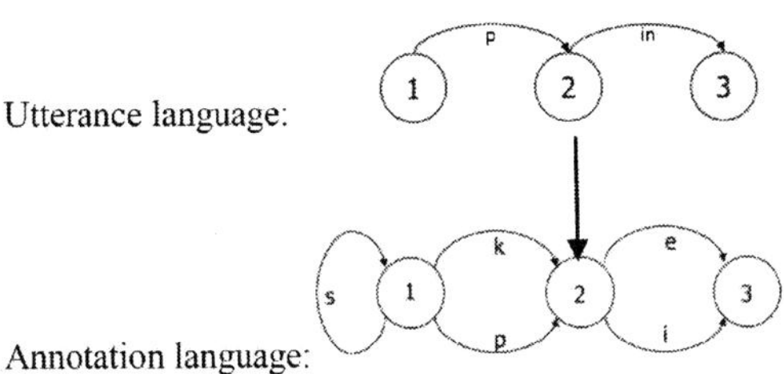

Figure 1: *FST Network Transfer*

PT and English PT are then each aligned with an utterance language transcript using a maximum likelihood alignment algorithm (Fig. 1 for the sample Cantonese sentence), in which the log probability of any given phoneme substitution is proportional to the Hamming distance between distinctive feature vectors corresponding to the two phonemes. Distinctive feature values for each phoneme are obtained from the Phoible phonological database (Moran et al., 2014); Table 2 shows four distinctive feature values corresponding to five different phonemes from the languages used in this work.

Suppose that $X = [x_1, \ldots, x_n]$ and $Y = [y_1, \ldots, y_n]$ are two phonemes whose distinctive features are $x_k \in \{0, 1\}$ and $y_k \in \{0, 1\}$ representing positive (1) and non-positive (0) distinctive feature values, respectively. The Hamming distance between these vectors is

$$D(X, Y) = \frac{1}{n} \sum_{f=1}^{n} |x_f - y_f|. \tag{1}$$

After the phonemes are aligned, they are converted to IPA symbols based on standard Mandarin and English orthography. The phone error rate (PER) derived from the phone alignments is hence computed as:

$$\text{PER} = 1 - \frac{\text{T}}{\text{M}}.$$

where T is the number of correct phone mappings based on IPA and M is the total number of the aligned phone mappings.

Phone error rates of these alignments had been reported in (Chen et al., 2016), where it is observed that Cantonese phone transcriptions recovered from Mandarin transcribers were much more accurate than those recovered from English transcribers.

3 Feature Weightings Analysis

Suppose we consider a weighted Hamming distance between phonemes (instead of an unweighted Hamming distance as shown in Equation 1):

$$\Delta(X, Y) = \sum_{f=1}^{n} G(f)|x_f - y_f|.$$

In order to define $\Delta(X, Y)$, it is necessary to choose some criterion for defining the feature weights $G(f)$. One such criterion, defined in (Nerbonne and Heeringa, 1997), is the information gain; we will not explore information gain further in this paper because it requires text in the utterance language. Mismatched crowdsourcing, however, provides us with an alternative measure of the distance between phonemes. Let t be a grapheme in the annotation language (English or Mandarin). Let $0 \leq S_X(t) \leq 1$ be the frequency with which utterance language phoneme X is aligned with annotation-language grapheme t. Then the distance between phonemes X and Y can be measured by the total variation distance (TVD) between their grapheme alignment distributions (Varshney et al., 2016),

$$B(X,Y) = \frac{1}{2}\sum_t |S_X(t) - S_Y(t)|.$$

TVD is defined in the range $0 \leq B(X,Y) \leq 1$. The more similar two phonemes are (as perceived by annotators who speak a given language), the more often they will be transcribed using the same grapheme, therefore the smaller will be the TVD between them. A reasonable model is that the probability of confusion, $1 - B(X,Y)$, is the product of individual distinctive feature confusion terms of the form $\exp(-G(f)|x_f - y_f|)$, therefore

$$1 - B(X,Y) = \exp(-\Delta(X,Y)).$$

Using this model, the vector of weights $G(f)$ is estimated as

$$G = \arg\min_G \|FG - B\|_2^2,$$

where $F(XY,i) = |x_i - y_i|$ is a matrix with a row for every pair of phonemes, and a column for each distinctive feature.

Features	Information gain weights
Low	2.9750
Back	2.9210
Tense	2.5247
Front	2.8905
Syllabic	2.8878
Tone	2.8878
Round	2.6673
Labial	2.6570
High	2.1660

Table 3: *Feature weighting targets for Cantonese phones (Information gain)*

Features	Weights predicted from Mandarin Transcribers
Front	0.3407
Low	0.2293
Tone	0.1698
High	0.1678
Tense	0.1678
Syllabic	0.1334
Back	0.1087
Labial	0.1087
Round	0.1087

Table 4: *Weights prediction for Cantonese from Mandarin transcriptions*

Table 3 shows the theoretical information gain of the distinctive feature weights computed from the phone occurrence frequencies of Cantonese. Tables 4 and 5 show the estimated feature weights from the TVD approximation. The list of features and the order for English and Mandarin are similar especially for front and low features. This demonstrates that, given the transcription data, we obtained the relative order of the weightings of the distinctive features to be similar to the actually information gain and important of the features in characterising phones.

Features	Weights predicted from English Transcribers
Front	0.3575
Low	0.1868
Tone	0.1216
High	0.0940
Tense	0.0940
Labial	0.0919
Round	0.0919
Back	0.0919
Syllabic	0.0630

Table 5: *Weights prediction for Cantonese from English transcriptions*

Can. Tones	C1	C2	C3	C4	C5	C6
C1	0	0.1668	0.0337	0.1946	0.1898	0.1221
C2		0	0.1352	0.0536	0.0322	0.0446
C3			0	0.1656	0.1617	0.0984
C4				0	0.0224	0.0724
C5					0	0.0676
C6						0

Table 6: *Total variation distance (TVD) between pairs of Cantonese tones, based on their alignment with Mandarin mismatched transcripts. The smaller the TVD between two tones, the more likely they are to be confused in an MAP decoding of the mismatched transcript.*

Next we apply the TVD analysis to the Cantonese tones (C1–C6) and Mandarin tones (M1–M4) with the tonal features described in (Chen et al., 2016). Table 6 shows the TVD between pairs of Cantonese tones, based on their alignments with Mandarin mismatched transcripts. We observe that Mandarin annotators have trouble creating a Pinyin transcript that distinguishes the Cantonese high vs. mid level tones (C1 and C3), or that distinguishes the low rising tone (C5) from the mid-rising (C2) or low falling (C4) tones.

Table 7 lists the raw probabilities on which Table 6 is based: the probabilities $p(M_k|C_k)$ that Cantonese utterance tone C_k is transcribed using Mandarin annotation tone M_k. We see that the Cantonese low falling (C4) and low rising (C5) tones are each most frequently annotated in Pinyin using the Mandarin low falling-rising tone (M3), whereas all three Cantonese level tones (C1, C3 and C6) are most frequently annotated by the Mandarin high level tone (M1).

CanTone vs ManTone	M1	M2	M3	M4
C1	0.568	0.105	0.270	0.055
C2	0.426	0.157	0.385	0.030
C3	0.562	0.104	0.304	0.029
C4	0.396	0.134	0.436	0.032
C5	0.400	0.151	0.413	0.033
C6	0.463	0.126	0.371	0.038

Table 7: *Mismatched crowdsourcing substitution probabilities $p(M_k|C_k)$ of Mandarin annotation tone M_k given Cantonese utterance tone C_k.*

4   Phonetic Clustering Algorithm

This section describes how we infer phone mappings between the transcriber languages and the target language. Specifically we describe a phonetic projection framework and clustering criteria with random projections. The problem is formulated as a bipartite graph clustering problem followed by segment classification. The clusters correspond to the segment list of the target language represented using binary feature vectors. This is similar to classification but we allow some segments appearing in English and Mandarin to not be mapped to any target segment. The experiment is evaluated with Cantonese. As illustrated in Figure 2, the task is to cluster the phone mappings in the data from two multilingual transcriber channels to be the phone classes in the target language based on the similarity of the distinctive features in the clusters and in the segment.

Suppose that we have mismatched transcripts in Mandarin and English orthography, but we do not have native Cantonese phone transcripts. Additionally, let us assume that we do not know the Cantonese phone set. Since we can no longer compute the TVD between Cantonese phone types, we instead compute the TVD between Cantonese phone tokens. Take one of the two probabilistic transcripts (English, say) to define the number of Cantonese phone tokens per utterance. Align the other PT to it (the Mandarin one). The Mandarin PT has one or two orthographic symbols (or a deletion symbol) aligned to every segment of the English PT; thus for each segment X, its substitution probability mass function (pmf) $S_X(t)$ has up to two nonzero entries.

We first aggregate these probabilities over all instances of the same English orthographic symbol, so that $S_X(t)$ is the probability that English orthographic symbol X is aligned to Mandarin Pinyin orthographic symbol t. We then build a matrix W whose (i, j)th element, w_{ij}, is the probability that English orthographic symbol i is aligned with Mandarin orthographic symbol j. In order to avoid losing tone information, we define the Mandarin orthography to be composed of Pinyin onsets and tone-annotated rhymes. Thus, the sequence $< hai3, ya2, you1, len1 >$ is decomposed into the 8 graphemes $< h, ai3, y, a2, y, ou1, l, en1 >$, which are aligned to the English orthographic sequence $< ch, an, h, eihn, n, uw, l, ah >$.

After constructing the matrix W, the next step involves merging the English (A's in full English segment set E) and Mandarin (B's in full Mandarin segment set M) clusters. We perform the following bipartite graph clustering using the normalized distances defined below.

Generally, the similarity between two sets A and B where $A \in E$ and $B \in M$ can be defined as:

$$W(A, B) = \sum_{i \epsilon A, j \epsilon B} w_{ij}.$$

Hence the distance and normalised distance between two clusters set A and B can be computed using:

$$d(A, B) = W(A, B^c) + W(A^c, B)$$
$$= \sum_{i \epsilon A, j \epsilon B^c} w_{ij} + \sum_{i \epsilon A^c, j \epsilon B} w_{ij}.$$

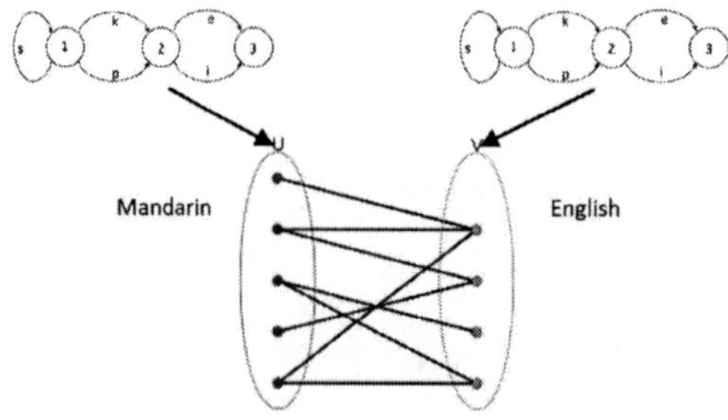

Figure 2: *From dynamic alignments to bipartite graph*

$$d_N(A, B) =$$

$$\frac{d(A, B)}{W(A, M) + W(E, B)} + \frac{d(A^c, B^c)}{W(A^c, M) + W(E, B^c)}.$$

where c is the conjugate sign of the set and the normalised distance is proposed to avoid the outliers in the set partioning. The final optimization criterion is then $\min\limits_{\pi(A,B)} d_N(A, B)$ where $\pi(A, B)$ denotes partitioning into the A and B clusters.

The clustering algorithm is shown in (Zha et al., 2001) to be equivalent to the singular vector decomposition problem. The procedure is summarized in an algorithm called Spectral Recursive Embedding (SRE): given a weighted bipartite graph $G = (X, Y, E)$ with its edge weight matrix W of the edge set E, we compute the scaled weight matrix and the second largest left and right singular vectors. Then we form partitions A for vertex set X, and B for vertex set Y as the first cluster for the target segment. Subsequently we recursively partition the subgraphs $G(A, B)$ and $G(A^c, B^c)$ until we test and obtain the same number of clusters as the number of segments of the target language in Phoible.

In the two-step graph clustering process for Cantonese from English and Mandarin transcriptions, we 1) group the Mandarin tonal phones with different tones into 25 clusters, 2) group the aligned English phones into 25 clusters, and 3) finally, group the clusters on the two sides of the bipartite graph into 29 clusters. As analyzed in Section 3, the tones in the Mandarin transcriptions will be able to help the Cantonese transcription prediction process. Feature weights, estimated in Section 3, are also used in the clustering mapping and selection. The clusters are chosen and tagged with the target segments based on the largest number of common distinctive features. Feature weights are employed when two clusters could be tagged as the same target segment. For example, let us consider two clusters A and B that could be mapped to the same target segment S. Suppose segments in cluster A are missing feature F_1 that appears in S while segments in cluster B are missing feature F_2 that also appears in S. If the feature weights determined for feature F_1 in Cantonese are less than the weights for feature F_2, then cluster A is tagged to be the target segment S.

5   Experimental Results and Analysis

This section evaluates our clustering based method on Cantonese transcribed by 2–6 English-speaking transcribers and 2–6 Mandarin-speaking transcribers. For Cantonese, we have 1 hour of Cantonese speech accompanied by native transcriptions that can be used as our evaluation data.

Our method is evaluated by computing the most probable Cantonese phone sequence (including tones) given knowledge of the sequence of bipartite graph clusters. Let X^ℓ be the reference label of the ℓth Cantonese phone in a native transcription, and let C^m be the cluster index, $1 \le C^m \le 29$, of the mth consecutive aligned set of Mandarin and English graphemes. The MAP Cantonese phone transcription is

$$[\hat{X}^{(1)}, \ldots, \hat{X}^{(M)}]$$

$$= \arg\max \prod_{m=1}^{M} p(X^{(m)}|X^{(m-1)})p(C^{(m)}|X^{(m)}).$$

where the language model $p(X^{(m)}|X^{(m-1)})$ is estimated from the grapheme-to-phoneme transduction of Cantonese text (Kong et al., 2016), and the misperception model $p(C^{(m)}|X^{(m)})$ is estimated using a separate training corpus with native and mismatched transcripts. The efficacy of the bipartite graph clustering algorithm could then be measured using the phone error rate (PER) between $\hat{X}$ and X. This could be compared with PERs of Cantonese transcripts recovered using only the English mismatched transcripts and with PERs of transcripts recovered using only Mandarin mismatched transcripts. All the target segments and transcription graphemes are converted into IPA phone set to compute phone error rates using the grapheme to phone conversion in (Hasegawa-Johnson, 2015). We also show PERs obtained using an FST union of the English and Mandarin mismatched transcript PTs, and from a majority

Cantonese **Phone Error Rate**	$N=2$	$N=3$	$N=6$
Majority Vote	65.1%	64.5%	63.7%
PT on English	64.3%	63.2%	62.7%
PT on Mandarin	47.4%	35.5%	30.9%
PT on E and M	43.1%	30.6%	29.5%
Clustering method	39.1%	25.5%	27.9%

Table 8: *Phone error rate (PER) for PT methods on Cantonese speech data. Here, N corresponds to the number of mismatched transcriptions for each utterance.*

voting algorithm that outputs a symbol only if the Mandarin and English PTs agree. All the above-mentioned PERs are shown in Table 8. We found the optimal number of transcribers for two individual transcriber channels is 3 that helps compensate the language bias and variance across transcribers (i.e., noise in the mismatched transcriptions). The error rate of the clustering method slightly increases when more transcribers' alignments are combined, possibly due to higher variance across a larger number of mismatched transcripts. This can be improved by averaging and selecting the n best intra aligned transcriptions for clustering.

The distinctive features corresponding to each cluster combining English and Mandarin phones are a good match to the closest segment in Cantonese. Tone perception by Mandarin speakers provides some information about the segments of the target tonal language. The average number of edges per segment in the probabilistic transcription FST combining English and Mandarin transcriptions is 4.6. Although this threshold was carefully tuned on the evaluation data, the PTs combining Mandarin and English transcripts did not outperform the bipartite graph clustering algorithm.

The key comparisons that we note from Table 8 are: 1) PERs using the clustering method compared against the PERs from the English, Mandarin and English+Mandarin systems, and 2) PERs using the clustering method compared against the simple aligned majority voting method. We observe that the clustering method is significantly more accurate than the simple majority voting method which needs to use phone mapping knowledge between the target and transcriber languages. Our clustering method also improves over a system that uses only Mandarin mismatched transcriptions which indicates that we are able to leverage useful information from the English mismatched transcriptions. When a larger number of transcribers are available, despite the increase in variability in transcriptions, we observe that the clustering method is able to maintain good PERs by averaging the transcription alignments in the clustering process.

6   Conclusion and Future Work

This paper presents an extension of the mismatched crowdsourcing framework that makes use of mismatched channels corresponding to different transcriber languages. We propose a phoneme clustering algorithm that effectively combines mismatched transcripts from English and Mandarin native speakers to predict phone transcriptions for Cantonese speech. Future work includes applying the predicted transcriptions and projected segments in recognition tasks involving tonal languages.

References

Wenda Chen, Mark Hasegawa-Johnson, and Nancy F Chen, 2016 "Mismatched Crowdsourcing based Language Perception for Under-resourced Languages, Procedia Computer Science, Volume 81, Pages 2329

Mark Hasegawa-Johnson, Preethi Jyothi, D. McCloy, M. Mirbagheri, G. di Liberto, A. Das, B. Ekin, C. Liu, V. Manohar, H. Tang, E.C. Lalor, N. Chen, P. Hager, T. Kekona, R. Sloan and A.K.C. Lee, 2016, ASR for Under-Resourced Languages from Probabilistic Transcription," in review

Preethi Jyothi and Mark Hasegawa-Johnson, 2016, Mismatched Crowdsourcing: A Novel Method for Acquiring Speech Transcriptions Using Non-Native Transcribers," in review.

Steven Moran, Daniel McCloy, and Richard Wright [eds]., PHOIBLE On Line. 2014." Leipzig: Max Planck Institute for Evolutionary Anthropology (Available on line at http://phoible.org. Accessed on 2016-07-21)

Xiang Kong, Preethi Jyothi, and Mark Hasegawa-Johnson, 2016, Performance Improvement of Probabilistic Transcriptions with Language-specific Constraints. Procedia Computer Science 81:30-36

Lav R. Varshney, Preethi Jyothi, and Mark Hasegawa- Johnson, 2016, Language Coverage for Mismatched Crowdsourcing, Information Theory and Applications (ITA) Workshop, San Diego, California.

Hongyuan Zha, Xiaofeng He, Chris Ding, Horst Simon, and Ming Gu, Bipartite Graph Partitioning and Data Clustering, 2001, Proceedings of the tenth international conference on information and knowledge management (CIKM 2001), pages 25-32

John Nerbonne and Wilbert Heeringa, Measuring Dialect Distance Phonetically, 1997, Proceedings of the Third Meeting of the ACL Special Interest Group in Computational Phonology

Mark Hasegawa-Johnson, 2015, SST Online Dictionary and G2P, http://www.isle.illinois.edu/sst/data/g2ps/

Improving the Morphological Analysis of Classical Sanskrit

Oliver Hellwig
Düsseldorf University, SFB 991
ohellwig@
phil-fak.uni-duesseldorf.de

Abstract

The paper describes a new tagset for the morphological disambiguation of Sanskrit, and compares the accuracy of two machine learning methods (CRF, deep recurrent neural networks) for this task, with a special focus on how to model the lexicographic information. It reports a significant improvement over previously published results.

1 Challenges of Sanskrit Linguistics and Related Research

Classical Sanskrit is a strongly inflecting Old Indo-Aryan language that developed out of earlier Vedic dialects in the middle of the first millenium BCE. Ever since, Sanskrit has been the main medium for transmitting the large corpus of religious, philosophical, scientific, and literary texts that shaped the intellectual history of ancient India.

Sanskrit poses considerable challenges for NLP at the levels of tokenization, lemmatization, and morphological analysis (Kulkarni and Shukla, 2009). These three steps are deeply intertwined in Sanskrit, because single word forms (*padas*) are merged by a set of phonetic rules called Sandhi "connection" into larger strings. In order to analyze a sentence at the morphological and lexical level, an NLP tool must be able to simultaneously resolve the Sandhis, and to detect the correct morphological and lexical path in the resulting lattice of word hypotheses. As a consequence, the tokenization of a sentence is guided by its lexical and morphological analyses. Due to these linguistic peculiarities, morphological ambiguity is introduced on three levels:

Inherent : Isolated Sanskrit forms are frequently ambiguous. The verbal form *gacchati*, for example, has three readings as 3rdSG.PR of the verb *gam* 'to go' ("(s)he / it goes"), L.SG.M. of the present participle of this verb ("in the going [some referent]"), and L.SG.N. of the same participle.

Sandhi : When morphologically unambiguous forms such as *draupadī* (N.SG.F. of *draupadī* 'name of a woman') are processed with Sandhi rules, they can become ambiguous. While the sentence *draupadī gacchati* 'Draupadī goes' allows only one reading of *draupadī*, the sentence *draupadī āgacchati* 'Draupadī arrives' is further processed by the Sandhi rule *ī* + *ā* = *yā*, resulting in *draupadyāgacchati*. When this string is analyzed with an NLP tool, the sequence *-yā-* can be resolved into (1) the "correct" source phonemes *ī* + *ā*, but also into (2) *i* + *ā*, (3) *ya* + *a*, (4) *ya* + *ā*, (5) *yā* + *a*, or (6) *yā* + *ā*, where solutions (1), (2), (5), and (6) represent lexico-morphologically, but not necessarily semantically valid readings.[1] The morphological analyzer (MA) has to decide between three readings *draupadī* (N.SG.), *draupadi* (V.SG.), and *draupadyā* (I.SG.), which are distinct in their un-Sandhied, phonetically disambiguated forms.

bahuvrīhi **compounds** : Sanskrit has a highly productive class of compounds called *bahuvrīhis* ("much rice"), which form possessive expressions. Compounds of this class behave like adjectives, because they inherit the inflectional information from their governing possessors. While the non-possessive

---

[1](2) "O Draupadī, he/she/it comes"; (5*) "With Draupadī ... in the not-going"; (6) "He/she/it arrives together with Draupadī"

Proceedings of the 6th Workshop on South and Southeast Asian Natural Language Processing,
pages 142–151, Osaka, Japan, December 11-17 2016.

compound *bahu-annam* 'much food' is inflected according to the grammatical class of its final member *anna* 'food' (neutre noun on short a), it takes over the inflectional class of the governing term *strī* 'woman', when used in the *bahuvrīhi* construction *bahu-annā*[2] *strī* 'a woman who has much food'. Morphological ambiguity is introduced in constructions such as *mahā-vṛkṣam udyānam* 'big-tree + garden', where the first element *mahā-vṛkṣam* has two readings:

1. possessive compound: "the garden that has (a) large tree(s)". *mahā-vṛkṣam* is N. or A.SG. following the selected morphological information of *udyānam* (N. or A.SG.N.), and its gender changes from M. to N.
2. non-possessive compound: "the big tree [and] the garden". *mahā-vṛkṣam* should preferably be analyzed as A.SG.M.

As in the case of Sandhi, resolving such cases correctly requires long-range contextual information.

Tagging Sanskrit texts requires a robust algorithm. Apart from the morphological disambiguities just described, the algorithm should be able to handle texts from a wide spectrum of domains, and from a timespan of over 2,500 years. Classical Sanskrit is generally assumed to be regulated by Pāṇini's grammar Aṣṭādhyāyī (Scharfe, 1977) on the phonetic, morphological, and – to a certain degree – the syntactic level, and by the large dictionaries such as the Amarakośa (approx. 3.-5. c. CE) and the Abhidhānacintāmaṇi (12. c. CE; see Katre (1991)) on the lexicographic level. However, the actual use in texts may frequently diverge from such an ideal language.[3]

Although better explored than Middle Indo-Aryan languages (see, for instance, Alfter and Knauth (2015)), Sanskrit is still a low-resource language from the perspective of NLP. Research on morphological disambiguation concentrates on building analyzers with a high coverage of valid word forms (Huet, 2005; Jha et al., 2009a; Mishra, 2009). Frameworks for analyzing complete sentences either rely on Finite State methods (Huet, 2006), or a combination of rule-based and statistical methods (Hellwig, 2015).

The present paper adopts a two-stage approach that resembles the methods proposed in Hajič and Hladká (1998). During the first stage, Sandhis are resolved, and the most probable lexical reading is detected using a factorized bigram language model. Morphological disambiguation, the topic of this paper, is performed during the second stage. At this point, the algorithm has access to the most probable lexical analysis of each word, and to the corresponding morphological reading(s) that are determined using a rule-based morphological analyzer. The experiments reported below deal with the question of how morphological ambiguities can be resolved in this second stage. It is important to keep in mind that the lexical and morphological information can contain errors, if the algorithm does not select the correct lexical reading in the first stage.

2 Method

2.1 Tag set

The inflectional morphology of a Sanskrit word can be described by five, partly incompatible categories. Nouns, adjectives, pronouns, and verbal participles are inflected by (1) eight cases, (2) three numbers (SG., DU., PL.), and (3) three genders (M., F., N.). Unmarked forms of these word classes are used in compound formation. Finite verbal forms are marked for number and (4) person (1st, 2nd, 3rd), and (5) by a complex system of tenses and modes. The rule based morphological analyzer produces fine-grained annotations that cover these five morphological categories. Because the classification methods used in this paper require a single output variable from a nominal scale, an obvious approach would use the Cartesian product of the five morphological categories as target variable. However, this approach unnecessarily complicates the learning process, because most feature combinations cannot cooccur in the morphological analysis of a single word. As a consequence, Hellwig (2015) reduced the tag set used

---

[2]*-ā* is the termination the N.SG. of feminine nouns and adjectives. *anna* cannot show this termination in non-possessive use.

[3]Examples are the dialect called Epic Sanskrit (Salomon, 1995), or the prolific use of Vedic forms in classical texts such as the 12th century Bhāgavatapurāṇa that deal with ritualistic and religious questions.

in morphological disambiguation by distinguishing between nominal and finite verbal inflection. While case, number, and gender information are used for nominally inflected forms, the tense-mode axis of the verbal system is reduced to a few coarse tense categories.

An evaluation of cooccurring morphological readings shows that this tag set can be reduced further without creating a significant amount of collisions, i.e. distinct morphological readings that are mapped to the same nominal output variable. This reduced tag set distinguishes the following output categories:

Tags 1-9 are occupied by finite verbal forms. Contrary to Hellwig (2015), tense and mode information is completely discarded during morphological disambiguation. Person and number are mapped to the first $3 \times 3 = 9$ tag classes.

10 : absolutive (*gatvā* 'having gone')

11 : infinitive (*gantum* 'in order to go')

12 : indeclinable words (adverbs, particles; cover term for tag C in the IL-POSTS tagset (Jha et al., 2009b))

13 : nominal forms in compounds, without gender distinction

14-86 : The last 8 (case) $\times 3$ (number) $\times 3$ (gender) $= 72$ tags describe inflected nominal forms, which are responsible for the majority of ambiguities and errors in this task (refer to Table 3).

The size of the new tagset is reduced by a factor of more than 4 when compared with the set proposed in Hellwig (2015).

2.2 Classifiers

This paper applies two types of sequential classifiers to the task of morphological disambiguation. First, it uses first-order Conditional Random Fields (CRF, Lafferty et al. (2001)), which have been applied successfully, among many other fields, for various tasks in Indian NLP (Hellwig, 2015; Pandian and Geetha, 2009).[4] The Viterbi decoding of the CRF has been modified in order to include the hard constraints generated by the morphological analyzer. Given a sequence of m words, and n possible tags for each word, the default implementation of Viterbi considers all n tags for each of the m words. The modified version only considers the proposals of the morphological analyzer for each of the m words, setting the output probabilities for the other options to 0.

CRFs are compared with the results obtained by using deep recurrent neural networks (NN). This paper implements a bidirectional architecture (Schuster and Paliwal, 1997) with Long Short-Term Memory units (LSTM, Hochreiter and Schmidhuber (1997)), which circumvent numerical problems of BPTT (Hochreiter et al., 2001). The NN consists of the following elements:

1. A fully connected input layer with an embedding size of 70, *tanh* activation, and a subsequent dropout layer with a dropout rate of 20% (Hinton et al., 2012)

2. Two bidirectional LSTM units

3. An output layer that is fully connected to the output of the second bidirectional LSTM.

The network is trained with the sentence-level log-likelihood criterion described in Collobert et al. (2011, 2530/31), by which transition probabilities between tags are integrated into the learning process. Weights are learned using gradient descent for 25 iterations and an initial learning rate of 0.01. The first 15 iterations don't apply any gradient descent optimization strategy, allowing the network to make large steps towards the (local) optimum. Iterations 16-25 are performed using Adagrad (Duchi et al., 2011).

---

[4]The software package `crfsuite` (`www.chokkan.org/software/crfsuite/`) is used for learning and decoding. Settings: optimization with L-BFGS, $L1 = 1$, $L2 = 2$, 100 iterations.

2.3 Features

The input layer of the NN contains at least one section in each of the following experiments. These sections receive (1) morphological, (2, optional) lexical, and (3, optional) word semantic information from the output of the morphological analyzer.

As mentioned above, the morphological analyzer generates at least one morphological reading for each word in an input sequence. These readings are encoded with the new tagset (Section 2.1), and directly used as input features for the NN. If a word has n out of 86 possible morphological readings, the first section of the input for the NN is a vector of length 86, in which the n positions representing the morphological readings are set to 1, and the remaining ones to 0. – For the CRF, all tags are combined into a single factor weighted with 1.0 (e.g., tags 15, 20, and 30 are combined into *morph_15_20_30*).

Previous research has put a strong focus on the question of how to provide (sparse) lexical information to machine learning methods. Therefore, this paper tests five different formats for encoding lexical information in the second section of the input layer:

none: This setting provides an unlexicalized baseline that is used for estimating the influence of lexical information on morphological disambiguation. No information is written in the lexical section.

1h: The lexical section is a sparse binary vector. The position corresponding to the current word w is set to 1, and all other positions are set to 0. The weights of the first layer are initialized with uniformly distributed random values from a small range around 0, and all weights in this layer are learned during training. Lemmata that occur less than five times in the training corpus, are mapped to an OOV entry in the input vector.

morfessor: In analogy to methods presented in Creutz et al. (2007) and Mousa et al. (2010), this setting uses sub-lexical representations of lexemes. Each nominal lemma occurring in the training part of the corpus and its frequency are passed to the tool `Morfessor` (Creutz and Lagus, 2007), and the resulting morphemes are used instead of the full lexical information. When setting the minimum length of a morpheme to two Sanskrit phonemes, `Morfessor` produces 11,021 morphemes out of 66,202 nominal lemmata, which reduces the size of the lexical input space by more than 83%. A closer inspection shows that many of the proposed morphemes are meaningful from the perspective of Sanskrit derivation morphology as, for instance, the set *ati-duś-cara* 'very difficult to perform', *ati-dur-dhara* 'very difficult to be administered', *ati-dur-dina* 'very bad weather', and *ati-dur-jaya* 'very difficult to be conquered'. Given the quality of such segmentations, one may expect that this setting strongly improves over the non-lexicalized baseline. – `Morfessor` features are fed into the NN in the same way as **1h**, except that more than one position may be set to 1 in the input vector. For CRF, each morpheme is presented as a separate input variable, such that the original lexeme is replaced by a decomposed representation.

w2v-sparse: The lexical section of the input layer has the same form as in **1h**, but the weights of the first layer are initialized with neural word embeddings generated from the training part of the corpus using the `word2vec` tool (Mikolov et al., 2011).[5] The w2v embeddings are meant to accelerate the training of the NN. – This setting is not meaningful for CRF, and no results are reported for it in Table 1.

w2v-dense: The same w2v embeddings are used as direct inputs to the NN, instead of initializing the embeddings as in **w2v-sparse**. As a consequence, the length of the lexical section equals the size of the learned embeddings (70 in the following experiments).

In addition to morphological and lexical information, the configuration **sem** associates each noun w with a distribution over 35 high-level word semantic categories S. The 35 dimensions of S are created by collapsing the hierarchical word semantic tree, with which parts of the DCS are annotated, to 35 top-level

---

[5] Training settings of `word2vec`: bow, embedding size: 70, window size: 8, negative sampling, minimal corpus frequency: 3

categories. The collapsing process is primarily guided by the weights[6] of the tree nodes, because nodes with high weights are assumed to represent central concepts that should not be merged into higher-level concepts. The categorization also involves a manual labeling that overrides some unsupervised weight-based decisions[7] and reorders parts of the tree.[8] The final 35 categories contain top-level concepts such as "person" (human beings, deities, animals acting like humans), "landscape" (mountains, lakes, rivers, ...), "quantities", or "movement". The feature vector for w is built by collecting all semantically annotated occurrences of w in the training part of the corpus, mapping each of the annotated concepts onto S, and setting its corresponding position in the 35 dimension binary feature vector to 1.

2.4 Data

All data are extracted from the Digital Corpus of Sanskrit (DCS), which contains 3,987,000 tokens with manually validated lexical and morphological annotations. The texts in the DCS cover the complete linguistic development of classical Sanskrit starting from late Vedic texts such as the Upaniṣads (5. c. BCE), and reaching up to Sanskrit texts from the 19. c. CE. Because morphological disambiguation operates at an intermediate level of the processing pipeline (refer to page 2), the complete corpus is re-analyzed, and the correct lexical and morphological analysis is stored for each word, along with its morphological readings. These data are used in two modes. When evaluating the influence of features and of the machine learning models, only one third of the data is used in *fast mode*. The final tests described in Section 3 are run on the complete data set (*full mode*). Data are split into $\frac{1}{10}$ for testing and $\frac{9}{10}$ for testing in both modes. To make different settings comparable, the train-test split does not involve a stochastic element.

3   Evaluation

This section reports how results are influenced by feature and model selection, and examines which linguistic phenomena are mainly responsible for errors made by the morphological disambiguation. If not mentioned otherwise, evaluation only considers the 42% of morphologically ambiguous forms. The "final" accuracy rate that also considers forms with only one possible solution is clearly higher (refer to the last row of Table 2).

Table 1 contrasts the results of CRF and LSTM for different lexicalizations in "fast mode". Remarkably, LSTM outperforms the CRF in all evaluation measures. A test with a higher-order CRF (not reported) shows that the accuracy of the CRF cannot be improved relevantly when wider ranges of output label transitions are considered, and increasing the range of input features also does not improve over the reported results.[9] So, the deep NN seems to be more appropriate for this task than a CRF.

Comparing the previous large and the new smaller tagset yields consistent results for CRF and LSTM.[10] While the previous tagset performs better for some low-frequency classes (higher F score), the new tagset produces a higher overall accuracy, and requires less time for training due to its lower dimensionality. In addition, Table 1 demonstrates the high influence of the lexical representation. While the unlexicalized variant (**none**) suffers especially from low recall, the values of **morfessor** are clearly closer to the lexicalized than to the unlexicalized version, indicating that this approach may turn out to be useful for (ancient) Indian languages for which no extensive lexical resources, but large unannotated corpora are available. Finally, the variants using word embeddings (**w2v-sparse** and **-dense**) produce lower accuracy rates than the one-hot-encodings. Adding the broad word-semantic classes further improves the accuracy of the **1h** encoding, although the difference to **1h** is not significant.

---

[6] The weight of a node is defined as the number of occurrences of the concept linked to the node, plus the sum of this number for all its subnodes.

[7] Example: Although the node "mountain" has a very high weight, it is further collapsed into a parent node "elements of the landscape", which covers related concepts such as "lake" or "river".

[8] Example: The subclasses of the concept "person" were widely scattered over the original tree and could, therefore, not be subsumed automatically under one common ancestor.

[9] A first-order CRF with a feature window of 7 instead of 5 words produces $P = 82.84$, $R = 64.13$, and $F = 68.71$.

[10] Results for the tagset used in Hellwig (2015) have been recalculated for this paper using the same settings as for the other experiments.

Lex.	CRF				LSTM			
	P	R	F	A	P	R	F	A
morfessor	80.54	64.21	68.61	86.27	81.98	71.27	74.13	88.55
none	75.4	58.31	62.13	82.34	76.35	60.96	63.97	83.33
1h	82.79	65.47	70.04	87.56	82.39	74.98	77.06	90.49
1h (old tagset)	86.21	68.64	72.56	87.11	82.81	76.41	77.3	89.89
1h sem	80.4	65.19	69.64	87.34	81.34	76.02	77.69	90.61
w2v-sparse	-	-	-	-	78.61	71.93	73.94	89.29
w2v-dense	72.86	59.05	62.84	82.24	79.52	69.9	72.64	88.99

Table 1: Macro-average P(recision), R(ecall) and F(-score), and A(ccuracy) for all words with more than one morphological reading, "fast mode". Note that macro-average measures tend to overemphasize (bad) results of small classes.

	CRF				LSTM			
	P	R	F	A	P	R	F	A
ambiguous	84.03	69.2	73.16	88.99	80.5	75.82	77.1	90.99
overall	90.46	79.68	82.62	95.17	87.36	83.11	84.5	96.01

Table 2: Macro-average PRF and accuracy on the full training set, features: **1h**. First row: Results for ambiguous words; second row: Results for all words.

To make the results comparable with those reported for other languages, the second row of Table 2 reports the performance of the two models when trained with the **1h** feature on the full data set. Remarkably, the CRF benefits more clearly from the increased training set, although its results are clearly worse than those of the LSTM.

Table 3, which splits the results of the best LSTM model from Table 1 according to coarse POS classes, confirms that the correct decisions were made when reducing the size of the tagset. The class of finite verbal forms, whose tense distinction strongly increased the size of the tagset, produce low error rates, while infinite declinable verbal forms are in a similar error range as adjectives and nouns.

To obtain a more detailed error analysis, all instances misclassified by CRF or LSTM have been stratified according to binned frequency classes of their lemmata.[11] The resulting data in Figure 1 allow for two interesting observations. First, the performance of CRF and LSTM differs strongly with regard to frequency classes. Although the LSTM consistently outperforms the CRF in all frequency classes, the error rates of the two models differ by a nearly constant factor for low (classes 1 and 2) and high frequency words (classes 7-9). For the intermediate classes 3-6, the error rate of the LSTM decreases appproximately linearly with the frequency class, while the error rate of the CRF increases sharply for class 3, before decreasing for more frequent words. Note that class 3 is the first class for which lexical information is fed into both models.[12] Contrary to the CRF, the LSTM seems to benefit from this

---

[11] The frequency class of word w with an observed frequency N is given by the rounded value of $\log(N)/\log(5)$.

[12] Class 1 contains all hapax legomena, and class 2 words with corpus frequencies between 2 and 4 occurrences. As remarked in Section 2.3, the experiments reported in Table 1 use a lexical frequency threshold of 5, such that class 3 is the first one for

POS	A(dj.)	I(nd.)	N(oun)	P(ron.)	V.fin.	V.inf.
Acc.	92.4	100	95.73	93.4	99.58	94.1

Table 3: Accuracy per coarse POS class for the best model from Table 1 for ambiguous and unambiguous words. Numbers are subsumed under the class A. V.fin.: finite verbal forms; V.inf.: infinite verbal forms

F.C.	Types	Tokens	E_{CRF}	E_{LSTM}
2	420	420	55	51
3	788	811	109	106
4	1683	1905	319	232
5	3085	5130	757	553
6	2424	10869	1473	1131
7	793	16188	2058	1590
8	83	7169	683	549
9	11	4101	466	409
10	1	2269	338	293

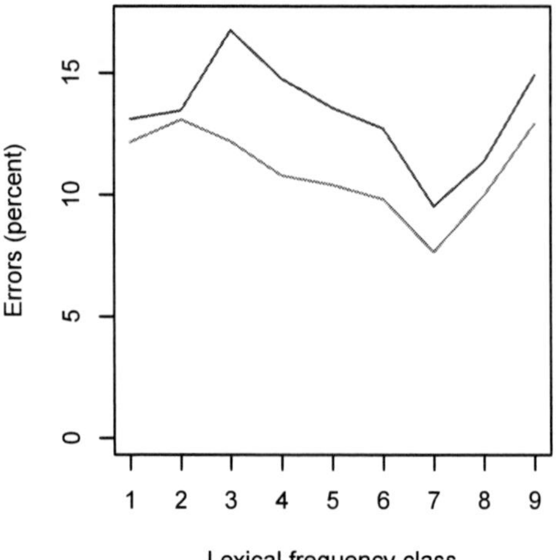

Figure 1: Number of lexical types and tokens, and of errors (E_{CRF}, E_{LSTM}) per logarithmized frequency class (F.C.; basis: 5). Right side: Percentual proportion of errors per frequency class for CRF (blue) and LSTM (red). Models = **1h** from Table 1.

information right from the beginning.

The second observation concerns the high frequency classes 8 and 9, for which both classifier types produce increasing error rates. The majority of errors in these two frequency classes is caused by a small set of personal (*tad* 'he/she/it', gender-neutral *mad* 'I' and *tvad* 'you'), demonstrative (*idam* 'this', *etad* 'this (here)'), and relative (*yad* 'which') pronouons, and by the quantifier *sarva* 'all', which is inflected like a pronoun. A closer inspection shows that ambiguities in case and gender assignment produce most of these errors. In 166 instances, for example, at least one of the models has made a wrong decision between N.SG.N. and A.SG.N. for one of the pronominal forms *tad*, *yad*, *etad*, and *idam*, or for forms such as *yasmin* 'in which', which can be analyzed either as masculine or as neuter of the locative singular. Some of the cases in which both models propose the same wrong analysis with high confidence values, actually give the correct reading of a misannotation in the corpus. Such results could be used for a future semi-automatic post-correction of the data.

Most of these errors, however, are caused by long-range constructions not detected by the model. The prose passage Viṣṇupurāṇa 4.12.17 provides a – rather usual – example of such a complex construction, where the morphological disambiguation was not able to establish the correct link between the A.SG.N. - *ratnam* and its predecessor ending in -*yugalam* (only relevant morphological information given; words to be linked and their morphological information are underlined):

tasmiṃś   ca   vidrute   'ti-trāsa-lola-āyata-locana-yugalaṃ   trāhi   trāhi
he:L.SG.M. and run away:L.SG.M. very-fear-restless-extended-eye-pair:Co....A.SG.N. protect:imper. protect

māṃ tāta-amba   bhrātar ity ākula-vilāpa-vidhuram   sa
me   father-mother brother so   agitated-lament-troubled:Co.-Co.-A.SG.N. he:N.SG.M.

rāja-kanyā-ratnam   adrākṣīt
king-daughter-jewel:Co.-Co.-A.SG.N. see:past, 3rd SG.

"After he (= a third person) had run away, he saw the jewel, which was the daughter of the king, whose pair of broad eyes was rolling due to (her) excessive fear, and which[13] was agitated by (her) confused lament (stating) 'Protect, protect me, o father, mother, brother'."

---

which lexical information is available.

[13]This word still refers to the "jewel".

Class	P	R	F
N.Sg.N.	**85.35**	**91.00**	**88.09**
A.Sg.N.	**84.26**	75.39	**79.58**
N.Pl.M.	94.18	98.27	**96.18**
A.Sg.M.	**85.54**	**84.55**	**85.04**
N.Sg.M.	**96.25**	96.18	**96.22**
G.Sg.M.	**93.46**	95.55	**94.50**
L.Sg.N.	92.12	89.38	90.73
N.Sg.F.	**93.61**	**91.83**	**92.72**
L.Sg.M.	86.92	89.69	88.28
I.Pl.M.	92.62	95.09	**93.84**
I.Sg.M.	89.88	**93.04**	**91.43**

Table 4: P, R, and F of the full LSTM model for the most frequent nominal categories. Bold numbers are higher than the best results reported in Hellwig (2015). Note that the F score may be better than in Hellwig (2015), even if neither P nor R are better, because Hellwig (2015) considers these values for two models.

Each of the three compounds ending on *-am* can be analyzed morphologically as N.Sg.N., A.Sg.N., or A.Sg.M.. The morphological disambiguation has labeled the morphologically ambiguous compounds ending on *vidhuram* and *ratnam* correctly as A.Sg.N. This decision was probably supported by the fact that the pronoun *sa* 'he' has only one morphological reading, and should therefore occupy the subject position of the singular verb, leaving the object slots free for the two accusative compounds. However, neither the LSTM nor the CRF were able to build the connection to the *bahuvrīhi* compound ending on *-yugalam* that forms the opening bracket around the direct speech.

Contracted forms of gender neutral personal pronouns constitute another high-frequency and error prone group. The pronouns of the first (*mad* 'I') and second person (*tvad* 'you') express their genitives and datives by morphologically unambiguous uncontracted (*mama* 'my', *mahyam* 'for me'; *tava* 'your', *tubhyam* 'for you'), and ambiguous contracted versions (*me* 'my, for me' and *te* 'your, for you'). In general, the use of dative and genitive becomes unstable in later and non-standard parts of the corpus, which may point to the linguistic influence of Middle and New Indo-Aryan languages. The passage Rāmāyaṇa, Utt., 57.28, for example, uses the genitive to express the receiver in the verbal frame of *dā* 'to give': *bhojanam ... mama* (G.Sg.!) *etad dātum icchasi* "You want to give me this food." The fact that the models are also trained on such non-standard instances may explain the high error rates for the contracted pronouns.

Table 4 presents precision, recall, and F scores for the most frequent morphological classes. Results are calculated from the output of the full LSTM model (Table 2). Comparing these values with the best results reported in Table 6 from Hellwig (2015) demonstrates that the LSTM clearly outperforms the published results, thereby setting a new standard for the morphological disambiguation of Sanskrit.

4 Conclusion

The paper has motivated and described a new tagset for the morphological disambiguation of Sanskrit, and had a closer look at the influence of lexical representation and model selection on the accuracy of morphological disambiguation. Using a reduced tagset, a combination of morphological, lexical, and semantic features, and a bidirectional deep neural network, the accuracy rates for morphological disambiguation could be improved significantly in comparison to previously published results. Future research should concentrate on better lexical representations for the numerous low-frequency lexemes, and on better integrating long-range linguistic structures that influence local morphological decisions.

References

David Alfter and Jürgen Knauth. 2015. Morphological analysis and generation for Pali. In *International Workshop on Systems and Frameworks for Computational Morphology*. Springer, pages 60–71.

Ronan Collobert, Jason Weston, Léon Bottou, Michael Karlen, Koray Kavukcuoglu, and Pavel Kuksa. 2011. Natural language processing (almost) from scratch. *Journal of Machine Learning Research* 12:2493–2537.

Mathias Creutz, Teemu Hirsimäki, Mikko Kurimo, Antti Puurula, Janne Pylkkönen, Vesa Siivola, Matti Varjokallio, Ebru Arisoy, Murat Saraçlar, and Andreas Stolcke. 2007. Morph-based speech recognition and modeling of out-of-vocabulary words across languages. *ACM Transactions on Speech and Language Processing (TSLP)* 5(1):1–27.

Mathias Creutz and Krista Lagus. 2007. Unsupervised models for morpheme segmentation and morphology learning. *ACM Transactions on Speech and Language Processing* 4(1).

John Duchi, Elad Hazan, and Yoram Singer. 2011. Adaptive subgradient methods for online learning and stochastic optimization. *Journal of Machine Learning Research* 12:2121–2159.

Jan Hajič and Barbora Hladká. 1998. Tagging inflective languages: Prediction of morphological categories for a rich, structured tagset. In *Proceedings of the 36th Annual Meeting of the ACL*. pages 483–490.

Oliver Hellwig. 2015. Morphological disambiguation of Classical Sanskrit. In Cerstin Mahlow and Michael Piotrowski, editors, *Systems and Frameworks for Computational Morphology*. Springer, Cham, pages 41–59.

Geoffrey E. Hinton, Nitish Srivastava, Alex Krizhevsky, Ilya Sutskever, and Ruslan R. Salakhutdinov. 2012. Improving neural networks by preventing co-adaptation of feature detectors. *arXiv preprint arXiv:1207.0580* .

Sepp Hochreiter, Yoshua Bengio, Paolo Frasconi, and Jürgen Schmidhuber. 2001. Gradient flow in recurrent nets: The difficulty of learning long-term dependencies. In S. C. Kremer and J. F. Kolen, editors, *A Field Guide to Dynamical Recurrent Neural Networks*.

Sepp Hochreiter and Jürgen Schmidhuber. 1997. Long Short-Term Memory. *Neural Computation* 9(8):1735–1780.

Gérard Huet. 2005. A functional toolkit for morphological and phonological processing, application to a Sanskrit tagger. *Journal of Functional Programming* 15(04):573–614.

Gérard Huet. 2006. Lexicon-directed segmentation and tagging of Sanskrit. In B. Tikkanen and H. Hettrich, editors, *Themes and Tasks in Old and Middle Indo-Aryan Linguistics*, Motilal Banarsidass, Delhi.

Girish Nath Jha, Muktanand Agrawal, Sudhir K. Mishra, Diwakar Mani, Diwakar Mishra, Manji Bhadra, Surjit K. Singh, et al. 2009a. Inflectional morphology analyzer for Sanskrit. In *Sanskrit Computational Linguistics*, Springer, pages 219–238.

Girish Nath Jha, Madhav Gopal, and Diwakar Mishra. 2009b. Annotating Sanskrit corpus: adapting IL-POSTS. In *Language and Technology Conference*. Springer, pages 371–379.

Sumitra M. Katre. 1991. Lexicography of Old Indo-Aryan: Vedic and Sanskrit. In Franz Josef Hausmann, Oskar Reichmann, Herbert Ernst Wiegand, and Ladislav Zgusta, editors, *Wörterbücher*, Walter de Gruyter, Berlin, pages 2487–2496.

Amba Kulkarni and Devanand Shukla. 2009. Sanskrit morphological analyser: Some issues. *Indian Linguistics* 70(1-4):169–177.

John D. Lafferty, Andrew McCallum, and Fernando C. N. Pereira. 2001. Conditional random fields: Probabilistic models for segmenting and labeling sequence data. In *Proceedings of the Eighteenth International Conference on Machine Learning*. pages 282–289.

Tomáš Mikolov, Anoop Deoras, Daniel Povey, Lukáš Burget, and Jan Černocký. 2011. Strategies for training large scale neural network language models. In *2011 IEEE Workshop on Automatic Speech Recognition and Understanding (ASRU)*. pages 196–201.

Anand Mishra. 2009. Simulating the Pāṇinian system of Sanskrit grammar. In *Sanskrit Computational Linguistics*, Springer, pages 127–138.

Amr El-Desoky Mousa, M Ali Basha Shaik, Ralf Schlüter, and Hermann Ney. 2010. Sub-lexical language models for German LVCSR. In *Spoken Language Technology Workshop (SLT)*. pages 171–176.

S. Lakshmana Pandian and T. V. Geetha. 2009. CRF models for Tamil part of speech tagging and chunking. In *Proceedings of the 22nd International Conference on Computer Processing of Oriental Languages*. Springer-Verlag, Berlin, Heidelberg, ICCPOL '09, pages 11–22.

Richard Salomon. 1995. On drawing socio-linguistic distinctions in Old Indo-Aryan: The question of Kṣatriya Sanskrit and related problems. In George Erdosy, editor, *The Indo-Aryans of Ancient South Asia. Language, Material Culture and Ethnicity*, Walter de Gruyter, Berlin, New York, pages 293–306.

Hartmut Scharfe. 1977. *Grammatical Literature*. A History of Indian Literature, Volume 5, Fasc. 2. Otto Harrassowitz, Wiesbaden.

M. Schuster and K.K. Paliwal. 1997. Bidirectional recurrent neural networks. *IEEE Transactions on Signal Processing* 45(11):2673–2681.

Query Translation for Cross-Language Information Retrieval using Multilingual Word Clusters

Paheli Bhattacharya, Pawan Goyal and Sudeshna Sarkar
Department of Computer Science and Engineering
Indian Institute of Technology Kharagpur
West Bengal, India
`paheli@iitkgp.ac.in`, `{pawang,sudeshna}@cse.iitkgp.ernet.in`

Abstract

In Cross-Language Information Retrieval, finding the appropriate translation of the source language query has always been a difficult problem to solve. We propose a technique towards solving this problem with the help of multilingual word clusters obtained from multilingual word embeddings. We use word embeddings of the languages projected to a common vector space on which a community-detection algorithm is applied to find clusters such that words that represent the same concept from different languages fall in the same group. We utilize these multilingual word clusters to perform query translation for Cross-Language Information Retrieval for three languages - English, Hindi and Bengali. We have experimented with the FIRE 2012 and Wikipedia datasets and have shown improvements over several standard methods like dictionary-based method, a transliteration-based model and Google Translate.

1   Introduction

With the advancement of the Web and availability of multilingual contents, searching over the Web is not limited only to one's native language but is extended to other languages as well. Relevant and adequate information may not always be available in only one particular language but may be spread across other languages. This gives rise to the necessity of Cross-Language Information Retrieval (CLIR, where only two languages are involved) and Multilingual Information Retrieval (MLIR, where more than two languages are involved), where the query and the documents do not belong to a single language only. Specifically, in CLIR, the user query is in a language different than the collection.

Since the language of the query is different from the language of the documents in CLIR and MLIR, a translation phase is necessary. Translating documents is a tedious task. So the general standard is to translate the query and we follow the query translation approach for CLIR. Common or popular approaches for query translation include, but are not limited to, leveraging bilingual or multilingual dictionaries, Statistical Machine Translation (SMT) systems, transliteration based models, graph-based models and online translation systems like Bing and Google Translate.

Each of the approaches have their own advantages and disadvantages. For instance, SMTs require parallel corpus and for languages such as Indian languages where such resources are scarce, SMTs are not very suitable. The dictionary based approaches require substantial word pair translations and suffer from coverage issues and data sparsity problems. We study the effectiveness of word embeddings in such a scenario where we want to have good quality translations that can improve CLIR performance in spite of having a scarcity in data-aligned resources.

Representing words using low dimensional vectors, called word embeddings, are now being widely used in many Natural Language Processing tasks. Each dimension of the vector represents a latent feature capturing useful properties. It has been seen that in the distributional space defined by the vector dimensions, syntactically and semantically similar words are close to each other. In the multilingual space, the objective is to have similar representations of similar words across different languages.

Proceedings of the 6th Workshop on South and Southeast Asian Natural Language Processing,
pages 152–162, Osaka, Japan, December 11-17 2016.

However, using the translations obtained from multilingual word embeddings directly has some draw-backs – words that are not much relevant to the source language word, may also come up as a translation. For instance, for the word "*desha*" (meaning, country) in Hindi, although correct translations like "country" and "democracy" were provided, irrelevant words like "aspiration" and "kind" also showed up as potential translations. Inclusion of such non-related words in a query greatly harms the IR performance. To address this problem, we propose to use multilingual clustering. In multilingual clustering, words from the same as well as across language, that more likely to represent similar concepts, fall in the same group. We use the multilingual embeddings to build these clusters. When multilingual clusters were used, candidate English translations besides "country" and "democracy" for our running example "*desha*" were "nation" and "cities". Our proposed method has shown significant improvements over dictionary-based method, a transliteration-based model and Google Translate.

The rest of the paper is organized as follows: Section 2 discusses recent work in the fields of Cross-Language Information Retrieval and Word Embeddinggs. In Section 3, we describe our proposed approach. The experimental settings and results have been covered in Section 4. Finally, we conclude in Section 5.

2 Related Work

2.1 Word Embeddings

Mikolov et. al (2013a) proposed a neural architecture that learns word representations by predicting neighbouring words. There are two main methods by which the distributed word representations can be learnt. One is the Continuous Bag-of-Words (CBOW) model that combines the representations of the surrounding words to predict the word in the middle. The second is the Skip-gram model that predicts the context of the target word in the same sentence. GloVe or Global Vectors (Pennington et al., 2014) is another unsupervised learning algorithm for obtaining word vectors.

2.2 Cross-lingual Vector Representations

The two major ways to learn word representations in the cross-lingual domain are to either first train the embeddings of the words separately for the languages and then project them to a common space (Faruqui and Dyer, 2014; Mikolov et al., 2013b) or co-learn the embeddings jointly for both monolingual and cross-lingual domains (Gouws et al., 2015; Luong et al., 2015).

Faruqui and Dyer (2014) uses Canonical Correlation Analysis (CCA) that maps words from two different languages in to a common, shared space. (Mikolov et al., 2013a) builds a translation matrix using linear regression that transforms the source language word vectors to the target language space. Huang et. al (2015) constructs translation invariant word embeddings by building on (Faruqui and Dyer, 2014). It performs matrix factorization where the matrices include a multilingual co-occurence matrix and other matrices based on the dictionary. Gouws and Søgaard (2015) uses a task-specific dictionary, i.e., a list of word pairs that are equivalent in some respect, depending on the task. Using a non-parallel corpora, given a sentence in one language, for each word in the sentence, equivalent words are substituted in its place. Then the CBOW model of the word2vec tool is employed.

Bilingual Bag-of-Words without Alignment (BilBOWA) (Gouws et al., 2015) uses monolingual datasets coupled with sentence aligned parallel data to learn word embeddings. They utilize the Skip-Gram model of word2vec to learn the monolingual features and a sampled bag-of-words technique for each parallel sentence as the cross-lingual objective. Chandar et al. (2014) shows that by learning to reconstruct the bag-of-words representations of aligned sentences, within and between languages, high-quality word representations can be learnt. They use an auto-encoder for this purpose.

Given an alignment link between a word w_1 in a language l_1 and a word w_2 in another language l_2, Luong et al. (2015) uses the word w_1 to predict the neighbours of the word w_2 and vice-versa. Klementiev et. al. (2012) induces distributed representations for a pair of languages jointly. They treat it as a multitask learning problem where each task corresponds to a single word and task relatedness is derived from co-occurence statistics in bilingual parallel data, with word alignments available.

2.3 Cross-Language Information Retrieval

Hull and Grefenstette (1996), Pirkola (1998), Ballesteros and Croft (1996) perform Cross-Language Information Retrieval through dictionary-based approaches. Littman et al. (1998) performs Latent Semantic Indexing on the term-document matrix. Statistical Machine Translations have also been tried out in (Schamoni et al., 2014; Türe et al., 2012b; Türe et al., 2012a; Sokolov et al., 2014). (Padariya et al., 2008; Chinnakotla et al., 2008) use transliteration for Out-of-Vocabulary words. In this method the dictionary-based technique is combined with a transliteration scheme in to a pageRank algorithm. We report their work as one of the baselines. Herbert et al. (2011) uses Wikipedia concepts along with Google Translate to translate the queries. By mining the cross-lingual links from the Wikipedia articles, a translation table is built. This is now coupled with translations from Google. Franco-Salvador et. al. (2014) leverages BabelNet, a multilingual semantic network for CLIR. Hosseinzadeh Vahid et al. (2015) uses Google and Bing to translate the queries and shows how the performances vary with translations from two different online systems.

Bhattacharya et. al (2016) uses word embeddings for Cross-Language Information Retrieval, learning word vectors from the document set. They also propose methods such that the query can be represented by a vector. We present their work as a baseline. Discriminative projection approaches for documents have also been applied to CLIR using Oriented Principal Component Analysis (OPCA), Coupled Probabilistic Latent Semantic Analysis (CPLSA) (Platt et al., 2010) and learning by Siamese Neural Network (S2Net) (Yih et al., 2011). Vulić and Moens (2015) uses word embeddings for CLIR. They collect document-aligned corpora and randomly merge and shuffle the pairs and feed them to the Skip-Gram architecture of word2vec. This way, they obtain cross-lingual word vectors, which they combine to obtain query vectors and document vectors. They perform IR by computing the cosine similarity between the query and the document vectors and ranking the documents according to the similarity.

3 Proposed Framework

We follow the query translation based approach towards Cross-Language Information Retrieval from Hindi to English and Bengali to English. We propose an approach for query translation using multilingual word clusters obtained from word embeddings.

Word embeddings serve as a potential tool for translation by bridging the gap between good quality translations and scarcity of data-aligned resources, like sentence-aligned parallel corpora and bilingual or multilingual dictionaries. Given a training corpus, word embeddings are able to generalize well over words that occur less frequently as well. Many words in Indian languages have been borrowed from English and have been added to the vocabulary, without any English translations like "*kaiMsara*" (meaning, Cancer, a disease). If a dictionary-based query translation is used for translating such terms, there is a high probability that the translations of such words shall be missing. Word embeddings on the other hand provide relevant translations like "cancer","disease","leukemia" for "*kaiMsara*".

To obtain multilingual word embeddings for the languages such that words that are similar across these languages have similar word vector representations, we use two state-of-the-art techniques to obtain these embeddings. The first approach is based on (Mikolov et al., 2013a) and (Mikolov et al., 2013b). The second approach is based on the idea of (Vulić and Moens, 2015). We use these methods since they use comparable and document-aligned corpora respectively, which are not very difficult to obtain. As described earlier, embedding methods requiring parallel corpora are difficult to get in resource-scarce languages. We describe the methods in Section 3.3.

In spite of multilingual embeddings being a powerful tool, translations obtained directly (by picking the top k target language words that have the highest cosine similarity with the source word) are sometimes irrelevant to the source language word. For instance, for the Hindi word "*pheMkanaa*" (meaning, throw) besides giving the correct translation "throw", the method also came up with not-so-relevant translations like "wash" and "splashing". In such situations, the performance of the CLIR system is greatly harmed. To deal with such scenarios, we propose the use of clustering. Multilingual clustering groups together similar words across languages that share the same concept. After the multilingual word embeddings have been obtained, we construct a graph $G = (V, E)$ from the word embeddings. V, set of vertices, represents words from the languages and E, set of edges, is formed if the cosine similarity between any two words (or vertices) is above a particular threshold and if so, then the weight of the edge is the cosine similarity value.

After such a graph has been constructed, we employ Louvain (Blondel et al., 2008), an efficient community-detection algorithm that runs in $O(nlogn)$ time. Applying Louvain on the above graph outputs clusters that contain words from all the languages that represent the same concept. More details on graph and cluster formation are provided in Section 3.4.

On clustering, words across languages that represent a certain concept will form dense clusters and edges representing a high cosine similarity value but an irrelevant translation will get overshadowed. Hence, the cluster containing *"pheMkanaa"* has similar and more related words like "hurl" and "dart" instead of "wash" and "splashing", which are now in a different cluster. These clusters are now used for the purpose of query translation for CLIR as described in Section 3.5.

3.1 Dataset

For obtaining multilingual word embeddings, we use two different approaches requiring two kinds of corpora: one approach requires comparable monolingual corpora for each of the three languages (English, Bengali and Hindi) and dictionaries containing Hindi-English and Bengali-English translations. The other approach requires document-aligned corpora for the three languages. The dataset details are as follows :

- Comparable Corpora : We have used FIRE (Forum for Information Retrieval Evaluation, developed as a South-Asian counterpart of CLEF, TREC, NTCIR) 2012 dataset [1]. The documents were obtained from the newspapers, 'The Telegraph' and 'BDNews24' for English; 'Amar Ujala' and 'Navbharat Times' for Hindi; 'Anandabazar Patrika' and 'BDNews24' for Bengali. There were 1,427,986 English; 1,164,526 Hindi and 500,122 Bengali documents.

- Document-Aligned Corpora: We have used the Wikipedia dumps[2] available for download for each of the three languages, English, Bengali and Hindi. In order to get the cross-lingual articles, we made use of the inter-wiki links that exist in the corresponding Wikipedia pages. There were 55,949 English-Hindi pages; 34,234 English-Bengali pages and 12,324 English-Bengali-Hindi pages.

- Cross-Language Information Retrieval: We used the FIRE 2012 queries for Hindi and Bengali for Hindi to English and Bengali to English CLIR. There were 50 queries with topics numbered from 176-225. We used the title fields for querying.

- Other resources: We used a Hindi-English dictionary[3] that had 26,485 translation-pairs, Bengali-English dictionary[4] containing 29,890 translation-pairs, Stopword lists[5] and an English Named-Entity Recognizer[6]. Louvain Method for community detection algorithm (Blondel et al., 2008) was used for clustering.

3.2 Pre-processing the Dataset

We perform the basic pre-processing tasks on the documents, like removing the html tags, sentence boundaries and reducing all the letters to lowercase (for English). We obtain word vectors from this document set. We count the term frequencies of the words and remove stopwords, top 50 most frequently occurring words and words below frequency of 20 (for Wikipedia dataset), 50 (for English and Bengali

---

[1] `http://fire.irsi.res.in/fire/data`
[2] `https://dumps.wikimedia.org/backup-index.html`
[3] `http://ltrc.iiit.ac.in/onlineServices/Dictionaries/Dict_Frame.html`
[4] `http://www.cfilt.iitb.ac.in/Downloads.html`
[5] `http://www.ranks.nl/stopwords`
[6] `http://nlp.stanford.edu/software/CRF-NER.shtml`

Table 1: Statistics of the number of words (vertices) used to create word clusters, separately for FIRE and Wikipedia Datasets

	Pair				Multi		
	English-Hindi		English-Bengali		English-Hindi-Bengali		
	English	Hindi	English	Bengali	English	Hindi	Bengali
FIRE	129,688	84,773	129,688	93,057	129,688	84,773	93,057
Wikipedia	106,746	35,361	77,302	24,794	50,620	16,534	13,490

Table 2: Statistics of the Bilingual and Multilingual Clusters

		# Levels		# Clusters	
		English-Hindi	English-Bengali	English-Hindi	English-Bengali
Pair	**FIRE**	5	5	403	384
	Wiki	4	4	19611	20627
Multi Wiki		5		406	

FIRE dataset) and 20 (for Hindi FIRE dataset). We choose these numbers so that we have balanced number of words for the three languages. We then obtain the embeddings of the remaining words.

3.3 Obtaining Multilingual Word Embeddings

For creating multilingual word clusters using an embedding based approach, we first need to obtain multilingual word vectors. Multilingual word vectors can be obtained from parallel corpora (Gouws et al., 2015), document-aligned corpora (Vulić and Moens, 2015) and comparable corpora using a dictionary (Mikolov et al., 2013b). Since, Hindi and Bengali are resource-scarce languages, parallel, sentence-aligned data are scarce and insufficient to train word vector models. Hence, we use the methods involving document-aligned corpora and comparable corpora using a dictionary for obtaining word embeddings and test their performance. We describe these two methods next.

3.3.1 Dictionary Projection based Approach using Comparable Corpora

We obtain monolingual word embeddings separately for English, Hindi and Bengali using the *word2vec* (Mikolov et al., 2013a) tool available for download [7]. We use the Continuous Bag-of-Words (CBOW) variant to learn the monolingual word embeddings, as it has been shown to work faster than Skip-Gram for large datasets.

For learning the projection function from the source languages (Hindi and Bengali) to the target language (English), we use the linear regression method similar to (Mikolov et al., 2013b). The idea is as follows: given a dictionary of translation word-pairs $\{x_i, y_i\}$ whose monolingual word vectors $x_i \in \mathbb{R}^{d_1}$ – a d_1- dimensional embedding, $y_i \in \mathbb{R}^{d_2}$ – a d_2- dimensional embedding, are known, the objective is to learn a translation matrix W such that the root mean square error between Wx_i and y_i is minimized. Once W has been learnt, it can now be used to project the entire vocabulary of the source language to the English space. The vectors of the words from all the three languages are now in a common vector space and can be used for translation.

3.3.2 Learning Embeddings together in a Joint Space using Document-Aligned Corpora

Vulić and Moens (2015) uses document-aligned corpora to learn bilingual embeddings. We use this approach and extend it for obtaining multilingual embeddings together in a joint space.

Let $D = \{(d_{s_1}, d_{t_1}), (d_{s_2}, d_{t_2}), \ldots, (d_{s_n}, d_{t_n})\}$ be the set of document-aligned, comparable corpora where (d_{s_i}, d_{t_i}) denotes a pair of aligned documents in source language s and target language t and n is the number of such aligned-document pairs constituting the corpus. In order to learn bilingual word embeddings, the first step is to merge the two document pairs (d_{s_i}, d_{t_i}) in to a "pseudo-bilingual"

---

[7]https://code.google.com/p/word2vec

document and remove sentence boundaries. Next, this bilingual document is randomly shuffled and is used as training for monolingual skip-gram model of *word2vec* (Vulić and Moens, 2015).

The idea of document-aligned "pairs" can be readily extended to document-aligned "triplets", where now there are three documents $(d_{e_i}, d_{h_i}, d_{b_i})$ in three languages that are document-aligned. In this case, we merge and shuffle the ith document-triplet and obtain embeddings for words from all the three languages.

3.4 Creating Graph and obtaining Clusters

After obtaining the multilingual embeddings separately by the two methods described above, we compute the cosine similarities between the word vectors. Now a graph $G = (V, E)$ is constructed, where the vertex set V represents words from both the languages and E defines the set of edges - an edge exists between two vertices if the cosine similarity value of the word embeddings of the two vertices is greater than or equal to a threshold of 0.5. The edge weights are the cosine similarity of the embeddings of the connecting vertices (words).

After the graphs have been obtained, we apply the Louvain algorithm for community detection (Blondel et al., 2008) separately for the graphs. Given a graph, Louvain looks for small clusters, optimizing the modularity in a local way. In the first pass, small communities are formed. In the subsequent passes, it combines communities from the lower level to create larger sized clusters. The iteration stops once maximum modularity is achieved. It performs hard clustering, that is, a word belongs to only one cluster. The algorithm runs pretty fast in $O(nlogn)$ time.

Table 1 shows word-count statistics that have been used as vertices to create clusters. "Pair" indicates that the words (or vertices) are from two languages while "Multi" indicates that the words (or vertices) are from three languages.

Table 2 shows the number of levels and number of clusters for each language pair on different corpora. Since, multilingual clusters using the dictionary-based approach were not used in our experiments due to poor performance, we do not report its statistics.

In lower levels, the number of clusters were more and words that should belong to the same cluster were scattered in other clusters. In the topmost level of clustering, although there were some clusters that had a large number of words and were unrelated, most of them had related words in the same cluster. On observing the bilingual and multilingual clusters closely, we find that the bilingual clusters were mostly small and contained words that were translations and/or transliterations of each other. For clusters that were large, the communities were well representative of the words. Our main focus was on multilingual clusters since the bigger objective of our work is to have an unified representation of words for Indian Languages. Following are some examples of clusters [8] :

- FIRE Hindi-English : (inflation, *mudraasphiiti*, money, *paise*, *rakama*, *dhanaraashi*, prices, cost)

- Wikipedia Multi : (*aarthika* (hi), currency, economics, *mudraasphiiti* (bn), inflation, *arthaniiti* (bn), *munaaphaa* (hi))

3.5 Query Translation from Word Clusters

After forming multilingual word clusters, we use them for the purpose of query translation in CLIR. Given a query Q = $q_1 q_2 \cdots q_n$ in Hindi or Bengali, we first find the cluster c_k to which the query word q_i belongs. We then extract all the English words from c_k and pick the top t most similar English words from the cluster c_k for the query word q_i. We repeat this step for all the query words and append them consecutively. Note that while the stopwords in the query are already filtered, the named-entities do not have the embeddings because of filtering of words below the threshold frequency. These named-entities are dealt separately, as described in the next section.

---

[8] All non-English words have been written in ITrans using `http://sanskritlibrary.org/transcodeText.html` Hindi words have been abbreviated as 'hi' and Bengali words as 'bn'.

Table 3: Performance of the Baseline Approaches for Hindi to English and Bengali to English CLIR on FIRE 2012 Dataset

		Hindi to English CLIR			Bengali to English CLIR		
		MAP	P5	P10	MAP	P5	P10
English Monolingual		0.3218	0.56	0.522	0.3218	0.56	0.522
Bhattacharya et al. (2016)	**FIRE**	0.2802	0.436	0.392	0.2368	0.334	0.318
	Wikipedia	0.1524	0.232	0.22	0.3027	0.448	0.402
Dictionary		0.1691	0.2048	0.2048	0.134	0.165	0.132
Chinnakotla et al. (2008)		0.2236	0.3347	0.3388	0.18	0.275	0.232
Google Translate		0.3566	0.576	0.522	0.294	0.524	0.48

3.6 Transliteration of Named Entities

Although most of the named-entities are filtered out in the pre-processing stage, some words like the names of political parties, e.g., *BJP, Congress* in Hindi and Bengali have embeddings and so we obtain similar words like the names of other political parties and also words like 'government' and 'parliament' in English. During our experiments, we observed that inclusion of such terms can harm the retrieval process and so we prefer to transliterate these. Since we did not have access to any Named-Entity Recognition (NER) tool for Hindi and Bengali, we resort to a transliteration based process similar to (Chinnakotla et al., 2008; Padariya et al., 2008). For each Hindi/Bengali character, we construct a table of its possible transliterations and also apply some language specific rules. Given a Hindi/Bengali query term h, we first transliterate it using the method described above and for each word e in the list of words returned as named entities by the NER tool for English, we apply the Minimum Edit Distance algorithm to h and e. If we find an e within a range of 0 to 1.5, we treat h as a named-entity and use the transliteration with the least distance. If no such e is returned, we consider it as a non-named entity and use the cluster based approach to obtain translation.

4 Experiments

We used Apache Solr version 4.1 as the monolingual retrieval engine. The similarity score between the query and the documents is the default TF-IDF Similarity [9]. The human relevance judgments were available from FIRE. Each query had about 500 documents that were manually judged as relevant (1) or non-relevant (0). We then used the trec-eval tool [10] for finding the Mean Average Precision (MAP), Precision at 5 (P5) and Precision at 10 (P10).

4.1 Baselines

In this section we describe the baseline methods we have used to compare our proposed approach.

- **English Monolingual**: FIRE provides corresponding queries for most Indian languages and also English. This baseline uses the English queries for retrieval.

- **Bhattacharya et al. (2016)**: In this approach, once the word vector of each query term projected in the target language (v) is obtained, cosine similarity between the vector embedding of each English word and v is computed, and the 3 best translations are picked. Although they obtained best results when the query as a whole was represented as a vector but our method involves translation at the cluster level and so we do not find such a comparison suitable. Hence, we report their result on query word vectors.

- **Dictionary**: This is the dictionary-based method where the query word translations have been obtained from the dictionary. For words that contain multiple translations, we include all of them.

---

[9]https://lucene.apache.org/core/3_5_0/api/core/org/apache/lucene/search/Similarity.html
[10]http://trec.nist.gov/trec_eval/

Table 4: Performance of the Proposed Cluster-based Approach for Hindi to English and Bengali to English CLIR on FIRE 2012 Dataset

Datasets		Methods	Hindi to English CLIR			Bengali to English CLIR		
			MAP	P5	P10	MAP	P5	P10
Pair En-Hi / En-Ben	FIRE	Cluster	0.352	0.4503	0.427	0.3038	0.478	0.418
		Cluster+DT	0.362	0.537	0.52	0.326	0.495	0.464
		Cluster+DT +GT	**0.452**	**0.627**	**0.578**	0.342	0.534	0.49
	Wikipedia	Cluster	0.2832	0.3760	0.35	0.3233	0.468	0.43
		Cluster+DT	0.324	0.408	0.386	0.361	0.482	0.458
		Cluster+DT +GT	0.42	0.526	0.501	0.389	0.517	0.487
Multi En-Ben-Hi	Wikipedia	Cluster	0.3014	0.446	0.37	0.3557	0.476	0.418
		Cluster+DT	0.356	0.541	0.510	0.396	0.538	0.501
		Cluster+DT+GT	0.432	0.575	0.538	**0.42**	**0.56**	**0.545**

Named entities are handled as in Section 3.6. If the translation of a query word is not present in the dictionary, it is ignored.

- **(Chinnakotla et al., 2008)** : The method proposed by (Chinnakotla et al., 2008) is used as a baseline.[11].

- **Google Translate** : Translations of the Hindi query to English have been obtained by using Google Translate.

4.2 Proposed Cluster-based Approach

We have experimented with various similarity thresholds and various levels of clustering and report the best results. We experimented with the following variants of our approach :

- **Cluster**: In this method, we simply pick the top 3 (experimentally chosen) most similar English words for each query term within the cluster and append them. We proportionally assign weights to each translation of a query term according to its similarity to the query word such that the weight of all the translations of a query term add up to 1. The named-entities were assigned a weight of 1.

- **Cluster + DT**: We combine translations from the dictionary as well as from the clusters. We first take translations from the dictionary, if a translation exists. If not, we take it only from clusters. In case translations exist in both, we assign 80% weightage to the cluster translations and 20% weightage to the dictionary translations. [12]

- **Cluster + DT + GT**: In this scheme, we combine translations from Google Translate as well as with the dictionary. We assign equal weightage to Cluster words and translations from Google, 40% each, and the rest to dictionary translations.

4.3 Results

Table 3 shows the baseline results for the CLIR task for Hindi to English and Bengali to English. The results of our proposed approached are in Table 4. For Hindi to English CLIR, dictionary-projection method performs the best and the performance improves when it is combined with dictionary translations and translations from Google. This is because the dictionary for Bengali-English was not as rich as Hindi-English. For Hindi-English the number of word pair translations trained on were 8714 and for

---

[11](Chinnakotla et al., 2008) is an improved version of (Padariya et al., 2008)

[12]We experimented with other weightages like 70%-30%, 90%-10%, but the 80%-20% division gives the best results.

Table 5: Some example queries and their performances

Query	Gloss	Translation Method	Translation	MAP	P5	P10
poliyo unmuulana abhiyaana	Polio eradication mission	No Cluster	vaccine polio campaign campaigns	0.4	0.55	0.48
		Wiki Pair Cluster	polio vaccine eradication mission	0.6	0.7	0.6
		Wiki Multi Cluster	polio infection prevention campaign	**0.85**	**1**	**0.9**
griisa iuro kaapa 2004 jaya	2004 Greece Euro Cup victory	No Cluster	Greece 2004 euro banknotes tournament champions victory win defeat	0.5	0.7	0.6
		Wiki Pair Cluster	Greece 2004 Euro euro trophy Football teams victory win winning	0.6	0.75	0.7
		Wiki Multi Cluster	Greece 2004 Euro trophy cup champions winner	**0.9**	**1**	**0.8**

Bengali-English the number was 6012. Multilingual word clusters perform better than bilingual word clusters when the multilingual embeddings have been learnt jointy using the Wikipedia document-aligned corpora suggesting that when another language is incorporated, cluster information improves and words in the clusters are more related with each other and aligned to the semantic information exhibited by the cluster.

Multilingual and bilingual word clusters formed using Wikipedia document-aligned data perform better for Bengali to English CLIR comapared to the dictionary-based approach using FIRE data. Multilingual word clusters alone performs well when compared in terms of MAP with Google Translate and shows improvements when combined with dictionary and Google Translate. The number of documents in Bengali from the FIRE dataset were less and this may be a probable cause for its poor performance.

Table 5 shows two example queries. The first query is for Hindi to English CLIR and the second query is for Bengali to English CLIR. For the first two translation methods, no translation is available for "*unmuulana*" (meaning, eradication) but multilingual clustering suggests the word "prevention". Also, for "*poliyo*", multilingual clustering comes up with more related word "infection" rather than "vaccine" since "polio" is primarily a disease/infection and vaccination is a medication and is secondary. For the second query, the word "*Euro*" is related to sports and not economics. No Cluster method wrongly predicts the context and suggests words like 'banknotes". On the other hand, pairwise clustering understands that "cup" is related to some sports, "football" to be more specific. Multilingual clustering restricts to a shorter query and hence translates to only "trophy" and "cup".

5   Conclusion and Future Extensions

In this paper, we proposed a method to cluster semantically similar words across languages, and evaluated it for query translation in the CLIR task. Experimental results confirm that it performs better than the dictionary method, English monolingual and transliteration based approaches. When combined with the dictionary and Google Translate in a hybrid model, it achieves the best performance. In future, we plan to extend the work for other Indian languages and obtain communities containing similar concept in multiple languages.

6 Acknowledgments

The authors would like to thank the anonymous reviewers for their valuable comments. This work is supported by the project "To Develop a Scientific Rationale of IELS (Indo-European Language Systems) Applying A) Computational Linguistics & B) Cognitive Geo-Spatial Mapping Approaches" funded by the Ministry of Human Resource Development (MHRD), India and conducted in Artificial Intelligence Laboratory, Indian Institute of Technology Kharagpur.

References

Lisa Ballesteros and W. Bruce Croft. 1996. Dictionary Methods for Cross-Lingual Information Retrieval. In *Proceedings of the 7th International Conference on Database and Expert Systems Applications*, DEXA '96, pages 791–801.

Paheli Bhattacharya, Pawan Goyal, and Sudeshna Sarkar. 2016. Using word embeddings for query translation for hindi to english cross language information retrieval. *Computación y Sistemas*, 20(3):435–447.

Vincent D Blondel, Jean-Loup Guillaume, Renaud Lambiotte, and Etienne Lefebvre. 2008. Fast Unfolding of Communities in Large Networks. *Journal of statistical mechanics: theory and experiment*, 2008(10):P10008.

Sarath Chandar, Stanislas Lauly, Hugo Larochelle, Mitesh Khapra, Balaraman Ravindran, Vikas C Raykar, and Amrita Saha. 2014. An autoencoder Approach to Learning Bilingual Word Representations. In *Advances in Neural Information Processing Systems*, pages 1853–1861.

Manoj Kumar Chinnakotla, Sagar Ranadive, Om P. Damani, and Pushpak Bhattacharyya. 2008. Hindi to English and Marathi to English Cross Language Information Retrieval Evaluation. In *8th Workshop of the Cross-Language Evaluation Forum, CLEF 2007, Budapest, Hungary, September 19-21, 2007, Revised Selected Papers*, pages 111–118.

Manaal Faruqui and Chris Dyer. 2014. Improving Vector Space Word Representations Using Multilingual Correlation. In *Proceedings of EACL*.

Marc Franco-Salvador, Paolo Rosso, and Roberto Navigli. 2014. A Knowledge-based Representation for Cross-Language Document Retrieval and Categorization. In *Proceedings of the 14th Conference of the European Chapter of the Association for Computational Linguistics (EACL 2014)*.

Stephan Gouws and Anders Søgaard. 2015. Simple task-specific bilingual word embeddings. *Proceedings of NAACL-HLT*, pages 1386–1390.

Stephan Gouws, Yoshua Bengio, and Greg Corrado. 2015. Bilbowa: Fast Bilingual Distributed Representations without Word Alignments. In *International Conference on Machine Learning (ICML)*.

Benjamin Herbert, György Szarvas, and Iryna Gurevych. 2011. Combining Query Translation Techniques to Improve Cross-language Information Retrieval. In *Proceedings of the 33rd European Conference on Advances in Information Retrieval*, ECIR'11, pages 712–715.

Ali Hosseinzadeh Vahid, Piyush Arora, Qun Liu, and Gareth J.F. Jones. 2015. A Comparative Study of Online Translation Services for Cross Language Information Retrieval. In *Proceedings of the 24th International Conference on World Wide Web*, pages 859–864.

Kejun Huang, Matt Gardner, Evangelos E. Papalexakis, Christos Faloutsos, Nikos D. Sidiropoulos, Tom M. Mitchell, Partha Pratim Talukdar, and Xiao Fu. 2015. Translation Invariant Word Embeddings. In *Proceedings of the 2015 Conference on Empirical Methods in Natural Language Processing, EMNLP 2015, Lisbon, Portugal, September 17-21, 2015*, pages 1084–1088. The Association for Computational Linguistics.

David A. Hull and Gregory Grefenstette. 1996. Querying across languages: A dictionary-based approach to multilingual information retrieval. In *Proceedings of the 19th Annual International ACM SIGIR Conference on Research and Development in Information Retrieval*, SIGIR '96, pages 49–57.

Alexandre Klementiev, Ivan Titov, and Binod Bhattarai. 2012. Inducing Crosslingual Distributed Representations of Words. In *COLING*.

Michael L. Littman, Susan T. Dumais, and Thomas K. Landauer, 1998. *Automatic Cross-Language Information Retrieval Using Latent Semantic Indexing*, pages 51–62.

Minh-Thang Luong, Hieu Pham, and Christopher D. Manning. 2015. Bilingual Word Representations with Monolingual Quality in Mind. In *NAACL Workshop on Vector Space Modeling for NLP*.

Tomas Mikolov, Kai Chen, Greg Corrado, and Jeffrey Dean. 2013a. Efficient estimation of word representations in vector space. *arXiv preprint arXiv:1301.3781*.

Tomas Mikolov, Quoc V. Le, and Ilya Sutskever. 2013b. Exploiting Similarities among Languages for Machine Translation. *CoRR*, abs/1309.4168.

Nilesh Padariya, Manoj Chinnakotla, Ajay Nagesh, and Om P Damani. 2008. Evaluation of Hindi to English, Marathi to English and English to Hindi CLIR at FIRE 2008. In *Working Notes of Forum for Information Retrieval and Evaluation (FIRE), 2008*.

Jeffrey Pennington, Richard Socher, and Christopher D. Manning. 2014. GloVe: Global Vectors for Word Representation. In *Empirical Methods in Natural Language Processing (EMNLP)*, pages 1532–1543.

Ari Pirkola. 1998. The Effects of Query Structure and Dictionary Setups in Dictionary-based Cross-language Information Retrieval. In *Proceedings of the 21st Annual International ACM SIGIR Conference on Research and Development in Information Retrieval*, SIGIR '98, pages 55–63.

John C. Platt, Kristina Toutanova, and Wen-tau Yih. 2010. Translingual document representations from discriminative projections. In *Proceedings of the 2010 Conference on Empirical Methods in Natural Language Processing*, EMNLP '10, pages 251–261.

Shigehiko Schamoni, Felix Hieber, Artem Sokolov, and Stefan Riezler. 2014. Learning Translational and Knowledge-based Similarities from Relevance Rankings for Cross-Language Retrieval. In *ACL*.

Artem Sokolov, Felix Hieber, and Stefan Riezler. 2014. Learning to Translate Queries for CLIR. In *Proceedings of the 37th International ACM SIGIR Conference on Research & Development in Information Retrieval*, SIGIR '14, pages 1179–1182.

Ferhan Türe, Jimmy Lin, and Douglas W Oard. 2012a. Looking inside the box: Context-sensitive translation for cross-language information retrieval. In *Proceedings of the 35th international ACM SIGIR conference on Research and development in information retrieval*, pages 1105–1106. ACM.

Ferhan Türe, Jimmy J Lin, and Douglas W Oard. 2012b. Combining Statistical Translation Techniques for Cross-Language Information Retrieval. In *COLING*, pages 2685–2702.

Ivan Vulić and Marie-Francine Moens. 2015. Monolingual and Cross-Lingual Information Retrieval Models Based on (Bilingual) Word Embeddings. In *Proceedings of the 38th International ACM SIGIR Conference on Research and Development in Information Retrieval*, pages 363–372. ACM.

Wen-tau Yih, Kristina Toutanova, John C. Platt, and Christopher Meek. 2011. Learning discriminative projections for text similarity measures. In *Proceedings of the Fifteenth Conference on Computational Natural Language Learning*, CoNLL '11, pages 247–256.

A study of attention-based Neural Machine Translation models on Indian Languages

Ayan Das, Pranay Yerra, Ken Kumar, Sudeshna Sarkar
Department of Computer Science and Engineering
Indian Institute of Technology, Kharagpur, WB, India
`ayan.das@cse.iitkgp.ernet.in`
`ypranay.hasan@cse.iitkgp.ernet.in`
`ken@iitkgp.ac.in`
`sudeshna@cse.iitkgp.ernet.in`

Abstract

Neural machine translation (NMT) models have recently been shown to be very successful in machine translation (MT). The use of LSTMs in machine translation has significantly improved the translation performance for longer sentences by being able to capture the context and long range correlations of the sentences in their hidden layers. The attention model based NMT system has become state-of-the-art, performing equal or better than other statistical MT approaches. In this paper, we studied the performance of the attention-model based NMT system on the Indian language pair, Hindi and Bengali. We analysed the types of errors that occur in morphologically rich languages when there is a scarcity of large parallel training corpus. We then carried out certain post-processing heuristic steps to improve the quality of the translated statements and suggest further measures.

1 Introduction

Deep Neural Network has been successfully applied to machine translation.The work of (Cho et al., 2014; Kalchbrenner and Blunsom, 2013; Sutskever et al., 2014) have shown that it is possible to build an end-to-end machine translation system using neural networks by introducing the *encoder-decoder* model. NMT systems have several advantages over the existing phrase-based statistical machine translation (SMT) systems (Koehn et al., 2007). The NMT systems do not assume any domain knowledge or linguistic features in source and target language sentences. Secondly, the entire encoder-decoder models are jointly trained to maximize the translation quality as opposed to the phrase-based SMT systems in which the individual components needs to be trained and tuned separately for optimal performance.

Although the NMT systems have several advantages, their performance is restricted in case of low-resource language pairs for which sufficiently large parallel corpora is not available and the language pairs whose syntaxes differ significantly. Morphological richness of language pairs poses another challenge for NMT systems that do not have any prior knowledge of the languages as it tends to increase the number of surface forms of the words due to inflectional attachments resulting in an increased vocabulary of the languages. Moreover, the inflectional forms have their semantic roles that have to be interpreted for proper translation. In order to enable the NMT systems to learn the roles of the inflectional forms automatically we need sufficiently large data. However, sufficiently large parallel data may not be available for low-resource morphologically rich language pairs. Most of the Indian languages are morphologically rich and there is lack of sufficiently large parallel corpus for Indian language pairs. Given our familiarity with Bengali and Hindi, we took up this task as a case-study and evaluated the performance of NMT models on Indian language pair-Hindi and Bengali. We then analyzed the resulting translated sentences and suggested post-processing heuristics to improve the quality of the translated sentences. We have proposed heuristics to rectify the incorrect translations of the named entities. We have also proposed a heuristic to translate and predict the position of untranslated source words.

Proceedings of the 6th Workshop on South and Southeast Asian Natural Language Processing,
pages 163–172, Osaka, Japan, December 11-17 2016.

2   Related work

Neural machine translation

Neural machine translation models attempt to optimize $p(e|f)$ directly by including feature extraction using a single neural network. The entire translation process is done using an encoder-decoder framework (Cho et al., 2014; Kalchbrenner and Blunsom, 2013; Sutskever et al., 2014) where the encoder encodes f into a continuous space representation and the decoder uses the encoding of f and decoding history to generate the target language sentence e. The encoders and decoders are essentially recurrent neural networks (RNNs)(Mikolov et al., 2010; Mikolov et al., 2011) or its gated versions (Gated Recurrent Unit (GRU) (Chung et al., 2014; Chung et al., 2015) or Long-Short Term Memory (LSTM) (Hochreiter and Schmidhuber, 1997)) capable of learning long-term dependencies.

Cho et al. (2014) proposed to use the final state of the hidden layer of the encoder as the encoding of the source sentence. Sundermeyer et al. (2014) used a bi-directional RNN in the encoder and used the concatenation of the final states of the hidden layers as the encoding of the source sentence. Sutskever et al. (2014) proposed to train the encoder using the source sentence in the reverse ordering of words and the decoder in the correct word ordering of target sentence.

Bahdanau et al. (2014) and Luong et al. (2015) have proposed the attention-based translation model. The encoder of the model is a bi-directional RNN (Schuster and Paliwal, 1997). The annotation vectors $\mathbf{h_j^T}$ (where $\mathbf{h_j}$ encodes the jth word with respect to the other words in the source sentence) are obtained by concatinating the two sequences of hidder layers $\overrightarrow{\mathbf{h_j^T}}$ and $\overleftarrow{\mathbf{h_j^T}}$ which are obtained by training the forward RNNs on the orginal sequence of input sentences and the backward RNNs on the reverse sequence of input sentences, such that $\mathbf{h_j^T} = [\overrightarrow{\mathbf{h_j^T}}; \overleftarrow{\mathbf{h_j^T}}]$. The decoder consists of a single layer GRU. At time step t, the alignment layer decides the relevance of the source words for the word to be predicted. The relevance (α_{tj}) of the jth annotation vector at time t is determined by a feed-forward neural network that takes the previous state of the hidden layer of the decoder ($\mathbf{s}_{t-1}$), embedding of the last predicted word ($\mathbf{y}_{t-1}$) and the jth annotation vector ($\mathbf{h}_j$) as input. The hidden state of the decoder at time t is computed as a function f_r of the previous hidden state $\mathbf{s}_t$, the context vector $\mathbf{c}_t$ and the previous predicted word $\mathbf{y}_{t-1}$, where f_r is a GRU and $\mathbf{c}_t$ is the context vector for the tth word is obtained as a sum of the annotation vectors weighted by the corresponding relevance scores.

$$\mathbf{s}_t = f_r(\mathbf{s}_{t-1}, y_{t-1}, c_t) \tag{1}$$

Finally, the conditional distribution over the words is obtained by using a deep output layer.

$$p(\mathbf{y}_t|\mathbf{y}_{t-1}, \mathbf{x}) \propto exp(\mathbf{y}_t^T(W_o f_o(\mathbf{s}_t, \mathbf{y}_{t-1}, \mathbf{c}_t) + b_o)) \tag{2}$$

where, $\mathbf{y}_t$ is the indicator vector corresponding to a word in the target vocabulary. W_o and b_o are the weights and bias of the deep layer and f_o is a single-layer feed-forward neural network with a two-way maxout layer (Goodfellow et al., 2013).

Once the model learns the conditional distribution, then given a source sentence we can find a translation that approximately maximizes the conditional probability using, for instance, a beam search algorithm.

3   Proposed Method

In this paper, we studied the performance of attention-model based NMT system (Bahdanau et al., 2014) on Bengali-Hindi language pair. The attention-based NMT models have shown near state-of-the-art performance for the language pairs, English-French and English-German. One of the advantages for these language pairs was the availability of good-quality, sentence aligned parallel corpora from WMT'14 dataset. We implemented the same attention-model based NMT system (Bahdanau et al., 2014) and studied its performance on the Indian language pair, Bengali and Hindi. Both Hindi and Bengali belong to the same family of language and share some high-level syntactic similarities such as Subject-Object-Verb (SOV) sentence structure which lead us to believe that the attention model will be useful for this language pair.

3.1 Resources used

Monolingual Hindi and Bengali corpora were used to train word2vec (Mikolov et al., 2013) to obtain the word embeddings. The monolingual Hindi corpus was obtained from the ILTP-DC (www.tdil-dc.in/) which consists of about 45 million sentences. The FIRE 2011 (http://www.isical.ac.in/ clia/2011/) monolingual Bengali news corpus consisting of about 3.5 million sentences was used to obtain the Bengali word vectors. The Bengali-Hindi parallel corpus was obtained from ILCI (sanskrit.jnu.ac.in/ilci), comprising of 50000 sentences obtained from tourism and health domains was used for the experiments. From the 50000 Bengali-Hindi parallel sentences, 49000 sentence pairs were randomly selected for training and remaining 1000 sentence pairs were used for testing. In order to reduce the size of the vocabulary we replaced all the numeric values by the 'NUM' token.

3.2 Our implementation of the Attention-Model

The attention-model based NMT model (Bahdanau et al., 2014) was implemented in Theano (Theano Development Team, 2016). The number of hidden layer units (n) was taken as 1000, the word embedding dimensionality as 620 and the size of the maxout hidden layer in the deep output was 500. The number of hidden units in the alignment model was 1000. We used gradient-clipping with a clipping threshold of 5. The model was trained using stochastic gradient descent with a learning rate of 0.0627 and batch size of 1. The model was run on a Nvidia Tesla K40C GPU machine.

4   Results

MOSES (a phrase-based SMT model) (Koehn et al., 2007) was used as a baseline system for comparison of the NMT model. The Bengali-Hindi parallel corpus obtained from ILCI (sanskrit.jnu.ac.in/ilci) comprising of 50000 sentences obtained from tourism and health domains was used for the experiments. From the 50000 Bengali-Hindi parallel sentences 49000 sentence pairs were randomly selected for training the model and remaining 1000 sentence pairs were used for testing. Out of the 49000 sentence-pairs in the training set, 15000 pairs (tuning set) were randomly selected for tuning the model parameter (weights) using MERT system (Minimum Error Rate Training) (Och, 2003) which searches for weights optimizing a given error measure which is BLEU score in our case. The SRILM (Stolcke, 2002) language model was trained using the entire training dataset comprising of 49000 sentence pairs.

We compared the performance of the attention-model based NMT system with that of the baseline MOSES phrase-based SMT system. We ran the NMT model for 25 epochs. Table 1 summarizes the results.

Table 1: Comparison of 1) attention-based NMT model and 2) MOSES phrase-based SMT system.

Translation model	BLEU score	Iterations
MOSES	14.35	-
Attention-based translation model	20.41	25

As the BLEU score suggests, the translation quality of the NMT system surpasses that of the MOSES (Koehn et al., 2007) by a significant margin. Out of the 1000 sentence pairs used for testing, we randomly picked up 8 sentences and present them in Appendix 1. We observe that in five of the eight examples the translation results of the attention model are clearly better than that produced by MOSES. The translation by MOSES is slightly better in two cases whereas in one example, both models have almost similar translation results. This was the general trend in all the test examples with the attention model performing relatively better than MOSES in cases of longer source sentences (Figure 1).

We also compared the BLEU score of our NMT model over 25 iterations with the MOSES system and saw that only after 5 iterations, the NMT model started performing better than MOSES (Figure 2).

5   Analysis

Our implementation of the attention based NMT model significantly outperforms MOSES in terms of BLEU scores. However on manual inspection of some random samples, we observed significant errors

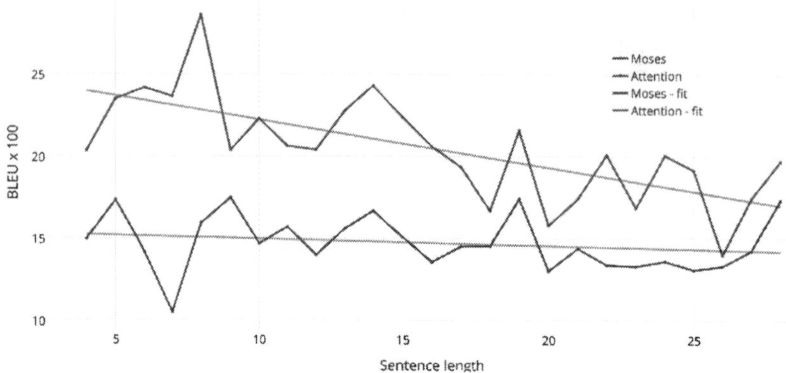

Figure 1: Variation of BLEU score with sentence length. The plot shows the BLEU score against the source sentence length.

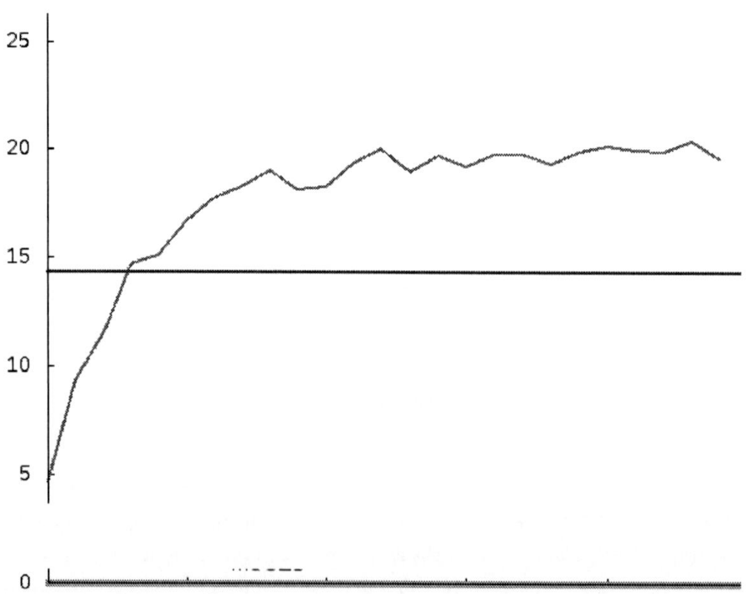

Figure 2: Comparison of BLEU score of the NMT model over 25 iterations with the baseline MOSES system.

in translation of named entities. Due to the limited size of the corpus, many named entities were absent from the vocabulary and hence the model was not able to find a suitable translation for them. Thus the quality of the translated sentences suffered. We propose the following algorithm as a post processing step in order to deal with named entities.

5.1 Dealing with named entities

Algorithm 1 summarizes the steps for correcting the errors due to wrong translation of the named entities for a test Bengali sentence.

Algorithm 1: Correction of errors due to wrong translation of the named entities

---

input : Bengali sentence ($B = \{b_1, b_2, \cdots, b_M\}$), translated Hindi sentence, word alignment scores (α values) for the translation

output: Corrected Hindi sentence

```
1  for each word b_j in B do
2  │   if b_j is named entity then
3  │   │   Tag b_j as NE
4  │   end
5  end
6  for each tagged b_j do
7  │   Transliterate the tagged b_j into the target language (Hindi) using any open-source transliteration
   │   tool.
8  │   Find the index i in the translated sentence for which the value of α_ij is maximum. /* This
   │       h_i corresponds to the word in the target language sentence
   │       whose translation has been most highly influenced by b_j.    */
9  │   Replace h_i with the transliterated word of b_j
10 end
```

The named entities in the test sentences were identified manually. For transliterating the Bengali words to Hindi we used a Bengali-Hindi transliterator developed at our institute. We are working on developing a good quality NER system for Bengali and automating the process of identification and transliteration of the Bengali named entities. On manually observing the target sentences after performing the heuristic, it was found that the overall quality of the translated sentences had gone up and they were more relevant to the context of the source sentences. However this post-processing step resulted in slight decrease in the BLEU score. Part of this may be due to the fact that direct transliteration of the named entities from the source language to the target language without stemming or lemmatization could not take into account the inflectional differences in the source and target language. In Appendix 2 we present five examples. Words like কচ্ছের (kachchh-of) in Bengali when transliterated directly into Hindi results in कच्छेर (kachchher), which is indeed the direct Hindi transliteration of the Bengali word including the inflection −of but fails to capture the context in which it is used and how it should be used (with proper inflection) in the target language sentence. Similarly in the third example sentence, the Bengali word এশিয়ান (Asiyan) transliterate directly to एशियान (Asiyan) in the target language but the word এশিয়াই (Asia-of) was more suited to the context of the sentence. But as we mentioned earlier, it was manually observed that the relevance of the target sentences in relation to the source sentences was found to be more than those of the translated sentences before correction.

5.2 The problem of untranslated words

The lack of sufficient amount of training data meant that we had to work with a limited vocabulary size for the source as well as the target language. This resulted in many phrases in the source sentences not getting translated simply because our model was not able to find words in the target language vocabulary for that phrase. Algorithm 2 summarizes the post-processing heuristic to deal with such untranslated words.

Algorithm 2: Prediction of translations for untranslated words

---

input : Bengali sentence ($B = \{b_1, b_2, \cdots, b_M\}$), translated Hindi sentence
       ($H = \{h_1, h_2, \cdots, h_N\}$), word alignment scores (α values) for the translation
output: Corrected Hindi sentence

1   **for** *each word in b_j in B* **do**
2   **if** b_j *is NOUN* **then**
3   *untranslated = false* **for** *all h_i in H* **do**
4   **if** $\alpha_{ij} > $ *threshold* **then**
5   *untranslated = true*
6   break
7   **end**
8   **end**
9   **if** *untranslated* **then**
10   Find the index i in the target sentence for which the value of α_{ij} is maximum.
11   Insert the transliteration of b_j in Hindi into the target sentence at the ith position.
12   **end**
13   **end**
14 **end**

The intuition behind this heuristic is very simple. The index which is most highly influenced by the untranslated word in the source sentence is the probable position for the translation of that word to occur. We simply transliterated those words and put them at position that they influence the most in the target sentence. We show five randomly selected examples in Appendix 3 ($\alpha_{ij} = 0.2$). Out of the five examples, we find that the quality of 4 sentences improved, while for one sentence, it did not improve much.

We observed that the NMT system is better at translating the postpositions than the SMT system. We need to further investigate this observation. The reason is not yet clear to us and we are working to find the explanation for this observation.

6   Conclusion

In this paper we showed that the performance of the attention-model based NMT system for the Indian language pair, Bengali and Hindi is better than the existing SMT model of MOSES. We then analysed the output translated sentences and observed that there were significant translation errors in case of named entites and rare words. In order to improve the results, we implemented certain post-processing heuristic steps and manually observed that we were able to make the translated sentences more relevant in context to the source sentences.

References

Dzmitry Bahdanau, Kyunghyun Cho, and Yoshua Bengio. 2014. Neural machine translation by jointly learning to align and translate. In *ICLR 2015*.

Kyunghyun Cho, Bart van Merrienboer, Caglar Gulcehre, Dzmitry Bahdanau, Fethi Bougares, Holger Schwenk, and Yoshua Bengio. 2014. Learning phrase representations using rnn encoder–decoder for statistical machine translation. In *Proceedings of the 2014 Conference on Empirical Methods in Natural Language Processing (EMNLP)*, pages 1724–1734, Doha, Qatar, October. Association for Computational Linguistics.

Junyoung Chung, Çaglar Gülçehre, KyungHyun Cho, and Yoshua Bengio. 2014. Empirical evaluation of gated recurrent neural networks on sequence modeling. *CoRR*, abs/1412.3555.

Junyoung Chung, Çaglar Gülçehre, KyungHyun Cho, and Yoshua Bengio. 2015. Gated feedback recurrent neural networks. *CoRR*, abs/1502.02367.

Ian J. Goodfellow, David Warde-Farley, Mehdi Mirza, Aaron C. Courville, and Yoshua Bengio. 2013. Maxout networks. In *Proceedings of the 30th International Conference on Machine Learning, ICML 2013, Atlanta, GA, USA, 16-21 June 2013*, pages 1319–1327.

Sepp Hochreiter and Jürgen Schmidhuber. 1997. Long short-term memory. *Neural Comput.*, 9(8):1735–1780, November.

Nal Kalchbrenner and Phil Blunsom. 2013. Recurrent continuous translation models. Seattle, October. Association for Computational Linguistics.

Philipp Koehn, Hieu Hoang, Alexandra Birch, Chris Callison-Burch, Marcello Federico, Nicola Bertoldi, Brooke Cowan, Wade Shen, Christine Moran, Richard Zens, Chris Dyer, Ondřej Bojar, Alexandra Constantin, and Evan Herbst. 2007. Moses: Open source toolkit for statistical machine translation. In *Proceedings of the 45th Annual Meeting of the ACL on Interactive Poster and Demonstration Sessions*, ACL '07, pages 177–180, Stroudsburg, PA, USA. Association for Computational Linguistics.

Minh-Thang Luong, Hieu Pham, and Christopher D. Manning. 2015. Effective approaches to attention-based neural machine translation. *CoRR*, abs/1508.04025.

Tomas Mikolov, Martin Karafiát, Lukás Burget, Jan Cernocký, and Sanjeev Khudanpur. 2010. Recurrent neural network based language model. In *INTERSPEECH 2010, 11th Annual Conference of the International Speech Communication Association, Makuhari, Chiba, Japan, September 26-30, 2010*, pages 1045–1048.

Tomas Mikolov, Stefan Kombrink, Lukás Burget, Jan Cernocký, and Sanjeev Khudanpur. 2011. Extensions of recurrent neural network language model. In *Proceedings of the IEEE International Conference on Acoustics, Speech, and Signal Processing, ICASSP 2011, May 22-27, 2011, Prague Congress Center, Prague, Czech Republic*, pages 5528–5531.

Tomas Mikolov, Ilya Sutskever, Kai Chen, Greg S Corrado, and Jeff Dean. 2013. Distributed representations of words and phrases and their compositionality. In C. J. C. Burges, L. Bottou, M. Welling, Z. Ghahramani, and K. Q. Weinberger, editors, *Advances in Neural Information Processing Systems 26*, pages 3111–3119. Curran Associates, Inc.

Franz Josef Och. 2003. Minimum error rate training in statistical machine translation. In *Proceedings of the 41st Annual Meeting on Association for Computational Linguistics - Volume 1*, ACL '03, pages 160–167, Stroudsburg, PA, USA. Association for Computational Linguistics.

M. Schuster and K.K. Paliwal. 1997. Bidirectional recurrent neural networks. *Trans. Sig. Proc.*, 45(11):2673–2681, November.

Andreas Stolcke. 2002. Srilm – an extensible language modeling toolkit. In *IN PROCEEDINGS OF THE 7TH INTERNATIONAL CONFERENCE ON SPOKEN LANGUAGE PROCESSING (ICSLP 2002*, pages 901–904.

Martin Sundermeyer, Tamer Alkhouli, Joern Wuebker, and Hermann Ney. 2014. Translation modeling with bidirectional recurrent neural networks. In *Proceedings of the 2014 Conference on Empirical Methods in Natural Language Processing (EMNLP)*, pages 14–25, Doha, Qatar, October. Association for Computational Linguistics.

Ilya Sutskever, Oriol Vinyals, and Quoc V Le. 2014. Sequence to sequence learning with neural networks. In *Advances in neural information processing systems*, pages 3104–3112.

Theano Development Team. 2016. Theano: A Python framework for fast computation of mathematical expressions. *arXiv e-prints*, abs/1605.02688, May.

Appendix A. Comparison of output of attention-based NMT model and MOSES.

Bengali	এরা হলেন সাধারণ বাজেটের পর্যটক ।
MOSES	ये चंदोला आम बजट वाला परयटक है ।
Attention-based TM	ये आम बजट के पर्यटक है ।
Ref. translation	ये सामान्य बजट के पर्यटक हैं ।
Bengali	পোর্ট ব্লেয়ারে পর্যটকদের থাকার জন্য ছোটো ছোটো হোটেল আর গেস্ট হাউসের ব্যবস্থা আছে ।
MOSES	पोर्ट ब्लेयर में पर्यटकों के ठहरने की के लिए छोटे छोटे होटल और गेस्ट हाउस के की व्यवस्था है है ।
Attention-based TM	पोर्ट ब्लेयर में पर्यटकों का ठहरने के लिए छोटे होटल होटल और गेस्ट हाउस की सुविधा है ।
Ref. translation	पोर्ट ब्लेयर में पर्यटकों के ठहरने के लिए छोटेछोटे होटल व गेस्ट हाउसों की व्यवस्था है ।
Bengali	পেটে চোট লাগলে ক্ষত হতে পারে যা মাংসপেশী ও হাড় পর্যন্ত পৌঁছে যায় আর পায়ে পুঁজ হতে পারে আঙুল গলে যেতে পারে বা কালো হয় যেতে পারে ।
MOSES	पेट में चोट लगने पर जख्म हो सकती है हो सकता है है जो की मांसपेशियाँ तथा की हड्डी तक पहुँच जाती है और पैरों में पीप हो सकती है हो सकता है गल के की अंगुलियों के जा सकता है या फिरि काले हो जा सकता है ।
Attention-based TM	पेट में चोट लगने पर जख्म हो सकते हैं जो मांसपेशियाँ तथा हड्डियाँ तक पहुँच हो और पैरों में मवाद हो पाती है या काले हो सकते है ।
Ref. translation	पेट में चोट लगने से नासूर बन सकता है जो मांसपेशियाँ व हड्डियों तक पहुँच जाता है और पैर में मवाद पड़ सकती हैं अँगुलियाँ गल सकती हैं या काली पड़ सकती हैं ।
Bengali	কম্প্যুটার যতই উন্নত বা বুদ্ধিমান হোক না কেন ও শুধু সেই কাজই করতে পারে যার বিধিটা আমরা স্বয়ং জানি ও ওকে দিয়েছি ।
MOSES	कंप्यूटर चाहे कितिना भी या कुशाग्र के उन्नत से ही क्यों न हो तथा सरिफ उस के काम ही कर सकता है जिसिसे में स्वयं ⬜⬜⬜⬜ हम जानते हैं तथा उसे दी और है ।
Attention-based TM	कंप्यूटर चाहे भी बेहतर या फायदेमंद साबति हो न हो या सरिफ वही काम कर सकते हैं जसि हम हम स्वयं जानते हैं ।
Ref. translation	कंप्यूटर चाहे कितिना ही उन्नत या चतुर क्यों न हो वह केवल वही काम कर सकता है जसिकी वधि हमें स्वयं ज्ञात है और जसि हमने कंप्यूटर को सखिा दिया है ।
Bengali	তেল চিকিৎসায় খনিজ তেলের কোনও ব্যবহার নেই কারণ তা ত্বকে প্রবেশ করতে পারে না ।
MOSES	तैलीय के इलाज में खनजि तेल के कसिी का इस्तेमाल नहीं है क्योंकि उसे त्वचा में के प्रवेश के लिए भी नहीं कर सकता ।
Attention-based TM	तैलीय चकितिसा में खनजि तेल का उपयोग न है क्योंकि यह त्वचा में प्रवेश नहीं है ।
Ref. translation	तैलीय चकितिसा में खनजि तेलों का कोई उपयोग नहीं क्योंकि वे त्वचा में प्रवेश नहीं कर सकते ।
Bengali	আমাকে বাইরে দাঁড়িয়ে থাকতে দেখে এক জন মহিলা এলেন আর মসজিদের ভেতর ডেকে নিয়ে গেলেন ।
MOSES	मुझे के बाहर खड़े हो महलिा से नरिणय लया था रह को देखकर के एक जॉन और मसजदि के के भीतर ले पड़े ।
Attention-based TM	मुझे बाहर खड़े होकर देखकर एक सौ आए थे और मसजदि को भीतर ले गए ।
Ref. translation	मुझे बाहर खड़ा देख कर एक महलिा आई और बुलाकर मसजदि के अंदर ले गई ।
Bengali	হেমারঘাট ঝিলে নৌকায় বসে ঝিল ভ্রমণ করা আর আশেপাশের প্রাকৃতিক দৃশ্য দেখতে ভালো লাগে ।
MOSES	हेमारघाट झील में नाव में बैठकर झील का भ्रमण कयिा और के आसपास के के प्राकृतिक दृश्य देखने को अच्छा लगता है है ।
Attention-based TM	बरैला झील में नौका में बैठकर झील भ्रमण करने और आसपास पराकृतकि दृश्यों को देखना अच्छा लगता है ।
Ref. translation	हेमारघाट झील में नाव में बैठकर झील का भ्रमण करना और आसपास के पराकृतकि दृश्यों को देखना बहुत अच्छा लगता है ।
Bengali	ভৈরবনাথ মন্দির সোন প্রয়াগ থেকে NUM কি মি পরে আর কেদারনাথ থেকে NUM কি মি আগে পায়ে হেঁটে হল এক অত্যন্ত গুরুত্বপূর্ণ তীর্থ এবং বিশ্রাম স্থল ।
MOSES	भैरवनाथ मंदरि सोन प्रयाग से NUM कमी की मी के बाद और केदारनाथ से NUM कमी की मी से पहले पैदल चलकर एक अत्यंत महत्त्वपूर्ण तीर्थ एवं वशिराम स्थल है ।
Attention-based TM	भैरवनाथ मंदरि सोन महादेव से NUM कमी आगे और केदारनाथ से NUM कमी आगे पैदल यात्रा अत्यंत महत्त्वपूर्ण तीर्थ है ।
Ref. translation	भैरवनाथ मंदरि सोनप्रयाग से NUM कमी आगे और केदारनाथ में NUM कमी पहले पैदल पड़ने वाला एक अत्यंत महत्वपूर्ण तीर्थ एवं वशिराम स्थल है ।

Appendix B. Example of sentences containing named entities before and after post-processing.

Table 2: Target sentences after transliterating the named entities in the source sentences

Bengali	কচ্ছের ছোটো মরুভূমি হল জাদুনগরী ।
Attention-based TM	कच्छ का छोटा रेगिस्तान भी है ।
After transliteration	कच्छेर का छोटा रेगिस्तान जादुनगरी है ।
Ref. translation	कच्छ का छोटा रेगिस्तान " जादुईनगरी " है ।
Bengali	এগুলির নাম হল কাফনি হিমবাহ পিওরী হিমবাহ লাবন হিমবাহ ও শলাঙ্গ হিমবাহ ।
Attention-based TM	इनके नाम है कि हिमनद ग्लेशयिर हिमनद हिमनद है ग्लेशयिर और हिमनदों ग्लेशयिर भी है ।
After transliteration	इनके नाम है काफनि हिमनद ग्लेशयिर पण्डिारी हिमनद लाबन ग्लेशयिर और शलाङ्ग ग्लेशयिर भी है ।
Ref. translation	इनके नाम हैं कफनी ग्लेशयिर पडिारी ग्लेशयिर लावन ग्लेशयिर और शलांग ग्लेशयिर ।
Bengali	তিনটি এশিয়ান গণ্ডারের মধ্যে পাওয়া সবথেকে বড় গণ্ডারটিকে দেখার জন্য পর্যটকদের বেশ ভিড় জমে ।
Attention-based TM	तीन चार गैंडे के पाए जाने के सबसे बड़े गाँव को देखने के लिए पर्यटकों की काफी भीड़ है ।
After transliteration	तीन एशियान गण्डारेर के पाए जाने के सबसे बड़े गाँव को देखने के लिए पर्यटकों की काफी भीड़ है ।
Ref. translation	तीनों एशियाई गैंडों में यहाँ पाया जाने वाला सब से बड़ा गैंडा देखने के लिए पर्यटकों की अच्छीखासी भीड़ जुटती है ।
Bengali	পোর্ট ব্লেয়ারে পর্যটকদের থাকার জন্য ছোটো ছোটো হোটেল আর গেস্ট হাউসের ব্যবস্থা আছে ।
Attention-based TM	पोर्ट ब्लेयर में पर्यटकों का ठहरने के लिए छोटे होटल होटल और गेस्ट हाउस की सुवधिा है ।
After transliteration	पोर्ट ब्लेयारे में पर्यटकों का ठहरने के लिए छोटे होटल होटल और गेस्ट हाउस की सुवधिा है ।
Ref. translation	पोर्ट ब्लेयर में पर्यटकों के ठहरने के लिए छोटेछोटे होटल व गेस्ट हाउसों की व्यवस्था है ।
Bengali	সম্পূর্ণ গ্যাঙ্গটক পারম্পরিক মুখোশ পরে লামারা নৃত্য করে ।
Attention-based TM	संपूर्ण पर्यटन पारम्परकि जीवन की पश्चात बाद लामाओं के नृत्य करते हैं ।
After transliteration	संपूर्ण ग्याङ्गटक पारम्परकि जीवन की पश्चात बाद लामारा के नृत्य करते हैं ।
Ref. translation	सम्पूर्ण गंगटोक में पारम्परकि मुखोटे पहने लामाओं द्वारा नृत्य किए जाते हैं ।

Appendix C.Example of sentences with untranslated words before and after post-processing.

Table 3: Target sentences after transliterating and inserting the untranslated words

Bengali	মুবারক মণ্ডী প্যালেস মহলে সবথেকে প্রাচীন ইমারত হল NUM সনের ।
Attention-based TM	मुबारक मंडी महल महल में सबसे प्राचीन इमारत NUM वीं सदी में है ।
After transliteration	मुबारक मंडी प्यालेस महल महल में सबसे प्राचीन हल इमारत NUM वीं सदी में है ।
Ref. translation	मुबारक मंडी पैलेस महल परिसर में सबसे प्राचीन इमारत NUM की है ।
Bengali	ওজন কমানো বা ত্বকের দেখাশোনা প্রসঙ্গ যাই হোক না কেন খাবারে তাজা ফল খাওয়ার পরামর্শ সব ব্যাপারেই দেওয়া যায় ।
Attention-based TM	वजन घटाना या त्वचा की देखभाल का चाहे चाहे क्यों न ताजे आहार को खाने की सलाह हमेशा ही दी जा है ।
After transliteration	वजन घटाना या त्वचा की देखभाल का चाहे चाहे क्यों न ताजे फल आहार को खाने की सलाह हमेशा ही दी जा है ।
Ref. translation	बात वजन घटाने की हो या त्वचा की देखभाल की खाने में ताजे फल खाने की सलाह सभी मामलों में दी जाती है ।
Bengali	পূজারী সাদা ধুতি সাদা পাঞ্জাবী ও মাথায় রাজস্থানী ভঙ্গীমায় পাগড়ী ধারণ করে খালি পায়ে মন্দির আসেন ।
Attention-based TM	पुजारी सफेद धोती सफेद तथा सरि में राजस्थानी रूप में धारण करके ऊपर से पैदल मंदिर हैं ।
After transliteration	पुजारी सफेद धोती सफेद पाञ्जाबी तथा सरि में राजस्थानी रूप में धारण करके ऊपर से पैदल मंदिर हैं ।
Ref. translation	पुजारी सफेद धोती सफेद कुर्ता व सरि पर राजस्थानी स्टाइल की पगड़ी धारण कर नंगे पैर मंदिर परिसर में आए ।
Bengali	হৃদ রোগ খুব ক্লান্ত হয়ে পড়া উত্তেজনা মেজাজ অস্থির বোধ করা প্রচণ্ড নিরাশা ঘুম কম হওয়া উচ্চ রক্তচাপ ইত্যাদি উত্তেজনাজনিত সাধারণ রোগ ।
Attention-based TM	दिल रोग रोग बहुत थक जाना उत्तेजना उत्तेजना का भय अत्यधिक गर्मी से कम नींद कम नींद उच्च रक्तचाप आदि आम तौर पर आम बीमारी है ।
After transliteration	दिल रोग रोग बहुत थक जाना उत्तेजना उत्तेजना का भय अत्यधिक गर्मी निराशा से कम नींद कम नींद उच्च रक्तचाप आदि आम तौर पर आम बीमारी है ।
Ref. translation	दिल की बीमारी बेहद थकान उत्तेजना के दौरे बारबार मूड बदलना बेचैनी की अवस्था घोर निराशा नींद कम आना उच्च रक्त चाप आदि तनाव की आम समस्याएँ है ।
Bengali	রক্তে অধিক শর্করা দীর্ঘকালীন জটিলতা ।
Attention-based TM	रक्त अधिक मात्रा अधिक जटलिताओं उत्पन्न होती है ।
After transliteration	रक्त अधिक मात्रा शर्करा अधिक जटलिताओं उत्पन्न होती है ।
Ref. translation	रक्त में शर्करा की अधिकता दीर्घकालीन जटलिताएँ ।

Comprehensive Part-Of-Speech Tag Set and SVM Based POS Tagger for Sinhala

Sandareka Fernando, Surangika Ranathunga, Sanath Jayasena, Gihan Dias
Department of Computer Science and Engineering
University of Moratuwa
Sri Lanka

`{sandarekaf,surangika,sanath,gihan}@cse.mrt.ac.lk`

Abstract

This paper presents a new comprehensive multi-level Part-Of-Speech tag set and a Support Vector Machine based Part-Of-Speech tagger for the Sinhala language. The currently available tag set for Sinhala has two limitations: the unavailability of tags to represent some word classes and the lack of tags to capture inflection based grammatical variations of words. The new tag set, presented in this paper overcomes both of these limitations. The accuracy of available Sinhala Part-Of-Speech taggers, which are based on Hidden Markov Models, still falls far behind state of the art. Our Support Vector Machine based tagger achieved an overall accuracy of 84.68% with 59.86% accuracy for unknown words and 87.12% for known words, when the test set contains 10% of unknown words.

1   Introduction

Sinhala, the official language of Sri Lanka, which is used by a 16 million odd population, is a morphologically rich and highly inflected language. Sinhala belongs to Indo-Aryan family of languages and has its own alphabet. Compared to the advancement in the area of computational linguistics, Sinhala language lacks many linguistic resources, holding back natural language processing research for the same (Manamini et al., 2016; Palihakkara et al.,2015). A standard and accurate Part-Of-Speech (POS) tagger is one such basic resource.

Automatic POS tagging requires two main resources: a comprehensive tag set and a tagger. Further, a manually annotated corpus is required to train the tagger, when using supervised learning techniques. Comprehensiveness of the tag set can be defined as the ability of the tag set to represent all word classes of the language. As such any grammatically correct sentence of the language can be tagged using the tag set. Quality of the manually tagged corpus is a measurement of how accurately the words are tagged manually. Comprehensiveness of the tag set and quality of the corpus directly affect the performance of tagger.

Some research has been carried out in Sinhala POS tagging. They use the UCSC Tag Set, which has three versions. The latest version consists of 29 tags (Gunasekara & Weerasinghe, 2016). However, a closer inspection reveals that this tag set is not comprehensive. There are some word classes in Sinhala that are not covered by this tag set. As reported by Gunasekara & Weerasinghe (2016), out of the 100,000 words in the manually POS tagged corpus, 3989 words do not fall into any category of the UCSC Tag Set, which means that even manual POS tagging cannot achieve 100% accuracy. This limitation has created unnecessary ambiguities in the tagged corpus, resulting some words being tagged as unknown and some words being tagged with multiple tags in different places even when they appear in the same context with a similar meaning. In addition, this tag set is not comprehensive enough to cover the inflection based grammatical variations of Sinhala language. Sinhala noun base forms are inflected by suffixing a morpheme to indicate number, definiteness and case. Finite Verbs are inflected based on person, tense, number and gender. UCSC Tag Set does not capture such grammatical features in inflected nouns and verbs. In this research, we designed a complete, multi-level tag set[1] for Sinhala that covers all word classes and grammatical variations of Sinhala words, with the help of Sinhala language experts. The new tag set resolves the identified limitations of the previous tag set.

---

[1] https://github.com/sandarekaf/SinhalaPOS/blob/master/Sinhala%20POS%20tags.pdf

Proceedings of the 6th Workshop on South and Southeast Asian Natural Language Processing,
pages 173–182, Osaka, Japan, December 11-17 2016.

Previous research on Sinhala POS taggers used Hidden Markov Model (HMM) based tagging models and a hybrid tagging model using HMM and morphological rules (Jayasuriya & Weerasinghe, 2013; Jayaweera & Dias, 2014; Gunasekara & Weerasinghe, 2016). The highest reported overall accuracy is 72% with 20% of average unknown words by the hybrid tagger. One reason for the low accuracy can be the ambiguities and limitations of the used tag set.

There are many other stochastic, rule based, and hybrid POS tagging techniques such as Support Vector Machines (SVM), Maximum Entropy, Brill Tagger, TnT and Neural Network based taggers that achieved higher accuracies (Ojha et al,2015; Antony & Soman, 2011; Kumar & Josan, 2010) when employed for other morphologically rich languages. Comparatively, SVM based taggers have provided promising results for POS tagging on other Indo-Aryan languages. SVM is a suitable method to use with a high dimensional feature space and it has proven results with a small training set. Given that Sinhala is an under-resourced language with a severe limitation in finding linguistic experts to prepare the annotated corpus, we opted to choose the SVM based approach.

This research is carried out as part of a larger initiative to build a computer assisted Sinhala to Tamil (another official language of Sri Lanka) translator for official documents. Based on the parent project, the corpus used for this research consists of official Sinhala documents such as official letters, annual reports and circulars. Creating a manually tagged corpus is a challenging task in Sinhala due to the lack of annotators with good knowledge in Sinhala linguistics.

Currently this study is carried out using a corpus of 70,000 words. We are continuously increasing the size of the corpus. The corpus is manually tagged using the second level of the new tag set that consists of 30 tags. The second level of the new tag set resolves the ambiguities of the previous tag set. From the third level onwards, separate tags are provided for each inflected form of a word. In Sinhala, inflecting factors are Number, Gender, Person, Animacy, Definiteness, Case and Tense. After tagging a word from a second level tag, expanding it to the third level based on above inflecting factors is straightforward and unambiguous. Thus, manually tagging at level 3 is straightforward and does not need high level of language skills. Automatic tagging at third level can also be done using a simple classification process followed by morphological analysis. Therefore, although we did not use the full tag set to annotate the corpus (due to time constraints and resource limitations), getting this done in a later stage is much straightforward.

An SVM based tagger was created using the SVM based sequential POS tagger generator provided by Giménez and Màrquez (2004a). Our tagger was successful in achieving an overall accuracy of 84.68%, with 87.12% and 59.86% accuracy for known words and unknown words, respectively. This accuracy was achieved when 10% of words are unknown words in the test set.

The rest of the paper is arranged as follows. Section two explains the current status of POS tagging research in Sinhala language and other south Asian languages. The new tag set is presented in detail in section three, explaining how it solves the problems identified in the previous tag set. Section four explains the corpus creation process. Section five explains the SVM based tagger and the selected feature set. Section six presents the experiment results and a discussion on the results. Finally section seven concludes the paper.

2   Literature Review

POS tagging related research done up to now for Sinhala language has used the UCSC Tag Set, which now has three versions. The latest version of UCSC Tag Set consists of 29 tags where 27 of them are language related tags. The remaining two tags are for Foreign Words and Symbols. Changes from the UCSC Tag Set Version 1 to Version 3 include addition of Common Noun Root tag and splitting the Verb Participle tag to four sub categories. All three versions of this tag set are hereafter collectively referred to as 'UCSC Tag Set', unless otherwise specifically referred to by the version number. UCSC Tag Set has two limitations. The main limitation is that some Sinhala words do not fall under any POS tag in the tag set, thus happens to be tagged as Unknown. Some examples are හැකි - hæki "can" ,යුතු - yuthu "should/must", නොහැකි - nohæki "cannot", කුමන - kumana "which", ඉටු - itu[2] ,සිදු - sidu[2] ,පත් - path[2] and බව - bava[2]. Such unknown words fall in to a small set of distinct categories that have special language characteristics, thus can be grouped under new tag categories. The second limitation is

---

[2] No comparable word in English

inflection based grammatical variations of words have not been captured in the tag set. For example, common nouns in Sinhala that get inflected based on cases (Nominative: ගස - gasa "the tree", Accusative :ගසක් - gasak "a tree", Dative :ගසට - gasata "to the tree", Genitive :ගසේ/ගසෙහි - gase/gasehi "in the tree", Instrumental :ගසෙන් - gasen "from the tree") are tagged under a single tag.

Previous research reported on creating Sinhala POS taggers (Jayasuriya & Weerasinghe,2013; Jayaweera & Dias, 2014; Gunasekara & Weerasinghe, 2016) has used the UCSC Tagged Corpus built from Sinhala newspaper articles which was tagged using the UCSC Tag Set. Jayasuriya and Weerasinghe (2013) used an HMM based statistical method to train a tagger and achieved 62% overall accuracy using an 80,000 word tagged corpus for training. Jayaweera & Dias (2014) reported an accuracy of 90% for known words. The accuracy for unknown words is not reported. Improving the previous work, Gunasekara and Weerasinghe (2016) have built a hybrid POS tagger using HMM based statistical tagging followed by a morphological rule based tag prediction technique for unknown words, and reported an overall tagging accuracy of 72% with 20% of average unknown words.

As seen above, very limited amount of research has been done on Sinhala POS tagging. Other south Asian languages (such as Hindi, Urdu, Bengali, Nepali, Bhojpuri, etc.) belonging to the same language family as Sinhala have comparably higher amount of research in the field of POS tagging (Modi & Nain, 2016; Joshi et al.,2013; Dandapat et al.,2007; Chakrabarti & CDAC, 2011; Gupta et al.,2016; Ekbal & Bandyopadhyay,2008; Shahi et al.,2013; Singh & Jha, 2015). These works have used different POS tagging techniques such as HMM, Maximum Entropy, Conditional Random Field(CRF) and SVM. Comparisons between the experimented POS tagging methodologies for south Asian languages have shown that, SVM based POS tagging method has shown promising results (Antony & Soman, 2011). For example, an SVM based tagger for Bengali has obtained an accuracy of 86.84% and found to be outperforming other tagging systems based on HMM, Maximum Entropy and CRF (Ekbal & Bandyopadhyay,2008). A POS tagger for Nepali, based on SVM has shown an accuracy of 93.27% and reported to be accurate than the TnT tagger (Shahi et al.,2013). POS tagger for Bhojpuri used an SVM based tagger with 87.67% accuracy when 3.7% words are unknown (Singh & Jha, 2015), where training is done using 10,440 tokens. Ojha et. al (2015) have done a comparison of two POS tagging methods: CRF and SVM for three Indo-Aryan languages : Hindi, Odia and Bhojpuri. Error rate in POS tagging is found to be lower in SVM for two languages except Bhojpuri. Similarly, English POS taggers based on SVM has achieved comparable results with the state of art (Giménez & Marquez, 2004b). Based on the above observations, SVM appears to be a promising option to create an accurate POS tagger.

3 Tag Set

This section describes the new comprehensive multi-level Sinhala tag set. This tag set was created based on the available tag set for Sinhala UCSC Tag Set. The UCSC Tag Set was improved based on the consultation with Sinhala language experts and some comparable tags were borrowed from the Penn Treebank tag set. The UCSC Tagged Corpus was taken as a reference to analyse language usage in creating the new tag set. The new tag set is defined in multiple levels, where in each new level, tags are divided in to sub tags based on inflecting factors or contextual definitions. The complete Sinhala POS tag set contains 148 tags. The hierarchical nature of the new tag set allows users to select the appropriate level of tagging for their application or purpose. Because of this multi-level nature, it was straightforward for us to tag the new corpus using only a 30 sub-set of this tag set.

3.1 Tags in Level One

Sinhala language has five primary top level parts of speech: Nouns (නාම - nāma), Adjectives (නාම විශේෂණ - nāma viśēṣaṇa), Verbs (ක්‍රියා - kriya), Adverbs (ක්‍රියා විශේෂණ - kriya viśēṣaṇa), and Nipāta (නිපාත).

3.2 Tags in Level Two

Each primary tag at level 1 is divided in to sub categories at level 2 based on context definitions.
Noun Categorization at Level Two
Nouns are divided in to 7 categories at secondary level based on the definition. Those are *Common Noun, Proper Noun, Pronoun, Noun in Compound Verb, Questioning Pronoun, Deterministic Pronoun,*

and *Question Based Pronoun*. From these, the first four tags are the most obvious and can be found in the UCSC Tag Set as well. The remaining three are newly introduced.

Common nouns in Sinhala are similar to common nouns in any other language and denote a class of objects or a concept. Similarly, *proper nouns* identify an exact entity (person, place or thing) and cannot have an indefinite form. *Pronouns*, similar to any other language, are words that can be substituted for a noun or a noun phrase. *Questioning pronouns*, a special category of pronouns, are words used to ask a question. This category is comparable to WH-Pronouns in Penn Treebank tag set. *Questioning pronoun* is a new tag introduced in the tag set. Sinhala examples for *questioning pronouns* are කුමක්ද - kumakda "what" ,කෙසේද - kesēda "how" ,කවදාද - kavadāda "when" and කොහේද - kohēdīda "where" . An example usage of a questioning pronoun කුමක්ද - kumakda "what" would be ඔබට අවශ්‍ය කුමක්ද? – obata avashaya kumakda? "What do you want?". As seen from the examples, all *questioning pronouns* in Sinhala end in letter 'ද'-'da'. In the UCSC annotated corpus that uses the UCSC Tag Set, these words have been broken down to two parts where the last letter 'ද'-'da' is separated. In the UCSC tagged corpus, 'ද'-'da' is tagged as particle. Tagging of the first part was also ambiguous. For example කුමක්ද - kumakda "what", is first broken up in to 'කුමක්' + 'ද', former part කුමක් - kumak "which" is tagged as Pronoun. At the same time, කුමක් - kumak "which" is tagged as unknown in some other places. We refer to this first part as *question base pronouns*. *Question base pronouns* are used to show the uncertainty of a noun/noun phrase of interest. As discussed above, *questioning pronouns* are created by adding the suffix 'ද'-'da' to *question base pronouns*. An example usage of *question base pronoun* කුමක් - kumak "what" would be ඔබ කුමක් කලේද? – oba kumak kaleda? "What did you do?". *Deterministic pronouns* are words built up from a combination of a determiner (discussed below) and a pronoun. For example සමහරෙක් - samaharek "some of them" is a word in Sinhala derived from සමහර - samahara "some", which is a determiner and දෙනෙක් - denek "them", which is a pronoun. Finally, *Noun in compound verb* is a common noun followed by a verb to build up a compound verb.

Adjective Categorization at Level Two

At the second level, adjectives are divided in to 3 categories: *adjective, adjectival noun* and *adjective in compound verb*. The whole purpose of an *adjective* is to describe a noun, and cannot be used as any other word type. This same tag is present in the UCSC Tag Set as well. *Adjectival noun* is a noun that acts as an adjective to describe another noun based on the context. Therefore the same word form can act as a *common noun* and *adjectival noun* based on the context. For example, පාසල් - pāsal "schools" is a *common noun* but in the phrase පාසල් වත්ත - pāsal vatta "school ground", පාසල් - pāsal "schools" is used to describe the වත්ත - vatta "ground", thus tagged as an *adjectival noun*. Another observation here is, adjectival nouns in Sinhala take the plural, base form of its related common noun. In contrast, English language uses the singular form of the common noun, even when it is used as a modifier of another noun. In the UCSC Tag Set Version 3, the base form of a common noun is identified as *common noun root* that is always plural. But *Common Noun Root* can either be used as a *common noun* alone, or as an *adjectival noun*. So in our new tag set, we use two tags, a*djectival noun* or c*ommon noun* to tag common noun roots, based on the context. *Adjectival noun* is a new tag introduced in our tag set. In contrast, in the Penn Treebank tagged corpus, as well as the UCSC tagged corpus, all adjectival nouns are tagged as some variation of *common noun*. Advantage of having an *adjectival noun* is it helps to identify noun phrases that need to be treated as a single entity. Finally, *adjective in compound verb* is an adjective followed by a verb to create a compound verb.

Verb Categorization at Level Two

Verbs are divided into five sub categories, based on the definition: *verb finite, verb participle, verbal noun, verb non-finite* and *modal auxiliary*. *Verb finite* refers to verbs used in a sentence ending. All other verb types are used in the middle of sentences. *Verbal noun* is an inflected form of a verb that acts as a noun. *Verb participle* is another inflected form of a verb that is used in a sentence to modify a noun, noun phrase, verb or a verb phrase. Thus it plays the same role as adjective or adverb. *Verb non-finite* contains all other inflected forms of the verb that do not belong to *verb finite, verb participle* and *verbal noun*. Sinhala has a set of words similar to English modal verbs: හැකි - hæki "Can", යුතු - yuthu "Should/ Must", නොහැකි - nohæki "Cannot". To cover this word group, *modal auxiliary* tag is borrowed from the Penn Treebank tag set. UCSC Tag Set has not defined this tag, and consequently, the corresponding words in the corpus have been marked as unknown.

Adverbs, similar to other languages, are words used to describe a verb, and are not divided in to sub categories at level two.

Nipātha Categorization at Level Two

Nipātha are further divided in to 8 categories: *Postposition, conjunction, particle, interjection, determiner, nipathana, case marker* and *preposition in compound verb*. *Postpositions* in Sinhala are words used after nouns, verbs and sometimes even after adjectives and adverbs to show their relationship to other words in order to build up a meaningful sentence. *Conjunctions* are words used to connect words, phrases or sentences. *Interjections* in Sinhala, similar to other languages, are words used to show the emotion or feeling. *Determiners* are words that are used before a noun to show which particular example of the noun is referred to. *Postposition, conjunction, particle, interjection* and *determiner* are present in the UCSC Tag Set as well. *Nipathana* is a special subset of *Nipātha*. Usually, *nipātha* words cannot be used alone. In contrast, *nipathana* can be used alone in some contexts, and can be used as a *postposition* as well if needed. Examples are ඇති - æti "enough/have/in[3]"and පුළුවන් - puluwan "able".

Sinhala nouns are morphologically inflected based on the case. A suffix is added to the noun to show the case. For animate nouns and inanimate singular nouns, suffix ට - ta is added for dative case, suffix ගේ - ge is added for genitive case and suffix ගෙන් - gen is added for instrumental case. For inanimate plural nouns, suffix වලට - valata is added for dative case, suffix වල - vala is added for genitive case and suffix වලින් - valin is added for instrumental case. According to Sinhala language rules, it is wrong to separate these case marking suffixes from the main noun (Dissanayaka, 2008; Dissanayaka, 2014). However, some Sinhala writers tend to separate this case marking suffix from the main noun. To cope with such cases, a POS tag called *case marker* is introduced. In the corpus tagged using the UCSC Tag Set, case markers have been handled in an ambiguous manner. For example, dative 'ට' case marking suffix is tagged as particle whereas dative 'වලට' case marking suffix is tagged as a noun. Finally, *preposition in compound verbs* are words that do not have a meaning by themselves but, when combined with another verb, make up a compound verb.

Compound Verbs

Three tags discussed above under Nouns, Verbs and Nipāta, deserve further discussion: *noun in compound verb, adjective in compound verb*, and *preposition in compound verb*. There are verbs in Sinhala that cannot be written using a single word, thus they need two words. These verb types are referred to as 'compound verbs' hereafter. Second word of a compound verb is always a verb type. Examples for such compound verbs are පාඩම් කරනවා - pāḍam karanavā "study" ,අඩු කරනවා - adu karanavā "reduce", අඩු වෙනවා - adu venavā "reducing" සිදු කරනවා - sidu karanavā "make something happen". The latter words of above examples, කරනවා - karanavā "doing" and වෙනවා venavā "happening" are verbs. When analyzing the former words, it can be a *common noun* as පාඩම් - pāḍam "lesson", an *adjective* as අඩු - adu "less/lesser" or a word that does not have a meaning on its own such as සිදු - sidu. Respectively, these three former words are tagged using *noun in compound verb, adjective in compound verb* and *preposition in compound verb*. *Noun in compound verb* and *adjective in compound verb* tags are present in UCSC Tag Set under the names *noun in kriya mula*, and *adjective in kriya mula*, respectively. Words that we categorize under *preposition in compound verb* are taken as unknown words in the UCSC Corpus. '*kriya mula*' in Sinhala means 'base verb' and it could be misleading. Thus we substituted the term *kriya mula* with the term *compound verb*.

Additional Tags at Level Two

Apart from the above discussed sub categorization of 5 primary tags, there are 5 other POS tags that are added to the tag set. These are *number, abbreviation, full stop, punctuation*, and *foreign word*, which are self-explanatory. Another special tag called *sentence ending* is introduced to mark all the words that end a sentence but do not belong to the category *verb finite*. In Sinhala, sentences can end in an inflected form of a *noun, adjective* or a *nipātha*. Examples are ගසකි - gasaki "a tree", which is a *noun*, සඳහායි - saňdahāyi "for" which is a *postposition* ,and විශේෂිතයි - viśēṣitayi "special", which is an *adjective*. In

---

[3] English meaning can vary based on the context

the UCSC Tag Set, these words are tagged using their original tag: *common noun, postposition,* and *adjective,* respectively.

These categorizations mark the second level of the tag set consisting of 30 tags.

3.3 Tags at Level Three

Nouns and verbs in Sinhala can be inflected based on number, gender, person, animacy, definiteness, case, and tense. From third level onwards, each tag at second level is further categorized based on inflection factors.

For example, *Common noun* can be inflected based on animacy (animate/ inanimate), gender (masculine/ feminine), number (singular/plural), definiteness (definite/indefinite) and case (nominative/accusative/dative/genitive /instrumental). *Finite verb* is further inflected based on person (first/second/third), tense (past/non past), number (singular/plural) and gender (masculine/ feminine).

As per the requirement, tag set can be extended up to more levels by taking the selected set of inflecting factors at each level. For example, one can do the third level classification only using animacy and gender for *common nouns*, and then further categorize each third level noun based on definiteness at fourth level. Granularity of categorization can be decided based on the requirements of the specific application. At the most fine grained level, our tag set contains a total of 148 tags.

Sentence ending tag holds the possibility of further categorization depending on its original word class such as Noun Finite, Adjective Finite and Nipātha Finite, which is not included in the current tag set and thus not used to tag the corpus.

There are some *postpositions* in Sinhala that can be inflected by suffixing a *particle*. For example, සඳහා - saṅdahā "for" can be inflected as සඳහාම - saṅdahāma "especially for" and සඳහාද - saṅdahāda "even for". Such inflections are not captured in this tag set.

4   Corpus Creation

This research is initiated as part of a larger project for creating a 'Sinhala to Tamil Machine assisted translation system for official documents in Sri Lanka'. Therefore, the corpus used for the research is built up using official documents used in various government organizations, such as official letters, circulars and annual reports.

A corpus of 70,000 words was created using official letters, circulars and annual reports. Corpus was manually annotated using the second level of the tag set, consisting of 30 tags. Training was given for each annotator before commencing annotation. Continuous feedback was provided for annotators to reduce errors.

Annotation was done by 7 annotators who are native Sinhala speakers. However, their Sinhala linguistic knowledge is naive. Due to the nature of their knowledge on the Sinhala language and human errors, annotators tend to make mistakes in tagging. Therefore a verification process was carried out on the initial phases of manually tagging during the training period of the annotators to overcome this limitation.

Table 1 shows the composition of the corpus in terms of frequency of frequencies of unique words. Our corpus of 70,000 words contains 12% of unique words.

No. of occurrences	1	2 - 5	6 -10	11 -50	51 - 100	100 – 200	200 – 300	300 – 400	400 - 500	> 500
% of unique words	49%	31%	7%	9%	1%	0.6%	0.2%	< 0.1%	< 0.1%	< 0.1%

Table 1: Word frequency of frequencies

Finally, it should be noted that we were able to assign a tag for each word in our corpus, unlike the corpus tagged with the UCSC Tag Set.

5   Tagger

SVM is a supervised machine learning algorithm for binary classification (Cortes & Vapnik, 1995). Given a set of training examples, where each instance is a vector in multidimensional space, SVM learns a Maximum Margin Hyperplane that separates positive examples from negative examples. Margin is the distance from the hyperplane to the nearest positive and negative examples in the vector space.

POS tagging is a multi-class classification problem. SVM, which by default is a binary classifier, is used to solve the multi-class classification problem by taking one POS tag at a time as positive class and rest of the tags as negative. Following this technique, the sequential POS tagger generator based on SVM (Giménez and Màrquez 2004a) was used to train a POS tagging model for Sinhala.

Three feature types are considered in tagger generation: word features, POS features, and lexicalized features. Word features are word unigrams, bigrams and trigrams. POS features are POS unigrams, bigrams and trigrams. Lexicalized features used for this experiment are prefixes, suffixes and word length. Lexicalized features related to English language that are based on character capitalization are irrelevant to Sinhala language.

A centred window of size N around the word to be disambiguated is considered in feature generation. N value 7 is used for feature generation in English (Giménez & Marquez, 2004b). But it may not be optimal for a language like Sinhala, which is highly inflected. To find out the best N value for Sinhala language, an experiment was done for N= 7, 5 and 3. From the 70,000 word corpus 55,000 words were used as training data and remaining 15,000 were used for testing. The tagger uses simple left-to-right tagging, so POS tags of following words are not decided at run time. To cope with this problem, ambiguity class tags are defined for proceeding context words. Ambiguity class for a word is a concatenation of all possible POS tags for that word. Each individual tag of ambiguity classes is taken as a 'May Be' binary feature. For example, if a word has an ambiguity class NN_VV (that word can be a Noun or a Verb), then May Be features are defined as "Following class May Be NN" and "Following class May Be VV". Feature set used for window size 3 is shown in Table 2.

To check the effect of ambiguity class related features, a tagger model is recreated with optimal window size. Features related to ambiguity classes (May Be's, POS unigrams for current and next (right) tag, and POS bigrams) were removed from the feature set. This is because those features use the ambiguity class of a specific word as its POS tag if its POS tag is not yet decided at run time. Finally, to analyze the effect of lexical features (prefixes, suffixes and word length), the experiment was carried out by removing them from the feature set.

Word Unigrams	w_{-1}, w_0, w_{+1}	Ambiguity Classes	a_0, a_1
Word Bigrams	$(w_{-1}, w_0)(w_{-1}, w_{+1}) (w_0, w_{+1})$	May Be's	m_0, m_1
Word Trigrams	(w_{-1}, w_0, w_{+1})	Prefixes	a(2), a(3), a(4)
POS Unigrams	p_{-1}	Suffixes	z(2), z(3), z(4)
POS Bigrams	(p_{-1}, a_{+1})	Word Length	L

Table 2: Feature set used in window size 3

6   Evaluation

Table 3 shows the performance of the tagger when features are generated using a centred window of size 7, 5 and 3. As observed, overall accuracy was increased when window size is reduced from 7 to 3. Sinhala words are inflected based on morphology. When compared with languages such as English, same information can be given using a lesser number of words. This may be the reason for increased accuracy when window size is decreasing. Further, the training time has drastically reduced when window size is reduced from 7 to 3. Based on these observations, window size 3 is selected for further experiments.

	N=7	N = 5	N= 3
Overall Accuracy	84.24%	84.43%	84.53%
Known Word Accuracy	86.50%	86.61%	86.78%
Unknown Word Accuracy	61.23%	62.26%	61.57%
Training Time (Sec)[4]	170	125	88
Tagging Time (Sec)	11	8	7

Table 3: Performance of SVM POS tagger for window size 7, 5 and 3

---

[4] Intel Core i3 CPU – 1.7GHz, RAM – 8GB

	Overall	Known word	Known unambiguous word	Known ambiguous word	Unknown word
Ambiguity class related features removed	84.68%	87.12%	91.98%	83.37%	59.86%
Lexical Features Removed	84.08%	87.13%	91.98%	83.39%	53.01%

Table 4: Accuracies with ambiguous and lexical features removed

Table 4 presents the accuracies of the tagger when ambiguous class related features and lexical features are omitted from the feature set, respectively. After removing ambiguous class related features from the features provided in Table 2, results provided an overall accuracy of 84.68% which is a further improvement. However, accuracy of unknown word tagging was reduced to 59.86%. Comparing results provided in Table 3 and Table 4, best unknown word accuracy is obtained when window size is 5 whereas best overall accuracy is obtained when window size is 3 and ambiguous class related features are omitted. Improvement in results for known word accuracy has contributed to the increase in the overall accuracy at this case. This opens up an interesting experiment to find out the reason behind unknown word accuracy decrement and known word accuracy increment, when features are generated from window of size 5 and 3, respectively.

When lexicalized features (prefixes, suffixes and word length) are removed from the feature set of window size 3, overall accuracy was reduced to 84.08%. This was due to the reduction in accuracy for unknown words to 53.01%. Therefore we can conclude that lexical features have contributed directly on determining POS tags for unknown words.

SVM based POS tagger for Sinhala was successful in obtaining an highest overall accuracy of 84.68% with known word accuracy of 87.12% and unknown word accuracy of 59.86% when test set contains 10% unknown words. Here, lexical features have helped improving the unknown word accuracy. Table 5 summarizes the feature set used to obtain the highest overall accuracy.

Word Unigrams	w_{-1}, w_0, w_{+1}	**Prefixes**	a(2), a(3), a(4)
Word Bigrams	$(w_{-1}, w_0)(w_{-1}, w_{+1})(w_0, w_{+1})$	**Suffixes**	z(2), z(3), z(4)
Word Trigrams	(w_{-1}, w_0, w_{+1})	**Word Length**	L
POS Unigrams	p_{-1}		

Table 5: Feature set used in obtaining the best results

Table 6 provides tagging accuracy per each language related POS tags. *Question pronoun, question base pronoun, modal auxiliary, pronoun, case marker, conjunction, postposition, particle, determiner* and *nipathana* have obtained tagging accuracy of 90% and above. Not surprisingly, these are closed class words. As discussed before, *common nouns* and *finite verbs* are two tags that will be further categorized based on inflection factors at third level tagging. These two tags have achieved 89% and 88% accuracy respectively at second level. Since third level tagging is straightforward and unambiguous, this will contribute to an increased accuracy of the tagger even when third level tagging is done. *Preposition in compound verb*, a new tag we introduced to tag set, has achieved 80% accuracy. Words belonging to this tag were tagged as Unknown in the UCSC tag set. Thus the new addition has contributed positively to POS tagging of Sinhala. *Adjectival noun*, again introduced in our tag set, has achieved a 67% of accuracy. This is due to ambiguity when the same word is used as an *adjectival noun* and *common noun* in two contexts. *Sentence ending*, another newly introduced tag has only achieved 48% accuracy. Accuracy of tagging *Adjectival Noun* and *sentence ending* can be improved by increasing the size of the corpus and avoiding the errors in manual tagging.

Tag	Accuracy	Tag	Accuracy	Tag	Accuracy
Question Pronoun	99%	Verbal Noun	91%	Preposition in Compound Verb	80%
Question Base Pronoun	99%	Determiner	90%	Adverb	72%
Conjunction	98%	Common Noun	89%	Proper Noun	72%
Modal Auxiliary	97%	Particle	89%	Adjective in Compound Verb	67%
Pronoun	95%	Finite Verbs	88%	Adjectival Noun	55%
Postposition	93%	Verb Non Finite	88%	Noun in Compound Verb	59%
Nipathana	95%	Verb participle	87%	Sentence Ending	48%
Case Marker	94%	Adjective	82%		

Table 6: Tagging accuracy per POS tag

7 Conclusion and Future Work

This study presented a comprehensive, multi-level Sinhala POS tag set. This tag set covers most of the word classes and inflection based grammatical variations of the language. The new tag set overcomes the identified ambiguities and limitations of the UCSC Tag Set. The new tag set was designed by analysing the UCSC Tag set and the UCSC tagged corpus, which was a corpus of news articles. The new tag set is then used to tag a corpus created from official documents, a different domain, and found to be successful. Further, an SVM based approach is followed in creating an automatic tagger for Sinhala, which is found to outperform existing taggers proposed for Sinhala language up to now.

The current accuracy of the tagger can be further improved by increasing the size of the corpus. Human errors in manual tagging has contributed to a certain percentage of errors in automatic tagging. The quality of the manually tagged corpus should be verified and improved further. Moreover, the tag set should be tested with other corpora of different domains to check the validity. Finally, the tagged corpus using the new tag set should be tested with advanced NLP tasks, such as machine translation, to evaluate the correctness and effect of the new tag set and the corpus tagged with it.

Acknowledgment

This research is funded by a Short Term Research Grant from University of Moratuwa. We would like to extend our gratitude to the language experts who helped in designing the new tag set, Professor J B Dissanayaka and Professor Sandagomi Koparahewa. We also thank Mr. Pasan Dissanayaka for his help in developing the verification tools for manual POS tagging, and annotators who did the manual tagging.

References

Antony, P. J., & Soman, K. P. (2011). Parts of speech tagging for Indian languages: a literature survey. International Journal of Computer Applications (0975-8887), 34(8), 22-29.

Chakrabarti, D., & CDAC, P. (2011). Layered parts of speech tagging for Bangla. Language in India, www. languageinindia. com, Special Volume: Problems of Parsing in Indian Languages.

Cortes, C., & Vapnik, V. (1995). Support-vector networks. Machine learning, 20(3), 273-297.

Dandapat, S., Sarkar, S., & Basu, A. (2007, June). Automatic part-of-speech tagging for Bengali: An approach for morphologically rich languages in a poor resource scenario. In Proceedings of the 45th Annual Meeting of the ACL on Interactive Poster and Demonstration Sessions (pp. 221-224). Association for Computational Linguistics.

Dissanayaka, J. B. (2014) Sinhala Reethiya 7 - Pada Nirmanaya. Sri Lanka: Sumitha Books.

Dissanayaka, J. B. (2008) Basaka Mahima 10; Nama Padaya. Sri Lanka: S. Godage & Brothers.

Ekbal, A., & Bandyopadhyay, S. (2008, December). Part of speech tagging in Bengali using support vector machines. In Proceedings of the International Conference on Information Technology, (pp. 106-111). IEEE.

Giménez, J., & Marquez, L. (2004a). SVMTool: A general POS tagger generator based on Support Vector Machines. In Proceedings of the 4th International Conference on Language Resources and Evaluation.

Giménez, J., & Marquez, L. (2004b). Fast and accurate part-of-speech tagging: The SVM approach revisited. Recent Advances in Natural Language Processing III, 153-162.

Gunasekara, N. A. K. B. D., & Weerasinghe, A. R. (2016). Hybrid Part of Speech Tagger for Sinhala Language. In Proceedings of the International Conference Advances in ICT for Emerging Regions (ICTer) (pp.41-48). IEEE.

Gupta, V., Joshi, N., & Mathur, I. (2016). POS tagger for Urdu using Stochastic approaches. In Proceedings of the Second International Conference on Information and Communication Technology for Competitive Strategies (p. 56). ACM.

Jayasuriya, M., & Weerasinghe, A. R. (2013). Learning a stochastic part of speech tagger for Sinhala. In Proceedings of the International Conference on Advances in ICT for Emerging Regions. (pp. 137-143). IEEE.

Jayaweera, A. J. P. M. P., & Dias, N. G. J. (2014). Hidden Markov Model Based Part of Speech Tagger for Sinhala Language. arXiv preprint arXiv:1407.2989.

Joshi, N., Darbari, H., & Mathur, I. (2013). HMM based POS tagger for Hindi. In Proceeding of the 2013 International Conference on Artificial Intelligence (pp. 341-349), Soft Computing.

Kumar, D., & Josan, G. S. (2010). Part of speech taggers for morphologically rich Indian languages: a survey. International Journal of Computer Applications, 6(5), 32-41.

Manamini, S. A. P. M., Ahamed, A. F., Rajapakshe, R. A. E. C., Reemal, G. H. A., Jayasena, S., Dias, G. V., & Ranathunga, S. (2016, April). Ananya-a Named-Entity-Recognition (NER) system for Sinhala language. In 2016 Moratuwa Engineering Research Conference (pp. 30-35). IEEE.

Modi, D., & Nain, N. (2016). Part-of-Speech Tagging of Hindi Corpus Using Rule-Based Method. In Proceedings of the International Conference on Recent Cognizance in Wireless Communication & Image Processing (pp. 241-247). Springer India.

Ojha, A. K., Behera, P., Singh, S., & Jha, G. N. (2015). Training & Evaluation of POS Taggers in Indo-Aryan Languages: A Case of Hindi, Odia and Bhojpuri. In the proceedings of 7th Language & Technology Conference: Human Language Technologies as a Challenge for Computer Science and Linguistics (pp. 524-529).

Palihakkara, S., Sahabandu, D., Shamsudeen, A., Bandara, C., & Ranathunga, S. Dialogue Act Recognition for Text-based Sinhala. In Proceedings of the 12th International Conference on Natural Language Processing.

Shahi, T. B., Dhamala, T. N., & Balami, B. (2013). Support vector machines based part of speech tagging for Nepali text. International Journal of Computer Applications, 70(24), 38-42.

Singh, S., & Jha, G. N. (2015, August). Statistical Tagger for Bhojpuri (employing Support Vector Machine)s. In Proceedings of the International Conference on Advances in Computing, Communications and Informatics (pp. 1524-1529). IEEE.

Align Me : A framework to generate Parallel Corpus Using OCRs & Bilingual Dictionaries

Priyam Bakliwal   **Devadath V V**   **C V Jawahar**

CVIT, International Institute of Information Technology, Hyderabad, India

Abstract

Multilingual processing tasks like statistical machine translation and cross language information retrieval rely mainly on availability of accurate parallel corpora. Manual construction of such corpus can be extremely expensive and time consuming. In this paper we present a simple yet efficient method to generate huge amount of reasonably accurate parallel corpus with minimal user efforts. We utilize the availability of large number of English books and their corresponding translations in other languages to build parallel corpus. Optical Character Recognition systems are used to digitize such books. We propose a robust dictionary based parallel corpus generation system for alignment of multilingual text at different levels of granularity (sentence, paragraphs, etc). We show the performance of our proposed method on a manually aligned dataset of 300 Hindi-English sentences and 100 English-Malayalam sentences.

1 Introduction

Parallel corpus is an inevitable resource for many language processing tasks like Statistical Machine Translation(SMT) and cross-lingual information retrieval. Such tasks require an *aligned parallel corpus* where each sentence in a source language is aligned to the corresponding translated sentence(s) in target language. The task of creating a sentence aligned parallel corpus is expensive and time consuming since it involves the task of manual translation. Major sources for creating parallel corpus are Parliamentary proceedings like Europarl corpus(Koehn, 2005), parallel sentences from web and translations of books/documents.

India is a multilingual, linguistically dense and diverse country with rich resources of information (Chaudhury et al., 2008a). Though Monolingual corpora are available, availability of parallel corpus is very limited in quantity for language pair other than Hindi-English. Indian parliament proceedings are available only in Hindi and English and not in any other languages. But there are numerous amount of books that are translated in more than one language which are not digitized but can be used as a reliable source to generate parallel sentences. In this work, we are trying to leverage the Optical Character Recognition systems for digitizing the books in English and their respective translations in other Indian languages. For solving the problem of sentence alignment, various methods have been proposed over the past three decades like (Gale and Church, 1993). Since our data is OCR-generated data, existing algorithms failed to fetch a good level of accuracy since the text to be aligned is noisy.

To the best of our knowledge, two main algorithms have been proposed for sentence alignment in noisy data. The first work *Bleualign* (Sennrich and Volk, 2010) proposed MT based method for aligning sentences from OCR-generated parallel texts which are noisy. They used MT system to initially translate the texts and then used BLEU score(Papineni et al., 2002) to calculate the sentence similarity which is the base for alignment. Following this method, (Gomes, 2016) proposed a new scoring function that discriminates parallel and non-parallel sentences based on the ratio of text covered by bilingual phrase-pairs from a Moses phrase table. The first approach requires an MT system with a reasonable performance (Sennrich and Volk, 2010) which in our case is only possible for Hindi-English pair. The second method needs the access to bilingual-phrase pairs where for Indian languages have only limited number of sentences in the parallel corpus to create phrase tables.

The SMT systems are very sensitive towards the quality of training data. We have not come across any work in the past that have a mechanism to detect the failures of alignment algorithm. We propose an Active Learning based solution that does validations along with text alignment. The key idea is, if an algorithm is able to detect its failures and give that to a human in the form of queries, one can significantly reduce the amount of human effort while consistently maintaining the output quality.

In this paper, we propose a dictionary based recursive alignment algorithm to align text at multiple levels (sentence, paragraph, *etc.*). This method is a self updating validation algorithm that can predict when the alignment is

Proceedings of the 6th Workshop on South and Southeast Asian Natural Language Processing,
pages 183–187, Osaka, Japan, December 11-17 2016.

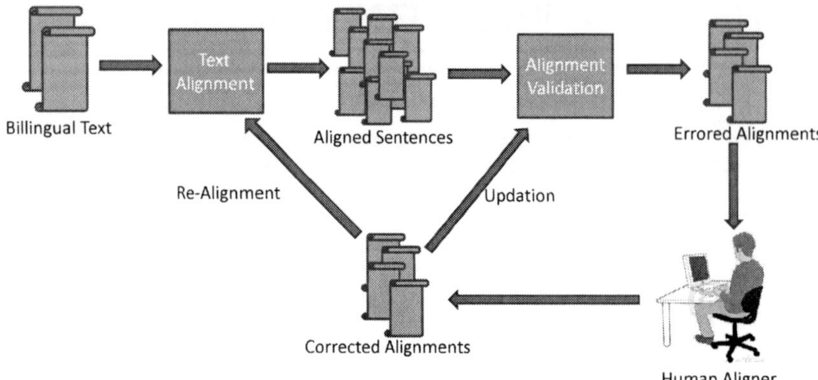

Figure 1: Block diagram of Align-Me framework. Given multilingual texts, an alignment algorithm is used to align the text. These aligned sentences are validated using length heuristics. Possible erroneous alignments are given to the user for corrections. These corrected alignments are used for updation of validation heuristics. In this way Align-Me aligns multilingual documents precisely with minimal user efforts.

done wrong. We show that the proposed framework can be used for precise alignment of multilingual sentences with minimal human effort.

2 Challenges for Data Creation & Sentence Alignment

These days the accuracy of OCR systems are very good. But still multiple errors occur while reading text due to font style difference, picture quality of book *etc.* Additional 1-to-many beads are introduced in our corpus by sentence boundaries being mis-recognized because of OCR or tokenization errors. There are several errors added in the form of spelling mistakes. Sentence alignment is further complicated by image captions, footnotes or advertisements that are not marked as such, and consequently considered part of the running text of the article. These text fragments typically occur at different positions in the two language versions, or only in one of them. They can be very disruptive to sentence alignment algorithms if they are not correctly recognized as deletions (1-to-0 or 0-to-1 beads), since a misalignment may cause consecutive sentences to be misaligned as well.

3 Algorithm

Align Me is an interactive framework that generates parallel corpus for two different languages given the parallel text (OCR data in our case) and a bilingual dictionary. As shown in Fig 1, the framework uses two separate algorithms: 'Alignment Algorithm' which align the sentences of the corpora and the 'Validation Algorithm' which detects where the former algorithm is failing. The sentences for which the alignment algorithm fails are given to the user for correction. Based on user corrections, the Validation algorithm updates itself for better prediction of the failures of the alignment algorithm.

We used the bilingual mappings released publicly by Indian Institute of Technology, Bombay (IIT, Bombay) for the initial alignment of text. These are dictionaries that contains root words of one language mapped to all its possible translationsin the other languages. There are 242 such dictionaries containing mappings of most of the Indian languages like Assamese, Bengali, Kannada, Gujarati, *etc.* Given the OCR generated parallel text T_{l1} and T_{l2} for language L_1 and L_2, we first find out all the words of language L_1 that occur exactly once in the T_{l1}. Further, We use a dictionary D_{l1-l2} to filter out the words from W_{l1} whose corresponding mapping in L_2 has occur only once. In this way we have a set of candidate aligned words C_{aw} in T_{l1} with their corresponding words in T_{l2}.

$$c_{aw} = \{(w_{l1}, w_{l2}) \mid \quad freq(w_{l1}) = freq(w_{l2}) = 1 \quad and \quad (w_{l1}, w_{l2}) \in D_{l1-l2}\} \quad (1)$$

It is observed that there exist a few erroneous items in word mappings found by Eq 1. Thus, we added another measure to validate the former mapping technique. We assume that the displacement of a word and its translation should not be large. We check that the relative position of two words w_{l1} and w_{l2} in the corresponding texts T_{l1} and T_{l1} should not differ more than a threshold τ.

$$f_{aw} = \{(w_{l1}, w_{l2}) \mid (w_{l1}, w_{l2}) \in C_{aw} \quad and \quad |(pos(w_{l1})/len(T_{l1}) - pos(w_{l2})/len(T_{l2}))| < \tau\} \quad (2)$$

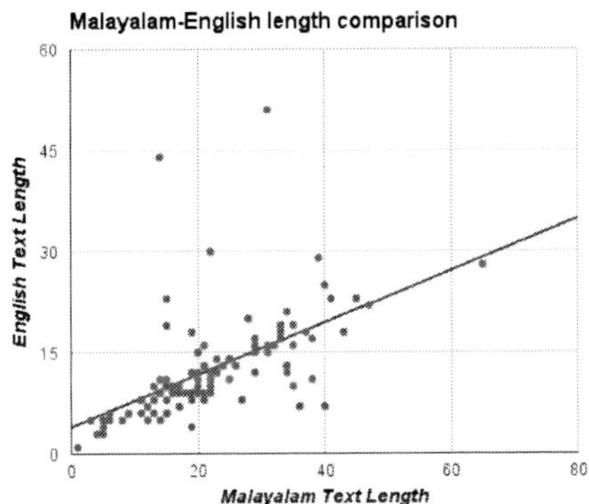

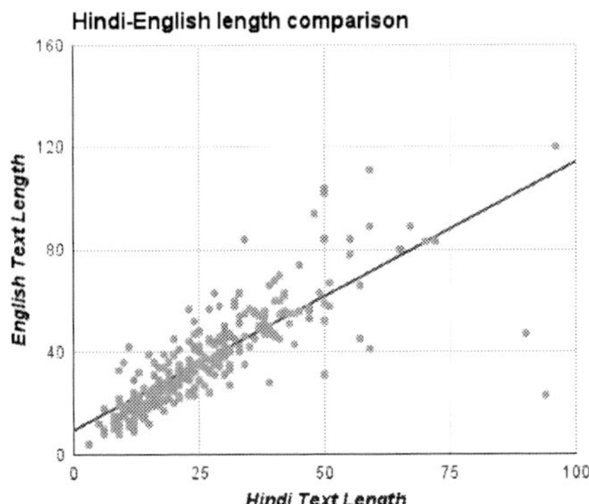

Figure 2: Comparison of number of words of 100 English-Malayalam sentences and 300 English-Hindi sentences. The figure shows that the count of words follow a nearly linear mapping.

where $pos(x)$ gives the position of a word in the text and $len(y)$ gives the length of the text. We consider the final word alignments f_{aw} as the correct alignments and use them as anchors to split the text. The next division of the text is done from the next separator. We use language specific sentence separators like "|", "?", "!" in Hindi and ".", "?", "!" in English.

Fig 2 shows that in spite of one-to-one or many-to-one mapping between sentences of two languages, the number of words in corresponding sentences mostly follow a linear mapping. This fact is used by our validation algorithm, we train a 'Linear Regressor' for the number of words present in the corresponding aligned texts of L_1 and L_2.

$$N_2 = a + b \times N_1 \tag{3}$$

where, N_1 and N_2 are number of words in aligned text of L_1 and L_2. We use the above trained Regressor to predict N_2 given N_1 for all the sentences aligned by the algorithm. The sentences where predicted number of words differs from that of original number of words by a certain threshold, are given to user for correction.

After the user corrections the Regressor is updated. These aligned texts are again given to the aligning algorithm for obtaining finer alignments. After each iteration we obtain finer annotations and an updated and more accurate Regressor.

4 Experiments & Results

To create the test data we digitized four books using OCR systems namely 'George Washington Man And Monument' and its Hindi translation and Kerala assembly Budget-speech of the year 2015 and its Malayalam translation. Due to the difference in writing styles of two authors, there is a huge difference between number of sentences present in the books and their respective translations. We have tested on 492 Hindi sentences and its corresponding 356 English sentences. We have aligned them manually to get 300 English-Hindi sentences. For English-Malayalam text we have used 140 Malayalam sentences and 165 English sentences. We created 100 English-Malayalam aligned sentences to validate the performance of proposed approach.

The approaches proposed in the past used various evaluation measures. Dan (1996) used block error to evaluate alignments. Chaudhary *et. al* (2008b) proposed a sentence based evaluation using Precision, Recall and F1-Measure. For the first level alignment of Hindi-English text we are getting 85.2% precision and 78% recall and for Malayalam-English text we are getting 96% precision and 85% recall.

To show the effectiveness of 'Active Learning' in the alignment task, we have used 'Word Level Error' than 'Sentence Level Error'. Even if a single word of a sentence have a mis-alignment, all the other words of that sentence are said to be aligned erroneously. We calculate 'Word Error Percentage' for both the languages as $(Number of Misaligned Words/Total Number of Words)$. In Fig 4 we show that our algorithm is able to detect correctly, the mis-aligned texts to be queried to the user. The figure shows the reduction in error with every user correction for two iterations on same text.

Fig 3 shows that Align-Me is effectively able to detect aligned texts of different modularities. With each iteration finer alignments are done. We also show that the proposed framework is immune to OCR system introduced errors. In the second iteration of Malayalam alignment, the algorithm handled 1-to-many beads introduced due to mis-recognition of sentence boundaries by OCR systems.

The UDF Government believes that this will help us achieve the vision that we have drawn up for the State in our perspective plan for 2030 and help us grow on par with more advanced regions of the world. For the implementation of these schemes under the seven thematic groups, Cabinet Sub Committees of concerned Ministers will be constituted wherever necessary. Empowered Committees chaired by the Chief Secretary with Secretaries will be formed to quickly implement decisions.	[Malayalam text]	Year by year this monument has grown, like a cairn to which each passer-by adds a stone. Pamphlet, speech, article and book; pebble, rubble, stone and boulder have piled up. Anecdote, monograph, panegyric: whatever the level and value of each contribution it has somehow — ironically, in the instance of more important contributions — smothered what it seeks to disclose.	जैसे-जैसे साल गुजरते चले गये, नई-नई कहानियां गढ़ी जाती रहीं । परिणामत: यह स्मारक ऊंचा उठता ही चला गया-ठीक उस समाधि की तरह जिस पर राह चलते लोग पत्थर रखते चले जाते है । इन पत्थरों के छोटे-छोटे टुकड़ों के " समान ही पुस्तिकाएं, भाषण, लेख और ग्रन्थ उस स्मारक के आकार को बढ़ाते ही रहे । परन्तु यह कितनी बिचित्र बात है कि इन भिन्न-भिन्न स्तर और मूल्यों की जीवन-झॉकियों, पाण्डित्यपूर्ण लेखों एवं प्रशस्तियो ने उनके जीवन के रहस्य को जितना खोजने की चेष्टा की, इस रहस्य के तार उतने ही उलझते चले गये ।
• The UDF Government believes that this will help us achieve the vision that we have drawn up for the State in our perspective plan for 2030 and help us grow on par with more advanced regions of the world. For the implementation of these schemes under the seven thematic groups, Cabinet Sub Committees of concerned Ministers will be constituted wherever necessary. • Empowered Committees chaired by the Chief Secretary with Secretaries will be formed to quickly implement decisions.	[Malayalam text]	• Year by year this monument has grown, like a cairn to which each passer-by adds a stone. • Pamphlet, speech, article and book; pebble, rubble, stone and boulder have piled up. • Anecdote, monograph, panegyric: whatever the level and value of each contribution it has somehow — ironically, in the instance of more important contributions — smothered what it seeks to disclose.	• जैसे-जैसे साल गुजरते चले गये, नई-नई कहानियां गढ़ी जाती रहीं । परिणामत: यह स्मारक ऊंचा उठता ही चला गया-ठीक उस समाधि की तरह जिस पर राह चलते लोग पत्थर रखते चले जाते है । • इन पत्थरों के छोटे-छोटे टुकड़ों के " समान ही पुस्तिकाएं, भाषण, लेख और ग्रन्थ उस स्मारक के आकार को बढ़ाते ही रहे । • परन्तु यह कितनी बिचित्र बात है कि इन भिन्न-भिन्न स्तर और मूल्यों की जीवन-झॉकियों, पाण्डित्यपूर्ण लेखों एवं प्रशस्तियो ने उनके जीवन के रहस्य को जितना खोजने की चेष्टा की, इस रहस्य के तार उतने ही उलझते चले गये ।

Figure 3: The above table shows the qualitative performance of Align-Me. The top row depicts the output of first iteration and bottom row depicts the output of second iteration. One can get aligned sentences at different levels depending on the requirement.

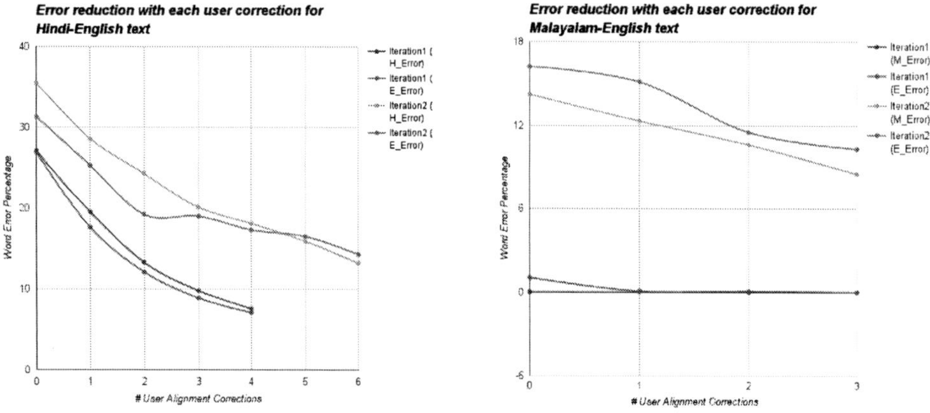

Figure 4: The above graph shows the reduction of 'Word Error Percentage' with every user annotation. We have calculated word errors for all the languages. 'H_Error', 'E_Error' and 'M_Error' are word errors for Hindi, English and Malayalam respectively. The error graph shows the fall of error for two iterations. It is evident that the validation algorithm is able to correctly determine the mis-aligned samples.

5 Conclusion & Future Directions

In this paper, we proposed Align Me as an efficient framework for generating huge corpus of parallel text using minimal user efforts. Our framework uses multilingual dictionaries to align the texts initially. At every step, the verification of the alignments is done using a validation algorithm which uses length based heuristics to determine possible mis-alignments. Experimental data depicts that length based heuristics work really well in cases where there are possible errors in the text-to-be-aligned. These heuristics also perform exceedingly well in cases when the number of sentences in both the languages vary by a huge count. In this approach, the human effort is reduced to a great extent as the framework queries only the misaligned sentences to the human annotator. The proposed approach can be utilized for generation of huge corpus for languages like Malayalam-English, Marathi-English, Hindi-Kannada *etc.* where there is huge paucity of aligned data. The performance of the method remains consistent even if the input data is noisy; this proves the high degree of robustness that the method offers.

As part of future work, we would like to use the proposed framework for generation of parallel corpus for other Indian languages as well. We are also trying to incorporate other factors like BLEU score for detection of mis-alignments.

References

Sriram Chaudhury, Dipti Misra Sharma, and Amba P Kulkarni. 2008a. Enhancing effectiveness of sentence alignment in parallel corpora: Using mt heuristics.

Sriram Chaudhury, Dipti Misra Sharma, and Amba P Kulkarni. 2008b. Enhancing effectiveness of sentence alignment in parallel corpora: Using mt heuristics. *ICON*.

William A Gale and Kenneth W Church. 1993. A program for aligning sentences in bilingual corpora. *Computational linguistics*, 19(1):75–102.

Luis Gomes. 2016. First steps towards coverage-based document alignment.

IIT. Bombay. Bilingual mappings (http://www.cfilt.iitb.ac.in/downloads.html).

Philipp Koehn. 2005. Europarl: A parallel corpus for statistical machine translation. In *MT summit*, volume 5, pages 79–86.

I Dan Melamed. 1996. A geometric approach to mapping bitext correspondence. *arXiv preprint cmp-lg/9609009*.

Kishore Papineni, Salim Roukos, Todd Ward, and Wei-Jing Zhu. 2002. Bleu: a method for automatic evaluation of machine translation. In *Proceedings of the 40th annual meeting on association for computational linguistics*, pages 311–318. Association for Computational Linguistics.

Rico Sennrich and Martin Volk. 2010. Mt-based sentence alignment for ocr-generated parallel texts.

Learning Indonesian-Chinese Lexicon
with Bilingual Word Embedding Models and Monolingual Signals

Xinying Qiu
CISCO School of Informatics
Guangdong University of Foreign Studies
Guangzhou, China
qiuxinying@gdufs.edu.cn

Gangqin Zhu
The Faculty of Asian Languages and Cultures
Guangdong University of Foreign Studies
Guangzhou, China
199210621@oamail.gdufs.edu.cn

Abstract

We present a research on learning Indonesian-Chinese bilingual lexicon using monolingual word embedding and bilingual seed lexicons to build shared bilingual word embedding space. We take the first attempt to examine the impact of different monolingual signals for the choice of seed lexicons on the model performance. We found that although monolingual signals alone do not seem to outperform signals coverings all words, the significant improvement for learning word translation of the same signal types may suggest that linguistic features possess value for further study in distinguishing the semantic margins of the shared word embedding space.

1 Introduction

We explore the latest development of bilingual lexicon learning (BLL) research and investigate their application on inducing Indonesian-Chinese lexicon. In particular, due to the limitation of parallel and comparable Indonesian-Chinese bilingual corpora, we study the state-of-the-art bilingual word embedding (BWE) models built with seed lexicons and monolingual corpora to project Indonesian and Chinese word pairs onto the same transformed space. We further explore the impact of Indonesian linguistic signals on these models to provide insights on the implications of monolingual signals and challenges for bilingual lexicon learning

Bilingual word embedding models have proven to be effective in many cross-lingual tasks such as document classification, POS tagging, and phrase generation. As illustrated in Figure 1, two sets of words (numbers and animals) in two languages (English and Spanish) have similar geometric arrangements. This is achieved by constructing wore embedding vectors for both languages and projecting the vectors down into two dimensions, rotated to show similarity. The Figure demonstrates that the relations between words are similar across languages. This finding inspired a series of research on generating a bilingual dictionary with cross-lingual word embedding space. The general steps involve 1) building a word space for each individual language; 2) projecting the two spaces into one shared space or from one to the other; and 3) learning or retrieving the target language word most similar to the source language word in the projection.

Our paper attempts to contribute to this line of research by examining the monolingual signals from Indonesian in building the bilingual word embedding model. The rest of the paper is organized as follows. In Section 2, we review the latest development in BLL with BWE. We summarize the related research and propose our research questions. In Section 3, we discuss details of our methodologies. We present our data preparation, experiment design, results and analysis in Section 4, and conclude with Section 5.

2 Research Framework and Related Work

Bilingual lexicon learning aims at enriching existing bilingual dictionaries and building new dictionaries to cross the language barriers between under-resourced languages and resourced languages. Many research endeavors such as the dictionary extraction from Wiktionary (Sérasset and Tchechmedjiev

Proceedings of the 6th Workshop on South and Southeast Asian Natural Language Processing,
pages 188–193, Osaka, Japan, December 11-17 2016.

(2014)), and the SisTec-embt Project (Al-Adhaileh et.al. (2002)) have explored the automatic dictionary construction methods and linguistics features for machine learning systems. To our limited knowledge, the electronic version of Indonesian-Chinese dictionary is currently only available as hardware devices for language learners, the content of which is not extractable as stand-alone softcopy. The hard-copy of Indonesian-Chinese dictionary is a little out-dated which makes the digitization work not much desirable. Both Google and Bing provide translation between Indonesian and Chinese (and vice versa), but with great deal of errors. Therefore, we find it a challenging research project to learn automatically Indonesian-Chinese lexicon, with many application opportunities for example, as building blocks for machine translation systems, document classification, and sentiment analysis. Our work is of explorative nature. We currently focus on learning simple vocables excluding collocations, and not restricted to specific domain or distinguishing senses. We aim at examining the performance of bilingual word embedding model complemented with monolingual signals in learning Indonesian-Chinese lexicon. We hope that the development and improvement of such models and algorithms would support the more efficient generation of large-volume and high quality bilingual dictionary.

We define our Indonesian-Chinese bilingual learning problem along the following dimensions: usage of monolingual word embedding and signals, bilingual signals, bilingual word embedding model, and learning algorithm, as inspired by the frameworks proposed by Upadhyay et al. (2016) and Vulic and Korhonen (2016).

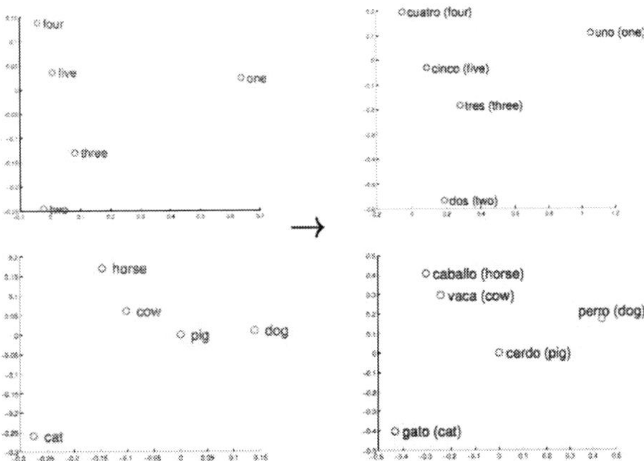

Figure 1: The idea behind transformation matrix. (from Mikilov et al. 2013)

Upadhyay et al. (2016) compared empirically some of the most recent development on cross-lingual models of word embeddings. They come up with a general schema as shown in Figure 2. Their empirical comparisons focus on the "bilingual corpus" component covering parallel corpus (Luong et. al. 2015), comparable corpus (Vulic and Moen, 2015), sentence-aligned corpus (Hermann and Blunsom, 2014), and bilingual lexicon (Faruqui and Dyer, 2014; Mikolov et al. 2013; Dinu et al. 2015). Their findings suggest that the most expensive supervision of training data such as word alignment may be more suitable for bilingual lexicon learning.

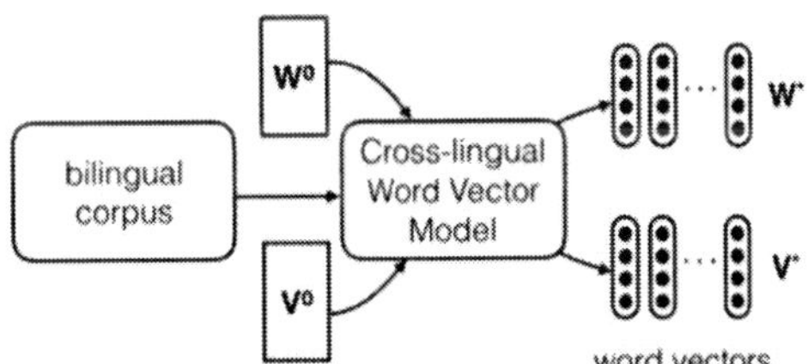

Figure 2: Cross-Lingual Word Embedding Schema as from Upadhyay et al. (2016)

Similarly, Vulic and Korhonen (2016) defined Bilingual Word Embedding (BWE) model as "induction of *a shared bilingual word embedding space (SBWES)*". They further proposed two desirable properties for BWE model as 1) usage of monolingual training sets tied with bilingual signals; and 2) inexpensive bilingual signal. In their setting, the "bilingual signals" are equivalent with the "bilingual corpus" in the schema by Upadhyay et al. (2016). The "monolingual training set" property is in consistent with Upadhyay et al. (2016) in their generalization of the loss function with monolingual corpora. The "inexpensive" requirement is in line with the "supervision cost" discussed by Upadhyay et al. (2016). They also suggest that for Bilingual Lexicon Learning, careful selection of seed lexicon (thus more expensive human supervision) may produce better results (Vulic and Korhonen (2016)).

By integrating these two frameworks, we demonstrate our research framework to induce Indonesian-Chinese lexicon as shown in Figure 3. Due to the lack of parallel and comparable corpora, and also because BLL is proven to be better supported with more expensive knowledge, we opt for using seed bilingual lexicon as our bilingual signal.

For learning algorithms, previous researchers have examined supervised or distantly supervised models (Irvine and Callison-Burch, 2015; Gouws and Sogaard, 2015), and unsupervised models (Mikolov et al. 2013; Luong et. al. 2015). Dinu et al. (2015) modified Mikolov's nearest neighbour method with zero-shot paradigm to correct the bilingual translations by considering the hubness of the candidate target language words. In this paper, we experiment with both Dinu's and Mikolov's unsupervised learning algorithms. We will explore the supervised learning approaches in our future work.

Many researchers have suggested that monolingual signals or features may impact on the learning the cross-lingual word embedding models, such as Irvine and Callison-Burch (2015), Vulic and Korhonen (2016) and Dinu et al. (2015). Inspired by the research discussed above, we propose to examine different monolingual signals to analyse their impact on bilingual word embedding models for Indonesian-Chinese lexicon learning.

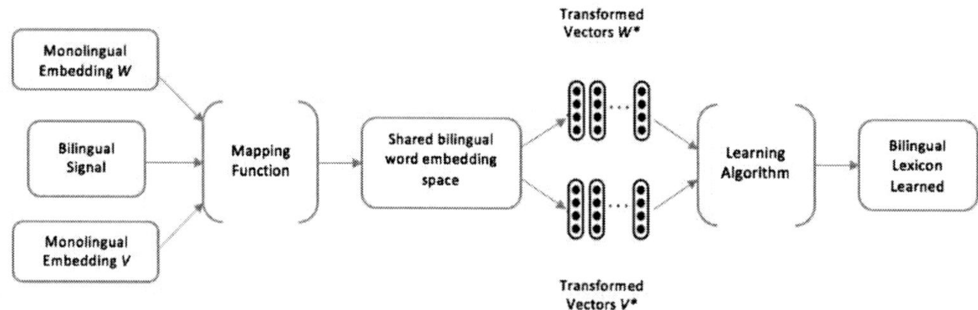

Figure 3: Our Research Framework

3 Methodologies

As discussed in Section 2, we choose the following methodologies within our proposed research framework:

1) We build monolingual embedding models for Indonesian and Chinese respectively. We use a seed Indonesian-Chinese lexicon as bilingual signals to tie up the monolingual word embeddings.

2) We experiment with Mikolov's mapping function to generate transformation matrix from which we could generate vectors of the two languages projected onto the same space. We also experiment with Dinu's method to mitigate the impact of hub vectors in the vector space.

3) Learning of translated Chinese words for the test data set is based on nearest neighbour retrieval. Evaluation method is the standard Precision@k for bilingual lexicon learning, with which we report results for k as 1, 5, and 10.

4) We examine the impact of the following monolingual signals on the performance of the word embedding models: nouns, root words, high-frequency words, and unambiguous words.

3.1 Mikolov's Mapping

Mikolov et al. (2013) proposed a method to use distributed representation of words and learns a linear mapping between vector space of different languages. More specifically, the model is as illustrated in the following equation:

$$\min_{W} \sum_{i=1}^{n} \|Wx_i - z_i\|^2$$

where W is the transformation matrix; x_i the vector of the source language word; z_i the vector of the target language word. When such a transformation matrix is learned, to retrieve the translation of a new word with its vector x, we may compute a new vector $z = Wx$, and find the nearest neighbour vector in the target language space.

3.2 Dinu's Hub-Correction

Dinu et al. (2015) proposed to improve over Mikolov's retrieval method by solving the *hubness* problem when retrieving target words with the following *globally-corrected* approach:

$$GC(x, T) = arg \min_{y \in T}(Rank_{y,P}(x) - \cos(x, y))$$

where x is the vector in the source language space; $Rank_{y,P}(x)$ measures the rank of x in the set of pivot vectors P with respect to its similarity to y in the target space; *cosine* score is used to break ties for the candidate target words.

3.3 Monolingual Signals

Inspired by previous research that discuss monolingual signals, the importance of seed lexicon choice, and the problem caused by "hub" words in the vector space, we propose to examine the following monolingual signals' impact on bilingual word embedding models.

Nouns: As we study "Kamus Besar Bahasa Indonesia" (the Grand Indonesian Dictionary), we found that out of the 7 POS tags available for Indonesian, the NOUN words take up the largest proportion of of 56.6%, with the second popular POS tag being VERB, taking up only 29.7% of Indonesian words. Considering this phenomenon, we experiment to see if words of NOUN type alone could serve as better monolingual signal in learning the bilingual word embedding models.

Root words: Indonesian is an agglutinative language, with many words derived as inflectional forms of root words with prefixes and/or suffixes attached. For example:

>*Root words:*   *Derived words:*
>kerja (work, *n.*) ----------> bekerja (work, *v.i.*); mengerjakan (work, *v.t.*);
>   pekerja (worker, *n.*); mempekerjakan (employment, *n.*);

We propose that by selecting root words and their Chinese translation as seed lexicon, we might be able to generate a more coherent transformation matrix that reduces the semantic similarity between word of inflectional variations within the bilingual word embedding space.

High-frequency words: Vulic and Korhonen (2016) suggested that words with higher frequency are more reliably translated to guarantee the quality of the seed lexicon. In addition to that, we also hypothesize that by selecting the more frequently used words to construct bilingual seed lexicons, we might be able to cover the more popularly discussed semantics in the transformation matrix.

Unambiguous words: The polysemy phenomenon in Indonesian languages may give us multiple translation entries for a single word in the seed lexicon. It is also quite common for a single Indonesian word to be matched with multiple similar Chinese translations. For example:

>*Polysemy:*
>   Peringatan ----> 纪念 (commemorate); 警告 (warning)
>*Multiple translations with similar meanings:*
>   Berkah ----- > 恩赐 (bestow), 祝福(blessing)

We hypothesize that by selecting highly unambiguous and monosemous translation pairs, we may be able generate vector space with more semantic margins between word vectors, and therefore improving the target word selection performance.

4   Experiments and Results

4.1   Data and Evaluation

For building monolingual word embedding models, we use Chinese and Indonesian Wikipedia articles as training set. We collected and processed the Chinese Wikipedia dump of Aug. 1 2016 and the Indonesian Wikipedia dump of July 20, 2016 and generate 727k Chinese word vectors and 190k Indonesian vectors.

For bilingual lexicons, we take the complete vocabulary from "Kamus Besar Bahasa Indonesia" (the Grand Indonesian Dictionary) and run the Google translation and Bing translation. Since both translation systems generate a great deal of errors, we take the same translation from both systems hoping for better accuracy. One of our authors (an Indonesian language teaching professor) manually filtered out the correct word-pairs from this translation set. We also take the vocabulary from the Indonesian language textbooks for Chinese learners to include with the word-pairs from the Grand Dictionary. Therefore, we have a collection of 10436 Indonesian-Chinese word-pair lexicon. Out of this base seed lexicon, we select nouns, root words, high-frequency words (as from the basic-level and medium-level Indonesian textbook for Chinese language learners), and highly-unambiguous words. The statistics are as follows:

All words	High-frequency	Nouns	Root-words	Unambiguous
10436	5037	4078	5493	2502

For each of the above 5 monolingual signals, we experiment with Mikolov's and Dinu's methodologies respectively. We take 10% of the data as test set, 90% as training set. We perform two types of experiment designs: <u>Design 1:</u> We build test data by randomly selecting 10% of all-words data. We build 5 training models with the five signal data without overlapping with the test set; <u>Design 2:</u> For each of 5 signal data, we randomly select 10% for testing, and the rest for training. In other words, each experiment is performed within the data of the same signal themselves.

These experiments evaluate the impact of signal for learning a general lexicon, and for learning lexicon of their own signal types. We evaluate performance with the standard Precisions @ 1, 5, and 10.

4.2   Results and Analysis

We first present some examples of learning results, with the correct translations retrieved in bold. There are many cases where the retrieved translation words rank as far as the hundredth.

Indonesian word: *Retrieved translation: rank: Chinese (English, cosine score)*
murid (student) -----> **#1: 学生 (student, 0.705)**; #2: 老师 (teacher, 0.636); #3: 女生(female student, 0.624); #4: 班级(class, 0.621); #5: 毕业生(graduates, 0.588)
gembira (happy) -----> #1: 难过(sad, 0.685); #2: 想念(yearn for, 0.669); #3: 伤心(grief, 0.663); #4: 吃惊(surprised, 0.643); **#5: 高兴(happy, 0.640)**

Table 1 presents results for testing on the same data set randomly selected from all-words lexicon, i.e. 1043 word-pairs. We find that the 4 special monolingual signals alone do not seem to improve the learning performance over the model built with all-words. The best performance is highlighted for "all-words" with Mikolov's method at 0.514 for precision at 10.
Table 2 presents results for testing within the same signal type. For the All-words data, this experiment design is the same as Design 1. We repeat it in the table for comparison purposes.

We have the following findings from Design 2:

1) NOUNs, root words, and highly unambiguous words all perform better in retrieving the correct translations for words of their own signal types.

2) Model with unambiguous words performs the best with a 0.632 precision at 10, much higher than even the all-words signal. We may infer that the better performance may come from the fact the transformation space is composed of highly distinguished vectors representing the drastic difference in words' semantics.

3) Dinu's method with hubness correction performs well with root words signal and test on its own data. This may be because root words data set support the elimination of similar target words that may push down the ranking of the correct translation.

		All words	High-Frequency	Nouns	Root words	Unambiguous
Mikolov's	Pre@1	0.244	0.213	0.204	0.201	0.217
	Pre@5	0.434	0.419	0.403	0.399	0.394
	Pre@10	**0.514**	0.509	0.474	0.478	0.472
Dinu's	Pre@1	0.248	0.223	0.201	0.218	0.227
	Pre@5	0.422	0.420	0.392	0.398	0.385
	Pre@10	0.481	0.470	0.443	0.449	0.435

Table 1: Design 1 -- Test on All-words Lexicon

		All words	High-Frequency	Nouns	Root words	Unambiguous
Mikolov's	Pre@1	0.244	0.110	0.266	0.265	0.318
	Pre@5	0.434	0.344	0.457	0.458	0.538
	Pre@10	**0.514**	0.407	**0.531**	0.529	**0.632**
Dinu's	Pre@1	0.248	0.114	0.269	0.272	0.323
	Pre@5	0.422	0.319	0.454	0.473	0.498
	Pre@10	0.481	0.392	0.529	**0.544**	0.516

Table 2: Design 2 – Test with data from the same signal type

5   Conclusions

We present a research on learning Indonesian-Chinese bilingual lexicon using monolingual word embedding and bilingual seed lexicons to build shared bilingual word embedding space. The aim of the work is to develop and improve bilingual lexicon learning models, as building block for research on machine translation and cross-language NLP. We apply the latest development on BWE framework and also take the first attempt to examine the possible impact of different monolingual signals for the choice of seed lexicons on the model performance. We found that although monolingual signals alone do not seem to outperform signals coverings all words, the significant improvement for learning word translation of the same signal types may suggest that linguistic features possess value for further study in distinguishing the semantic margins of the shared word embedding space. For our future work, we plan on studying the impact of word senses, collocation, and other lexical features on the BWE model.

References:
Sérasset G, Tchechmedjiev A. Dbnary: Wiktionary as Linked Data for 12 Language Editions with Enhanced Translation Relations. 3rd Workshop on Linked Data in Linguistics. 2014.
Al-Adhaileh M H, Kong T E, Yusoff Z. A synchronization structure of SSTC and its applications in machine translation. Proceedings of the 2002 COLING workshop on Machine translation in Asia. Volume 16. 2002
Mikolov T., Quoc V. Le, and Ilya Sutskever. Exploiting similarities among languages for machine translation. CoRR, abs/1309.4168. 2013.
Upadhyay S, Faruqui M, Dyer C, et al. Cross-lingual Models of Word Embeddings: An Empirical Comparison[J]. arXiv preprint arXiv:1604.00425, 2016.
Vulic I, Korhonen A. On the Role of Seed Lexicons in Learning Bilingual Word Embeddings. ACL, 2016.
Luong T, Pham H, Manning C D. Bilingual word representations with monolingual quality in mind. Proceedings of the 1st Workshop on Vector Space Modeling for Natural Language Processing. 2015: 151-159.
Vulic´ I and Marie-Francine Moens. Bilingual word embeddings from non-parallel document-aligned data applied to bilingual lexicon induction. In Proc. of ACL, 2015
Hermann K. and Phil Blunsom. Multi-lingual models for compositional distributed semantics. In ACL, 2014.
Faruqui M, Dyer C. Improving vector space word representations using multilingual correlation. In ACL, 2014.
Dinu G, Lazaridou A, Baroni M. Improving zero-shot learning by mitigating the hubness problem. ICLR, 2015.
Irvine A, Callison-Burch C. Discriminative Bilingual Lexicon Induction. Computational Linguistics, 2015, 1(1).
Gouws S, Søgaard A. Simple task-specific bilingual word embeddings. Proceedings of NAACL-HLT. 2015: 1386-1390.

Creating rich online dictionaries for the Lao↔French language pair, reusable for Machine Translation

Vincent Berment
INaLCO, Paris
Vincent.Berment@inalco.fr

Abstract

In this paper, we present how we generated two rich online bilingual dictionaries — Lao-French and French-Lao — from unstructured dictionaries in Microsoft Word files. Then we shortly discuss the possible reuse of the lexical data for Machine Translation projects.

1   Introduction

The creation of a dictionary with a large coverage is a very difficult and time-consuming task, when starting more or less from scratch. At INaLCO (Oriental Studies Institute, Paris, France), where the Lao language is taught, two dictionaries were recently published almost at the same time, making an outstanding milestone because of their coverage and their quality compared to the previous ones. We detail hereafter how we transformed them into digital resources.

2   Available bilingual dictionaries containing the Lao language

Bilingual resources with Lao as one of the languages are relatively rare and often poor. The main ones to our knowledge are (list limited to general bilingual dictionaries with more than 300 pages ; this list simply shows how scarce are the Lao-NL bilingual dictionaries):

Authors	Date	Languages	Pages
SOUKBANDITH Bounmy	1983	English-Lao and Lao-English	719 p.
KERR Allen D.	1992	Lao-English	XX-1223 p.
PATTERSON William Lorenzo, SEVERINO Mario E.	1995	Lao-English	826 p.
SISAVEUY Souvanny	1996	English-Lao	901 p.
KANGPHACHANPHENG, Keo, VILAYSACK Vilayphan, KOUNLAPHAN Vongnathi	1996	English-Lao and Lao-English	1033 p., ill., 522 p.
BOUARAVONG Phone, CHIEMSISOURAJ Chanthaphilit, CHANTHAPHONE Vanhnolack	1999	English-Lao	508 p.
BOUARAVONG Phone, CHIEMSISOURAJ Chanthaphilit, CHANTHAPHONE Vanhnolack	2000	English-Lao and Lao-English	739 p.
MARCUS Russell	2000	English-Lao and Lao-English	416 p.
MINGBUAPHA Khamphan, BECKER Benjawan Poomsan	2003	English-Lao and Lao-English	780 p.
REINHORN Marc	1970	Lao-French	49-2150 p.
NGINN Somchine Pierre	1980	French-Lao	VI-910 p.
SOUKHAVONG Souphaphone, SOUKHAVONG Khamsay	1985	Lao-French	[14]-581 p.
SIMANA Suksavang	1994	Lao-French-English	429 p.
INTHAMONE Lamvieng	2011	Lao-French	1523 p.

Proceedings of the 6th Workshop on South and Southeast Asian Natural Language Processing,
pages 194–197, Osaka, Japan, December 11-17 2016.

Authors	Date	Languages	Pages
REINHORN Marc, BERMENT Vincent	2013	French-Lao	1729 p.
MOREV, L.N. VASILYEVA, V.H. PLUM, U.Y. (МОРЕВ Л.Н., ВАСИЛЬЕВА В.Х., ПЛАМ Ю.Я.)	1982	Lao-Russian	952 p.
MOREV, L.N., KEDAYTENE E.I., MITROKHIN V.I. (МОРЕВ, Л. Н., КЕДАЙТЕНЕ, Е. И., МИТРОХИНА В. И.)	1987	Russian-Lao	352 p.
SISAENGCHAN Thongsit, AMPHAI Vognobuntham	199?	Lao-Magyar	604 p.
LÊ Duy Luong	1992	Vietnamese-Lao	742 p.
PHAM Duc Duong, HOANG Tung Son, TRUONG Duy Hoa	1995	Lao-Vietnamese	835 p.
PROMPRAPHAN Waranon, SAYAVONG Somseng, McCARTHY Robert (Kasetsart University, Department of linguistics)	2000	Lao-Thai-English	XVII-762 p.
WIRAPHONG Misathan	2000	Lao-Thai	XXIV-428 p.
VIRACHIT Khamphanh, OUDOM Kikèo, PHONEKA-SEUMSOUK Kidèng	2000	Khmer-Lao	XII-1246 p.
HOUANGBINH Sisouvanh	2000	Lao-Chinese	1523 p.
INTHAVONGSA Kèo, et al.	2000	Lao-Japanese	XI-410 p.
SULAVAN Khamluan, KINGSADA Thongpheth, COSTELLO Nancy A.	1998	Katu-Lao-English	363 p.
PREISIG Elisabeth, SIMANA Suksavang, SAYGNA-VONG Somseng	1994	Kmhmu-Lao-French-English	68-429 p.
TAYANIN Damrong, SVANTESSON Jan-Ölof, LIN-DELL Kristina, SAYAVONG Somseng, KINGSADA Thongpheth	1994	Kmhmu-Lao	501 p.

Figure 1: Bilingual dictionaries including Lao (from Bernard Gay, 2003 [1], with additions)

The number of pages provides (to a certain extent) a possibility to compare the quantity of lexical information between the dictionaries, but it does not allow evaluating their quality. The content is actually often limited to an entry, a part of speech, a pronunciation and only one word (thus one sense) as the translation. Moreover, some dictionaries are obviously partial or integral plagiarisms.

As for the available online bilingual dictionaries, the main ones are with English:
- http://sealang.net/lao/dictionary.htm
  - Lao ↔ English (both directions)
  - Derives from Kerr and from Patterson/Severino dictionaries
- http://www.seasite.niu.edu/Lao/LDictionary/default.aspx
  - Lao → English
- https://translate.google.fr
  - Lao ↔ English (both directions, through English for the other languages)
and for French:
- http://laosoftware.com/
  - Lao ↔ French (both directions)
  - Relies on Paul Jadin's dictionary

3 From unstructured dictionaries to clean databases with fine structures

3.1 The original dictionaries in Microsoft Word files

Recently, two relatively rich dictionaries (~40,000 entries, ~60,000 word-senses, ~15,000 expressions, many details including POS, examples, glosses, special plural forms, synonyms...) between Lao and French ([2], [3]) brought the opportunity to provide them as digital resources, as we were allowed to use their original Microsoft Word files. In both cases, the dictionary was made of one file per initial letter. Altogether, the authors spent about 40-50 years to produce these two dictionaries.

3.2 Step 1: Parsing the Word files

The first step towards constructing the database was to parse as finely as possible the Word files, in order to discover their fine-grained structure ("microstructure"). We used Claude Del Vigna's "saint-jean" compiler that generates parsers in C++. This task was quite complex as this structure could sometimes lack regularity or rigor. Actually, this step also included manual modifications in the files when parsing failed, in order to make the structure rigorously regular. A simple example among hundreds or thousands: the POS could vary from entry to entry, giving (for "*verbe transitif*") sometimes "vt", "vt.", "v.t.", or even "v .t." (with a white space inside). This step has certainly been the longest one, due to this iterative process, and also because the structure discovery itself was also iterative. The rarest types of lexical information drove us to modify the parser every time they occurred, and also to reparse the parts already successfully parsed with the previous version of the parser.

In order to exploit the style information available in the Word files, we chose to embed the parser in a Word addin[1]. A Word addin is a DLL library that is automatically loaded when Microsoft Word starts. This library must be placed in a specific directory (configurable in Word) and have ".wll" as file extension (instead of the usual ".dll"). Doing so, we could use the font name, size, and style to characterize the different elements. For example, the legacy (non-Unicode) fonts used to write the parts in Lao language are never used for French, so these parts could be assigned the categories of either entry (Lao→French) or translation (French→Lao) or example in Lao... This was indeed very useful and even simply made the parsing possible.

3.3 Step 2: Generating the lexical database

The WLL was written in C++ and was compiled and linked with the SQLITE[2] code to generate the lexical database. The generated tables are directly derived from the dictionary structure. Here is an example for the French→Lao dictionary (without the tables used to describe the examples).

- Vedette (the main table with the lemma and an index for linking the other tables)
    - NumeroEntree (entry id)
    - Vedette (lemma)
- Entree (table containing miscellaneous information for the entry)
    - NumeroEntree (entry id)
    - NumeroDeSens (sense id French)
    - CMS (POS)
    - Correlat (reference to other entries in the dictionary)
    - Exemple (example)
    - Pluriel (special plural forms)
    - Locution (in case the entry is part of a frozen expression)
    - CommentaireParentheses (gloss)
    - LocutionEtoile (gloss in case the entry is part of a frozen expression)
    - CMSLocutionEtoile (POS in case the entry is part of a frozen expression)
    - Synonyme (synonym)
- Renvoi (table linking an entry to another, for example in case of multiple spellings)
    - NumeroEntree (entry id)
    - NumeroDeSensLao (sense id of the Lao translation referred to)
    - Renvoi (lemma of the reference entry)

---

[1] https://support.microsoft.com/en-us/kb/190057 (see http://www.wordaddins.com/ for recent versions of Word).
[2] https://sqlite.org/

- `Traductions` (table containing the translations)
  - `NumeroEntree` (entry id)
  - `NumeroDeSensLao` (sense id Lao)
  - `Traduction` (translation)
  - `Commentaire` (comment in Lao associated to the translation)
  - `Abreviation` (abbreviation in Lao associated to the translation)

3.4 Step 3: Cleaning the lexical database

A meticulous verification step followed the generation of the database. Some errors still remained and had to be fixed. Then, we still had to transform into Unicode the parts that were initially written with non-Unicode fonts. This was the case for the parts written in Lao as well as the IPA transcriptions (for the Lao→French dictionary only).

Nota: An ongoing work is currently being done by Lamvieng Inthamone to refine the structure of the Lao-French dictionary, so that the two dictionaries will be at the same level. This is done in an Excel file extracted from the cleaned database.

3.5 Step 4: Creating the software for the online dictionary look-up

The last step was to make the dictionaries available online. As we wanted to provide the users with the possibility, for the Lao→French direction, to submit strings containing more than one word (it is not always easy to know where a word starts and ends, as there are no spaces between words in Lao), the first thing to do was to embed a word segmenter in the translation process. We chose the general-purpose segmenter MOTOR (see [4], [5]) and embedded it as the initial phase of the translation pipeline from Lao to French. In order to make the translations consistent with the segmentation, the segmenter was configured with the list of entries of the Lao→French dictionary. Then, when a string contains several Lao words, several requests are done in AJAX towards the server.

The dictionaries are available at http://laosoftware.com/HeloiseTest/Dicolofr/indexnew.htm.

4 Conclusion

The Lao-French and French-Lao dictionaries are available online since early 2016 and the first feedbacks are very positive. Now, the next step will be to use the associated lexical databases to bootstrap the creation of dictionaries for Lao→French and French→Lao machine translation systems. This can be done semi-automatically by associating the lemmas in French with the lexical units of the existing analysis and generation modules of French. The examples in the dictionaries, which are most generally multi-word expressions, can be associated to the existing MWEs of the analysers or added when absent.

Another interesting use of the lexical databases would be to link the Lao words to words in other languages, thanks to existing dictionaries between French and other languages, or using interlingual lexical units such as WordNet synsets[3] or UNL Universal Words[4]. A further possibility would be to build MT systems between Lao and many other languages using UNL graphs as pivot representations.

References

[1] Gay, B. (2003). Les sources contemporaines du lao / Contemporary sources on Lao : 1976-2003. ACRS (Singapour) / Institut de Recherches sur la Culture (Laos) Comité National des Sciences (Laos) 2003. 1385 p.

[2] Inthamone, L. (2011). Nouveau Dictionnaire Lao-Français. You Feng. 1523 p.

[3] Reinhorn, M. ; Berment, V. (2013). Dictionnaire Français-Lao. You Feng. 1729 p.

[4] de Malézieux, G. ; Bosc, A. ; Berment, V. (2014). RBMT as an alternative to SMT for under-resourced languages. WSSANLP 2014, 23 August 2014, Dublin.

[5] Berment, V. (2014). Some thoughts on how to address commercially unprofitable languages and language pairs. keynote speech, WSSANLP 2014, 23 August 2014, Dublin.

---

[3] Here is the WOLF (*WOrdnet Libre du Français*) French WordNet: http://alpage.inria.fr/~sagot/wolf.html.
[4] Resources are here: https://github.com/dikonov/Universal-Dictionary-of-Concepts/tree/master/data/csv.

Author Index

Abdul Hameed, Riyafa, 124
Akasegawa, Shiro, 114
Albacea, Eliezer, 74

Bakliwal, Priyam, 183
Batista-Navarro, Riza Theresa, 74
Behera, Pitambar, 64, 103
Berment, Vincent, 194
Bhattacharya, Paheli, 152
Biswas, Arindam, 93
Bojar, Ondřej, 54

Chen, Nancy, 133
Chen, Wenda, 133

Das, Ayan, 33, 163
Dias, Gihan, 44, 124, 173

Fernando, Sandareka, 124, 173

Goyal, Pawan, 1, 152
Gridach, Mourad, 23

Hasegawa-Johnson, Mark, 133
Hellwig, Oliver, 142

Ihalapathirana, Anusha, 124
Iwahashi, Naoto, 11

Jawahar, C V, 183
Jawaid, Bushra, 54
Jayasena, Sanath, 124, 173
Jha, Girish, 64
Jyothi, Preethi, 133

Kadupitiya, Jcs, 44
Kamran, Amir, 54
Kanapathipillai, Shujeevan, 83
Krishna, Amrith, 1
Kumar, Apurv, 1
Kumar, Ken, 163
Kyaw Thu, Ye, 11

Lahiri, Shibamouli, 93
Lapitan, Fermin Roberto, 74

Mourya, Neha, 103

Muzaffar, Sharmin, 64

Nishioka, Miki, 114

Ojha, Atul kr., 64

Pa Pa, Win, 11
Pandey, Vandana, 103
Pathirennehelage, Nadeeshani, 124
Phani, Shanta, 93

Qiu, Xinying, 188

Ranathunga, Surangika, 44, 124, 173

Sagisaka, Yoshinori, 11
Saha, Agnivo, 33
Sarkar, Sudeshna, 33, 152, 163
Satuluri, Pavankumar, 1
Sharma, Shubham, 1

V V, Devadath, 183
Varshney, Lav, 133

Weerasinghe, Ruwan, 83
Welgama, Viraj, 83

Yerra, Pranay, 163

Zhu, Gangqin, 188
Ziyad Mohamed, Maryam, 124

Association for Computational Linguistics
209 N. Eighth Street
Stroudsburg, Pennsylvania 18360

ISBN 978-1-5108-3317-3